CHARLIE BROWN
ALL TIED UP

Other *Peanuts* Kids' Collections

Snoopy: Cowabunga!
Charlie Brown and Friends
Charlie Brown: Pow!
Woodstock: Master of Disguise
Snoopy: Contact!
Snoopy: Party Animal
Charlie Brown: Here We Go Again
Snoopy to the Rescue
Snoopy: What's Wrong with Dog Lips?
I'm Not Your Sweet Babboo!
Snoopy: Boogie Down!
Lucy: Speak Out!

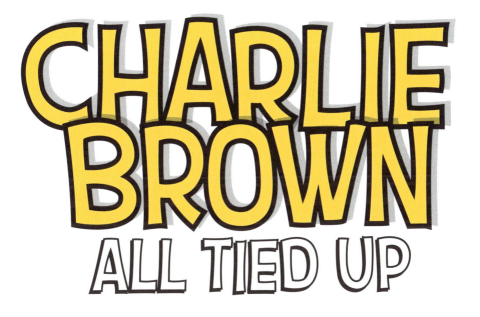

CHARLIE BROWN ALL TIED UP

A  Collection

CHARLES M. SCHULZ

Andrews McMeel
PUBLISHING®

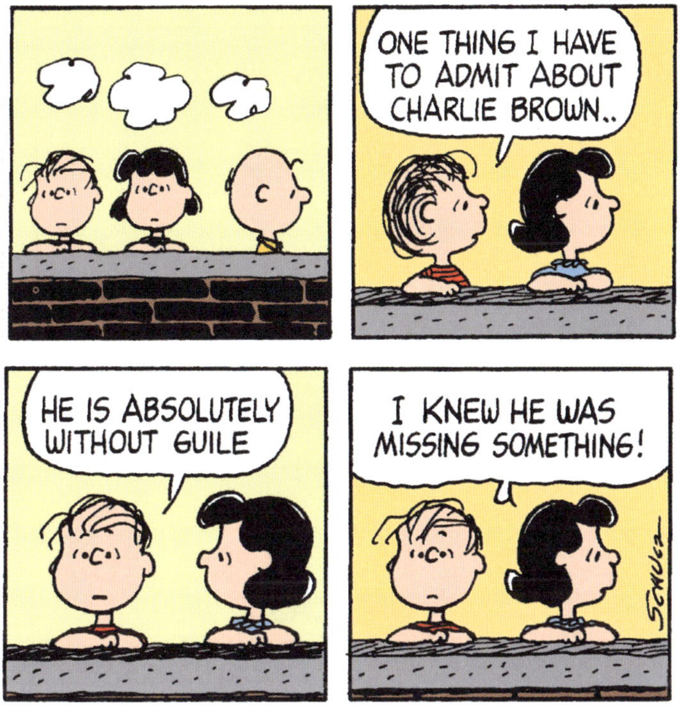
ONE THING I HAVE TO ADMIT ABOUT CHARLIE BROWN..
HE IS ABSOLUTELY WITHOUT GUILE
I KNEW HE WAS MISSING SOMETHING!

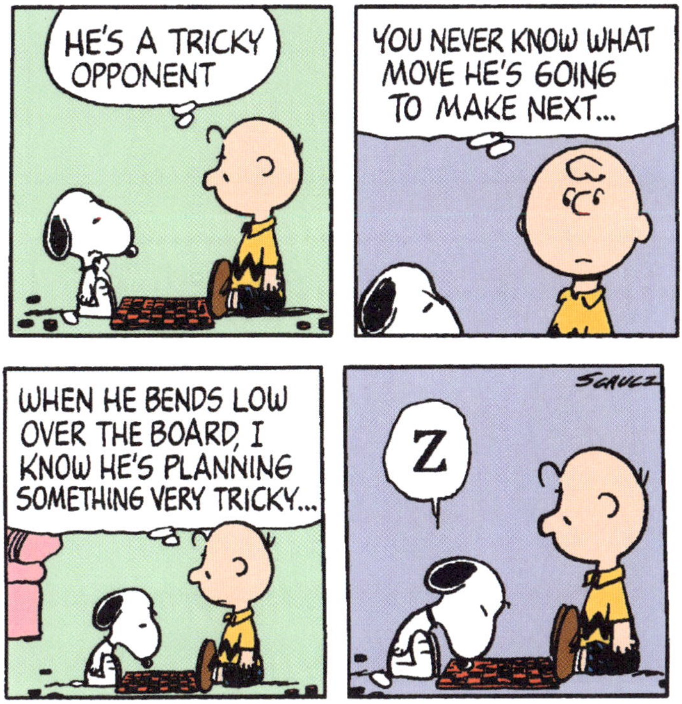
HE'S A TRICKY OPPONENT
YOU NEVER KNOW WHAT MOVE HE'S GOING TO MAKE NEXT...
WHEN HE BENDS LOW OVER THE BOARD, I KNOW HE'S PLANNING SOMETHING VERY TRICKY...
Z

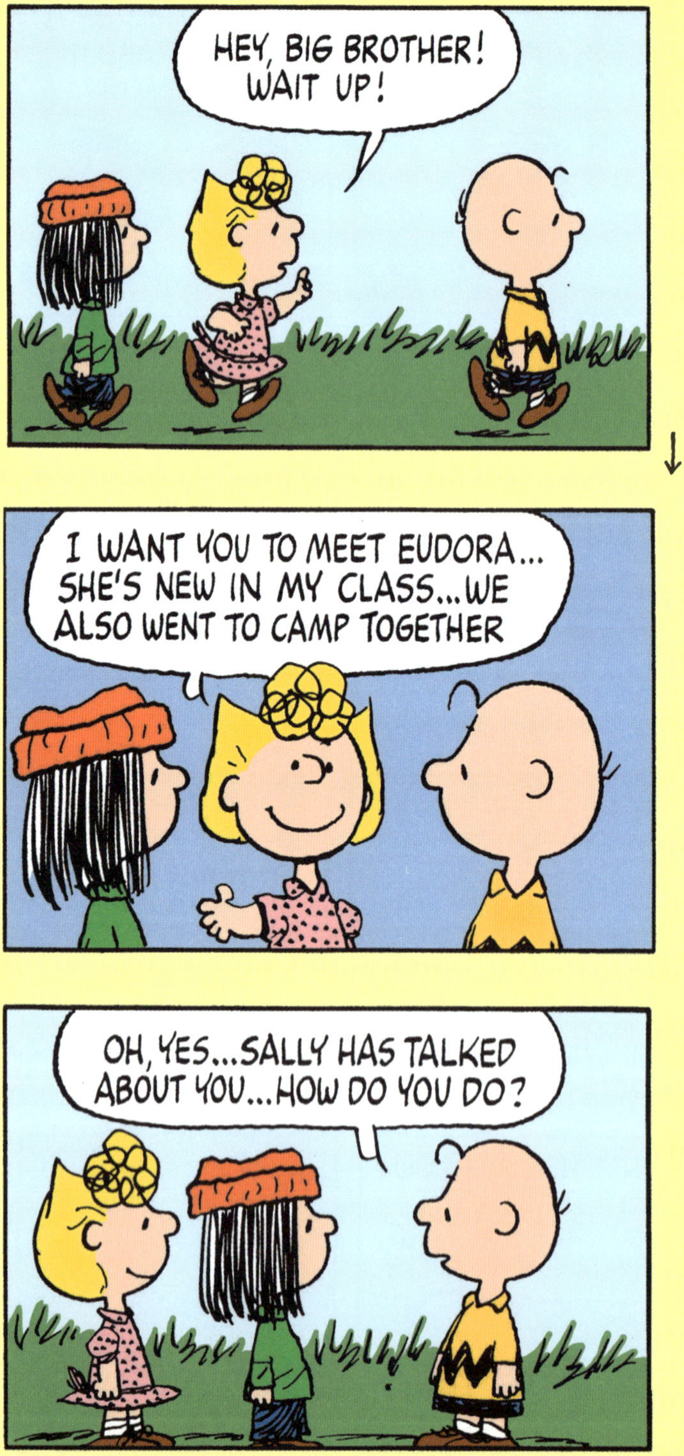
HEY, BIG BROTHER! WAIT UP!
I WANT YOU TO MEET EUDORA... SHE'S NEW IN MY CLASS...WE ALSO WENT TO CAMP TOGETHER
OH, YES...SALLY HAS TALKED ABOUT YOU...HOW DO YOU DO?

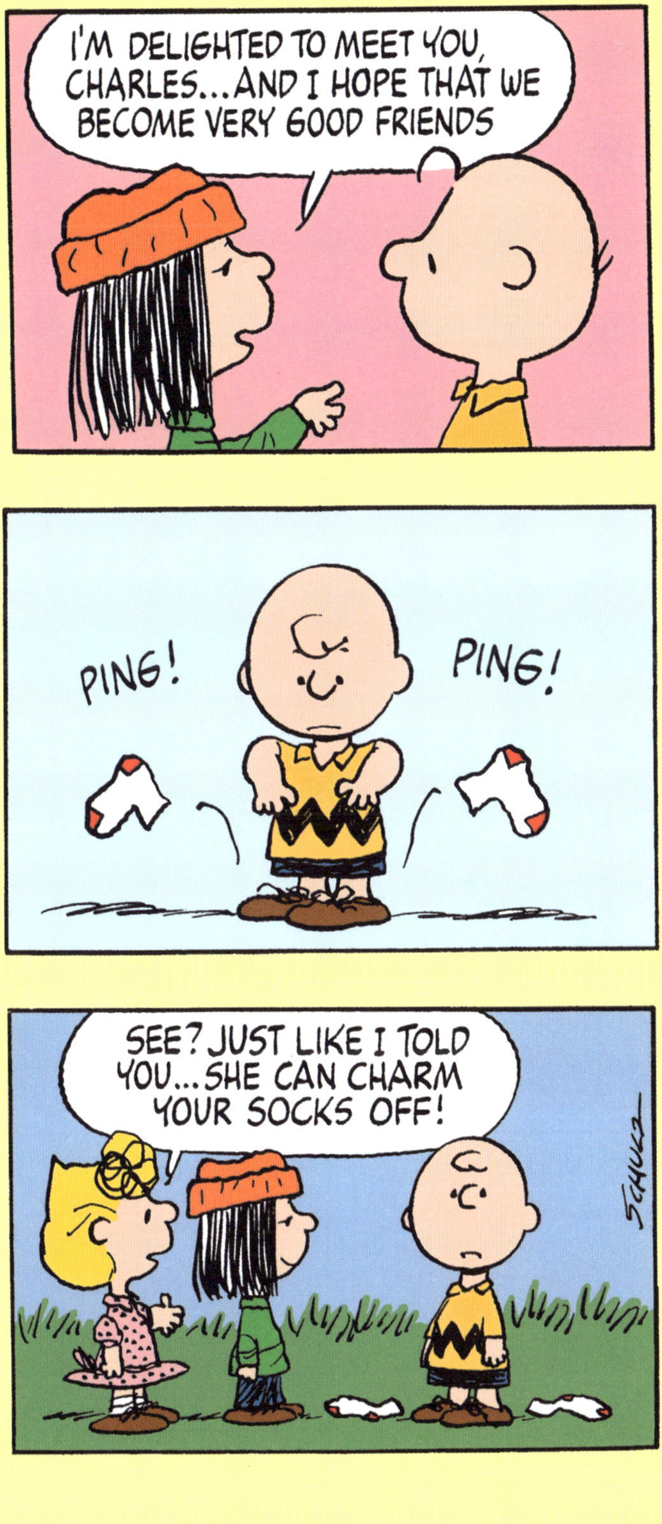
I'M DELIGHTED TO MEET YOU, CHARLES...AND I HOPE THAT WE BECOME VERY GOOD FRIENDS
PING!
PING!
SEE? JUST LIKE I TOLD YOU...SHE CAN CHARM YOUR SOCKS OFF!
SCHULZ

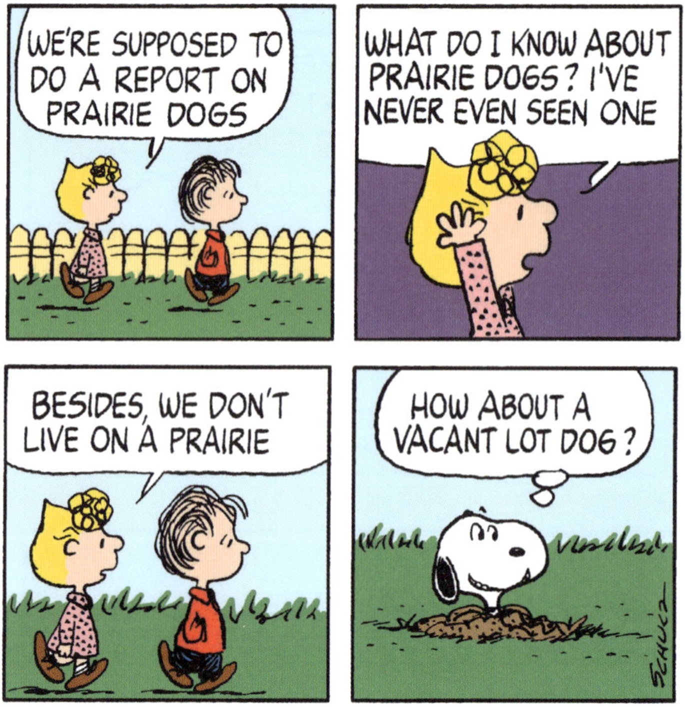
WE'RE SUPPOSED TO DO A REPORT ON PRAIRIE DOGS
WHAT DO I KNOW ABOUT PRAIRIE DOGS? I'VE NEVER EVEN SEEN ONE
BESIDES, WE DON'T LIVE ON A PRAIRIE
HOW ABOUT A VACANT LOT DOG?
SCHULZ

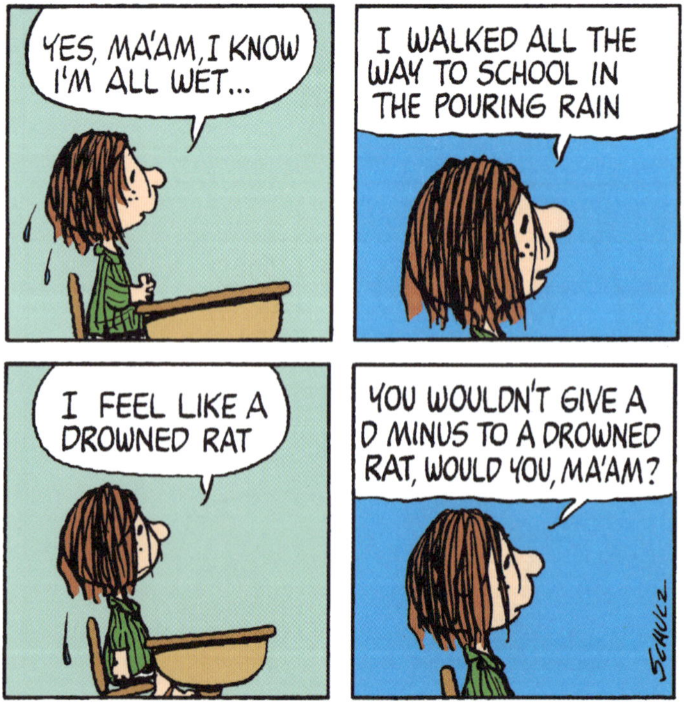
YES, MA'AM, I KNOW I'M ALL WET...
I WALKED ALL THE WAY TO SCHOOL IN THE POURING RAIN
I FEEL LIKE A DROWNED RAT
YOU WOULDN'T GIVE A D MINUS TO A DROWNED RAT, WOULD YOU, MA'AM?
SCHULZ

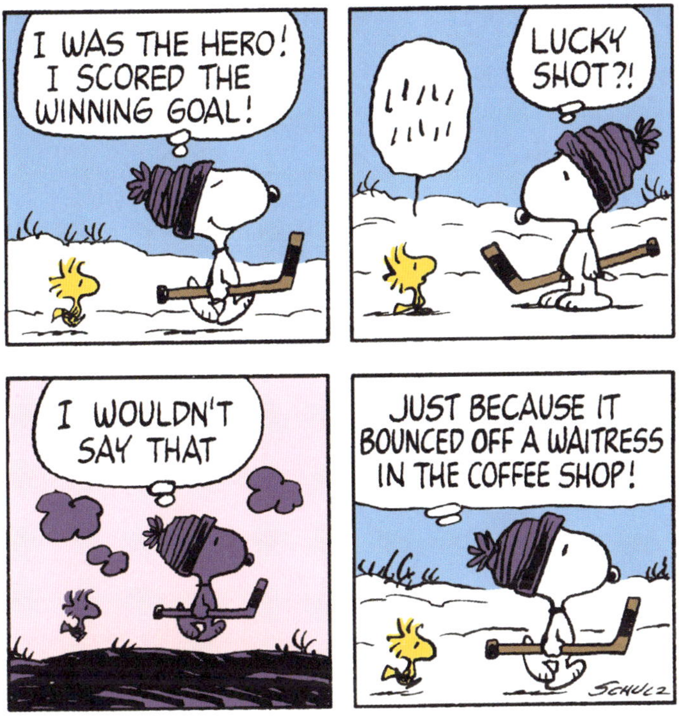
I WAS THE HERO! I SCORED THE WINNING GOAL!
LUCKY SHOT?!
I WOULDN'T SAY THAT
JUST BECAUSE IT BOUNCED OFF A WAITRESS IN THE COFFEE SHOP!
SCHULZ

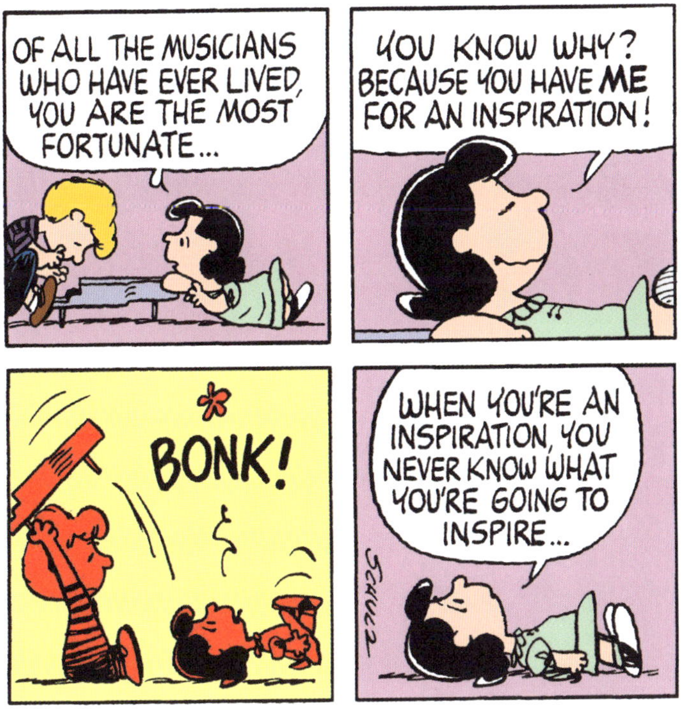
OF ALL THE MUSICIANS WHO HAVE EVER LIVED, YOU ARE THE MOST FORTUNATE...
YOU KNOW WHY? BECAUSE YOU HAVE **ME** FOR AN INSPIRATION!
BONK!
WHEN YOU'RE AN INSPIRATION, YOU NEVER KNOW WHAT YOU'RE GOING TO INSPIRE...
SCHULZ

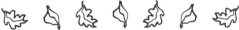

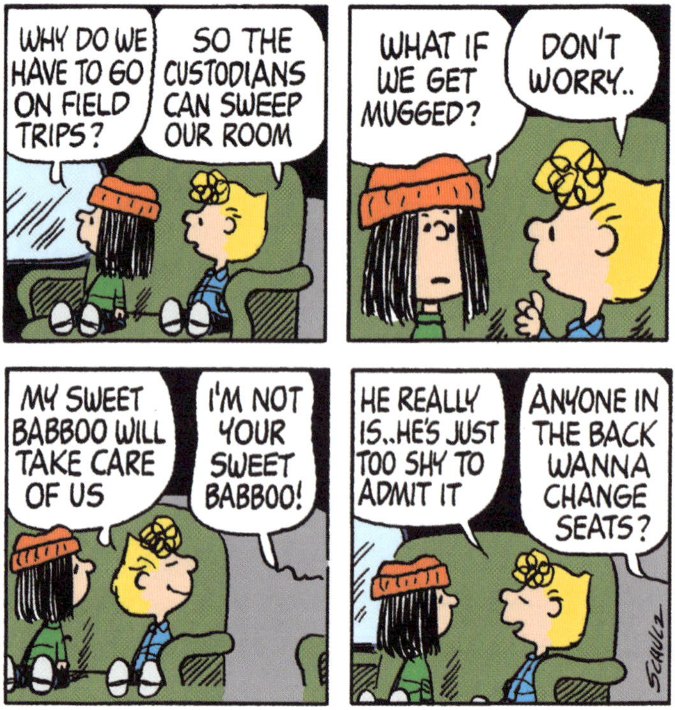
WHY DO WE HAVE TO GO ON FIELD TRIPS?
SO THE CUSTODIANS CAN SWEEP OUR ROOM
WHAT IF WE GET MUGGED?
DON'T WORRY..
MY SWEET BABBOO WILL TAKE CARE OF US
I'M NOT YOUR SWEET BABBOO!
HE REALLY IS..HE'S JUST TOO SHY TO ADMIT IT
ANYONE IN THE BACK WANNA CHANGE SEATS?
SCHULZ

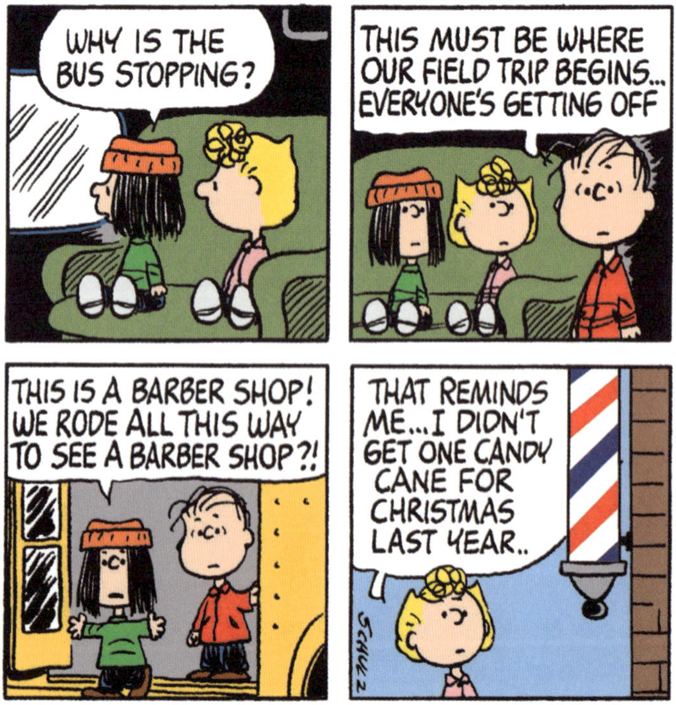
WHY IS THE BUS STOPPING?
THIS MUST BE WHERE OUR FIELD TRIP BEGINS... EVERYONE'S GETTING OFF
THIS IS A BARBER SHOP! WE RODE ALL THIS WAY TO SEE A BARBER SHOP?!
THAT REMINDS ME...I DIDN'T GET ONE CANDY CANE FOR CHRISTMAS LAST YEAR..
SCHULZ

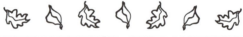

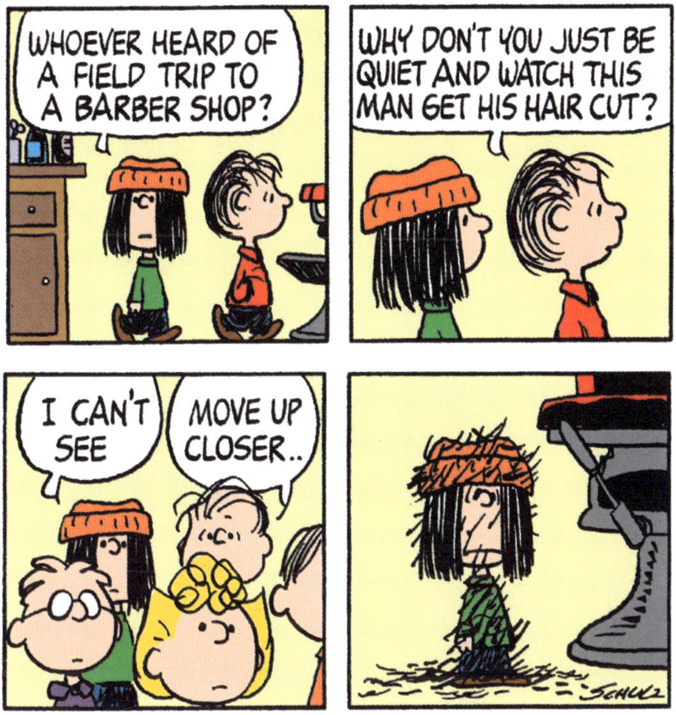
WHOEVER HEARD OF A FIELD TRIP TO A BARBER SHOP?
WHY DON'T YOU JUST BE QUIET AND WATCH THIS MAN GET HIS HAIR CUT?
I CAN'T SEE
MOVE UP CLOSER..

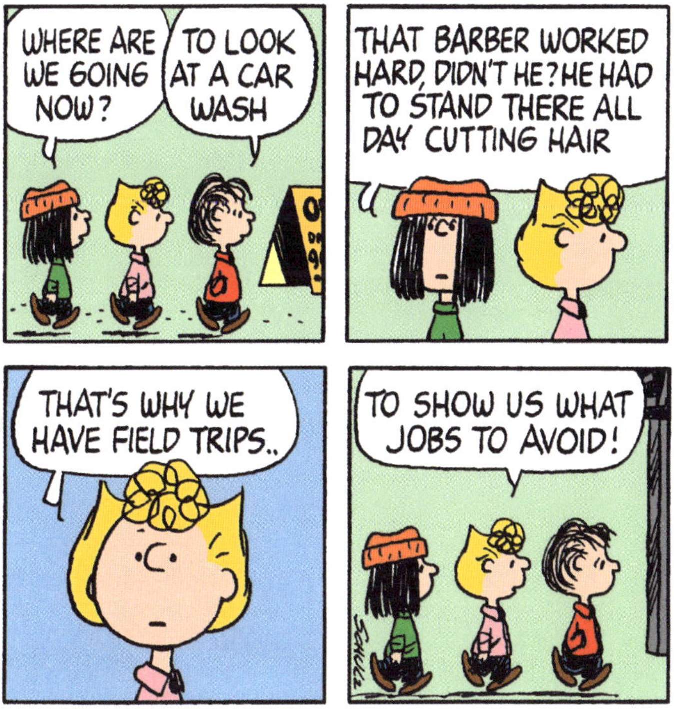
WHERE ARE WE GOING NOW?
TO LOOK AT A CAR WASH
THAT BARBER WORKED HARD, DIDN'T HE? HE HAD TO STAND THERE ALL DAY CUTTING HAIR
THAT'S WHY WE HAVE FIELD TRIPS..
TO SHOW US WHAT JOBS TO AVOID!

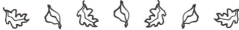

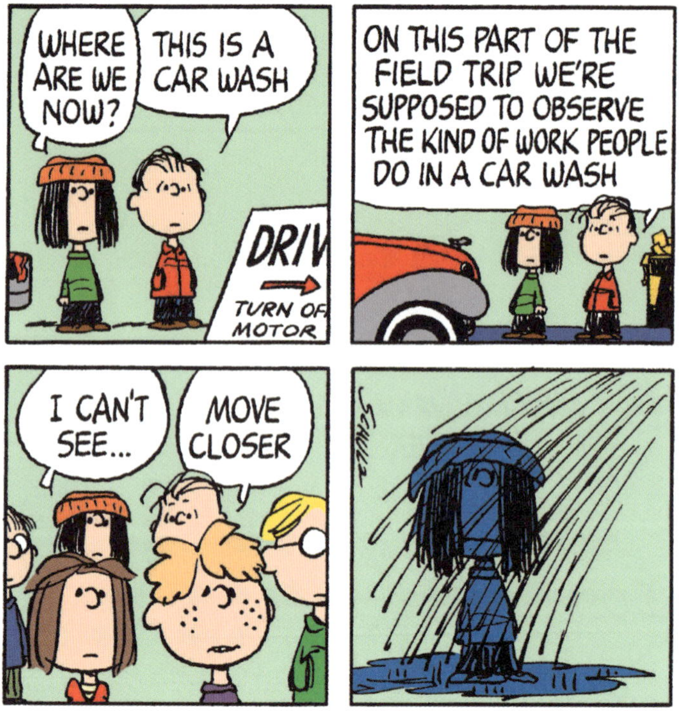
WHERE ARE WE NOW?
THIS IS A CAR WASH
DRIV
TURN OF
MOTOR
ON THIS PART OF THE FIELD TRIP WE'RE SUPPOSED TO OBSERVE THE KIND OF WORK PEOPLE DO IN A CAR WASH
I CAN'T SEE...
MOVE CLOSER
SCHULZ

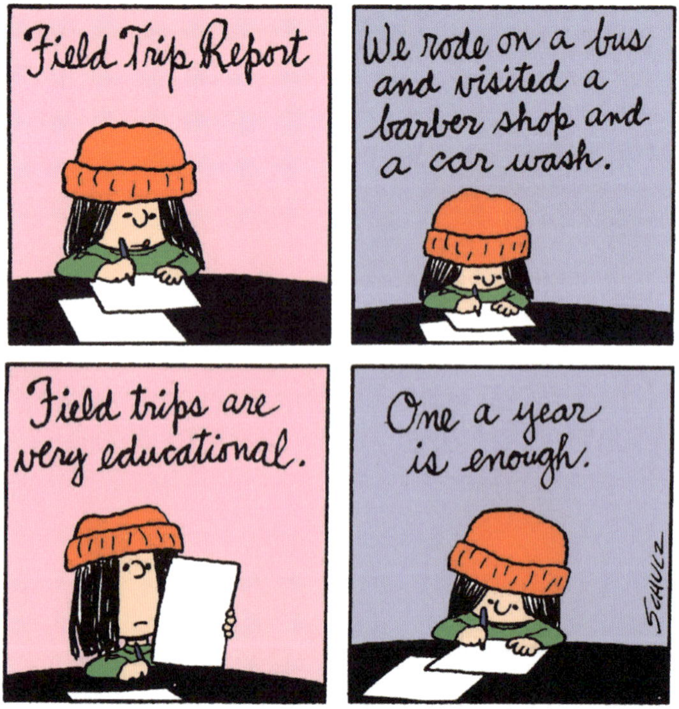
Field Trip Report
We rode on a bus and visited a barber shop and a car wash.
Field trips are very educational.
One a year is enough.
SCHULZ

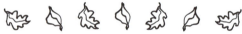

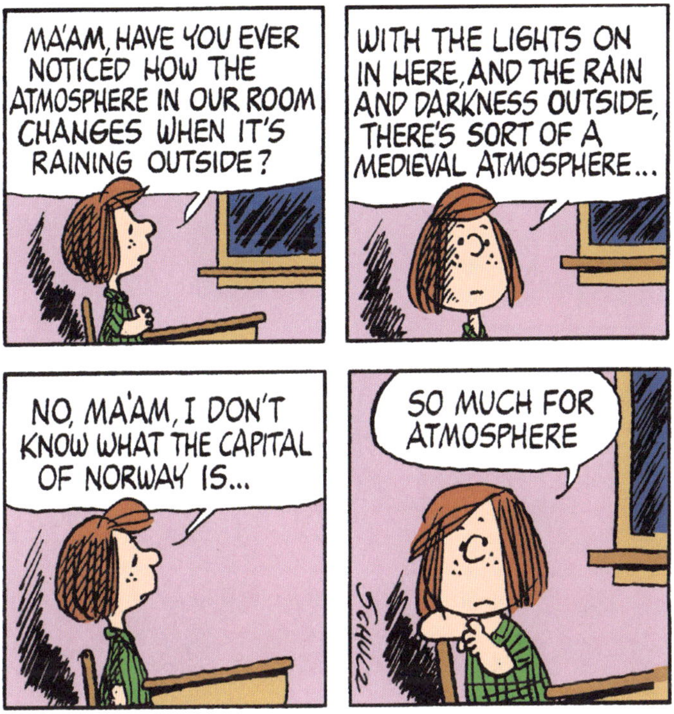
MA'AM, HAVE YOU EVER NOTICED HOW THE ATMOSPHERE IN OUR ROOM CHANGES WHEN IT'S RAINING OUTSIDE?
WITH THE LIGHTS ON IN HERE, AND THE RAIN AND DARKNESS OUTSIDE, THERE'S SORT OF A MEDIEVAL ATMOSPHERE...
NO, MA'AM, I DON'T KNOW WHAT THE CAPITAL OF NORWAY IS...
SO MUCH FOR ATMOSPHERE

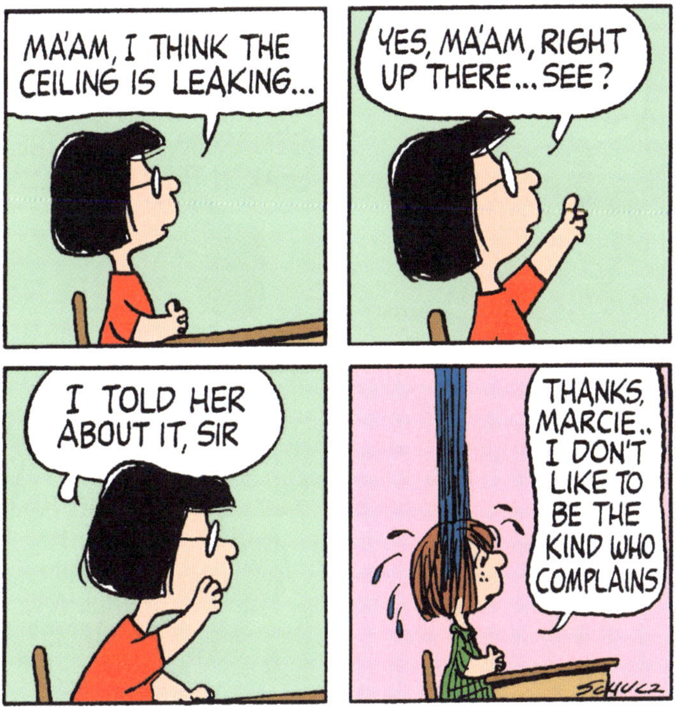
MA'AM, I THINK THE CEILING IS LEAKING...
YES, MA'AM, RIGHT UP THERE... SEE?
I TOLD HER ABOUT IT, SIR
THANKS, MARCIE.. I DON'T LIKE TO BE THE KIND WHO COMPLAINS

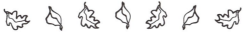

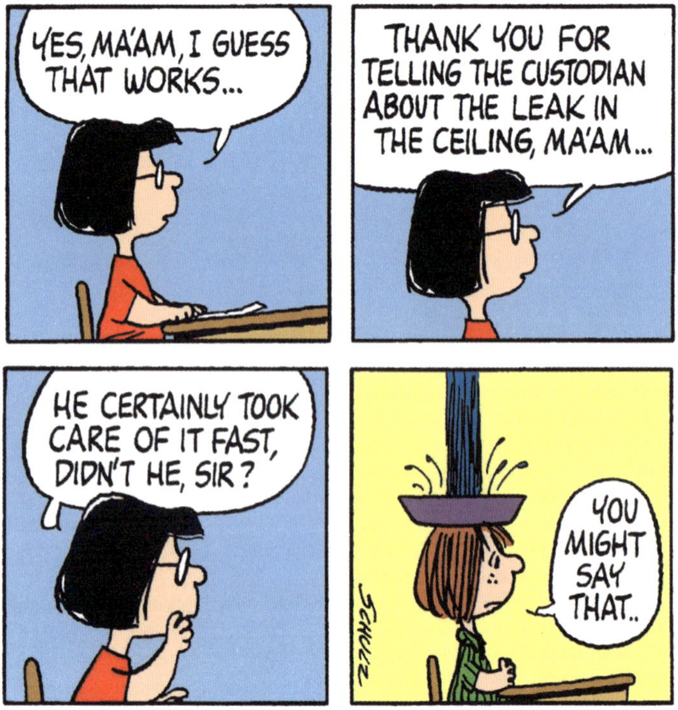
YES, MA'AM, I GUESS THAT WORKS...
THANK YOU FOR TELLING THE CUSTODIAN ABOUT THE LEAK IN THE CEILING, MA'AM...
HE CERTAINLY TOOK CARE OF IT FAST, DIDN'T HE, SIR?
YOU MIGHT SAY THAT..

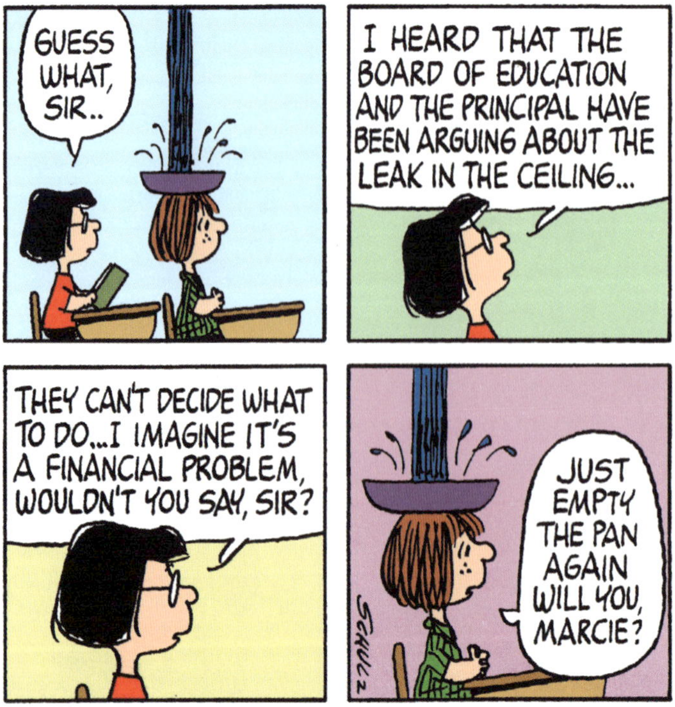
GUESS WHAT, SIR..
I HEARD THAT THE BOARD OF EDUCATION AND THE PRINCIPAL HAVE BEEN ARGUING ABOUT THE LEAK IN THE CEILING...
THEY CAN'T DECIDE WHAT TO DO...I IMAGINE IT'S A FINANCIAL PROBLEM, WOULDN'T YOU SAY, SIR?
JUST EMPTY THE PAN AGAIN WILL YOU, MARCIE?

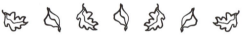

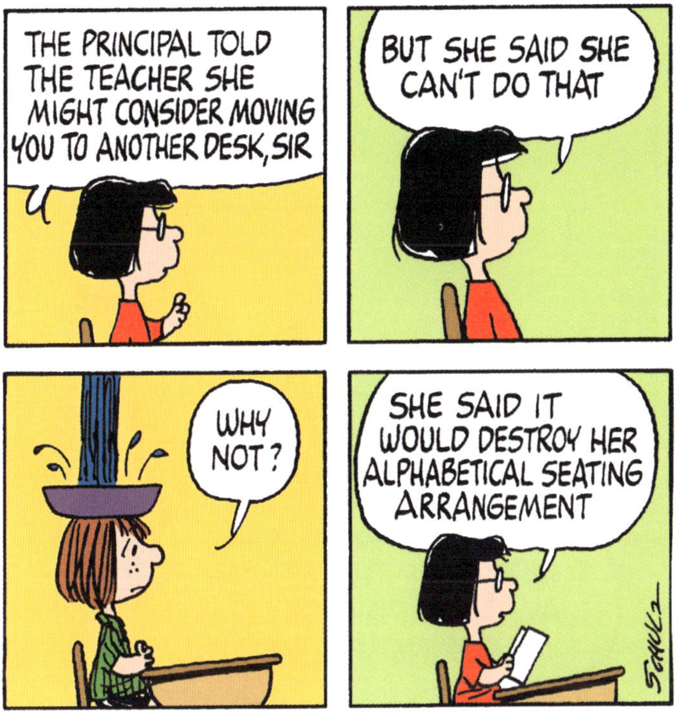
THE PRINCIPAL TOLD THE TEACHER SHE MIGHT CONSIDER MOVING YOU TO ANOTHER DESK, SIR
BUT SHE SAID SHE CAN'T DO THAT
WHY NOT?
SHE SAID IT WOULD DESTROY HER ALPHABETICAL SEATING ARRANGEMENT
SCHULZ

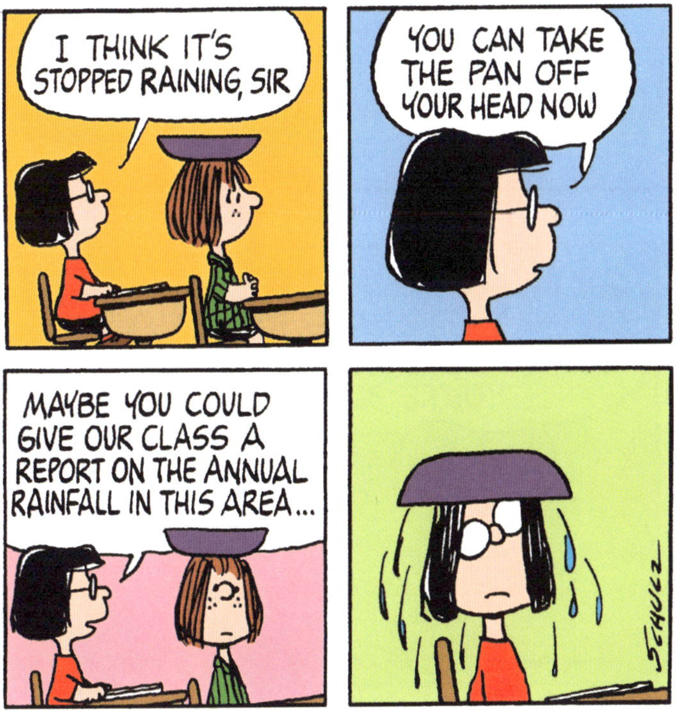
I THINK IT'S STOPPED RAINING, SIR
YOU CAN TAKE THE PAN OFF YOUR HEAD NOW
MAYBE YOU COULD GIVE OUR CLASS A REPORT ON THE ANNUAL RAINFALL IN THIS AREA...
SCHULZ

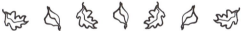

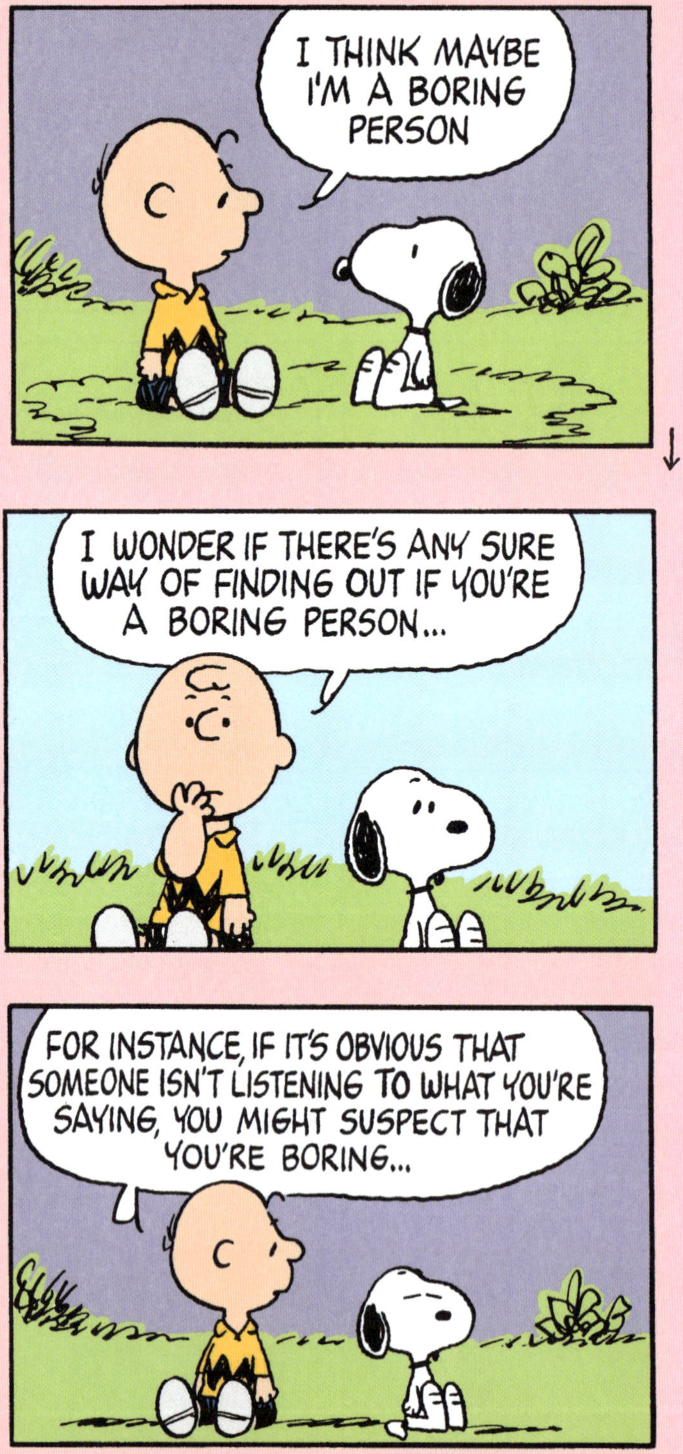
I THINK MAYBE I'M A BORING PERSON
I WONDER IF THERE'S ANY SURE WAY OF FINDING OUT IF YOU'RE A BORING PERSON...
FOR INSTANCE, IF IT'S OBVIOUS THAT SOMEONE ISN'T LISTENING TO WHAT YOU'RE SAYING, YOU MIGHT SUSPECT THAT YOU'RE BORING...

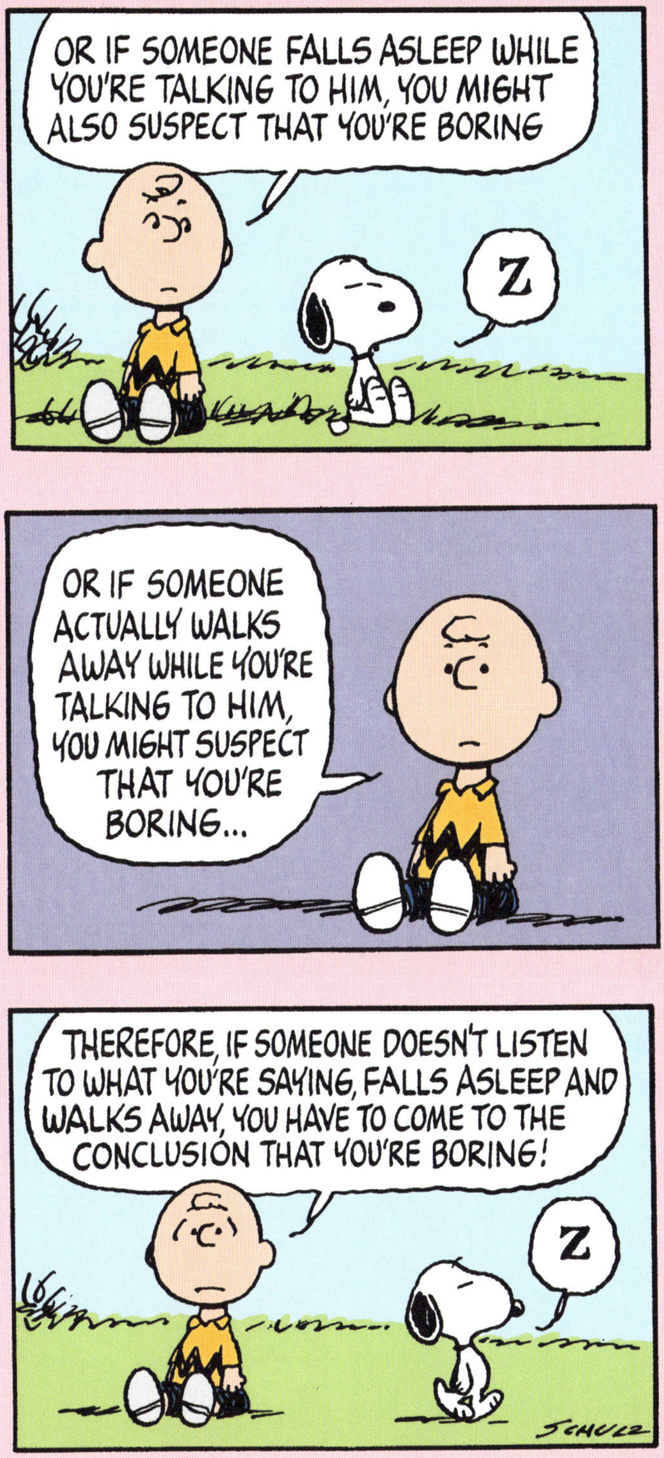
OR IF SOMEONE FALLS ASLEEP WHILE YOU'RE TALKING TO HIM, YOU MIGHT ALSO SUSPECT THAT YOU'RE BORING
Z
OR IF SOMEONE ACTUALLY WALKS AWAY WHILE YOU'RE TALKING TO HIM, YOU MIGHT SUSPECT THAT YOU'RE BORING...
THEREFORE, IF SOMEONE DOESN'T LISTEN TO WHAT YOU'RE SAYING, FALLS ASLEEP AND WALKS AWAY, YOU HAVE TO COME TO THE CONCLUSION THAT YOU'RE BORING!
Z
SCHULZ

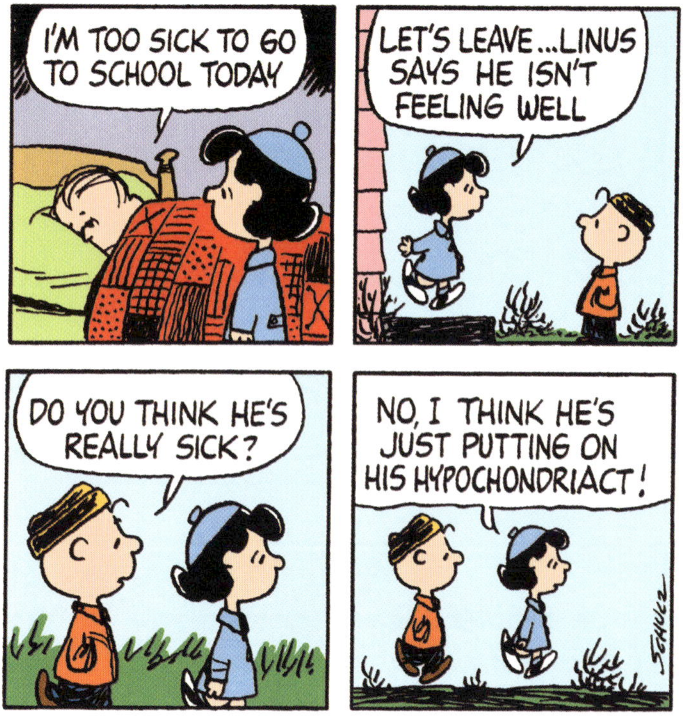
I'M TOO SICK TO GO TO SCHOOL TODAY
LET'S LEAVE...LINUS SAYS HE ISN'T FEELING WELL
DO YOU THINK HE'S REALLY SICK?
NO, I THINK HE'S JUST PUTTING ON HIS HYPOCHONDRIACT!

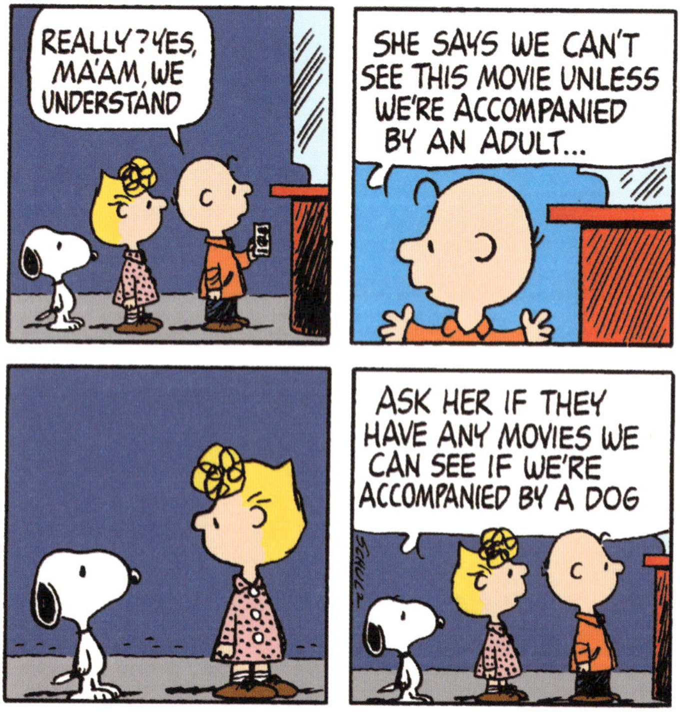
REALLY? YES, MA'AM, WE UNDERSTAND
SHE SAYS WE CAN'T SEE THIS MOVIE UNLESS WE'RE ACCOMPANIED BY AN ADULT...
ASK HER IF THEY HAVE ANY MOVIES WE CAN SEE IF WE'RE ACCOMPANIED BY A DOG

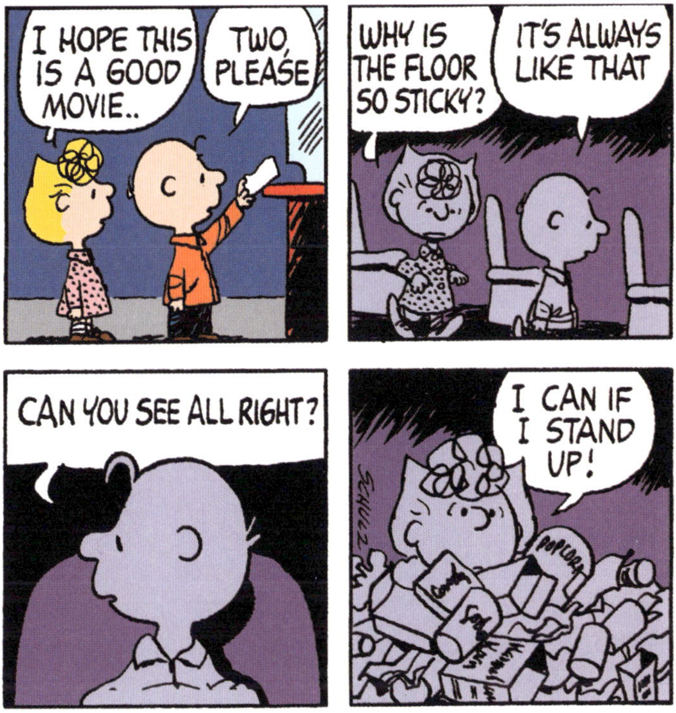
I HOPE THIS IS A GOOD MOVIE..
TWO, PLEASE
WHY IS THE FLOOR SO STICKY?
IT'S ALWAYS LIKE THAT
CAN YOU SEE ALL RIGHT?
I CAN IF I STAND UP!

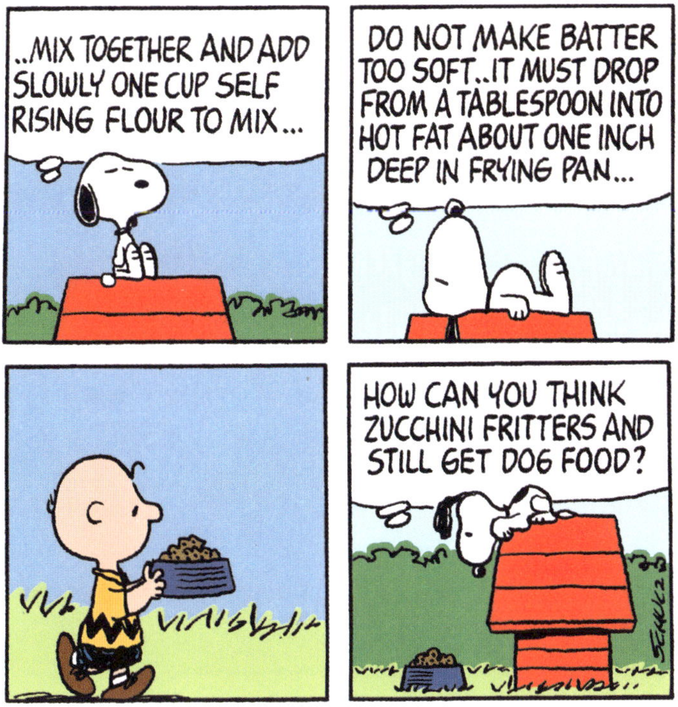
..MIX TOGETHER AND ADD SLOWLY ONE CUP SELF RISING FLOUR TO MIX...
DO NOT MAKE BATTER TOO SOFT..IT MUST DROP FROM A TABLESPOON INTO HOT FAT ABOUT ONE INCH DEEP IN FRYING PAN...
HOW CAN YOU THINK ZUCCHINI FRITTERS AND STILL GET DOG FOOD?

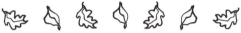

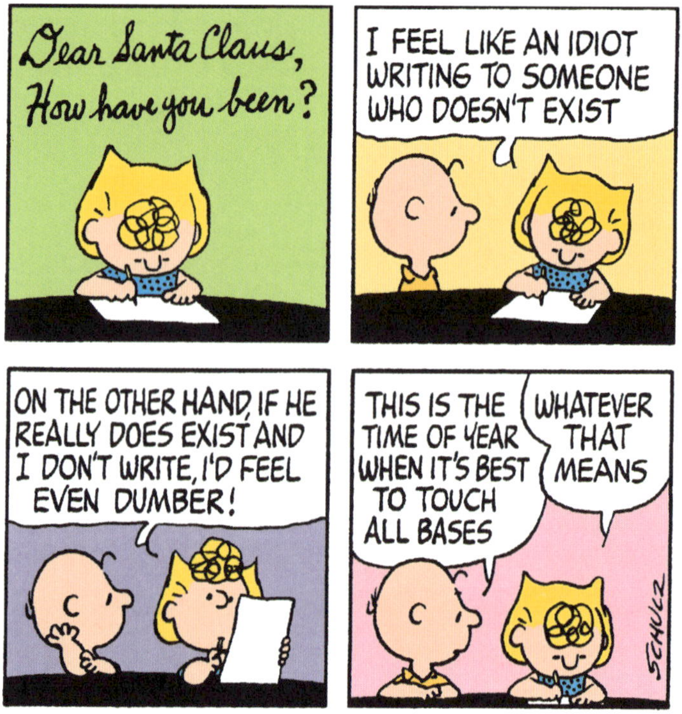
Dear Santa Claus,
How have you been?
I FEEL LIKE AN IDIOT WRITING TO SOMEONE WHO DOESN'T EXIST
ON THE OTHER HAND, IF HE REALLY DOES EXIST AND I DON'T WRITE, I'D FEEL EVEN DUMBER!
THIS IS THE TIME OF YEAR WHEN IT'S BEST TO TOUCH ALL BASES
WHATEVER THAT MEANS
SCHULZ

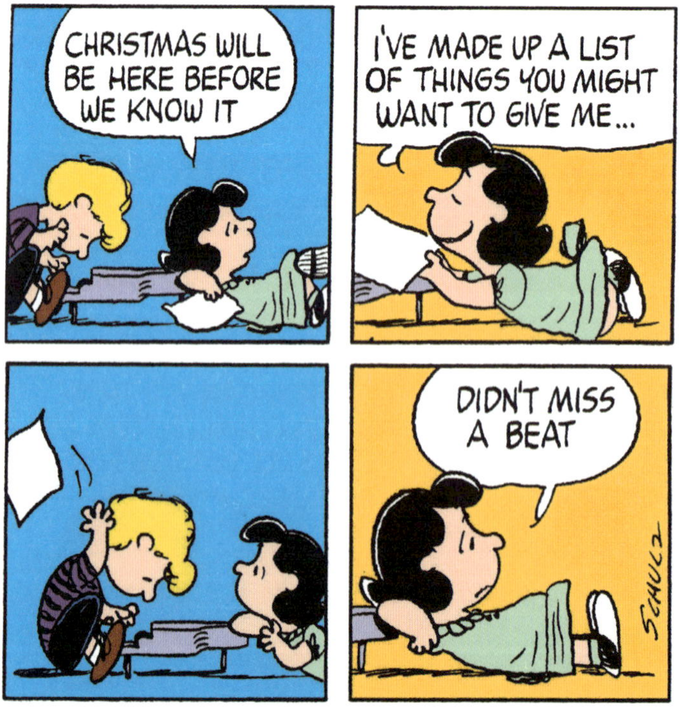
CHRISTMAS WILL BE HERE BEFORE WE KNOW IT
I'VE MADE UP A LIST OF THINGS YOU MIGHT WANT TO GIVE ME...
DIDN'T MISS A BEAT
SCHULZ

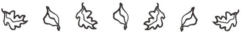

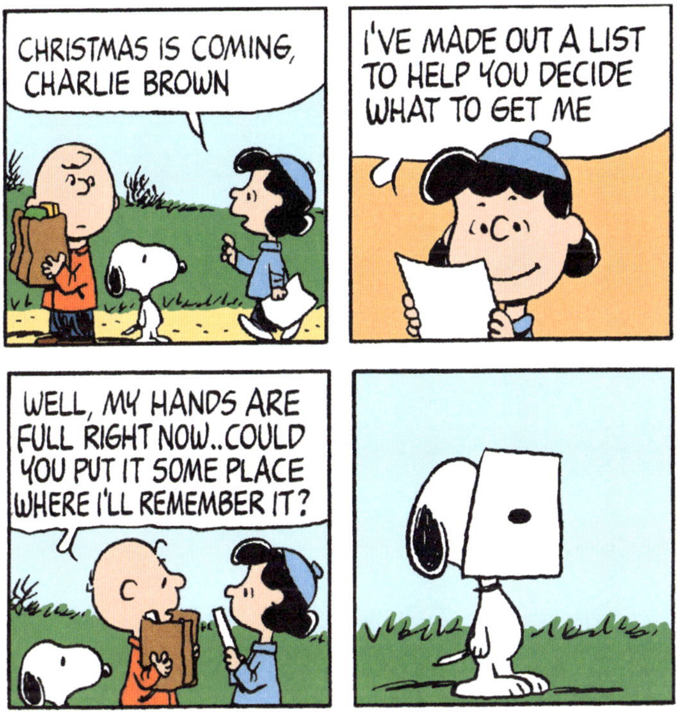
CHRISTMAS IS COMING, CHARLIE BROWN
I'VE MADE OUT A LIST TO HELP YOU DECIDE WHAT TO GET ME
WELL, MY HANDS ARE FULL RIGHT NOW..COULD YOU PUT IT SOME PLACE WHERE I'LL REMEMBER IT?

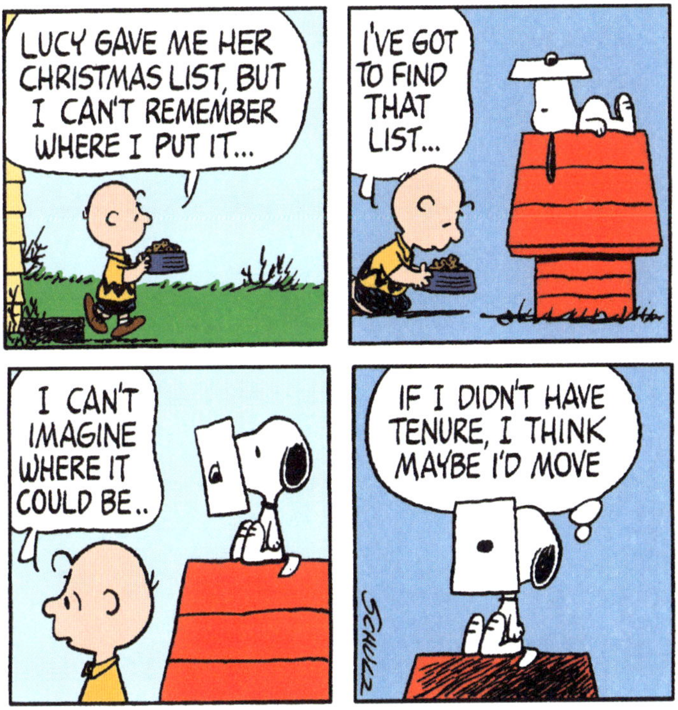
LUCY GAVE ME HER CHRISTMAS LIST, BUT I CAN'T REMEMBER WHERE I PUT IT...
I'VE GOT TO FIND THAT LIST...
I CAN'T IMAGINE WHERE IT COULD BE..
IF I DIDN'T HAVE TENURE, I THINK MAYBE I'D MOVE
SCHULZ

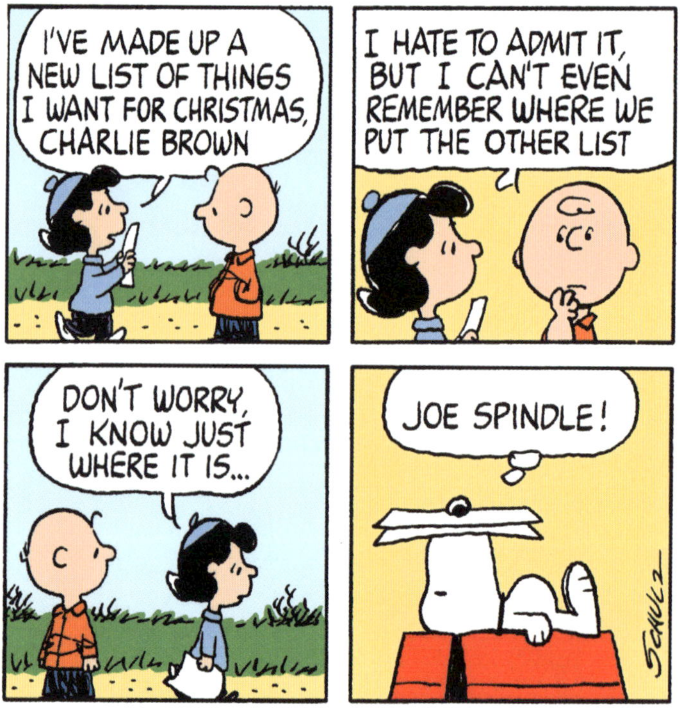
I'VE MADE UP A NEW LIST OF THINGS I WANT FOR CHRISTMAS, CHARLIE BROWN
I HATE TO ADMIT IT, BUT I CAN'T EVEN REMEMBER WHERE WE PUT THE OTHER LIST
DON'T WORRY, I KNOW JUST WHERE IT IS...
JOE SPINDLE!
SCHULZ

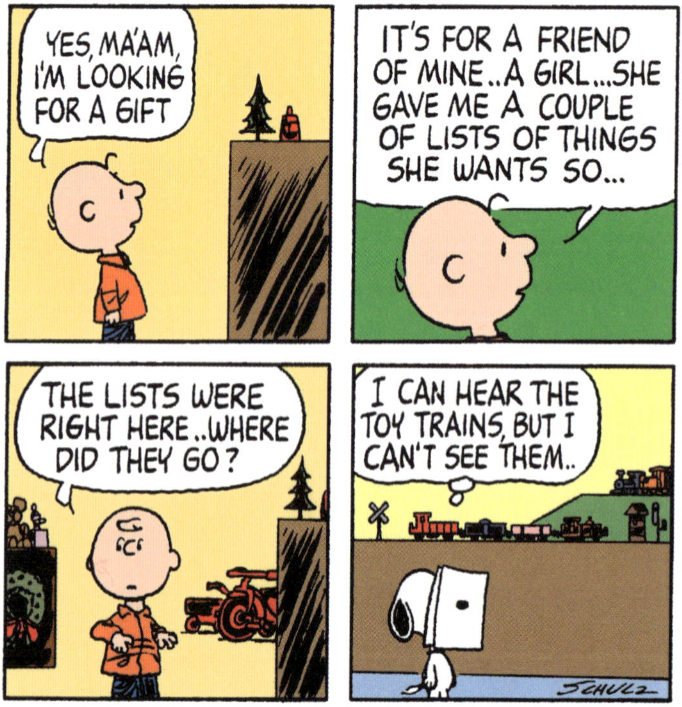
YES, MA'AM, I'M LOOKING FOR A GIFT
IT'S FOR A FRIEND OF MINE..A GIRL...SHE GAVE ME A COUPLE OF LISTS OF THINGS SHE WANTS SO...
THE LISTS WERE RIGHT HERE..WHERE DID THEY GO?
I CAN HEAR THE TOY TRAINS, BUT I CAN'T SEE THEM..
SCHULZ

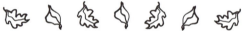

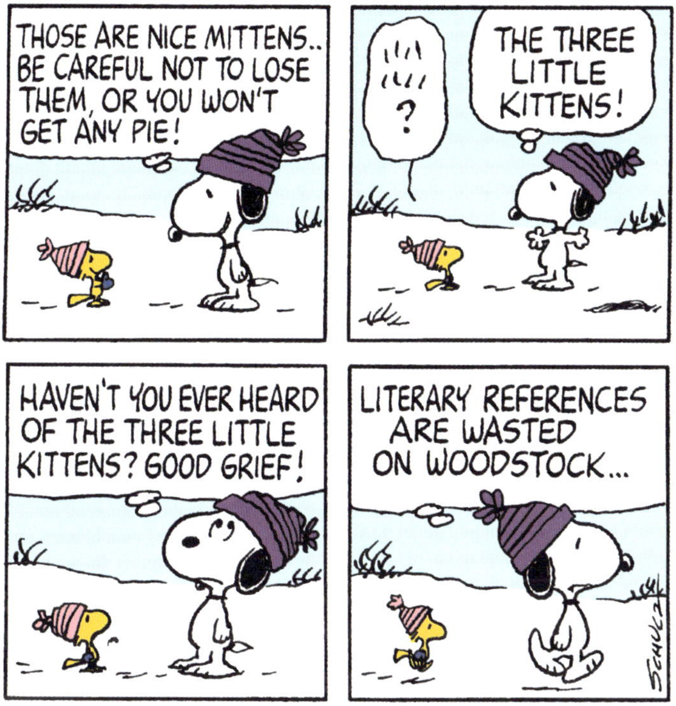
THOSE ARE NICE MITTENS.. BE CAREFUL NOT TO LOSE THEM, OR YOU WON'T GET ANY PIE!
?
THE THREE LITTLE KITTENS!
HAVEN'T YOU EVER HEARD OF THE THREE LITTLE KITTENS? GOOD GRIEF!
LITERARY REFERENCES ARE WASTED ON WOODSTOCK...

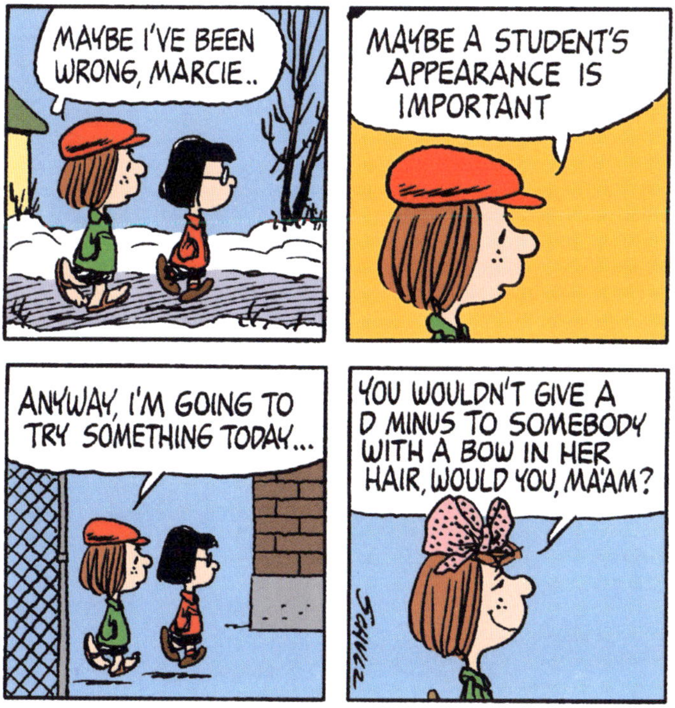
MAYBE I'VE BEEN WRONG, MARCIE..
MAYBE A STUDENT'S APPEARANCE IS IMPORTANT
ANYWAY, I'M GOING TO TRY SOMETHING TODAY...
YOU WOULDN'T GIVE A D MINUS TO SOMEBODY WITH A BOW IN HER HAIR, WOULD YOU, MA'AM?

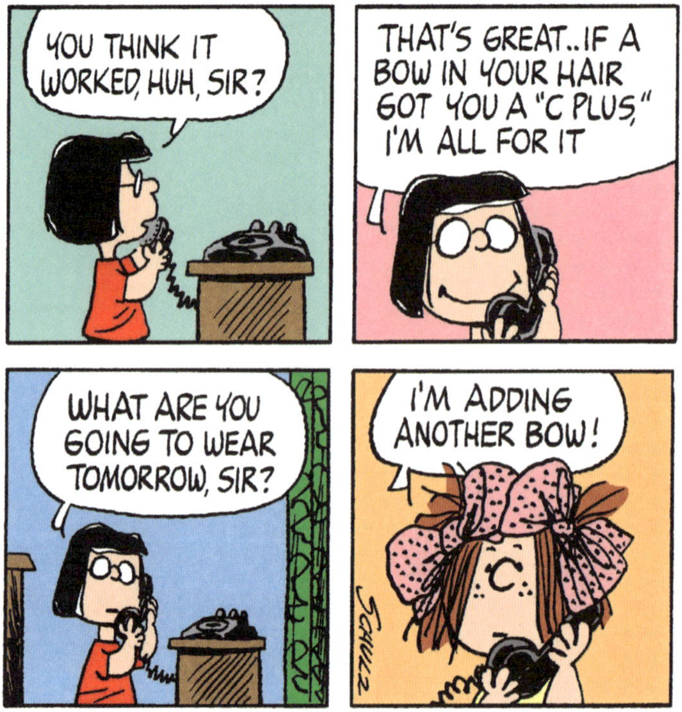
YOU THINK IT WORKED, HUH, SIR?
THAT'S GREAT..IF A BOW IN YOUR HAIR GOT YOU A "C PLUS," I'M ALL FOR IT
WHAT ARE YOU GOING TO WEAR TOMORROW, SIR?
I'M ADDING ANOTHER BOW!
SCHULZ

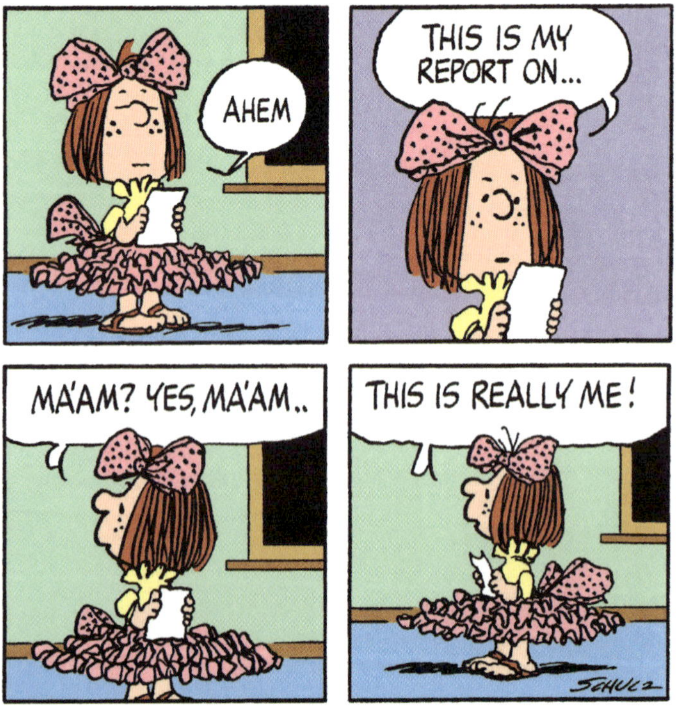
AHEM
THIS IS MY REPORT ON...
MA'AM? YES, MA'AM..
THIS IS REALLY ME!
SCHULZ

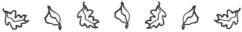

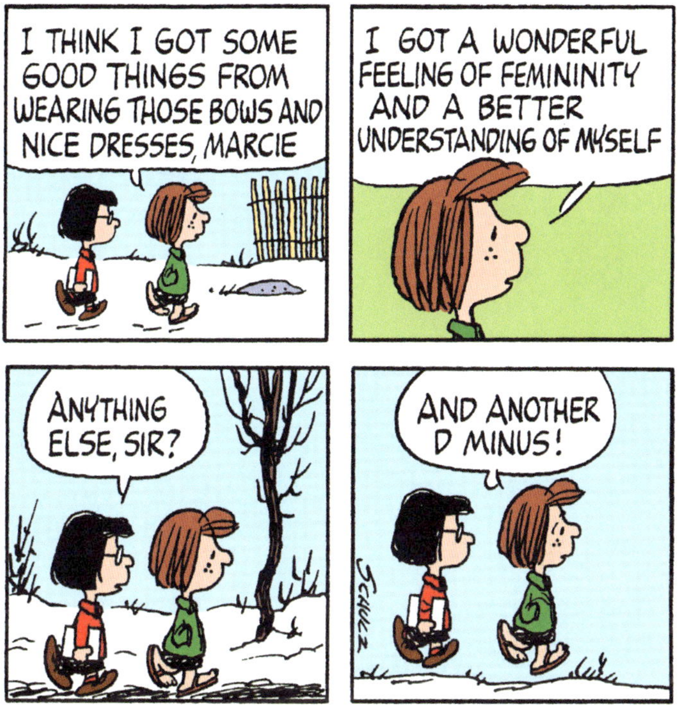
I THINK I GOT SOME GOOD THINGS FROM WEARING THOSE BOWS AND NICE DRESSES, MARCIE
I GOT A WONDERFUL FEELING OF FEMININITY AND A BETTER UNDERSTANDING OF MYSELF
ANYTHING ELSE, SIR?
AND ANOTHER D MINUS!
SCHULZ

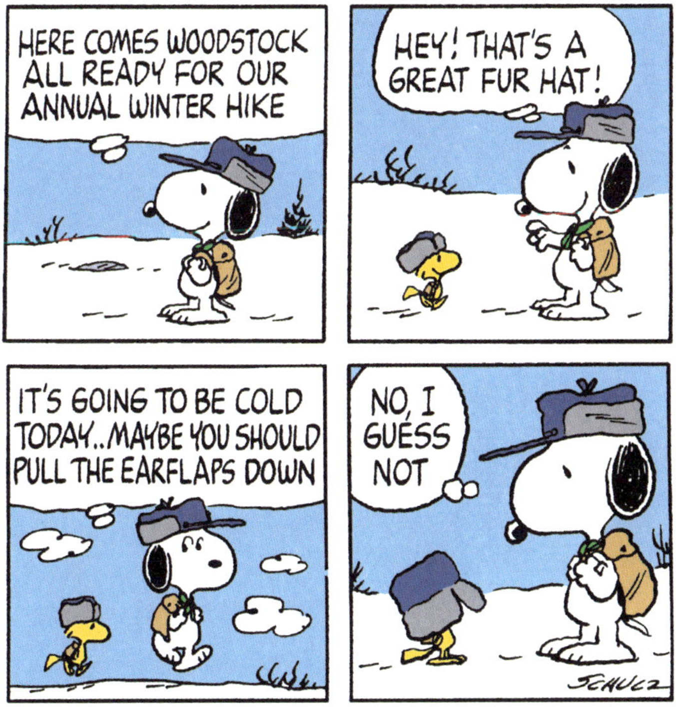
HERE COMES WOODSTOCK ALL READY FOR OUR ANNUAL WINTER HIKE
HEY! THAT'S A GREAT FUR HAT!
IT'S GOING TO BE COLD TODAY..MAYBE YOU SHOULD PULL THE EARFLAPS DOWN
NO, I GUESS NOT
SCHULZ

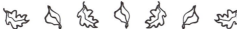

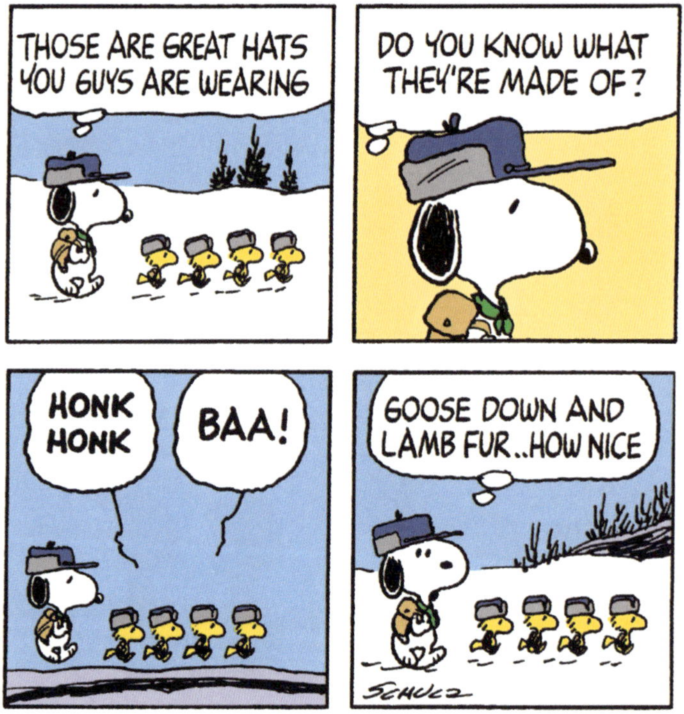
THOSE ARE GREAT HATS YOU GUYS ARE WEARING
DO YOU KNOW WHAT THEY'RE MADE OF?
HONK HONK
BAA!
GOOSE DOWN AND LAMB FUR..HOW NICE
SCHULZ

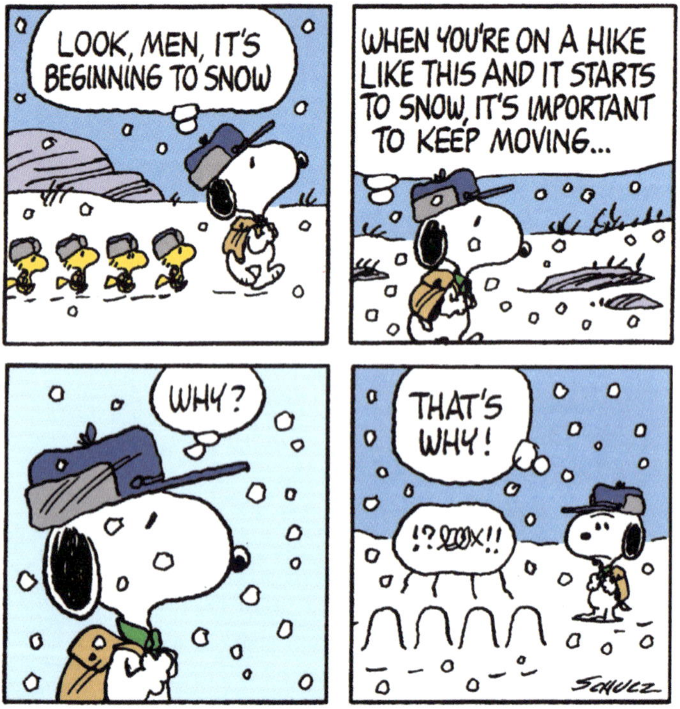
LOOK, MEN, IT'S BEGINNING TO SNOW
WHEN YOU'RE ON A HIKE LIKE THIS AND IT STARTS TO SNOW, IT'S IMPORTANT TO KEEP MOVING...
WHY?
THAT'S WHY!
SCHULZ

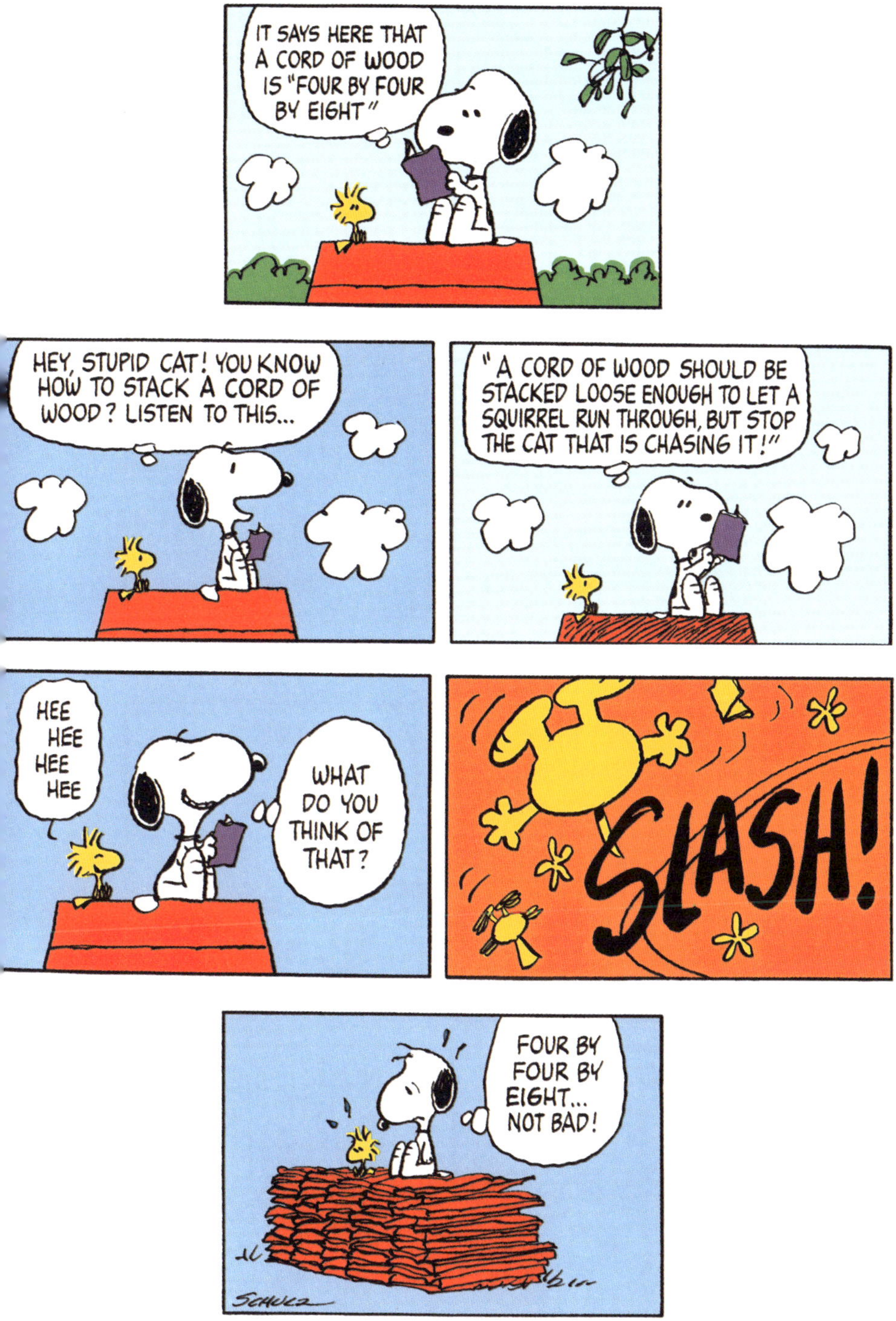
IT SAYS HERE THAT A CORD OF WOOD IS "FOUR BY FOUR BY EIGHT"
HEY, STUPID CAT! YOU KNOW HOW TO STACK A CORD OF WOOD? LISTEN TO THIS...
"A CORD OF WOOD SHOULD BE STACKED LOOSE ENOUGH TO LET A SQUIRREL RUN THROUGH, BUT STOP THE CAT THAT IS CHASING IT!"
HEE HEE HEE HEE
WHAT DO YOU THINK OF THAT?
SLASH!
FOUR BY FOUR BY EIGHT... NOT BAD!
SCHULZ

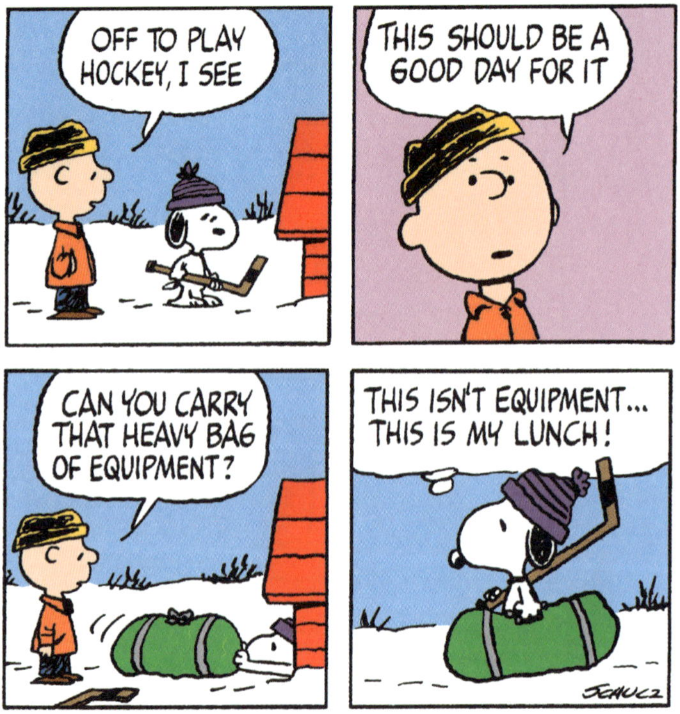
OFF TO PLAY HOCKEY, I SEE
THIS SHOULD BE A GOOD DAY FOR IT
CAN YOU CARRY THAT HEAVY BAG OF EQUIPMENT?
THIS ISN'T EQUIPMENT... THIS IS MY LUNCH!
SCHULZ

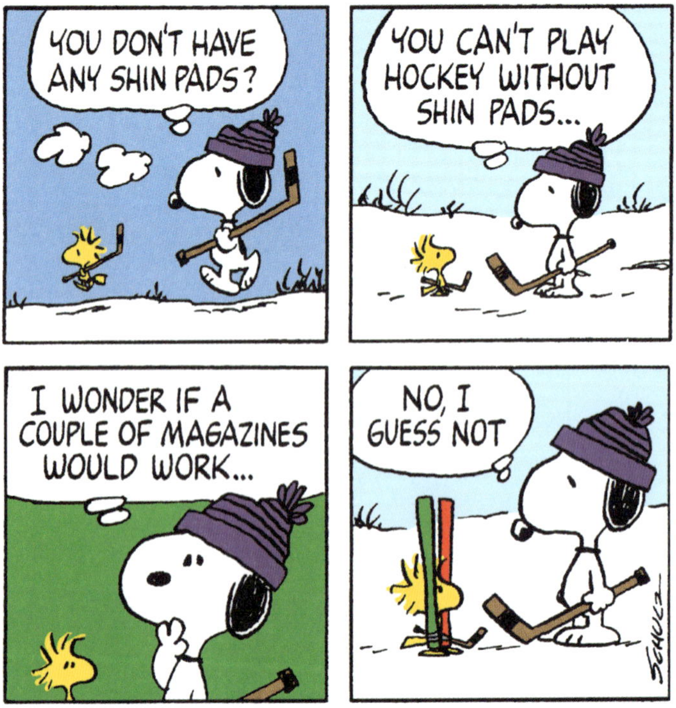
YOU DON'T HAVE ANY SHIN PADS?
YOU CAN'T PLAY HOCKEY WITHOUT SHIN PADS...
I WONDER IF A COUPLE OF MAGAZINES WOULD WORK...
NO, I GUESS NOT
SCHULZ

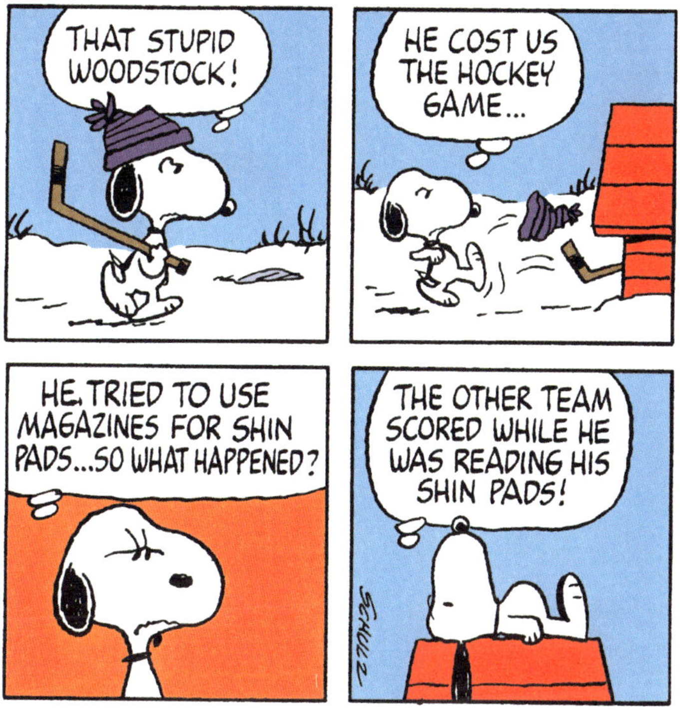
THAT STUPID WOODSTOCK!
HE COST US THE HOCKEY GAME...
HE TRIED TO USE MAGAZINES FOR SHIN PADS...SO WHAT HAPPENED?
THE OTHER TEAM SCORED WHILE HE WAS READING HIS SHIN PADS!
SCHULZ

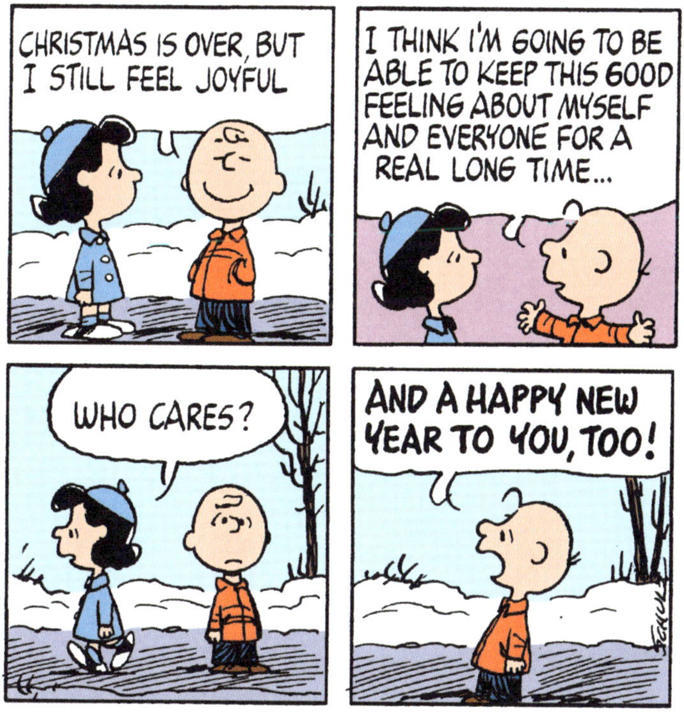
CHRISTMAS IS OVER, BUT I STILL FEEL JOYFUL
I THINK I'M GOING TO BE ABLE TO KEEP THIS GOOD FEELING ABOUT MYSELF AND EVERYONE FOR A REAL LONG TIME...
WHO CARES?
AND A HAPPY NEW YEAR TO YOU, TOO!
SCHULZ

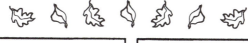

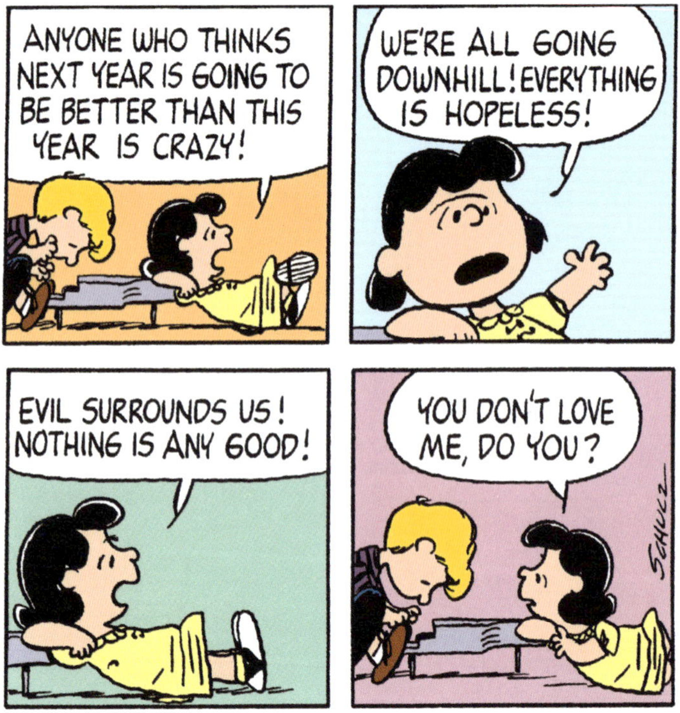
ANYONE WHO THINKS NEXT YEAR IS GOING TO BE BETTER THAN THIS YEAR IS CRAZY!
WE'RE ALL GOING DOWNHILL! EVERYTHING IS HOPELESS!
EVIL SURROUNDS US! NOTHING IS ANY GOOD!
YOU DON'T LOVE ME, DO YOU?
SCHULZ

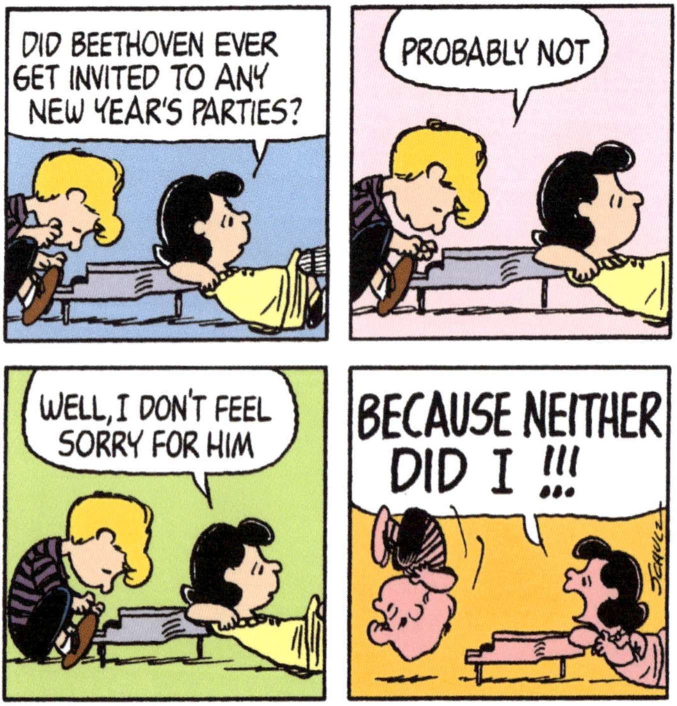
DID BEETHOVEN EVER GET INVITED TO ANY NEW YEAR'S PARTIES?
PROBABLY NOT
WELL, I DON'T FEEL SORRY FOR HIM
BECAUSE NEITHER DID I !!!
SCHULZ

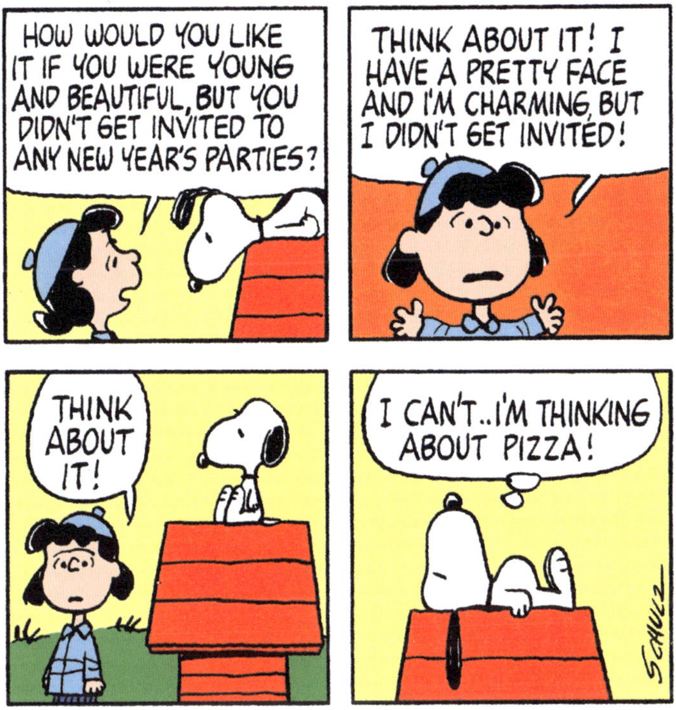
HOW WOULD YOU LIKE IT IF YOU WERE YOUNG AND BEAUTIFUL, BUT YOU DIDN'T GET INVITED TO ANY NEW YEAR'S PARTIES?
THINK ABOUT IT! I HAVE A PRETTY FACE AND I'M CHARMING, BUT I DIDN'T GET INVITED!
THINK ABOUT IT!
I CAN'T..I'M THINKING ABOUT PIZZA!
SCHULZ

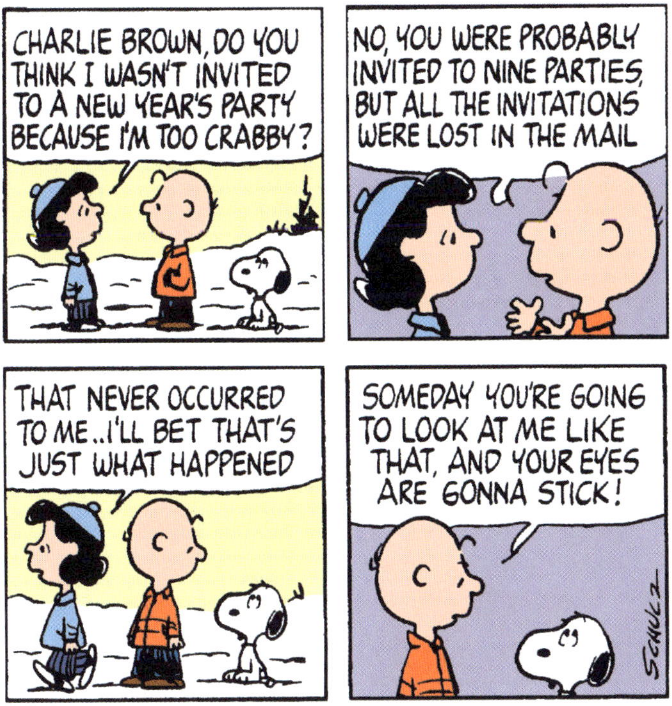
CHARLIE BROWN, DO YOU THINK I WASN'T INVITED TO A NEW YEAR'S PARTY BECAUSE I'M TOO CRABBY?
NO, YOU WERE PROBABLY INVITED TO NINE PARTIES, BUT ALL THE INVITATIONS WERE LOST IN THE MAIL
THAT NEVER OCCURRED TO ME..I'LL BET THAT'S JUST WHAT HAPPENED
SOMEDAY YOU'RE GOING TO LOOK AT ME LIKE THAT, AND YOUR EYES ARE GONNA STICK!
SCHULZ

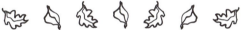

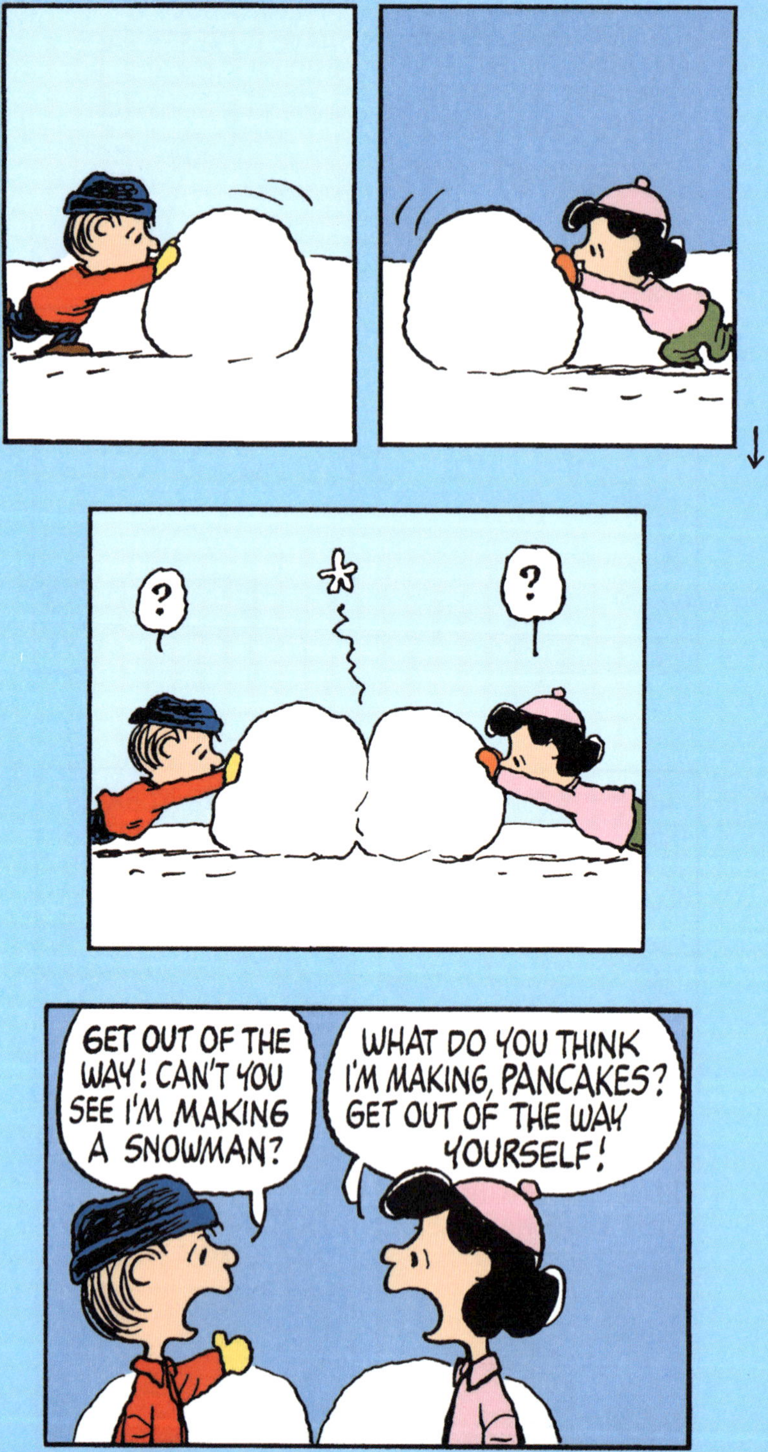
?
?
GET OUT OF THE WAY! CAN'T YOU SEE I'M MAKING A SNOWMAN?
WHAT DO YOU THINK I'M MAKING, PANCAKES? GET OUT OF THE WAY YOURSELF!

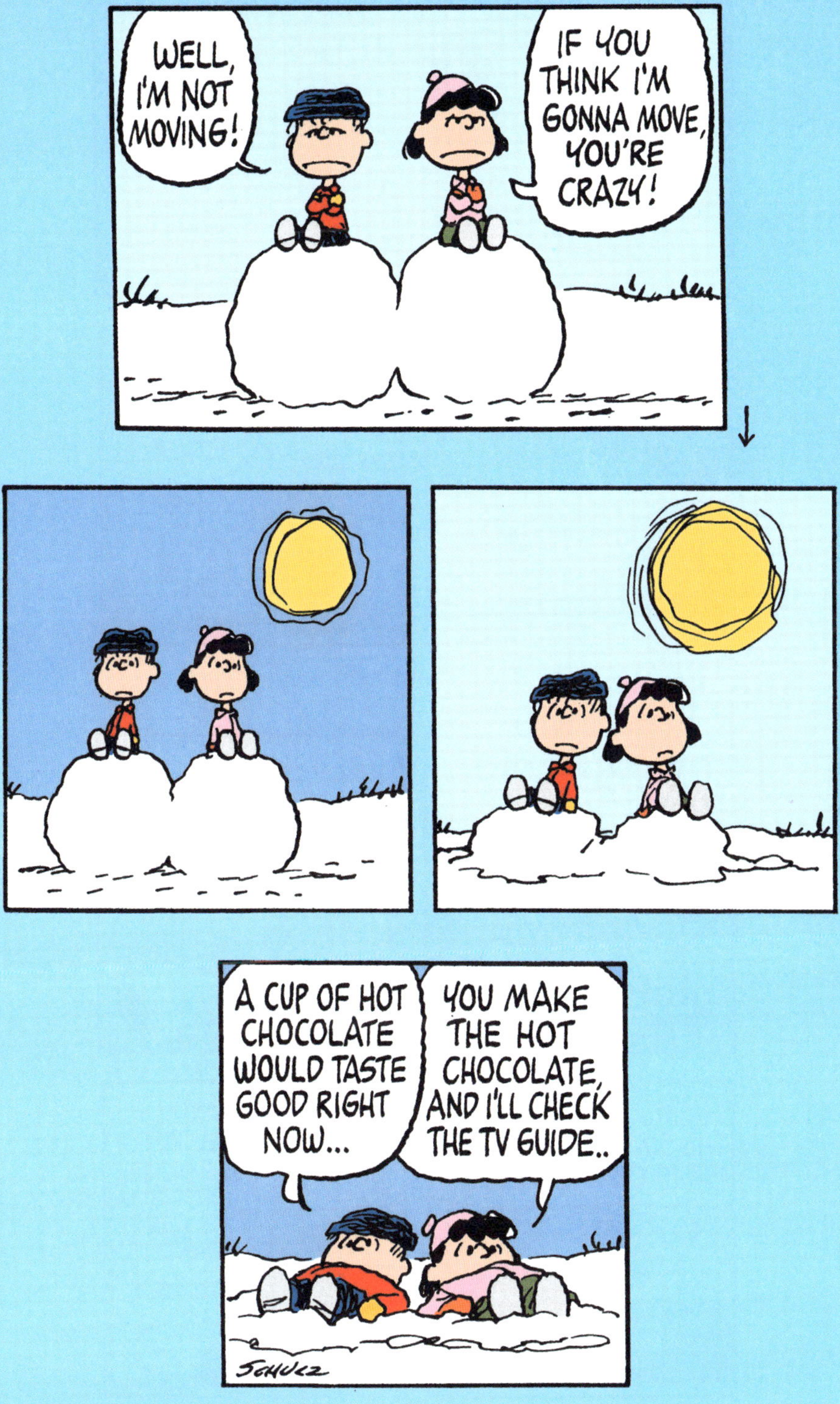
WELL, I'M NOT MOVING!
IF YOU THINK I'M GONNA MOVE, YOU'RE CRAZY!
A CUP OF HOT CHOCOLATE WOULD TASTE GOOD RIGHT NOW...
YOU MAKE THE HOT CHOCOLATE, AND I'LL CHECK THE TV GUIDE..
SCHULZ

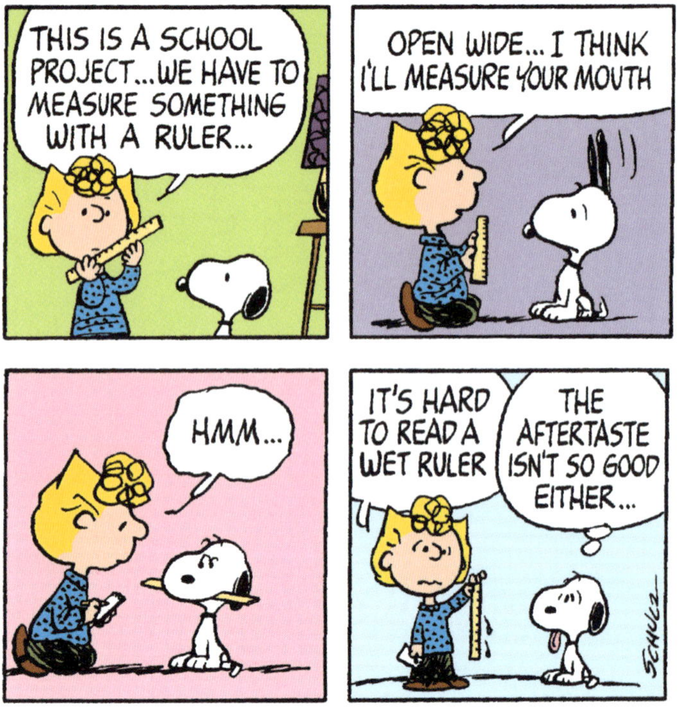
THIS IS A SCHOOL PROJECT...WE HAVE TO MEASURE SOMETHING WITH A RULER...
OPEN WIDE... I THINK I'LL MEASURE YOUR MOUTH
HMM...
IT'S HARD TO READ A WET RULER
THE AFTERTASTE ISN'T SO GOOD EITHER...
SCHULZ

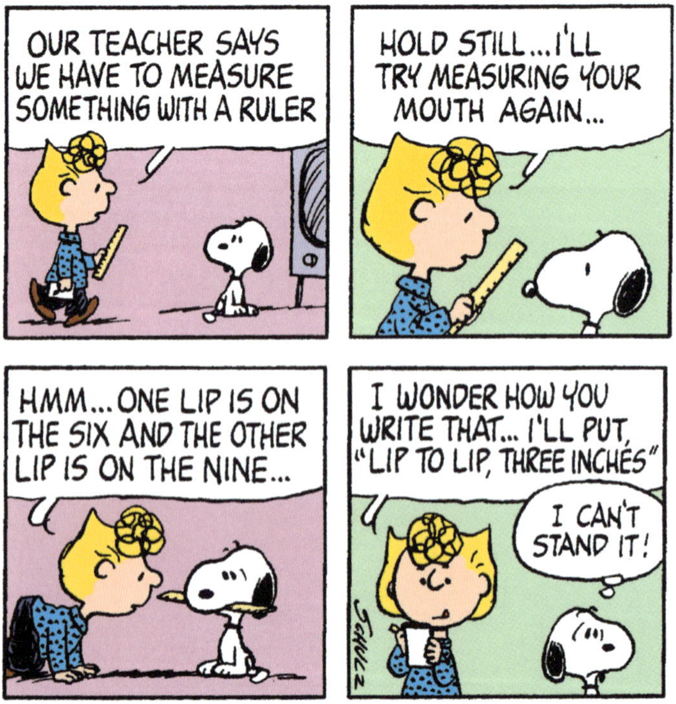
OUR TEACHER SAYS WE HAVE TO MEASURE SOMETHING WITH A RULER
HOLD STILL...I'LL TRY MEASURING YOUR MOUTH AGAIN...
HMM...ONE LIP IS ON THE SIX AND THE OTHER LIP IS ON THE NINE...
I WONDER HOW YOU WRITE THAT... I'LL PUT, "LIP TO LIP, THREE INCHES"
I CAN'T STAND IT!
SCHULZ

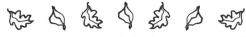

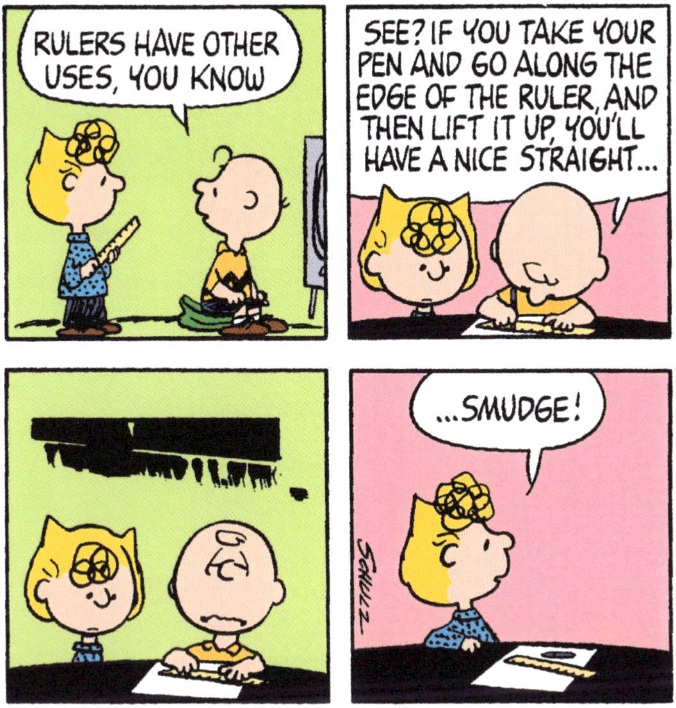
RULERS HAVE OTHER USES, YOU KNOW
SEE? IF YOU TAKE YOUR PEN AND GO ALONG THE EDGE OF THE RULER, AND THEN LIFT IT UP, YOU'LL HAVE A NICE STRAIGHT...
...SMUDGE!
SCHULZ

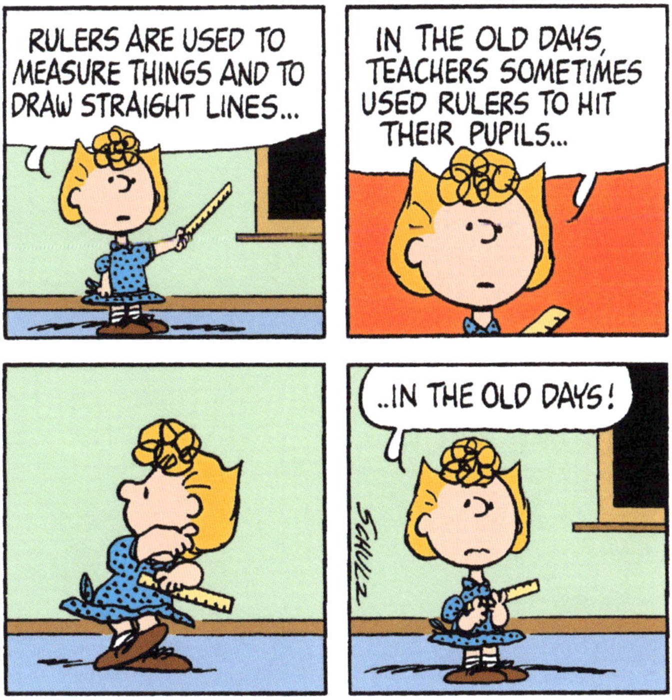
RULERS ARE USED TO MEASURE THINGS AND TO DRAW STRAIGHT LINES...
IN THE OLD DAYS, TEACHERS SOMETIMES USED RULERS TO HIT THEIR PUPILS...
..IN THE OLD DAYS!
SCHULZ

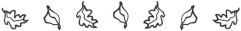

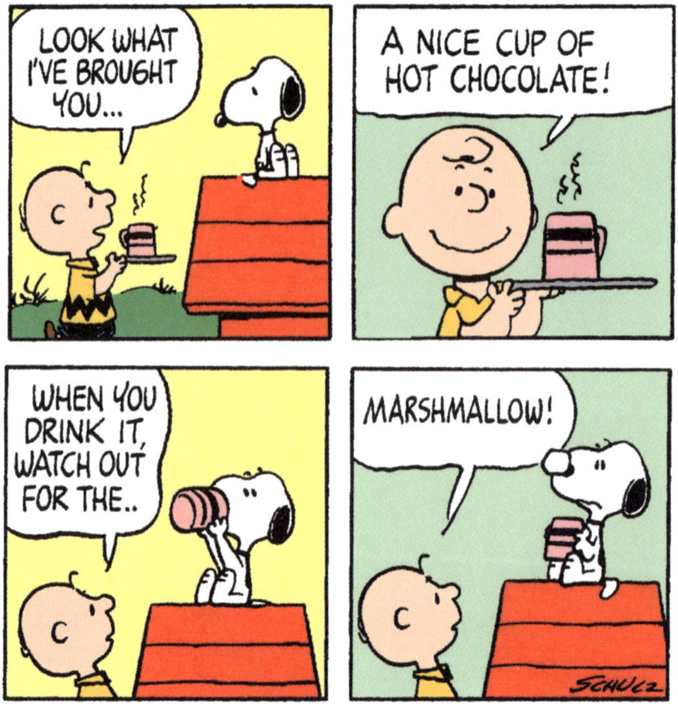
LOOK WHAT I'VE BROUGHT YOU...
A NICE CUP OF HOT CHOCOLATE!
WHEN YOU DRINK IT, WATCH OUT FOR THE..
MARSHMALLOW!

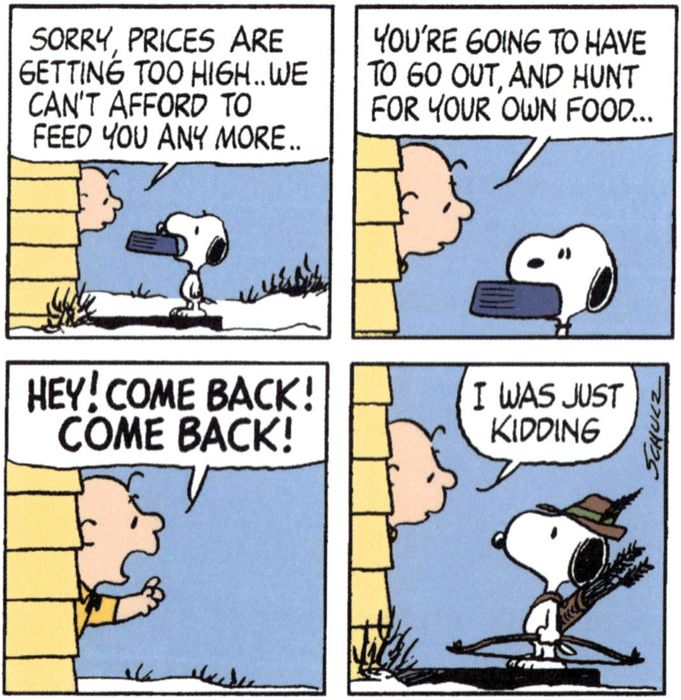
SORRY, PRICES ARE GETTING TOO HIGH..WE CAN'T AFFORD TO FEED YOU ANY MORE..
YOU'RE GOING TO HAVE TO GO OUT, AND HUNT FOR YOUR OWN FOOD...
HEY! COME BACK! COME BACK!
I WAS JUST KIDDING

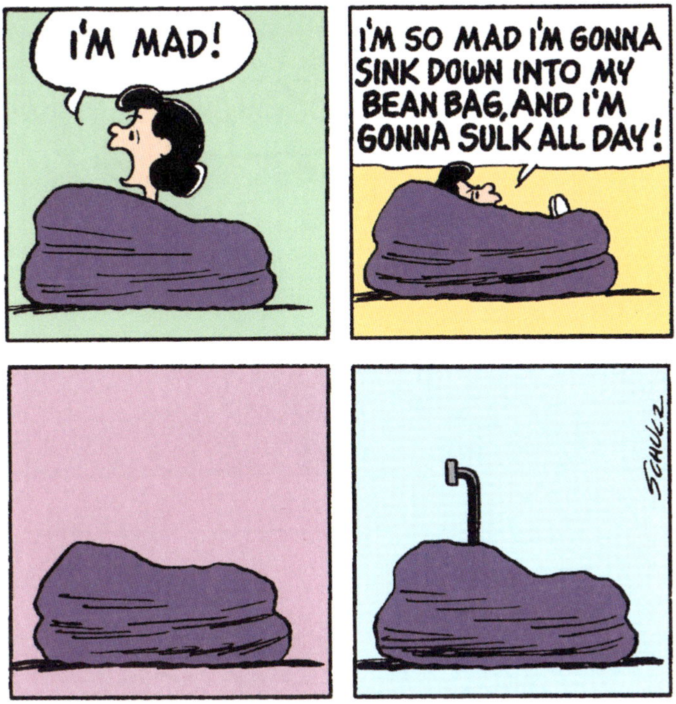
I'M MAD!
I'M SO MAD I'M GONNA SINK DOWN INTO MY BEAN BAG, AND I'M GONNA SULK ALL DAY!
SCHULZ

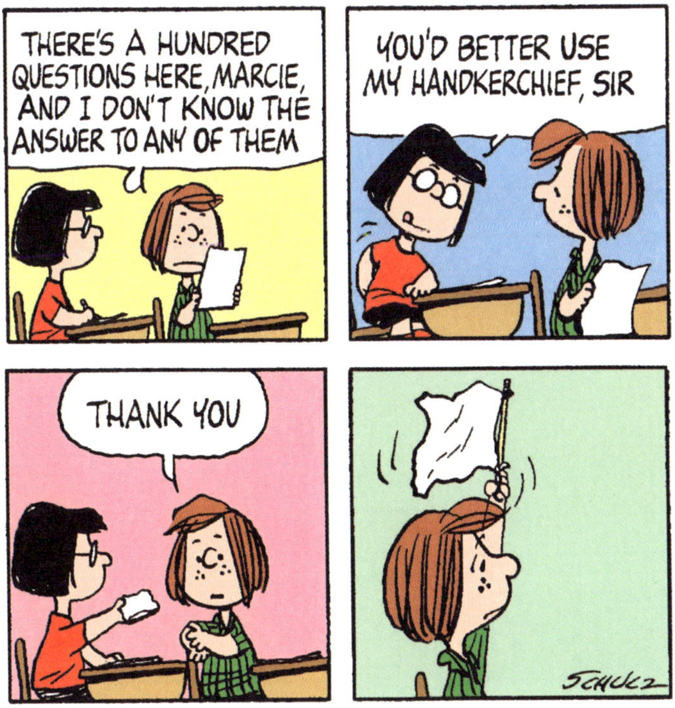
THERE'S A HUNDRED QUESTIONS HERE, MARCIE, AND I DON'T KNOW THE ANSWER TO ANY OF THEM
YOU'D BETTER USE MY HANDKERCHIEF, SIR
THANK YOU
SCHULZ

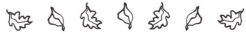

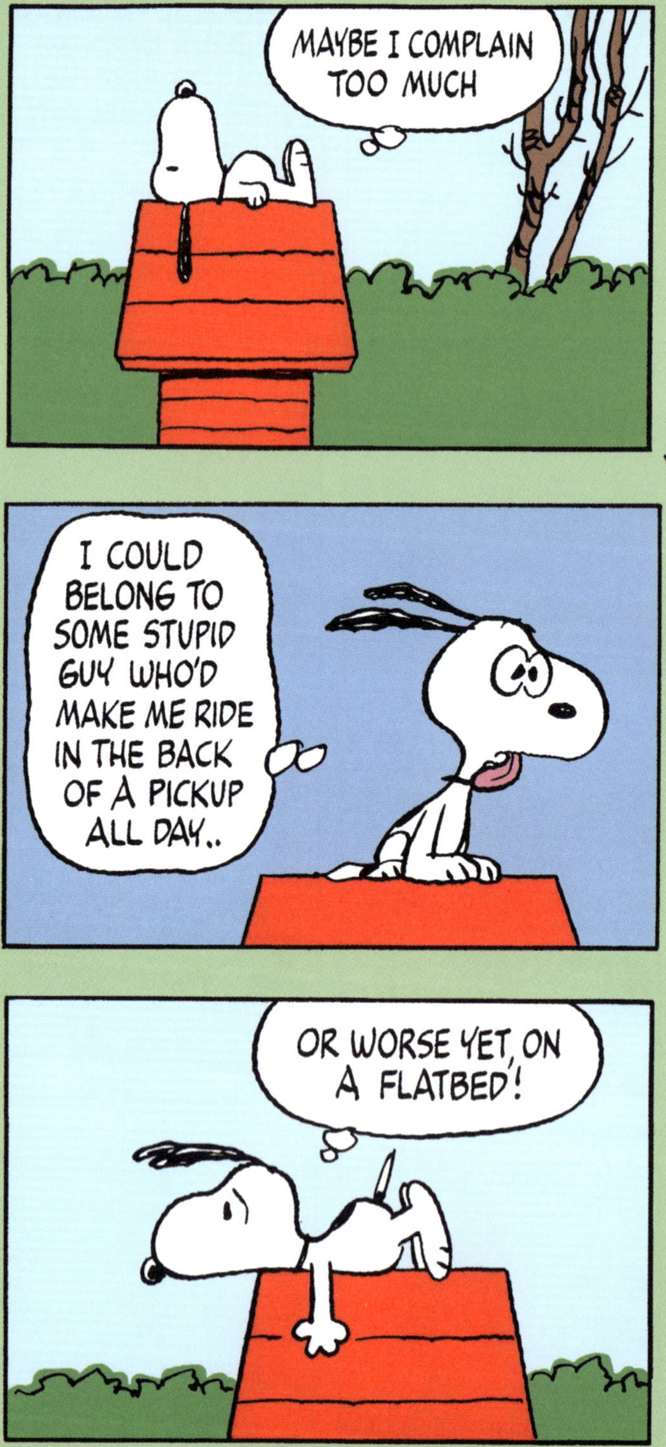
MAYBE I COMPLAIN TOO MUCH
I COULD BELONG TO SOME STUPID GUY WHO'D MAKE ME RIDE IN THE BACK OF A PICKUP ALL DAY..
OR WORSE YET, ON A FLATBED!

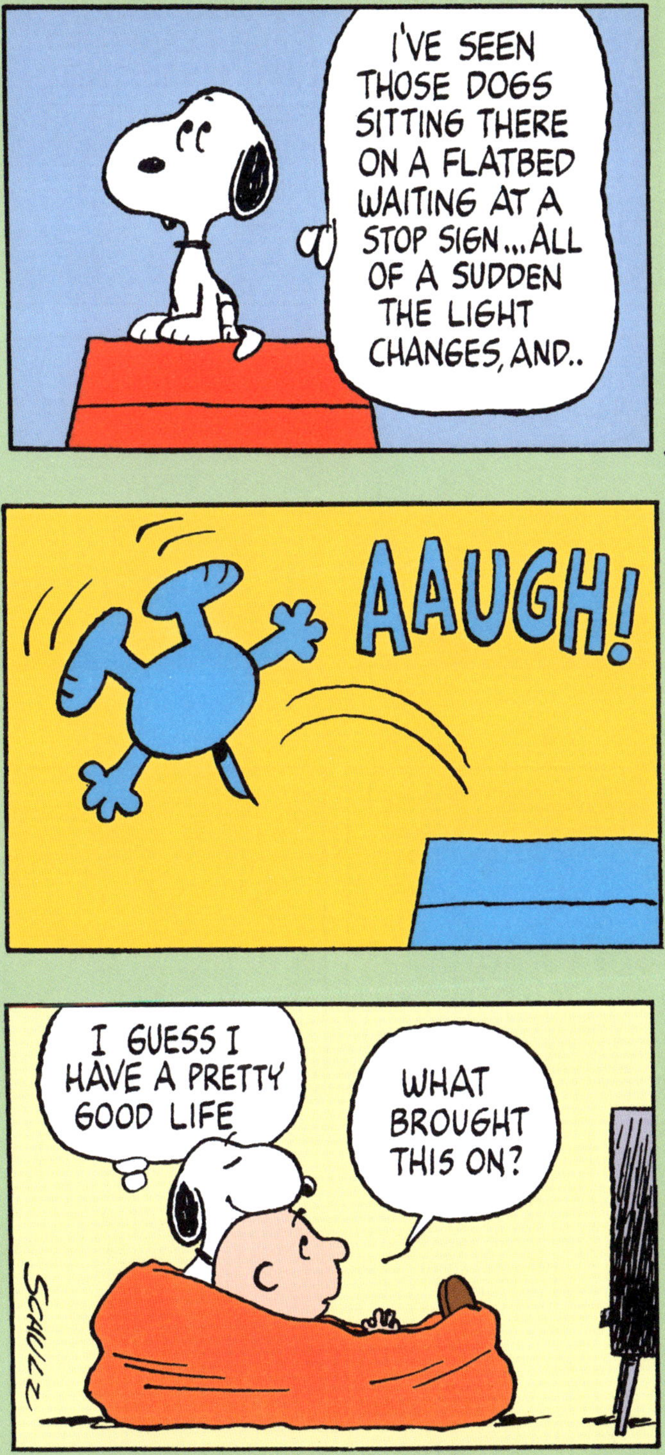
I'VE SEEN THOSE DOGS SITTING THERE ON A FLATBED WAITING AT A STOP SIGN...ALL OF A SUDDEN THE LIGHT CHANGES, AND..
AAUGH!
I GUESS I HAVE A PRETTY GOOD LIFE
WHAT BROUGHT THIS ON?
SCHULZ

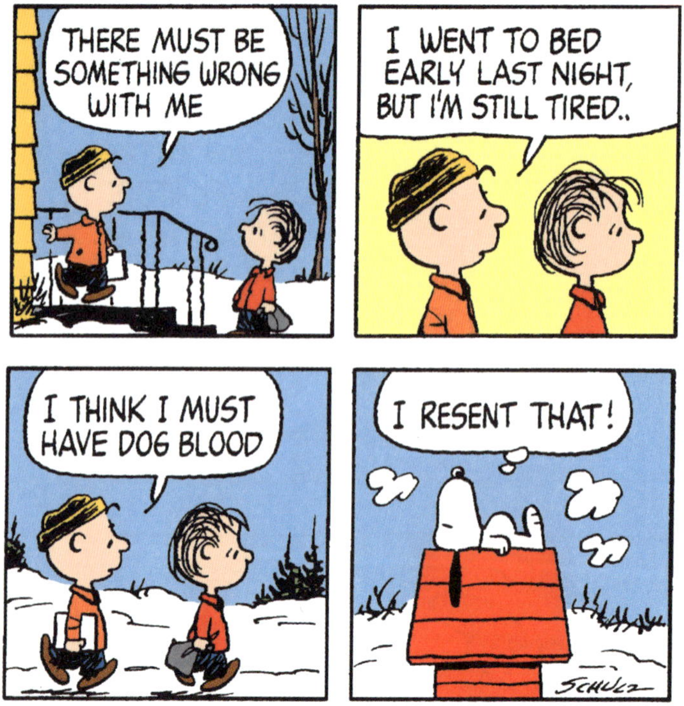
THERE MUST BE SOMETHING WRONG WITH ME
I WENT TO BED EARLY LAST NIGHT, BUT I'M STILL TIRED..
I THINK I MUST HAVE DOG BLOOD
I RESENT THAT!
SCHULZ

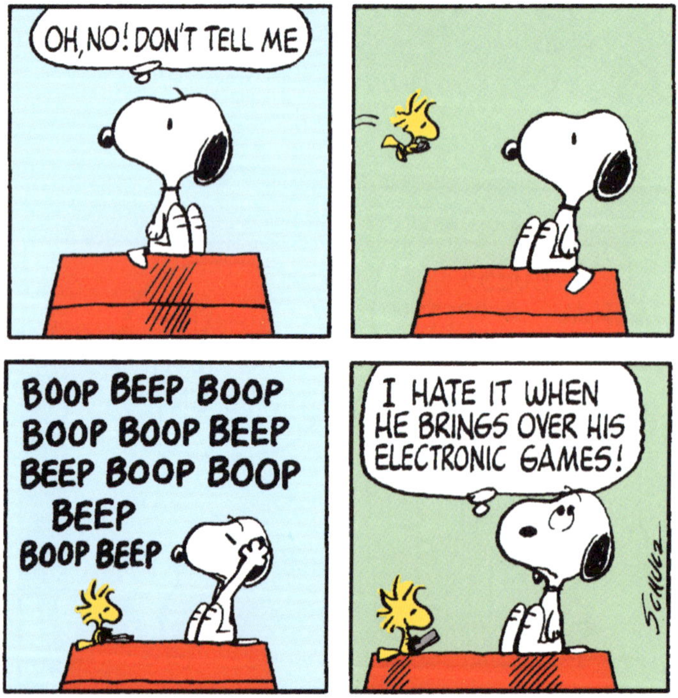
OH, NO! DON'T TELL ME
BOOP BEEP BOOP
BOOP BOOP BEEP
BEEP BOOP BOOP
BEEP
BOOP BEEP
I HATE IT WHEN HE BRINGS OVER HIS ELECTRONIC GAMES!
SCHULZ

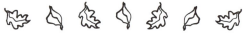

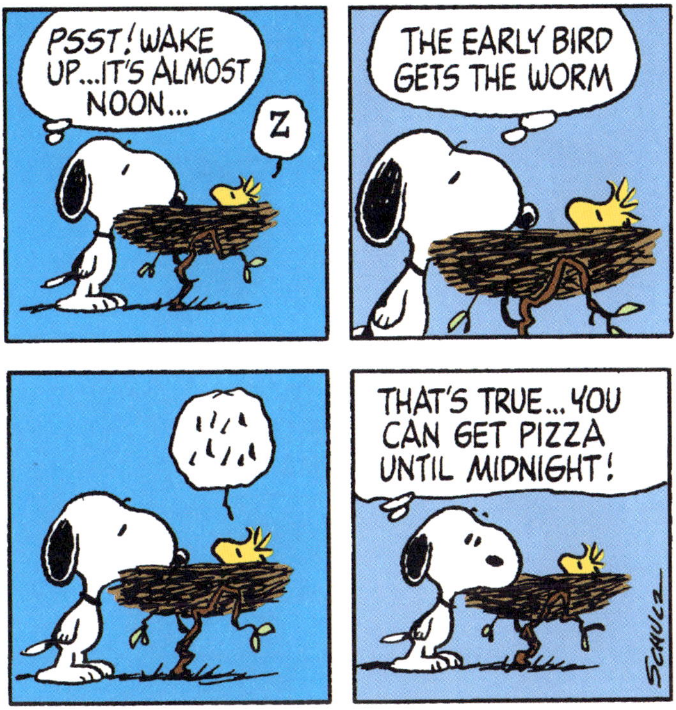
PSST! WAKE UP...IT'S ALMOST NOON...
Z
THE EARLY BIRD GETS THE WORM
THAT'S TRUE... YOU CAN GET PIZZA UNTIL MIDNIGHT!
SCHULZ

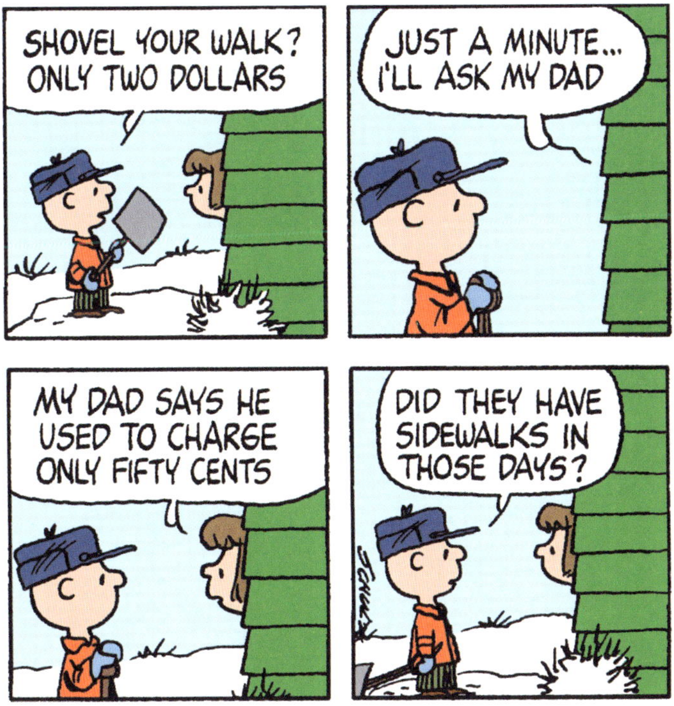
SHOVEL YOUR WALK? ONLY TWO DOLLARS
JUST A MINUTE... I'LL ASK MY DAD
MY DAD SAYS HE USED TO CHARGE ONLY FIFTY CENTS
DID THEY HAVE SIDEWALKS IN THOSE DAYS?
SCHULZ

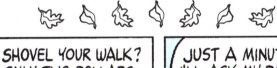

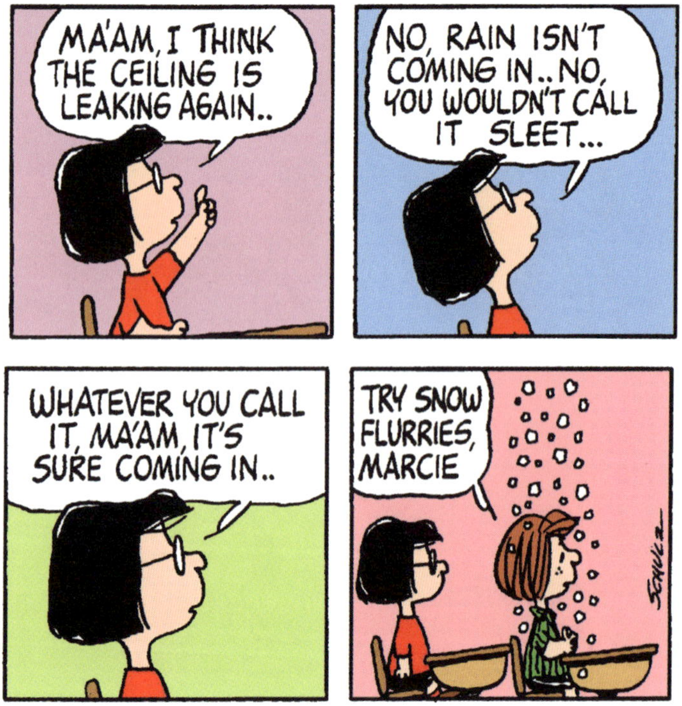
MA'AM, I THINK THE CEILING IS LEAKING AGAIN..
NO, RAIN ISN'T COMING IN.. NO, YOU WOULDN'T CALL IT SLEET...
WHATEVER YOU CALL IT, MA'AM, IT'S SURE COMING IN..
TRY SNOW FLURRIES, MARCIE
SCHULZ

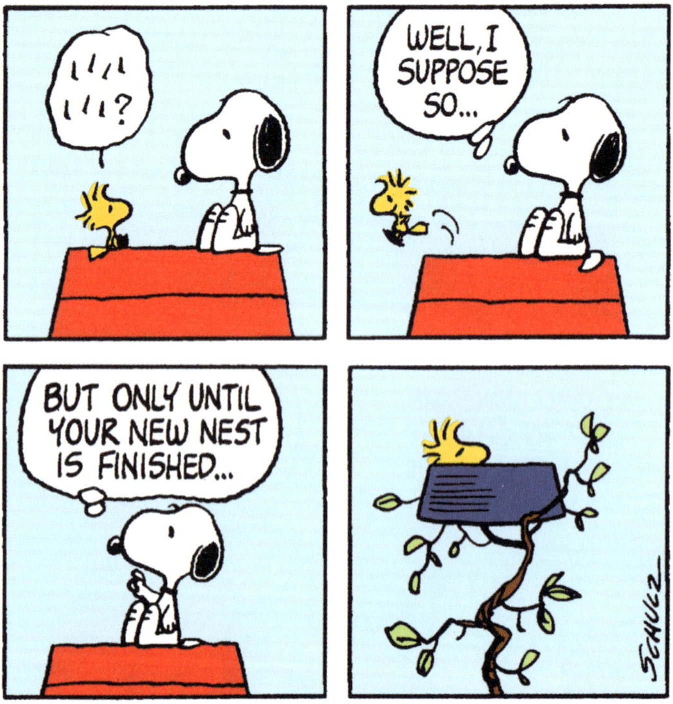
WELL, I SUPPOSE SO...
BUT ONLY UNTIL YOUR NEW NEST IS FINISHED...
SCHULZ

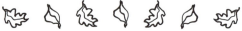

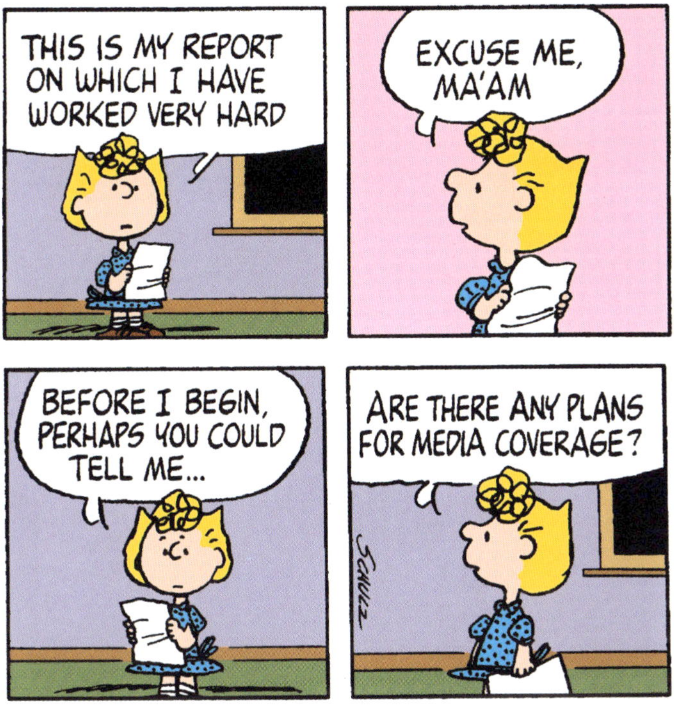
THIS IS MY REPORT ON WHICH I HAVE WORKED VERY HARD
EXCUSE ME, MA'AM
BEFORE I BEGIN, PERHAPS YOU COULD TELL ME...
ARE THERE ANY PLANS FOR MEDIA COVERAGE?

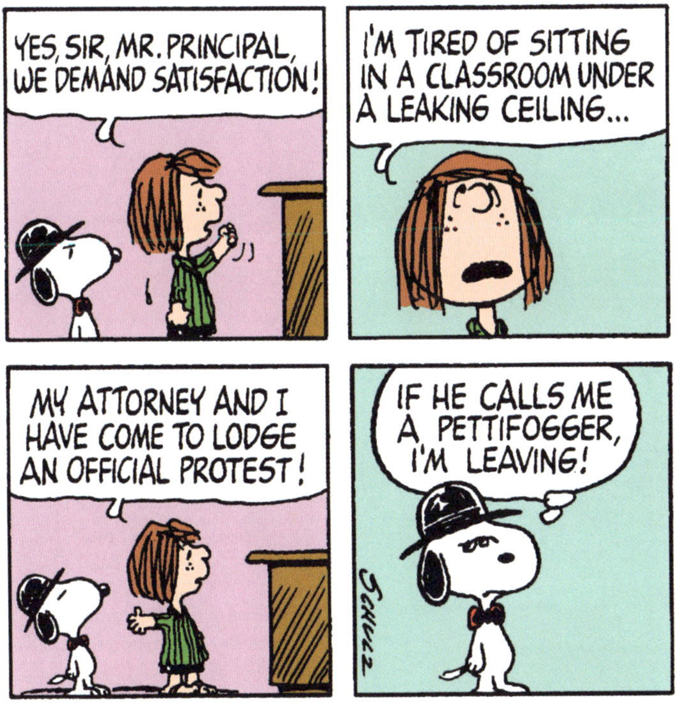
YES, SIR, MR. PRINCIPAL, WE DEMAND SATISFACTION!
I'M TIRED OF SITTING IN A CLASSROOM UNDER A LEAKING CEILING...
MY ATTORNEY AND I HAVE COME TO LODGE AN OFFICIAL PROTEST!
IF HE CALLS ME A PETTIFOGGER, I'M LEAVING!

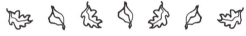

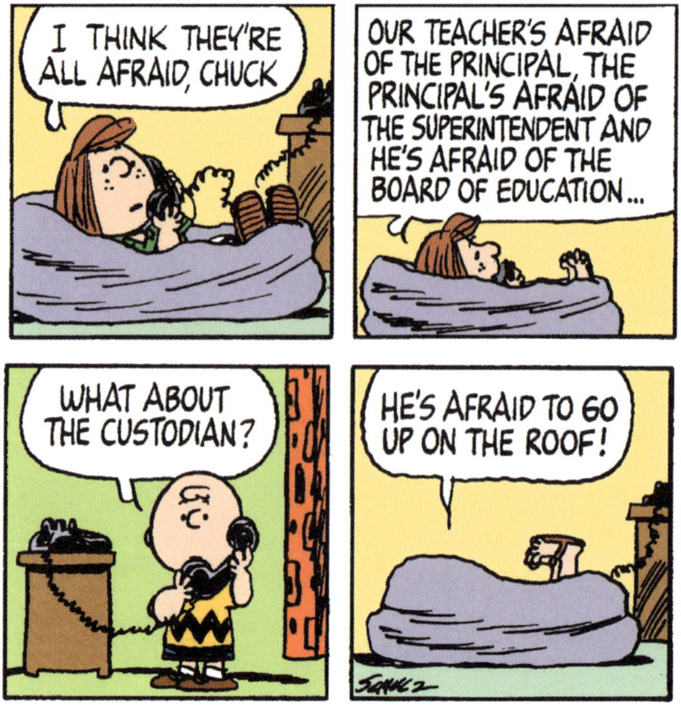
I THINK THEY'RE ALL AFRAID, CHUCK
OUR TEACHER'S AFRAID OF THE PRINCIPAL, THE PRINCIPAL'S AFRAID OF THE SUPERINTENDENT AND HE'S AFRAID OF THE BOARD OF EDUCATION...
WHAT ABOUT THE CUSTODIAN?
HE'S AFRAID TO GO UP ON THE ROOF!
SCHULZ

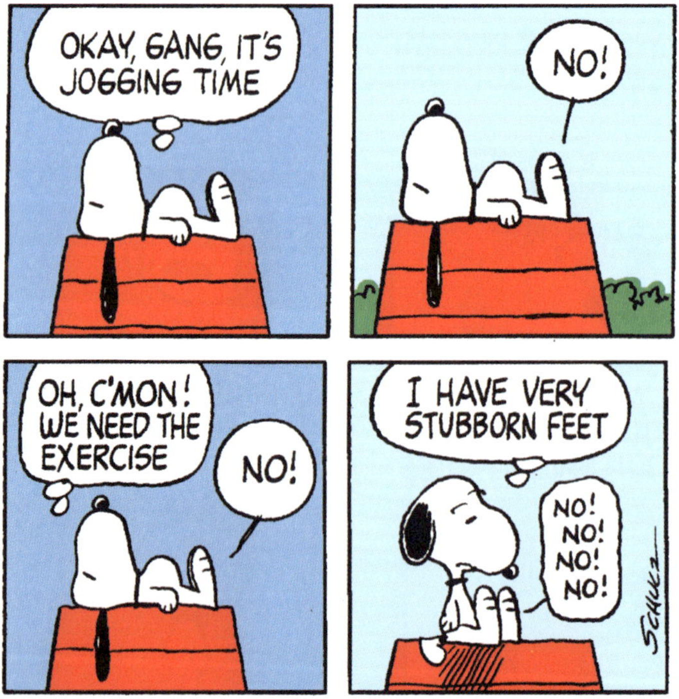
OKAY, GANG, IT'S JOGGING TIME
NO!
OH, C'MON! WE NEED THE EXERCISE
NO!
I HAVE VERY STUBBORN FEET
NO! NO! NO! NO!
SCHULZ

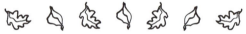

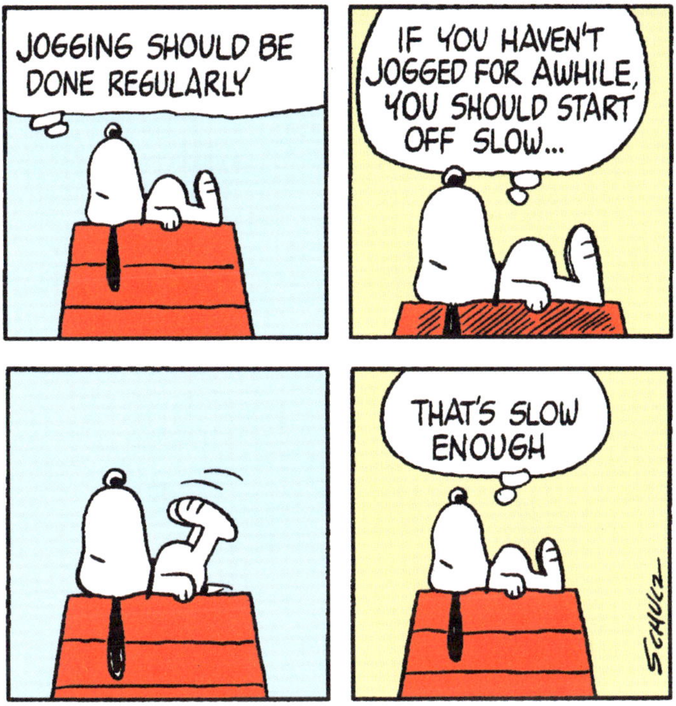
JOGGING SHOULD BE DONE REGULARLY
IF YOU HAVEN'T JOGGED FOR AWHILE, YOU SHOULD START OFF SLOW...
THAT'S SLOW ENOUGH
SCHULZ

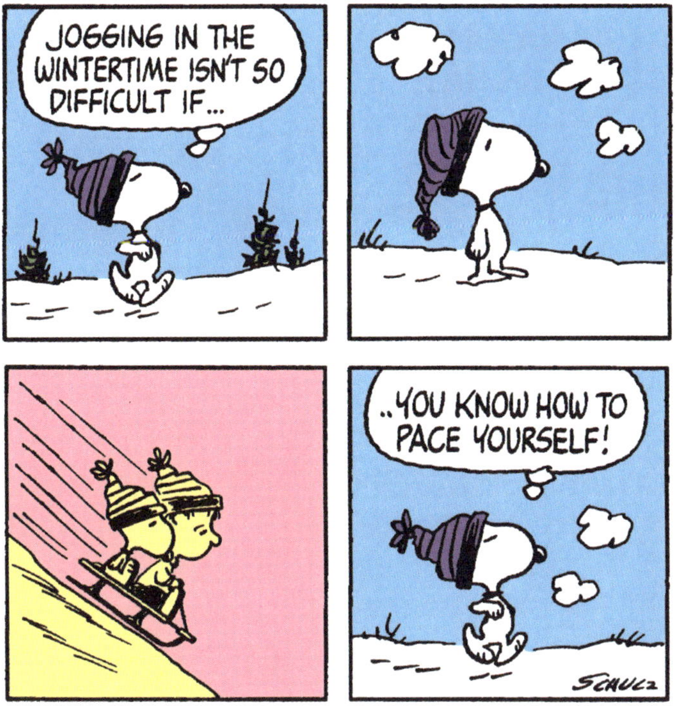
JOGGING IN THE WINTERTIME ISN'T SO DIFFICULT IF...
..YOU KNOW HOW TO PACE YOURSELF!
SCHULZ

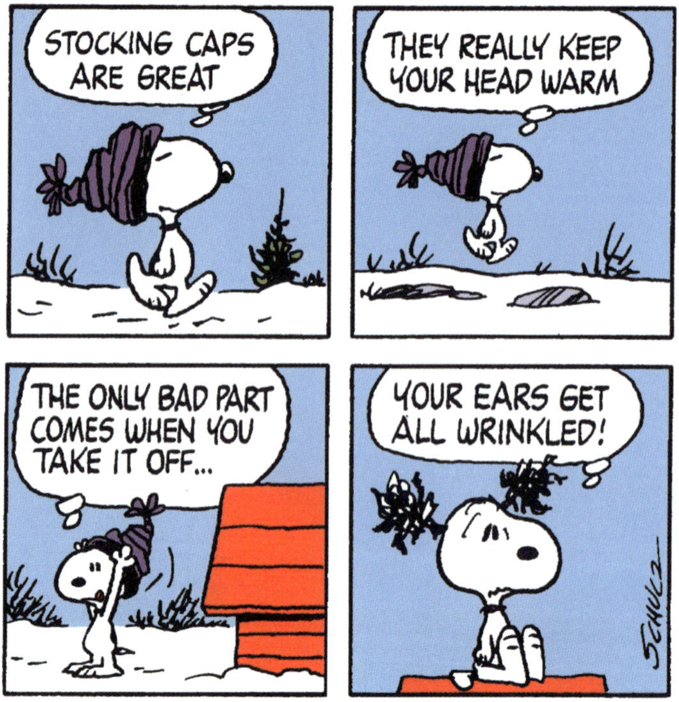
STOCKING CAPS ARE GREAT
THEY REALLY KEEP YOUR HEAD WARM
THE ONLY BAD PART COMES WHEN YOU TAKE IT OFF...
YOUR EARS GET ALL WRINKLED!
SCHULZ

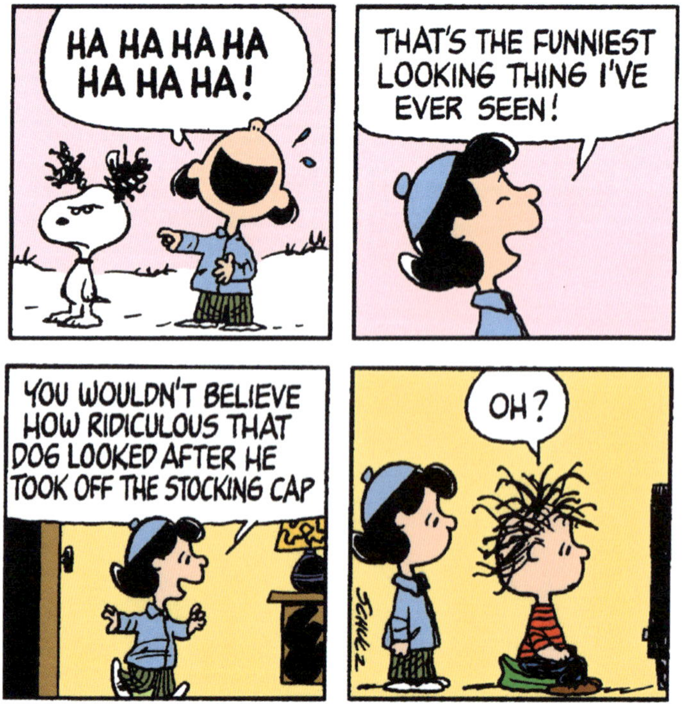
HA HA HA HA HA HA HA!
THAT'S THE FUNNIEST LOOKING THING I'VE EVER SEEN!
YOU WOULDN'T BELIEVE HOW RIDICULOUS THAT DOG LOOKED AFTER HE TOOK OFF THE STOCKING CAP
OH?
SCHULZ

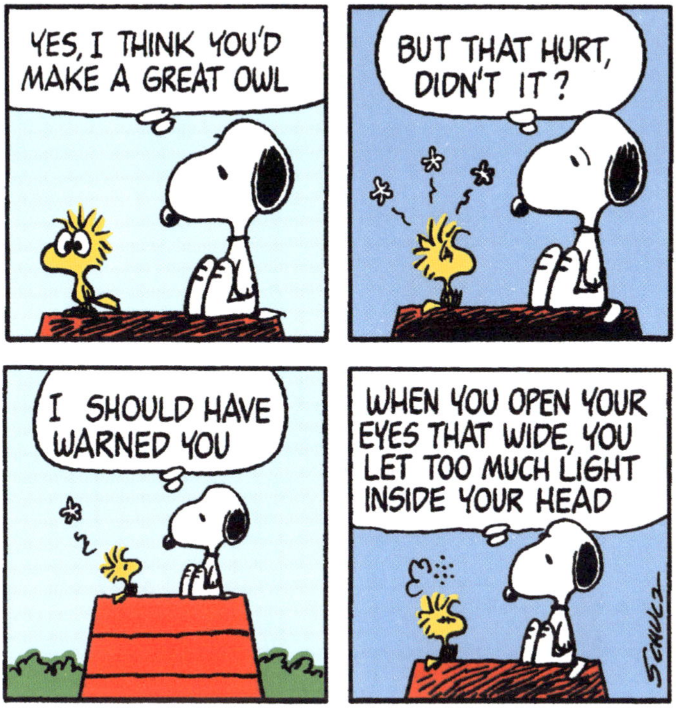
YES, I THINK YOU'D MAKE A GREAT OWL
BUT THAT HURT, DIDN'T IT ?
I SHOULD HAVE WARNED YOU
WHEN YOU OPEN YOUR EYES THAT WIDE, YOU LET TOO MUCH LIGHT INSIDE YOUR HEAD

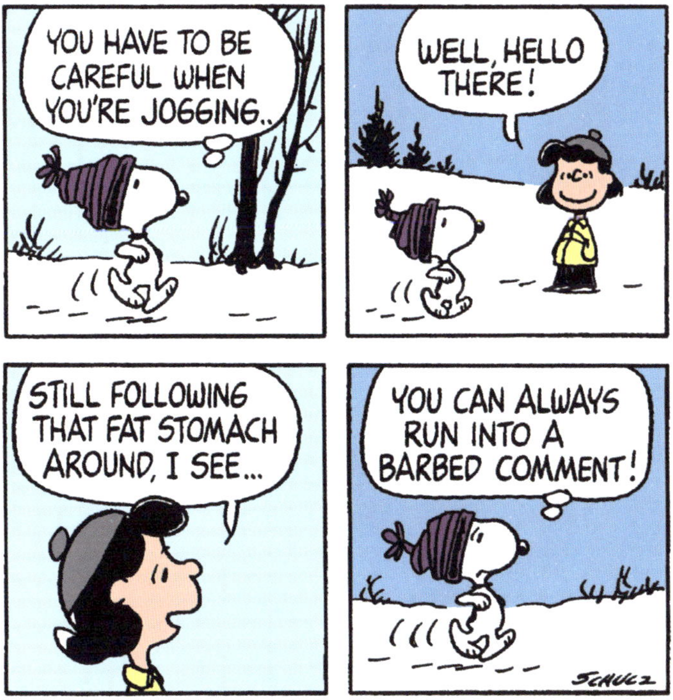
YOU HAVE TO BE CAREFUL WHEN YOU'RE JOGGING..
WELL, HELLO THERE!
STILL FOLLOWING THAT FAT STOMACH AROUND, I SEE...
YOU CAN ALWAYS RUN INTO A BARBED COMMENT!

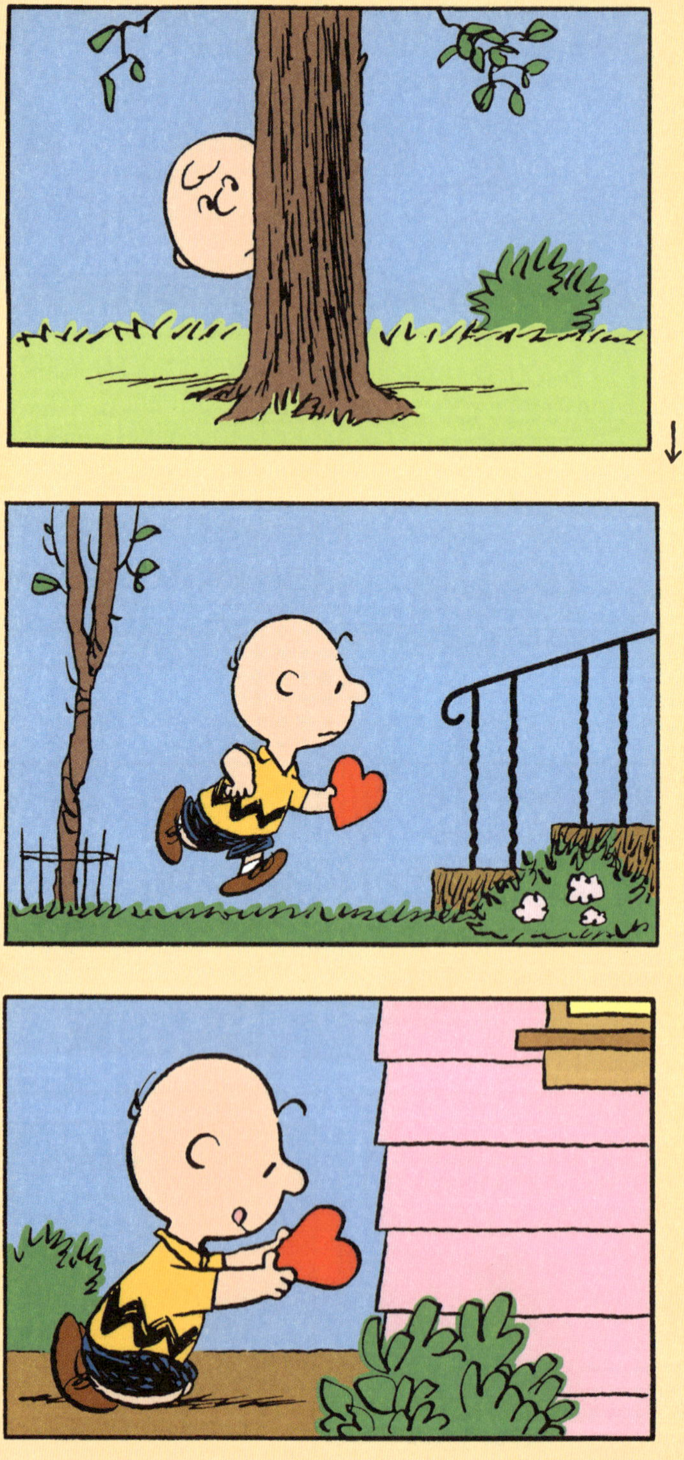

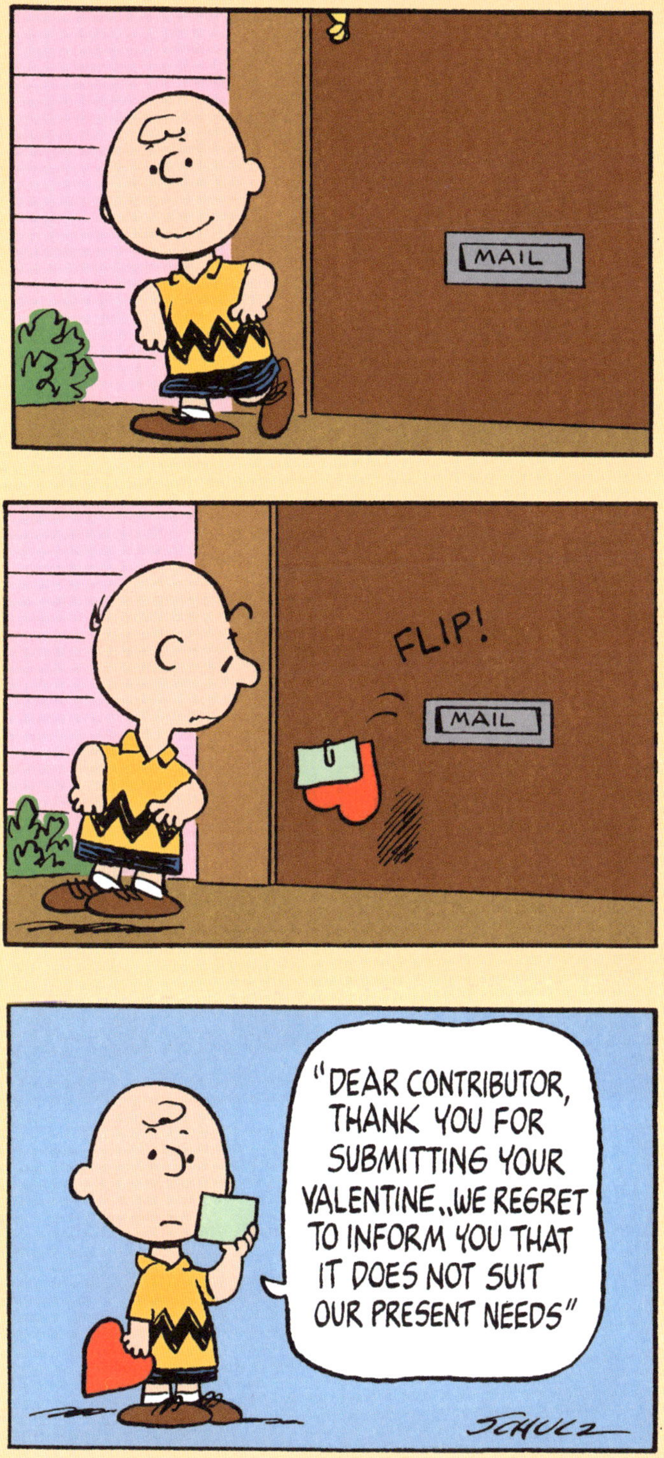
MAIL
FLIP!
MAIL
"DEAR CONTRIBUTOR, THANK YOU FOR SUBMITTING YOUR VALENTINE..WE REGRET TO INFORM YOU THAT IT DOES NOT SUIT OUR PRESENT NEEDS"
SCHULZ

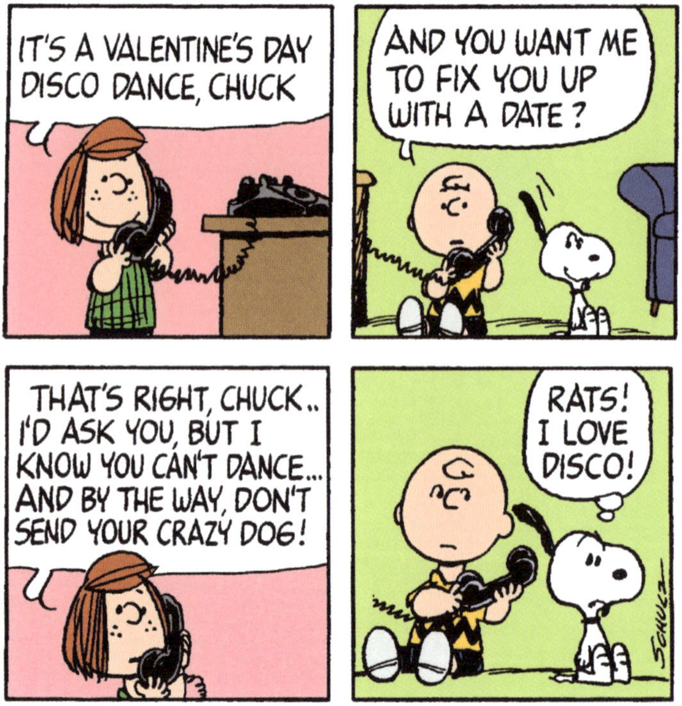
IT'S A VALENTINE'S DAY DISCO DANCE, CHUCK
AND YOU WANT ME TO FIX YOU UP WITH A DATE?
THAT'S RIGHT, CHUCK.. I'D ASK YOU, BUT I KNOW YOU CAN'T DANCE... AND BY THE WAY, DON'T SEND YOUR CRAZY DOG!
RATS! I LOVE DISCO!
SCHULZ

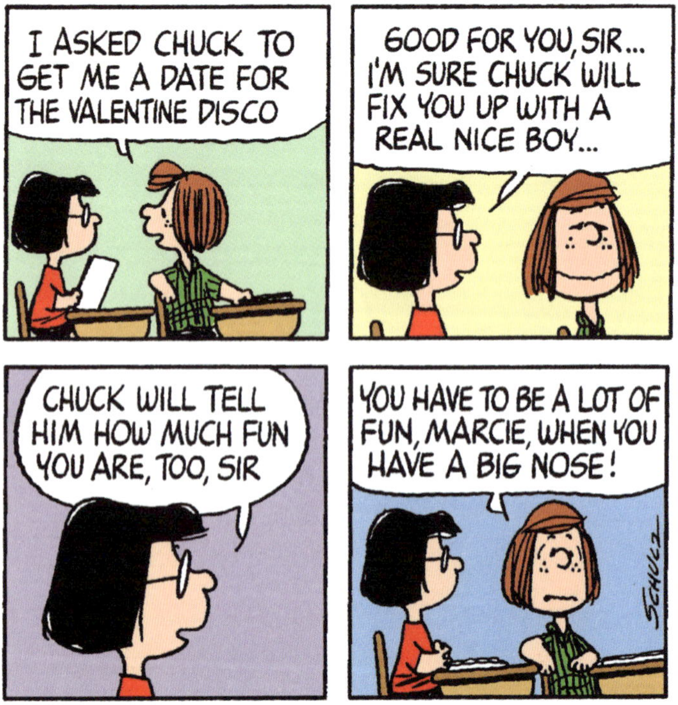
I ASKED CHUCK TO GET ME A DATE FOR THE VALENTINE DISCO
GOOD FOR YOU, SIR... I'M SURE CHUCK WILL FIX YOU UP WITH A REAL NICE BOY...
CHUCK WILL TELL HIM HOW MUCH FUN YOU ARE, TOO, SIR
YOU HAVE TO BE A LOT OF FUN, MARCIE, WHEN YOU HAVE A BIG NOSE!
SCHULZ

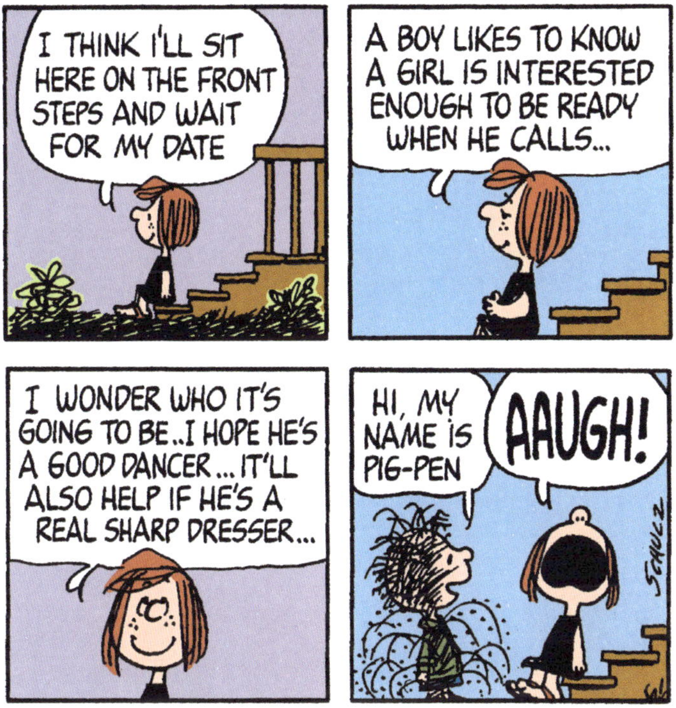
I THINK I'LL SIT HERE ON THE FRONT STEPS AND WAIT FOR MY DATE
A BOY LIKES TO KNOW A GIRL IS INTERESTED ENOUGH TO BE READY WHEN HE CALLS...
I WONDER WHO IT'S GOING TO BE..I HOPE HE'S A GOOD DANCER... IT'LL ALSO HELP IF HE'S A REAL SHARP DRESSER...
HI, MY NAME IS PIG-PEN
AAUGH!

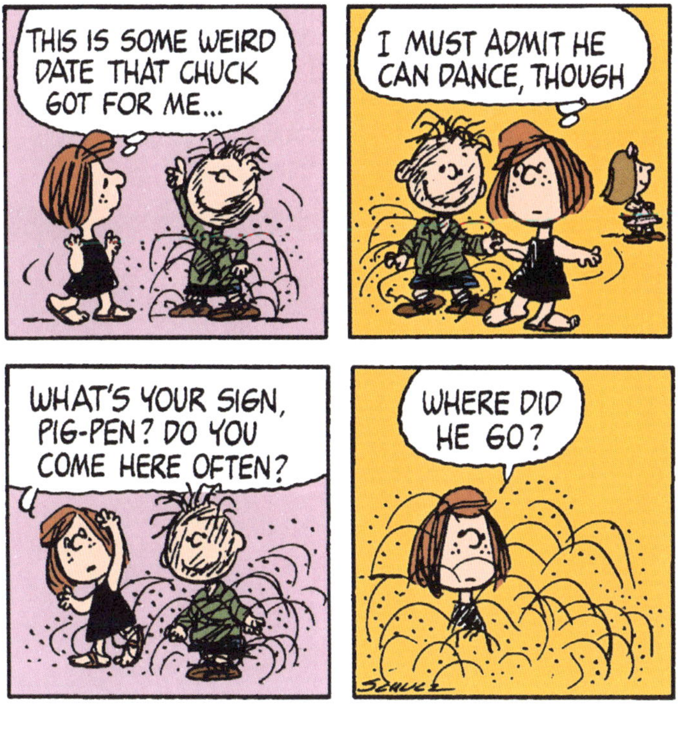
THIS IS SOME WEIRD DATE THAT CHUCK GOT FOR ME...
I MUST ADMIT HE CAN DANCE, THOUGH
WHAT'S YOUR SIGN, PIG-PEN? DO YOU COME HERE OFTEN?
WHERE DID HE GO?

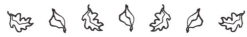

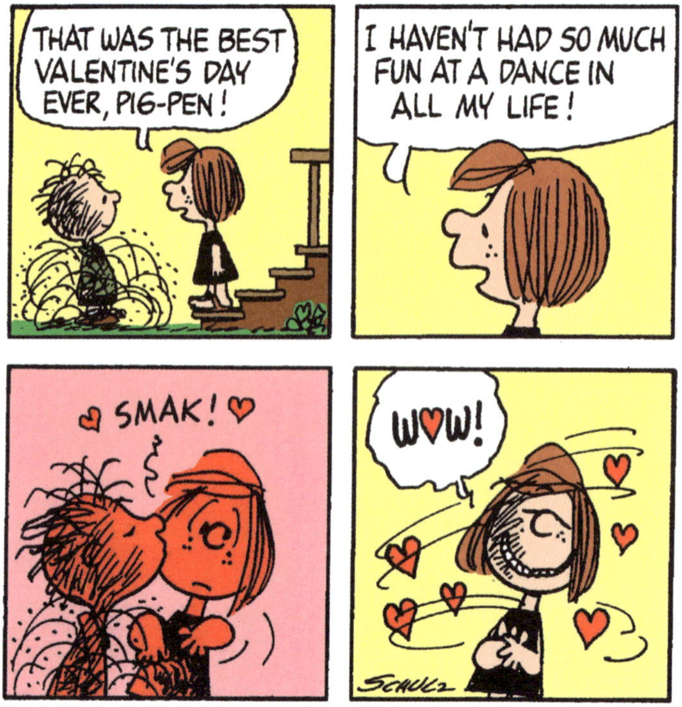
THAT WAS THE BEST VALENTINE'S DAY EVER, PIG-PEN!
I HAVEN'T HAD SO MUCH FUN AT A DANCE IN ALL MY LIFE!
SMAK!
WOW!
SCHULZ

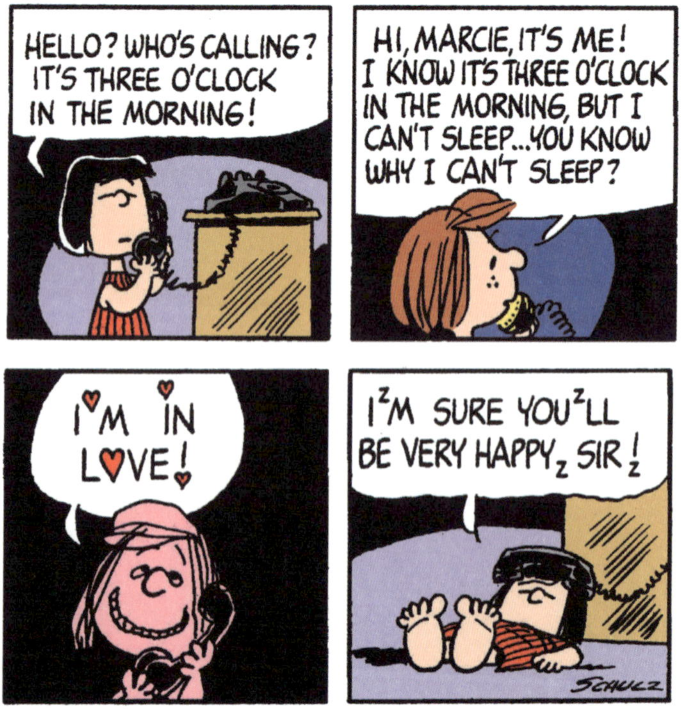
HELLO? WHO'S CALLING? IT'S THREE O'CLOCK IN THE MORNING!
HI, MARCIE, IT'S ME! I KNOW IT'S THREE O'CLOCK IN THE MORNING, BUT I CAN'T SLEEP...YOU KNOW WHY I CAN'T SLEEP?
I'M IN LOVE!
I'M SURE YOU'LL BE VERY HAPPY, SIR!
SCHULZ

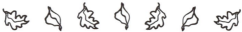

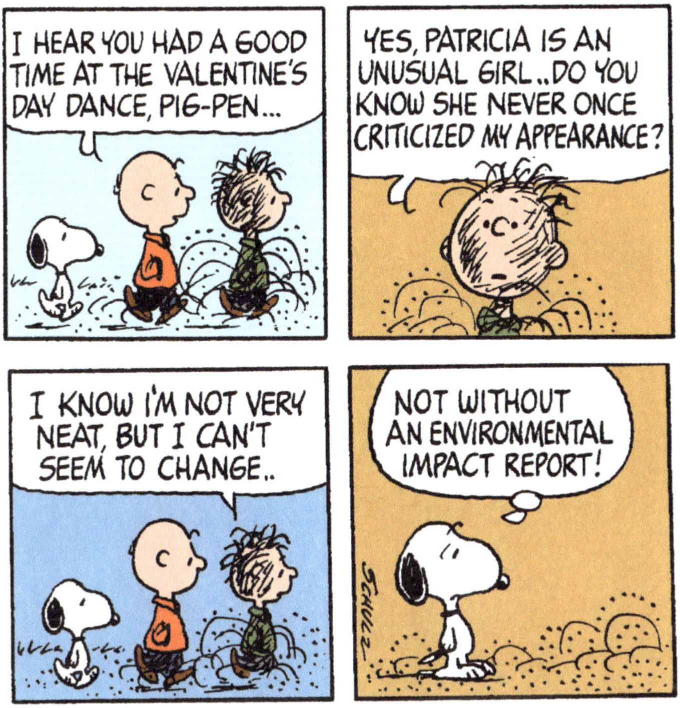
I HEAR YOU HAD A GOOD TIME AT THE VALENTINE'S DAY DANCE, PIG-PEN...
YES, PATRICIA IS AN UNUSUAL GIRL..DO YOU KNOW SHE NEVER ONCE CRITICIZED MY APPEARANCE?
I KNOW I'M NOT VERY NEAT, BUT I CAN'T SEEM TO CHANGE..
NOT WITHOUT AN ENVIRONMENTAL IMPACT REPORT!
SCHULZ

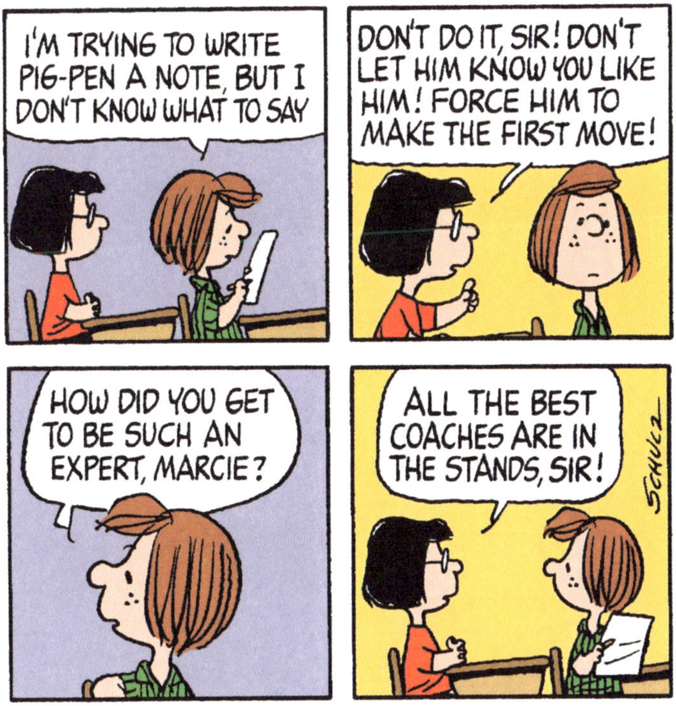
I'M TRYING TO WRITE PIG-PEN A NOTE, BUT I DON'T KNOW WHAT TO SAY
DON'T DO IT, SIR! DON'T LET HIM KNOW YOU LIKE HIM! FORCE HIM TO MAKE THE FIRST MOVE!
HOW DID YOU GET TO BE SUCH AN EXPERT, MARCIE?
ALL THE BEST COACHES ARE IN THE STANDS, SIR!
SCHULZ

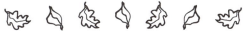

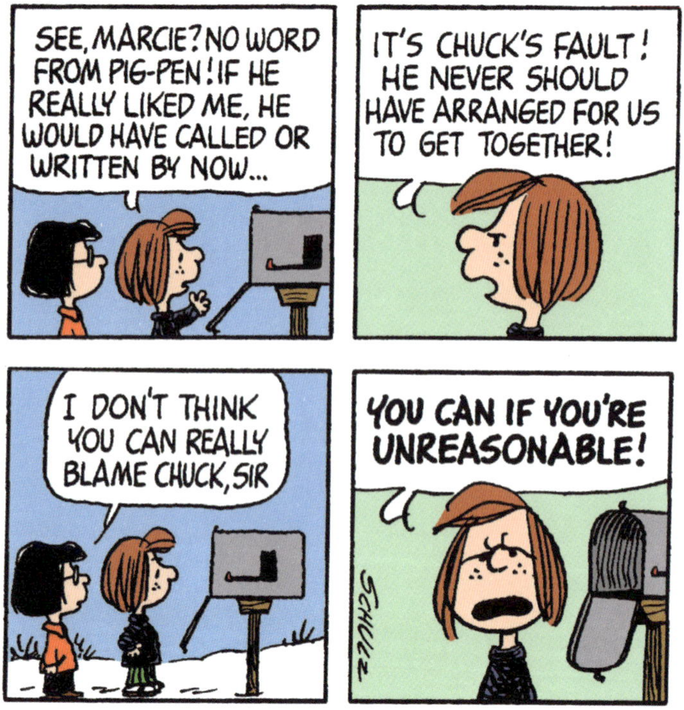
SEE, MARCIE? NO WORD FROM PIG-PEN! IF HE REALLY LIKED ME, HE WOULD HAVE CALLED OR WRITTEN BY NOW...
IT'S CHUCK'S FAULT! HE NEVER SHOULD HAVE ARRANGED FOR US TO GET TOGETHER!
I DON'T THINK YOU CAN REALLY BLAME CHUCK, SIR
YOU CAN IF YOU'RE UNREASONABLE!
SCHULZ

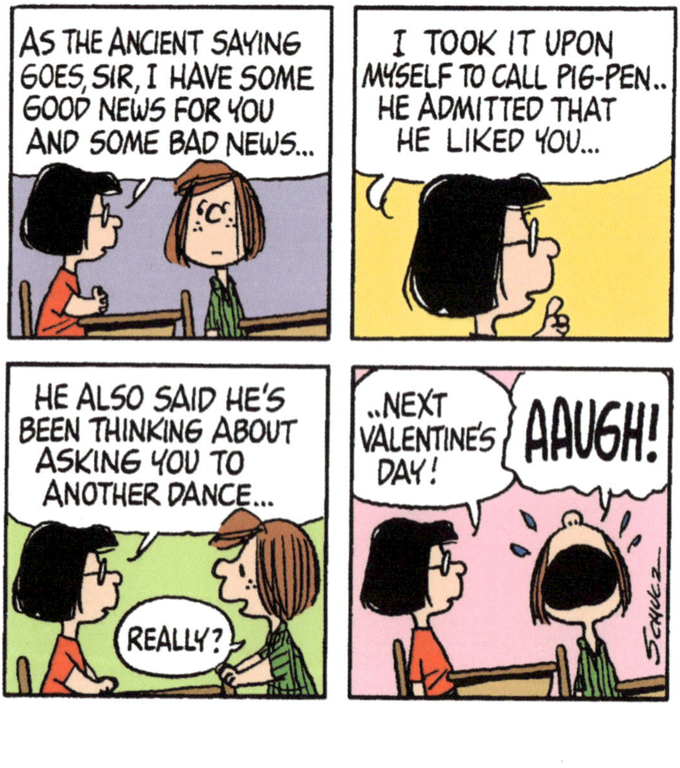
AS THE ANCIENT SAYING GOES, SIR, I HAVE SOME GOOD NEWS FOR YOU AND SOME BAD NEWS...
I TOOK IT UPON MYSELF TO CALL PIG-PEN.. HE ADMITTED THAT HE LIKED YOU...
HE ALSO SAID HE'S BEEN THINKING ABOUT ASKING YOU TO ANOTHER DANCE...
REALLY?
..NEXT VALENTINE'S DAY!
AAUGH!
SCHULZ

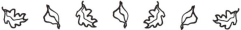

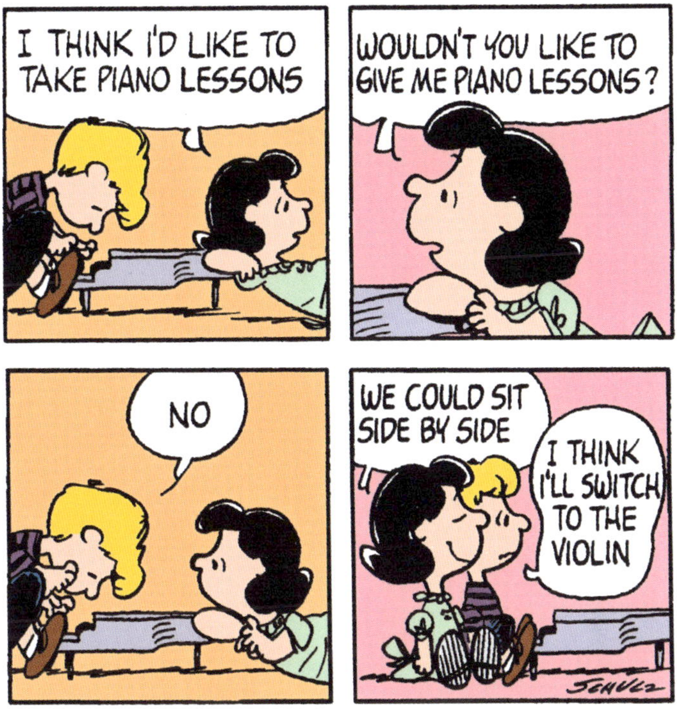
I THINK I'D LIKE TO TAKE PIANO LESSONS
WOULDN'T YOU LIKE TO GIVE ME PIANO LESSONS?
NO
WE COULD SIT SIDE BY SIDE
I THINK I'LL SWITCH TO THE VIOLIN
SCHULZ

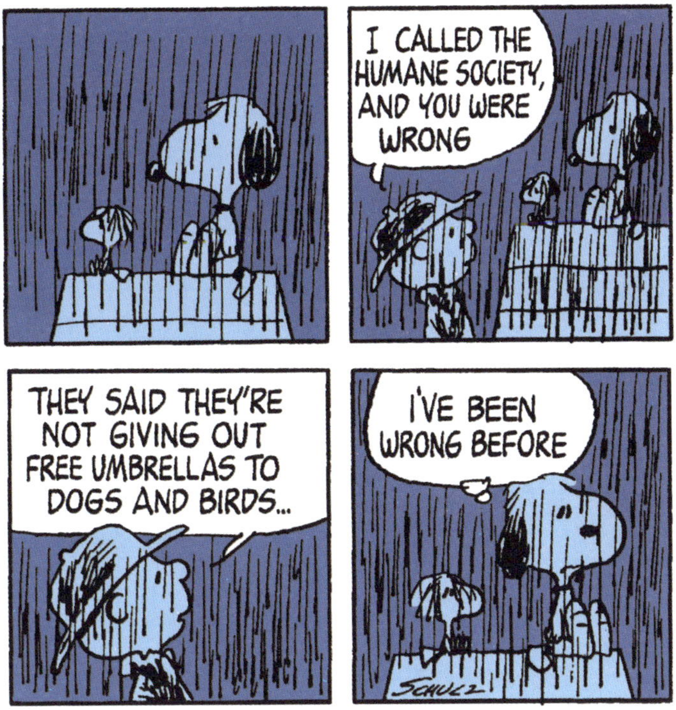
I CALLED THE HUMANE SOCIETY, AND YOU WERE WRONG
THEY SAID THEY'RE NOT GIVING OUT FREE UMBRELLAS TO DOGS AND BIRDS...
I'VE BEEN WRONG BEFORE
SCHULZ

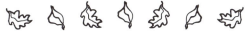

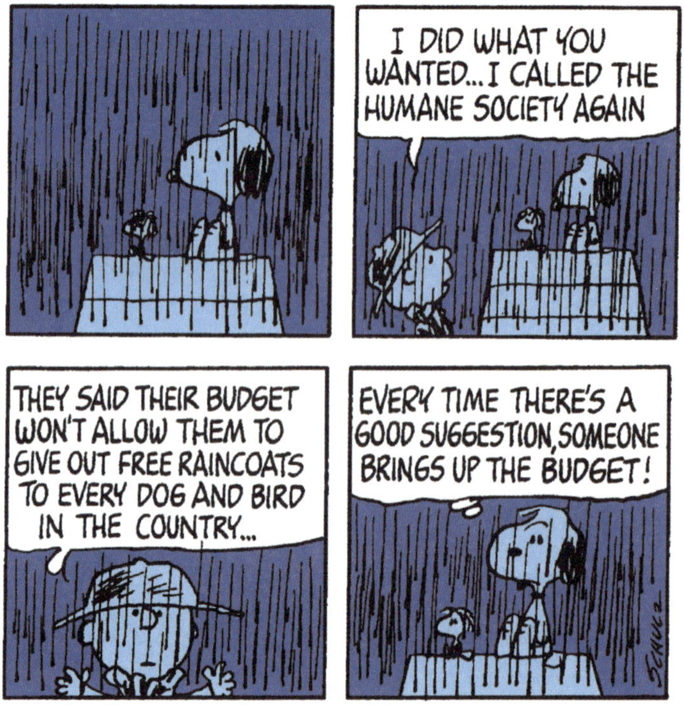
I DID WHAT YOU WANTED...I CALLED THE HUMANE SOCIETY AGAIN
THEY SAID THEIR BUDGET WON'T ALLOW THEM TO GIVE OUT FREE RAINCOATS TO EVERY DOG AND BIRD IN THE COUNTRY...
EVERY TIME THERE'S A GOOD SUGGESTION, SOMEONE BRINGS UP THE BUDGET!

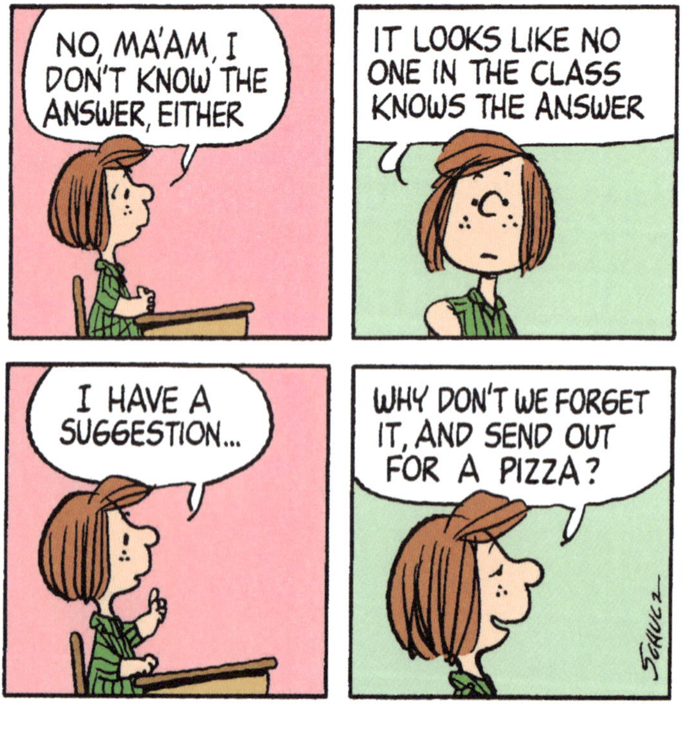
NO, MA'AM, I DON'T KNOW THE ANSWER, EITHER
IT LOOKS LIKE NO ONE IN THE CLASS KNOWS THE ANSWER
I HAVE A SUGGESTION...
WHY DON'T WE FORGET IT, AND SEND OUT FOR A PIZZA?

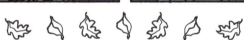

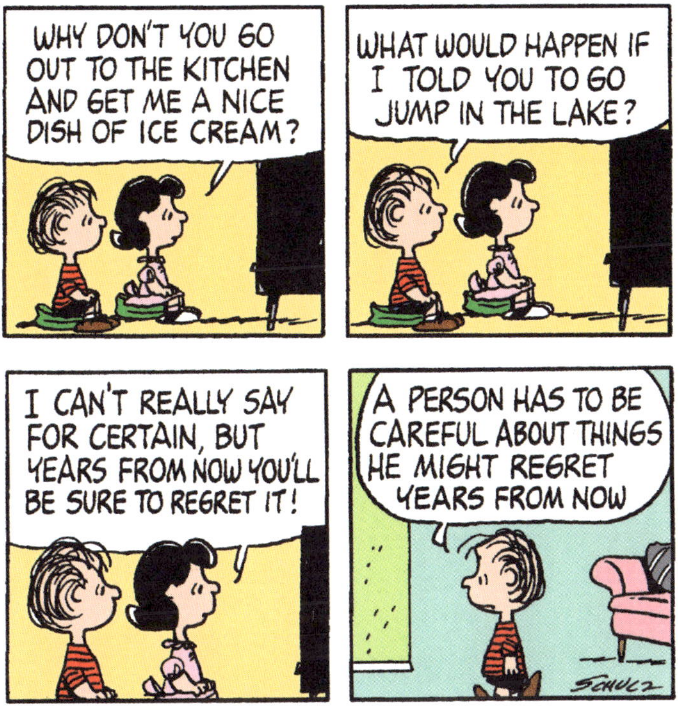
WHY DON'T YOU GO OUT TO THE KITCHEN AND GET ME A NICE DISH OF ICE CREAM?
WHAT WOULD HAPPEN IF I TOLD YOU TO GO JUMP IN THE LAKE?
I CAN'T REALLY SAY FOR CERTAIN, BUT YEARS FROM NOW YOU'LL BE SURE TO REGRET IT!
A PERSON HAS TO BE CAREFUL ABOUT THINGS HE MIGHT REGRET YEARS FROM NOW
SCHULZ

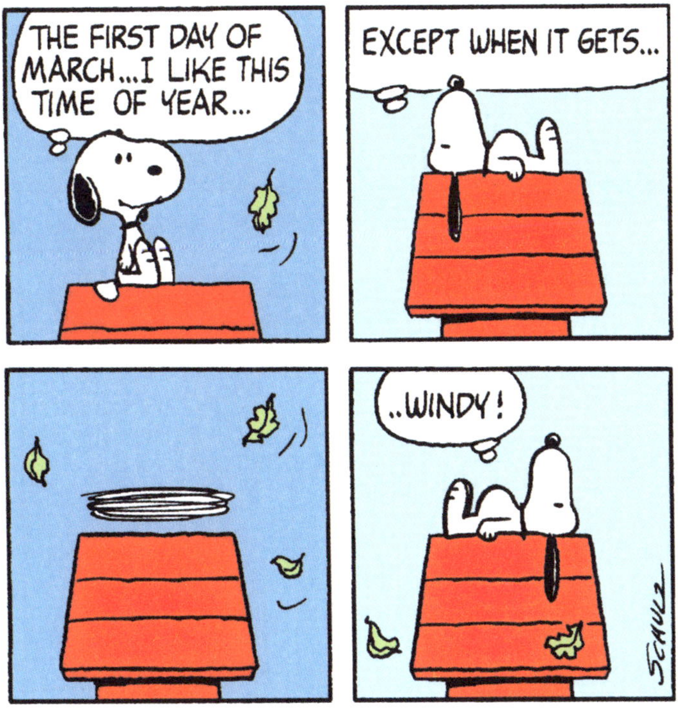
THE FIRST DAY OF MARCH...I LIKE THIS TIME OF YEAR...
EXCEPT WHEN IT GETS...
..WINDY!
SCHULZ

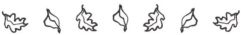

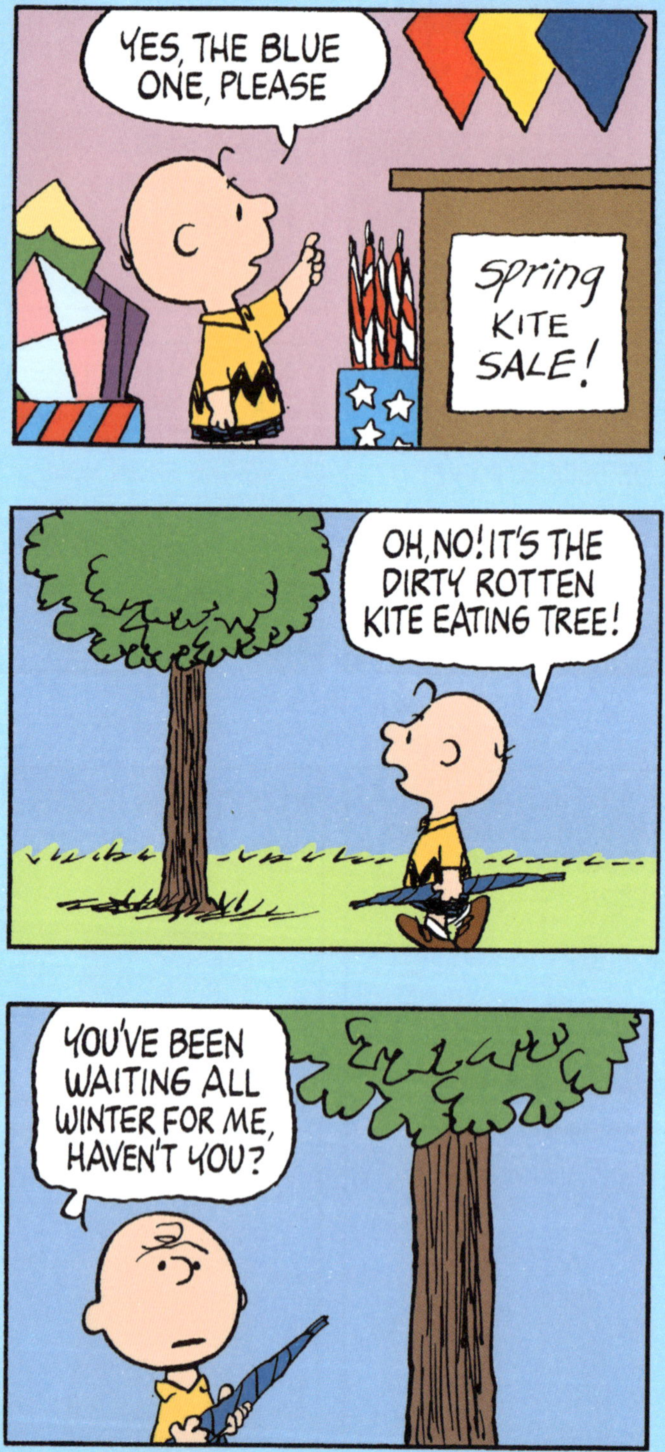
YES, THE BLUE ONE, PLEASE
Spring KITE SALE!
OH, NO! IT'S THE DIRTY ROTTEN KITE EATING TREE!
YOU'VE BEEN WAITING ALL WINTER FOR ME, HAVEN'T YOU?

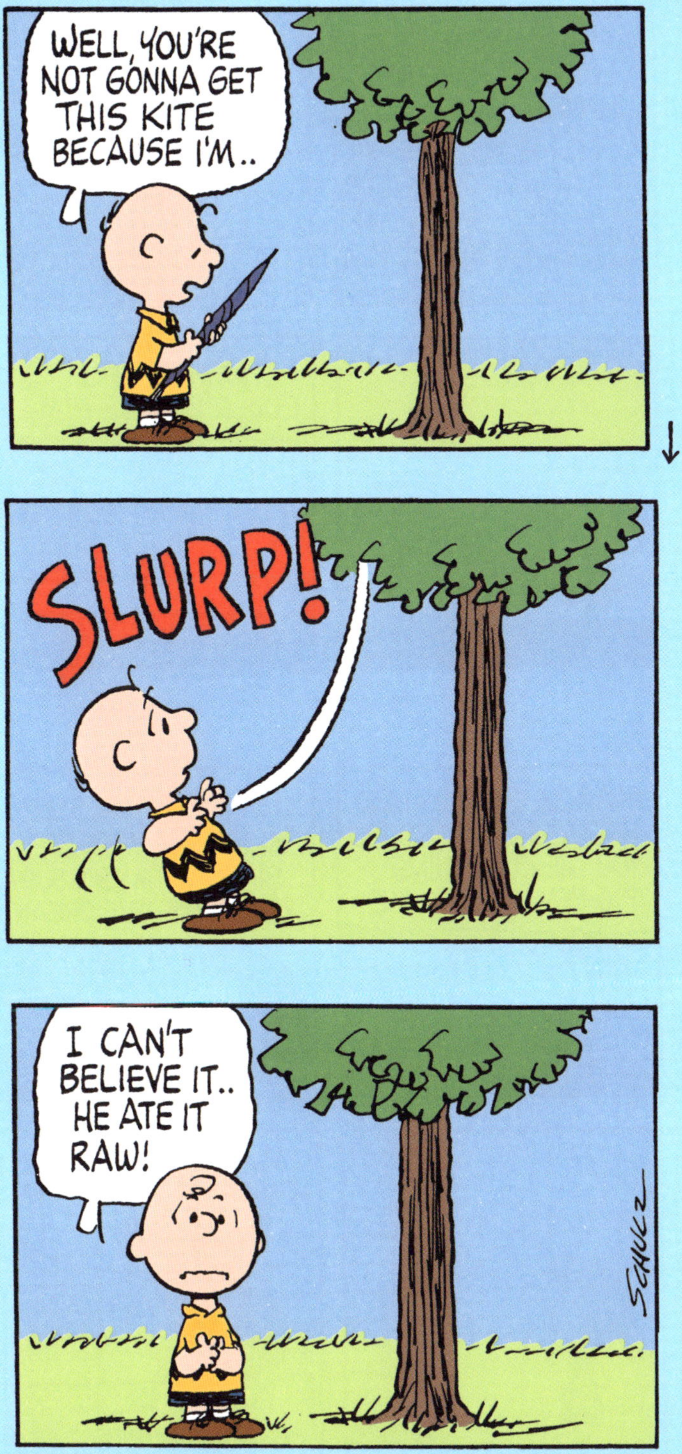
WELL, YOU'RE NOT GONNA GET THIS KITE BECAUSE I'M..
SLURP!
I CAN'T BELIEVE IT.. HE ATE IT RAW!
SCHULZ

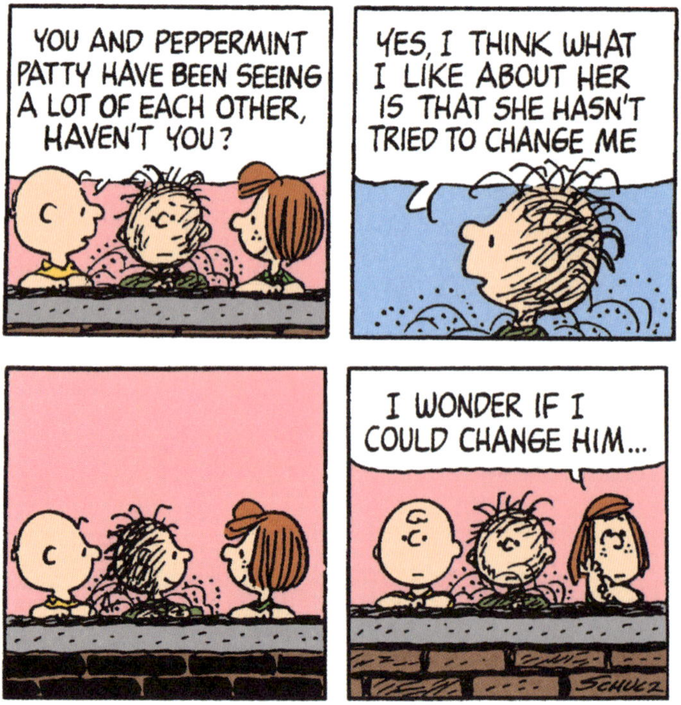
YOU AND PEPPERMINT PATTY HAVE BEEN SEEING A LOT OF EACH OTHER, HAVEN'T YOU?
YES, I THINK WHAT I LIKE ABOUT HER IS THAT SHE HASN'T TRIED TO CHANGE ME
I WONDER IF I COULD CHANGE HIM...

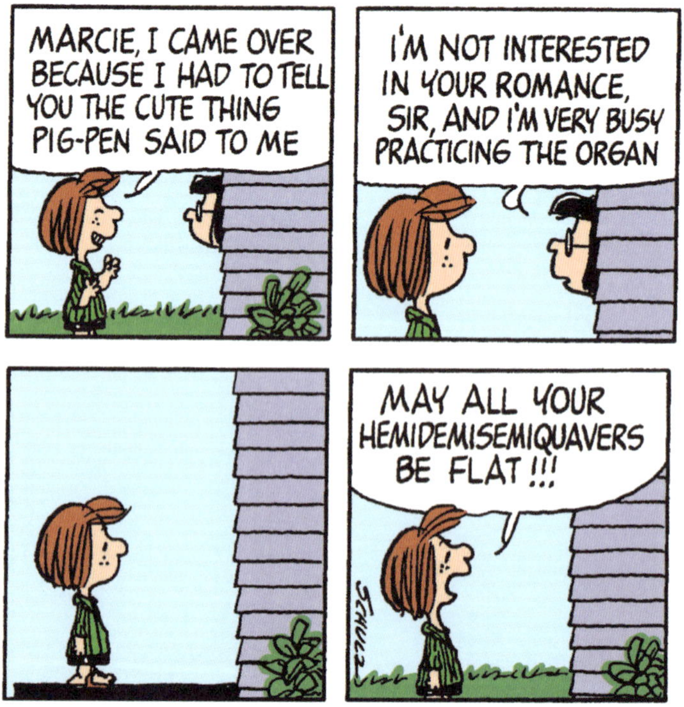
MARCIE, I CAME OVER BECAUSE I HAD TO TELL YOU THE CUTE THING PIG-PEN SAID TO ME
I'M NOT INTERESTED IN YOUR ROMANCE, SIR, AND I'M VERY BUSY PRACTICING THE ORGAN
MAY ALL YOUR HEMIDEMISEMIQUAVERS BE FLAT!!!

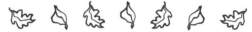

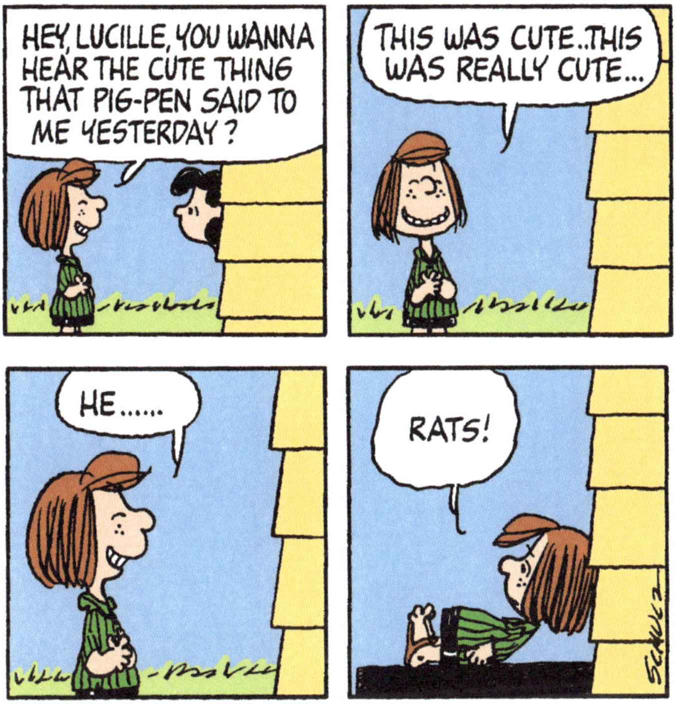
HEY, LUCILLE, YOU WANNA HEAR THE CUTE THING THAT PIG-PEN SAID TO ME YESTERDAY?
THIS WAS CUTE..THIS WAS REALLY CUTE...
HE......
RATS!

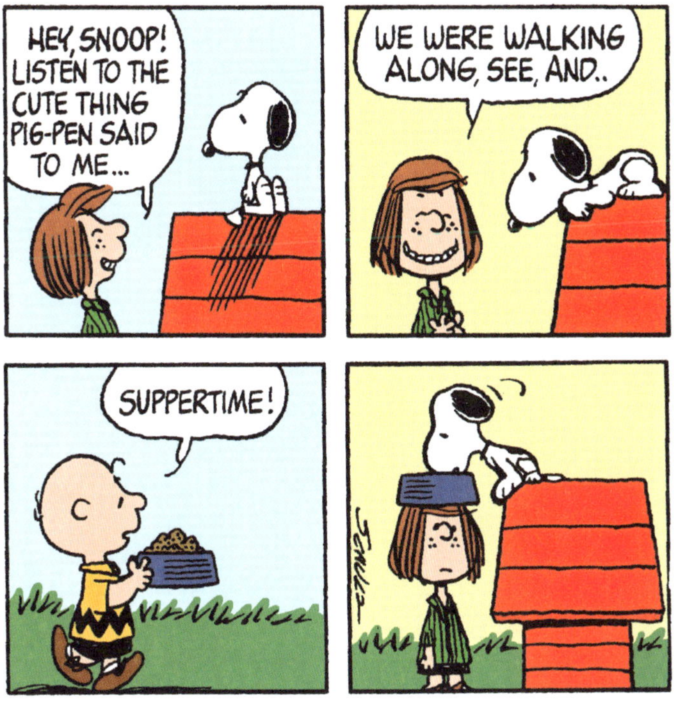
HEY, SNOOP! LISTEN TO THE CUTE THING PIG-PEN SAID TO ME...
WE WERE WALKING ALONG, SEE, AND..
SUPPERTIME!

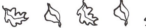

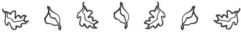

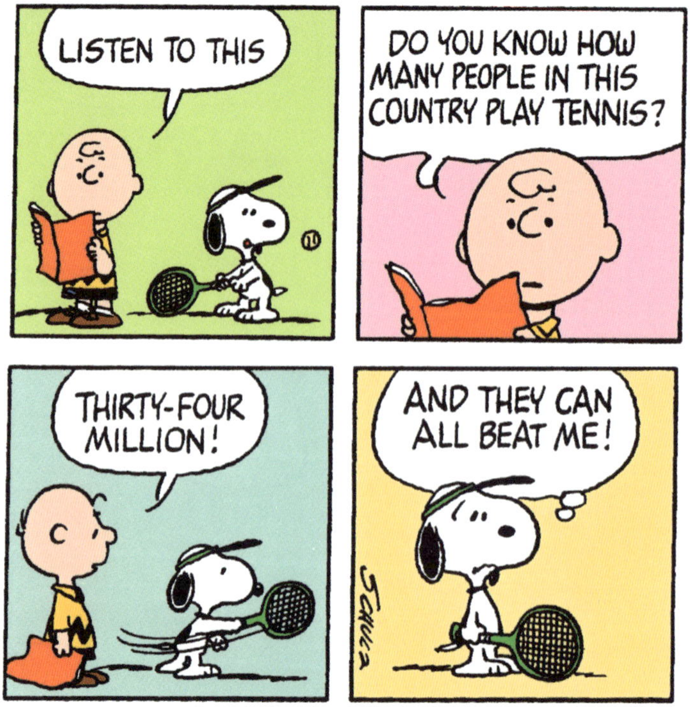
LISTEN TO THIS
DO YOU KNOW HOW MANY PEOPLE IN THIS COUNTRY PLAY TENNIS?
THIRTY-FOUR MILLION!
AND THEY CAN ALL BEAT ME!
SCHULZ

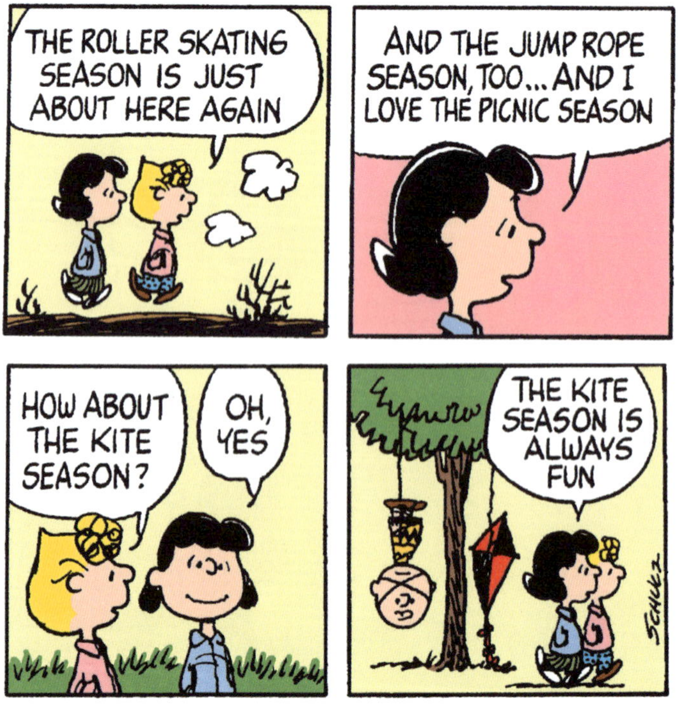
THE ROLLER SKATING SEASON IS JUST ABOUT HERE AGAIN
AND THE JUMP ROPE SEASON, TOO... AND I LOVE THE PICNIC SEASON
HOW ABOUT THE KITE SEASON?
OH, YES
THE KITE SEASON IS ALWAYS FUN
SCHULZ

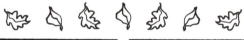

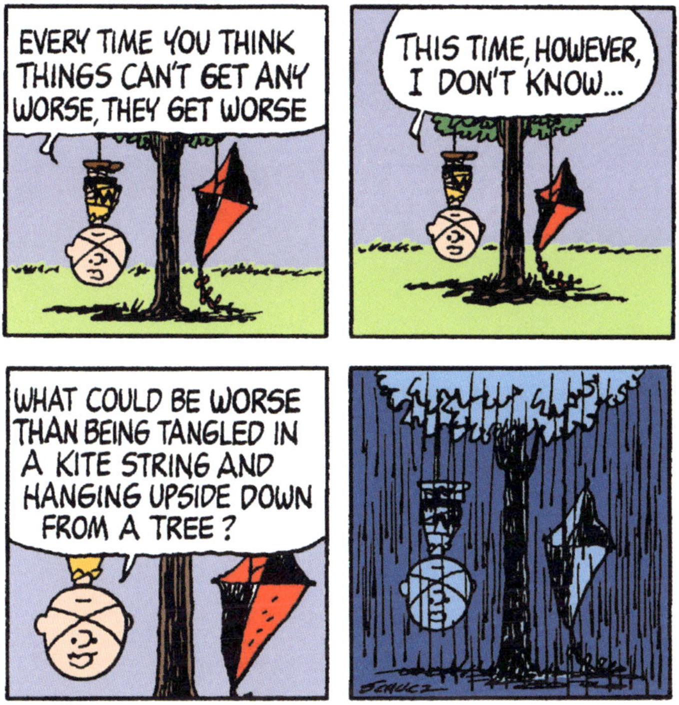
EVERY TIME YOU THINK THINGS CAN'T GET ANY WORSE, THEY GET WORSE
THIS TIME, HOWEVER, I DON'T KNOW...
WHAT COULD BE WORSE THAN BEING TANGLED IN A KITE STRING AND HANGING UPSIDE DOWN FROM A TREE?

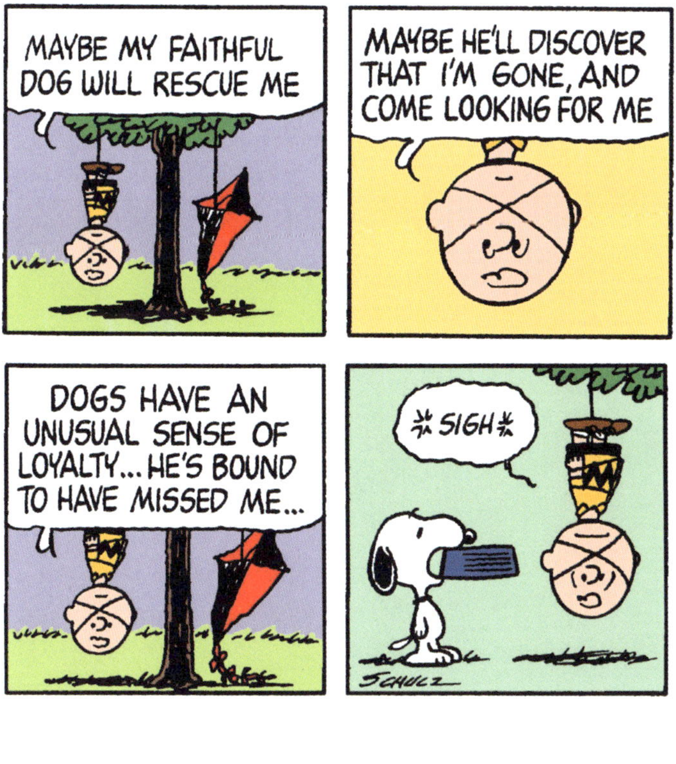
MAYBE MY FAITHFUL DOG WILL RESCUE ME
MAYBE HE'LL DISCOVER THAT I'M GONE, AND COME LOOKING FOR ME
DOGS HAVE AN UNUSUAL SENSE OF LOYALTY... HE'S BOUND TO HAVE MISSED ME...
SIGH

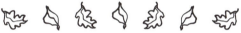

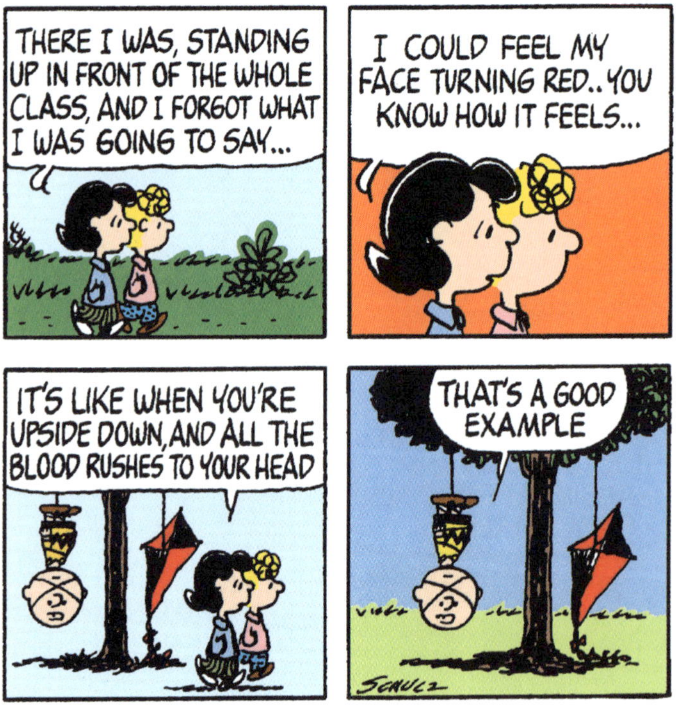
THERE I WAS, STANDING UP IN FRONT OF THE WHOLE CLASS, AND I FORGOT WHAT I WAS GOING TO SAY...
I COULD FEEL MY FACE TURNING RED.. YOU KNOW HOW IT FEELS...
IT'S LIKE WHEN YOU'RE UPSIDE DOWN, AND ALL THE BLOOD RUSHES TO YOUR HEAD
THAT'S A GOOD EXAMPLE
SCHULZ

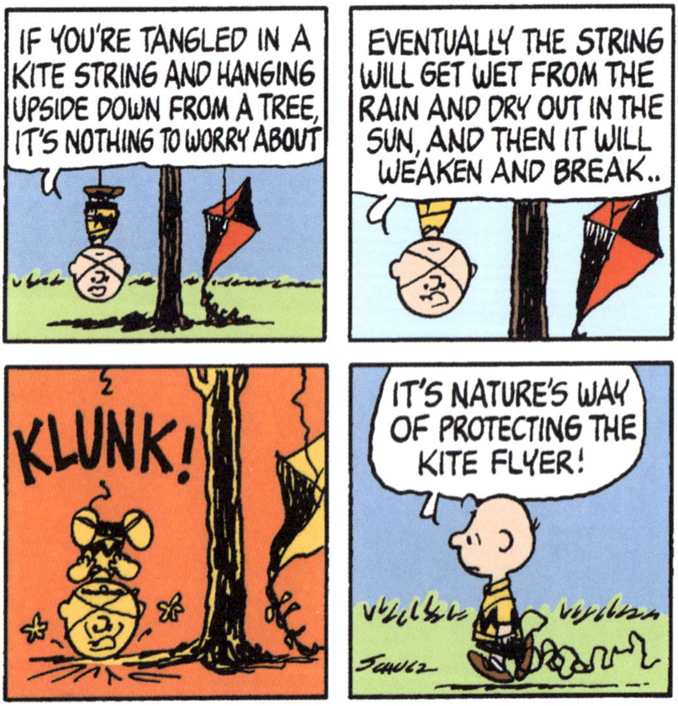
IF YOU'RE TANGLED IN A KITE STRING AND HANGING UPSIDE DOWN FROM A TREE, IT'S NOTHING TO WORRY ABOUT
EVENTUALLY THE STRING WILL GET WET FROM THE RAIN AND DRY OUT IN THE SUN, AND THEN IT WILL WEAKEN AND BREAK..
KLUNK!
IT'S NATURE'S WAY OF PROTECTING THE KITE FLYER!
SCHULZ

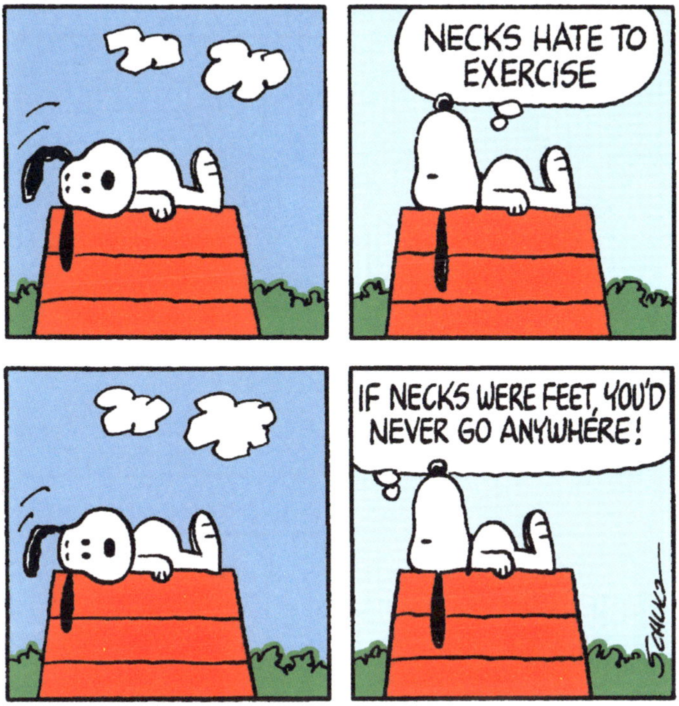
NECKS HATE TO EXERCISE
IF NECKS WERE FEET, YOU'D NEVER GO ANYWHERE!

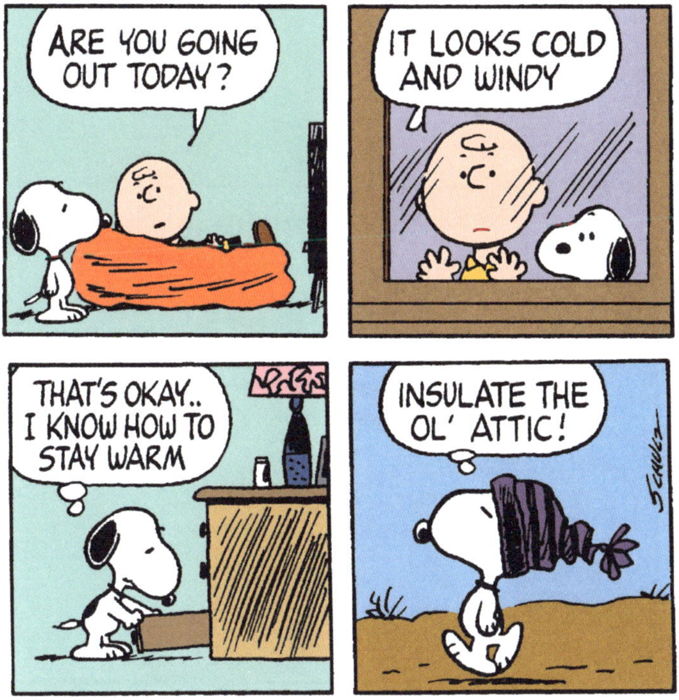
ARE YOU GOING OUT TODAY?
IT LOOKS COLD AND WINDY
THAT'S OKAY.. I KNOW HOW TO STAY WARM
INSULATE THE OL' ATTIC!

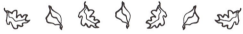

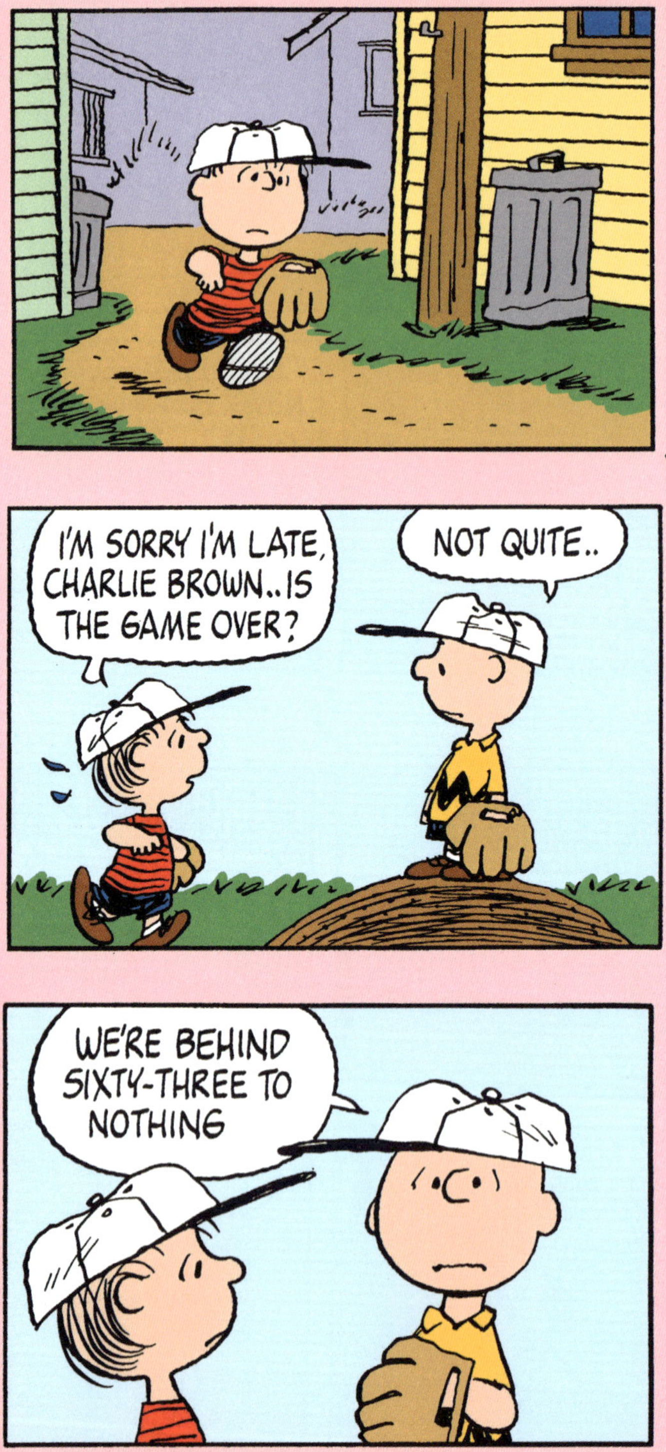
I'M SORRY I'M LATE, CHARLIE BROWN..IS THE GAME OVER?
NOT QUITE..
WE'RE BEHIND SIXTY-THREE TO NOTHING

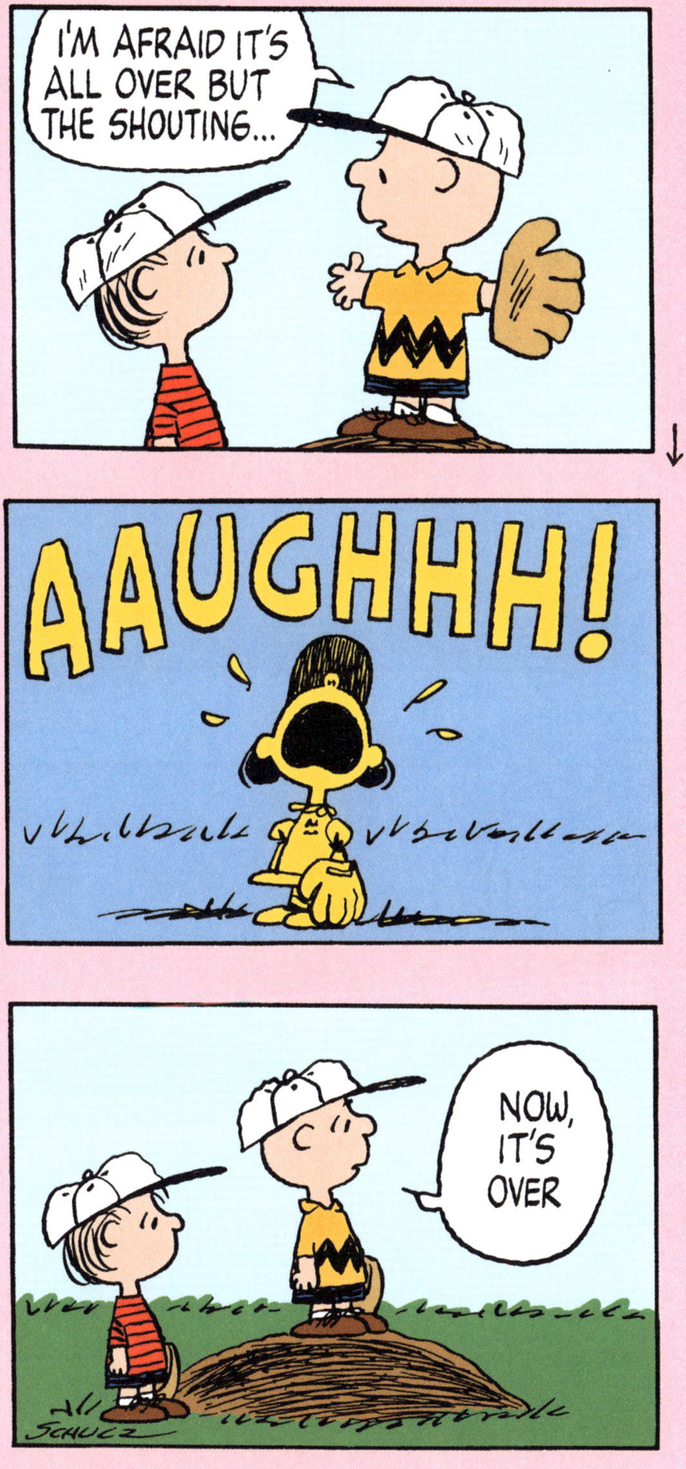
I'M AFRAID IT'S ALL OVER BUT THE SHOUTING...
AAUGHHH!
NOW, IT'S OVER
SCHULZ

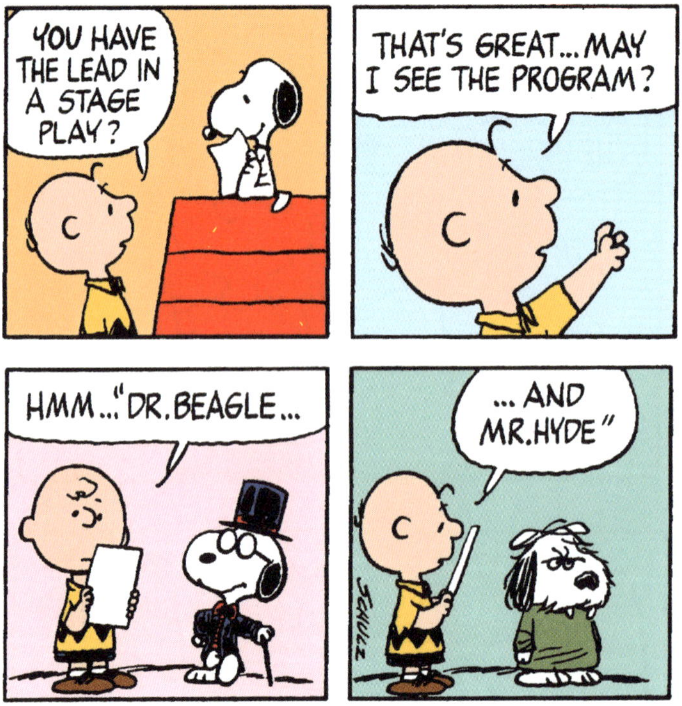
YOU HAVE THE LEAD IN A STAGE PLAY?
THAT'S GREAT... MAY I SEE THE PROGRAM?
HMM... "DR. BEAGLE...
... AND MR. HYDE"

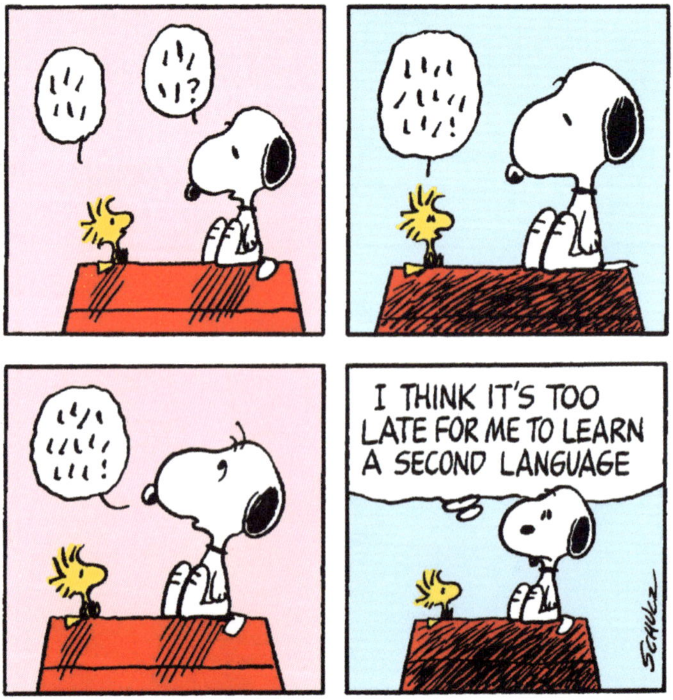
I THINK IT'S TOO LATE FOR ME TO LEARN A SECOND LANGUAGE

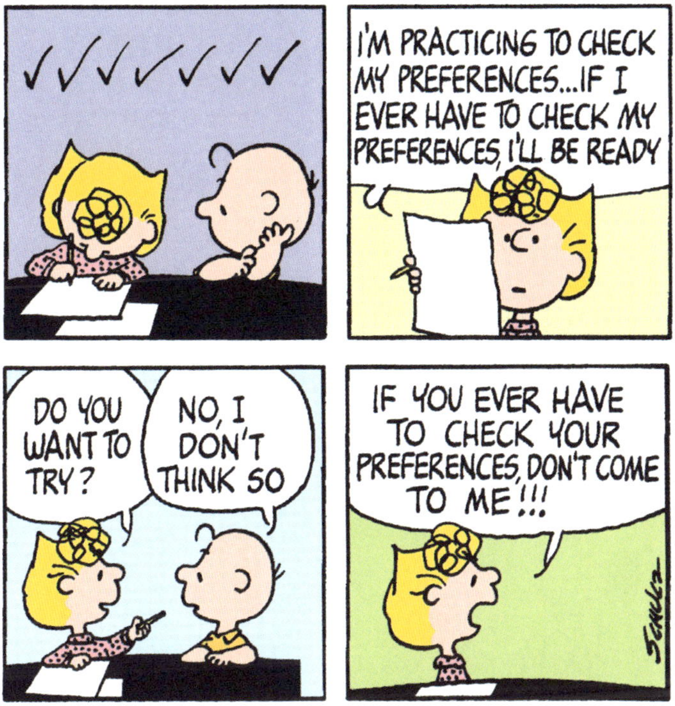
I'M PRACTICING TO CHECK MY PREFERENCES...IF I EVER HAVE TO CHECK MY PREFERENCES, I'LL BE READY
DO YOU WANT TO TRY?
NO, I DON'T THINK SO
IF YOU EVER HAVE TO CHECK YOUR PREFERENCES, DON'T COME TO ME!!!
SCHULZ

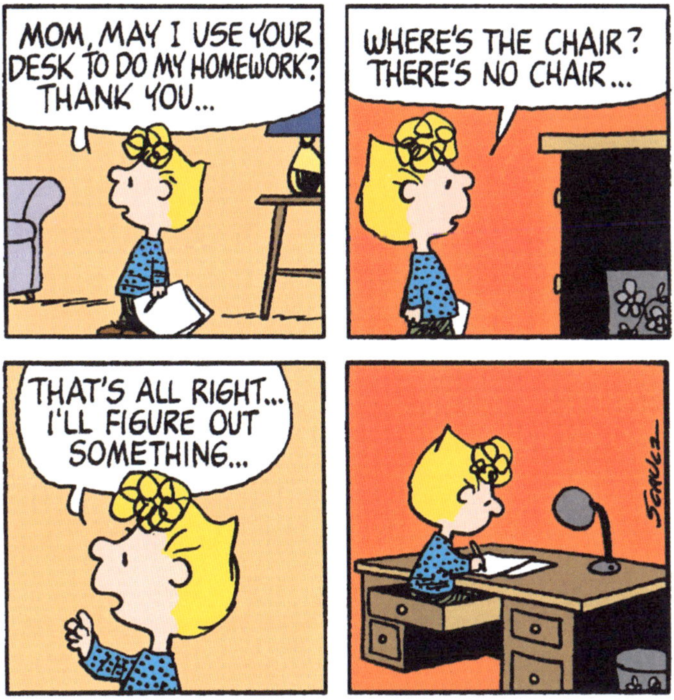
MOM, MAY I USE YOUR DESK TO DO MY HOMEWORK? THANK YOU...
WHERE'S THE CHAIR? THERE'S NO CHAIR...
THAT'S ALL RIGHT... I'LL FIGURE OUT SOMETHING...
SCHULZ

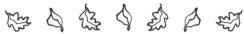

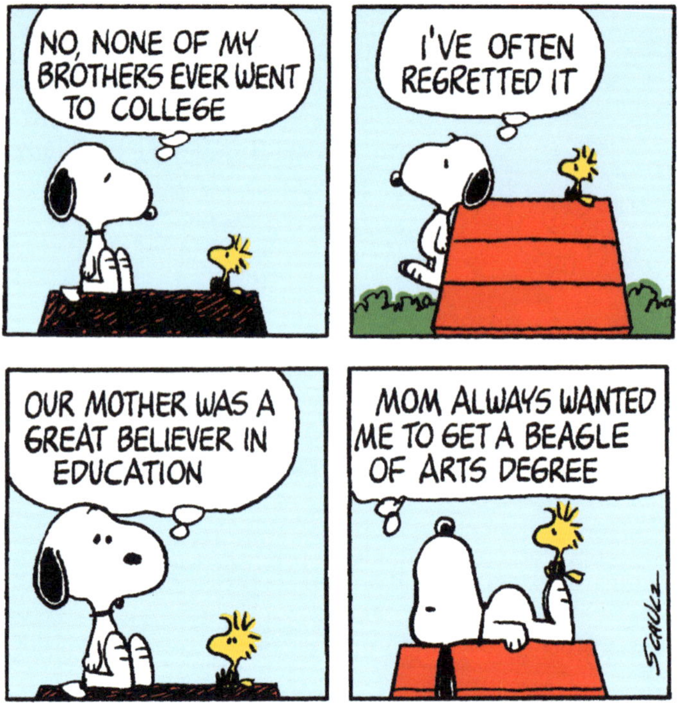
NO, NONE OF MY BROTHERS EVER WENT TO COLLEGE
I'VE OFTEN REGRETTED IT
OUR MOTHER WAS A GREAT BELIEVER IN EDUCATION
MOM ALWAYS WANTED ME TO GET A BEAGLE OF ARTS DEGREE
SCHULZ

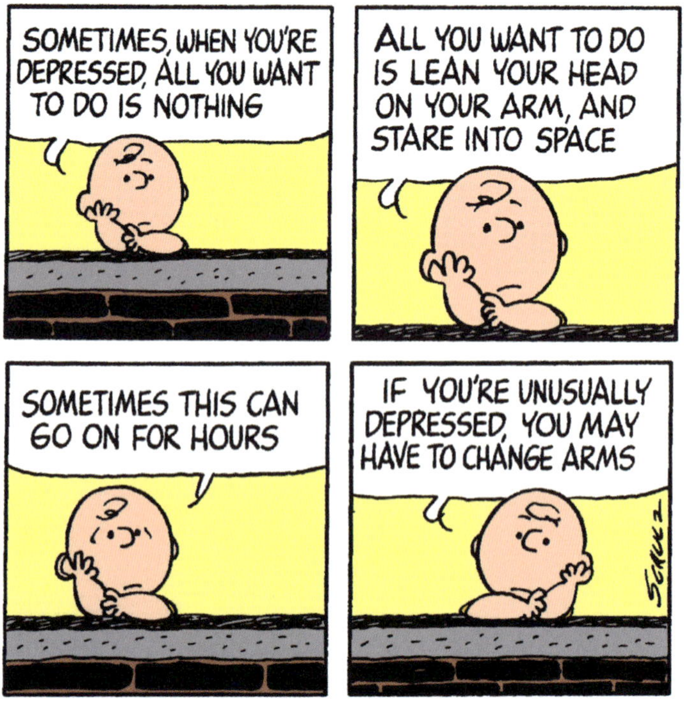
SOMETIMES, WHEN YOU'RE DEPRESSED, ALL YOU WANT TO DO IS NOTHING
ALL YOU WANT TO DO IS LEAN YOUR HEAD ON YOUR ARM, AND STARE INTO SPACE
SOMETIMES THIS CAN GO ON FOR HOURS
IF YOU'RE UNUSUALLY DEPRESSED, YOU MAY HAVE TO CHANGE ARMS
SCHULZ

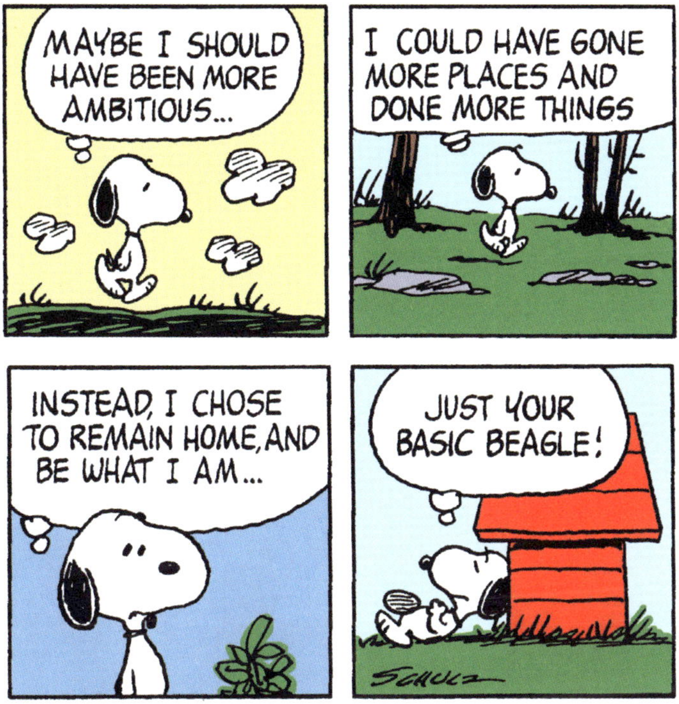
MAYBE I SHOULD HAVE BEEN MORE AMBITIOUS...
I COULD HAVE GONE MORE PLACES AND DONE MORE THINGS
INSTEAD, I CHOSE TO REMAIN HOME, AND BE WHAT I AM...
JUST YOUR BASIC BEAGLE!

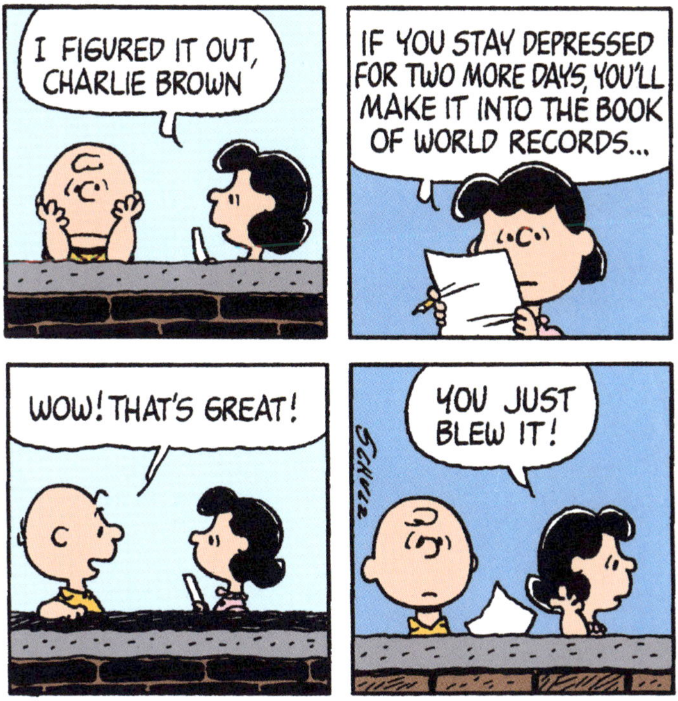
I FIGURED IT OUT, CHARLIE BROWN
IF YOU STAY DEPRESSED FOR TWO MORE DAYS, YOU'LL MAKE IT INTO THE BOOK OF WORLD RECORDS...
WOW! THAT'S GREAT!
YOU JUST BLEW IT!

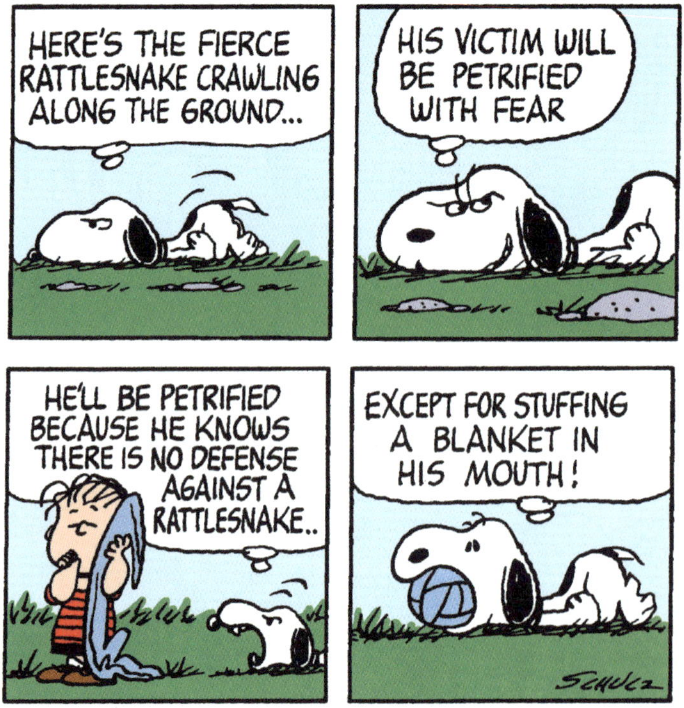
HERE'S THE FIERCE RATTLESNAKE CRAWLING ALONG THE GROUND...
HIS VICTIM WILL BE PETRIFIED WITH FEAR
HE'LL BE PETRIFIED BECAUSE HE KNOWS THERE IS NO DEFENSE AGAINST A RATTLESNAKE..
EXCEPT FOR STUFFING A BLANKET IN HIS MOUTH!
SCHULZ

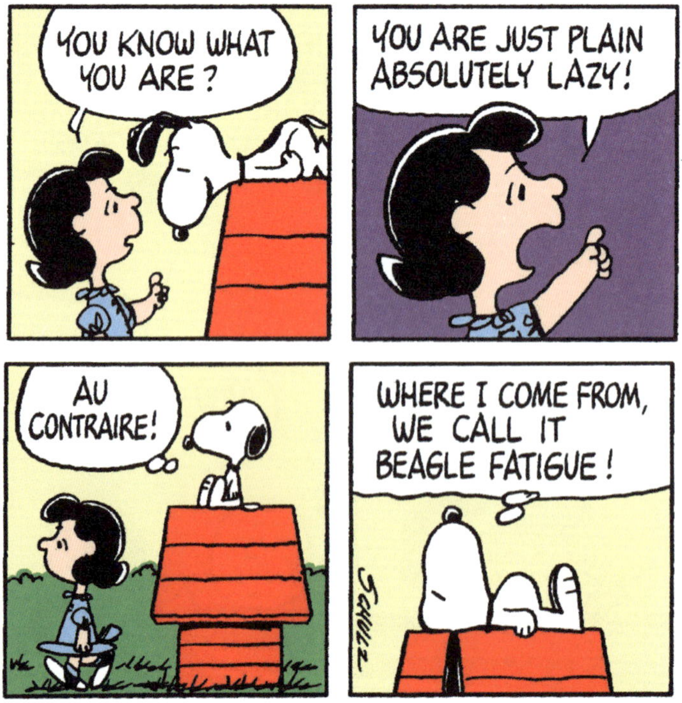
YOU KNOW WHAT YOU ARE?
YOU ARE JUST PLAIN ABSOLUTELY LAZY!
AU CONTRAIRE!
WHERE I COME FROM, WE CALL IT BEAGLE FATIGUE!
SCHULZ

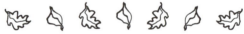

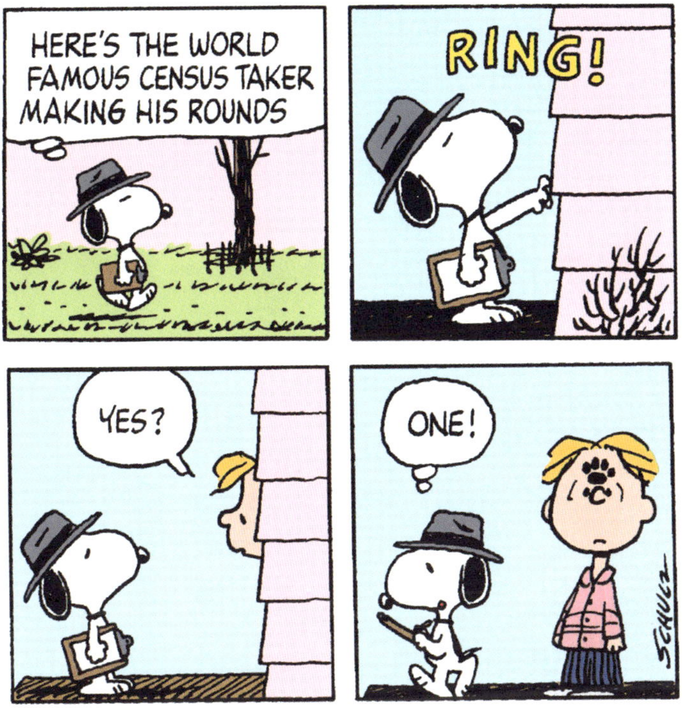
HERE'S THE WORLD FAMOUS CENSUS TAKER MAKING HIS ROUNDS
RING!
YES?
ONE!
SCHULZ

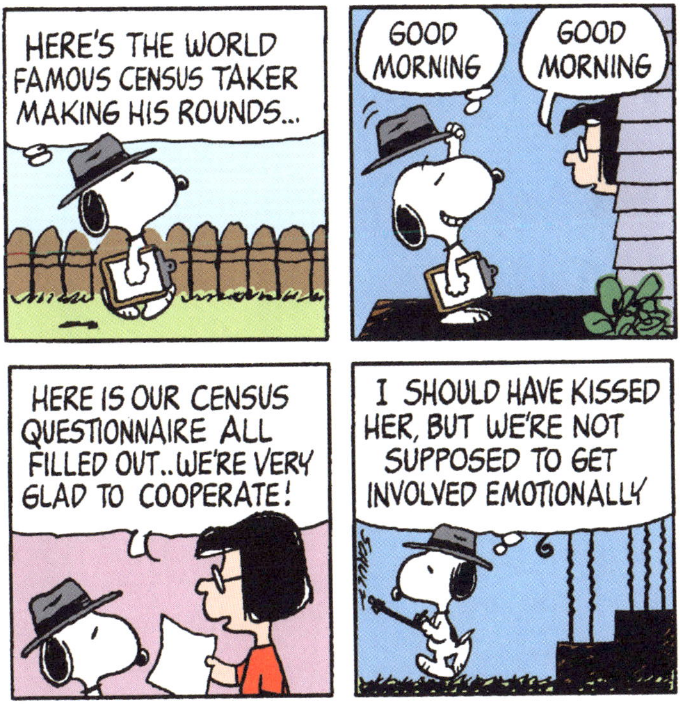
HERE'S THE WORLD FAMOUS CENSUS TAKER MAKING HIS ROUNDS...
GOOD MORNING
GOOD MORNING
HERE IS OUR CENSUS QUESTIONNAIRE ALL FILLED OUT..WE'RE VERY GLAD TO COOPERATE!
I SHOULD HAVE KISSED HER, BUT WE'RE NOT SUPPOSED TO GET INVOLVED EMOTIONALLY
SCHULZ

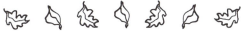

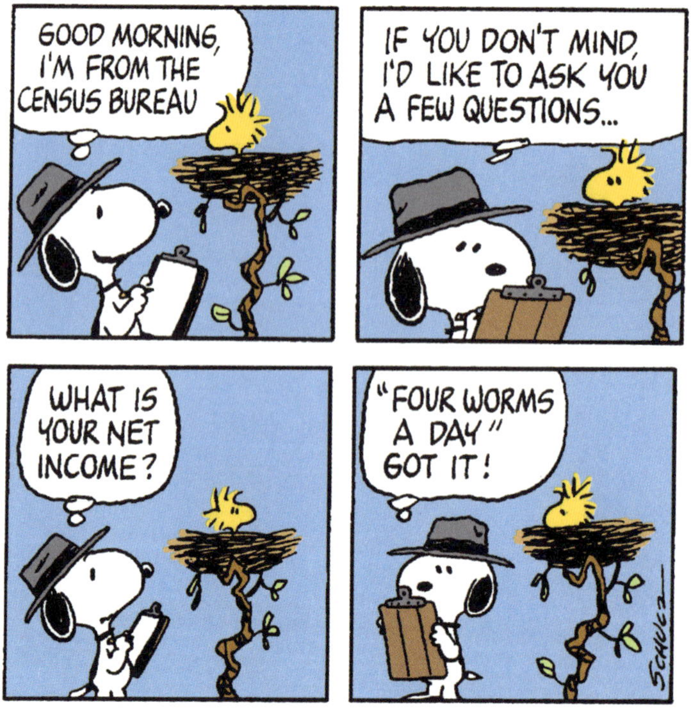
GOOD MORNING, I'M FROM THE CENSUS BUREAU
IF YOU DON'T MIND, I'D LIKE TO ASK YOU A FEW QUESTIONS...
WHAT IS YOUR NET INCOME?
"FOUR WORMS A DAY" GOT IT!
SCHULZ

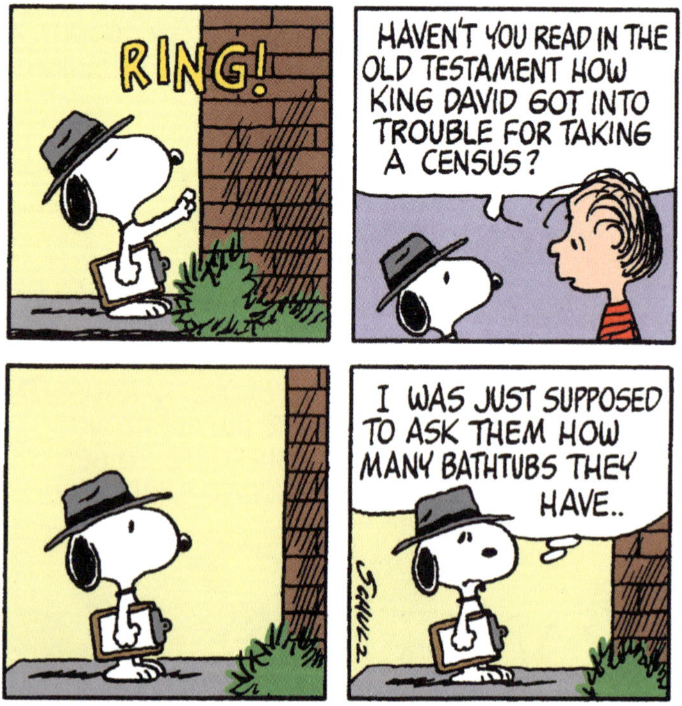
RING!
HAVEN'T YOU READ IN THE OLD TESTAMENT HOW KING DAVID GOT INTO TROUBLE FOR TAKING A CENSUS?
I WAS JUST SUPPOSED TO ASK THEM HOW MANY BATHTUBS THEY HAVE..
SCHULZ

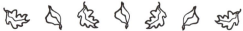

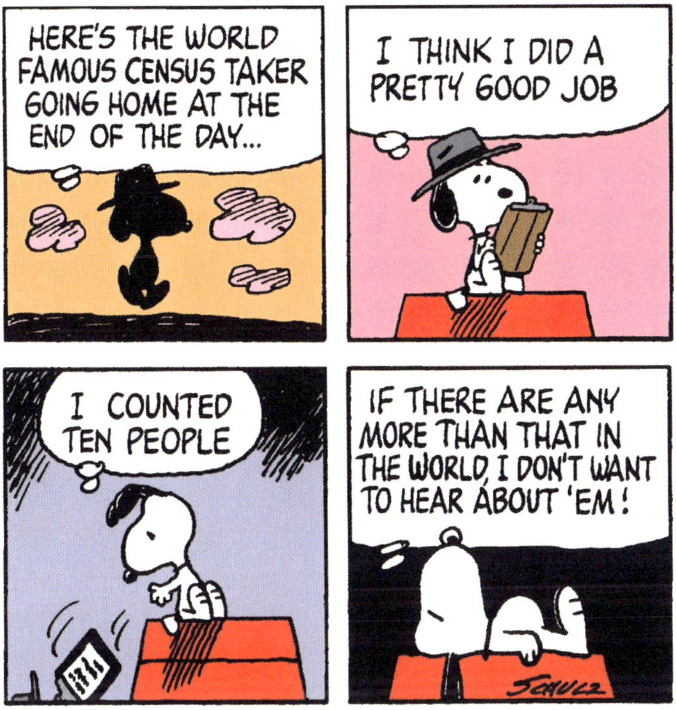
HERE'S THE WORLD FAMOUS CENSUS TAKER GOING HOME AT THE END OF THE DAY...
I THINK I DID A PRETTY GOOD JOB
I COUNTED TEN PEOPLE
IF THERE ARE ANY MORE THAN THAT IN THE WORLD, I DON'T WANT TO HEAR ABOUT 'EM!
SCHULZ

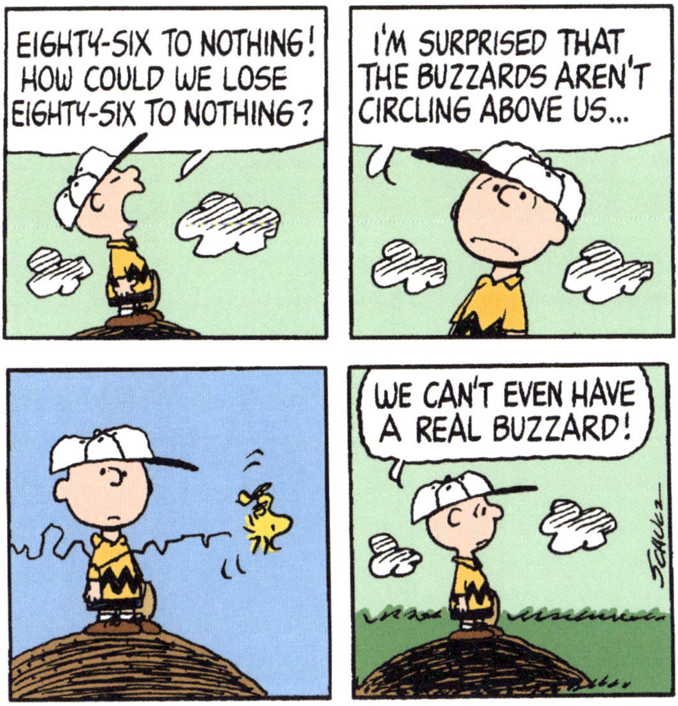
EIGHTY-SIX TO NOTHING! HOW COULD WE LOSE EIGHTY-SIX TO NOTHING?
I'M SURPRISED THAT THE BUZZARDS AREN'T CIRCLING ABOVE US...
WE CAN'T EVEN HAVE A REAL BUZZARD!
SCHULZ

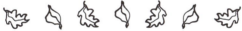

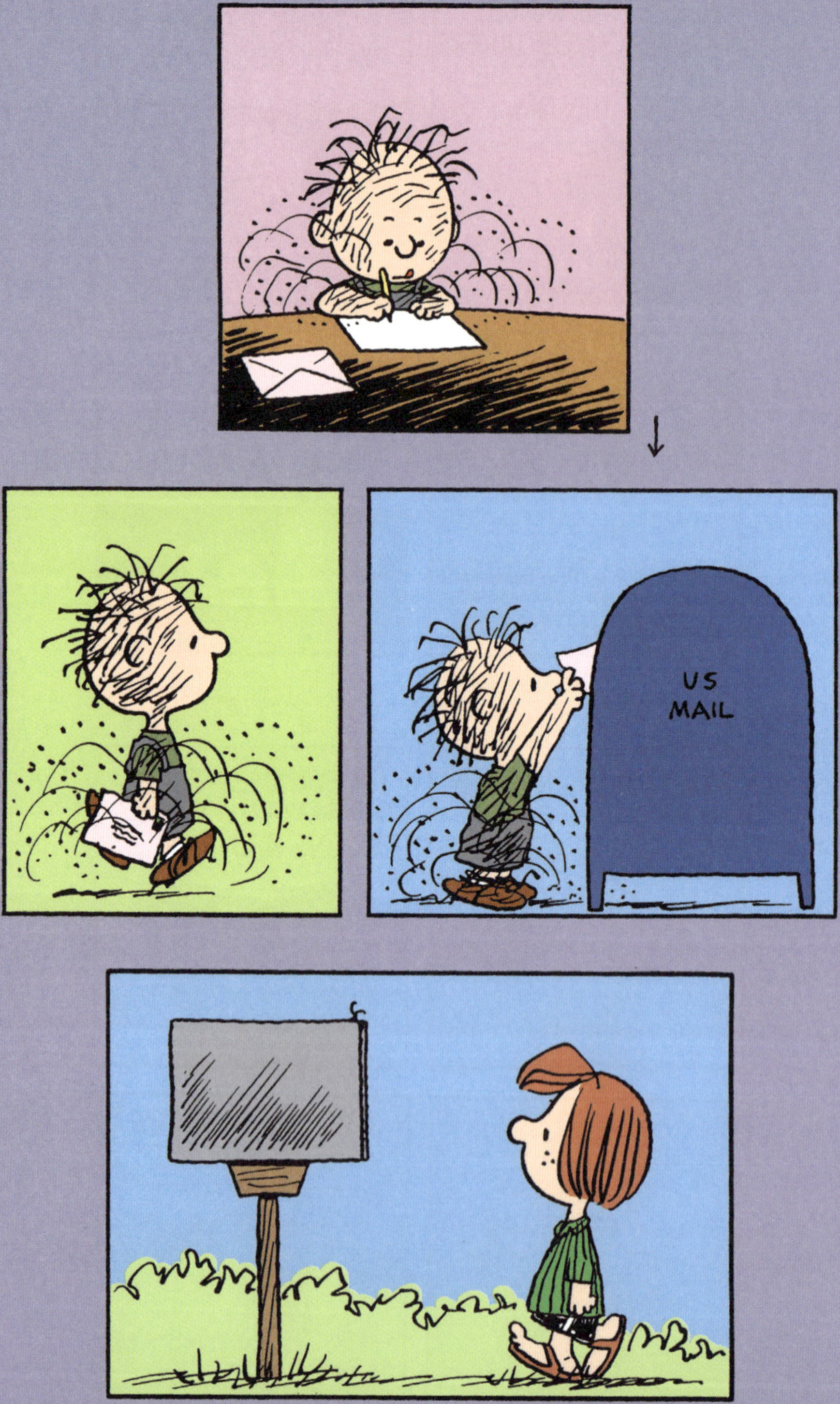
US MAIL

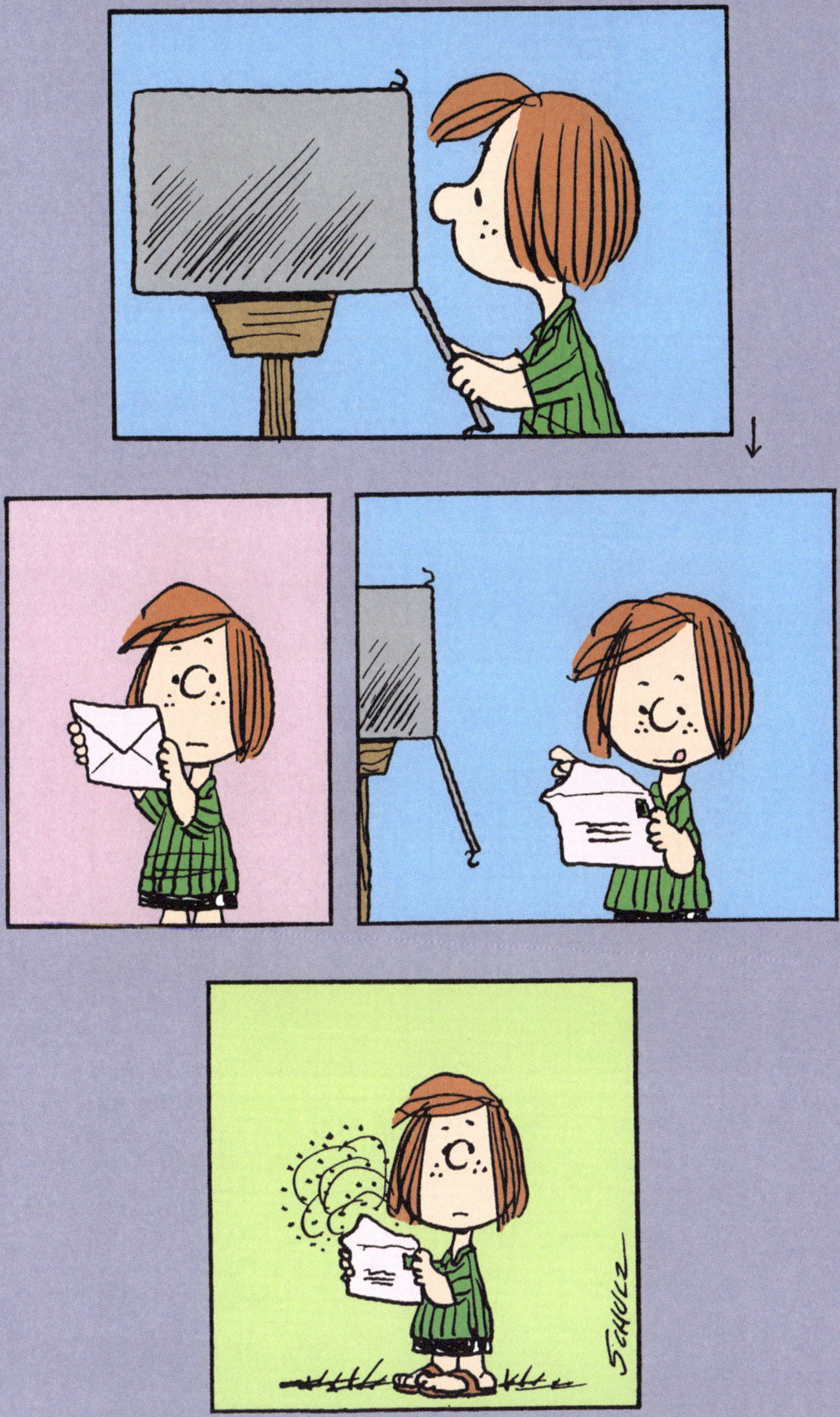
SCHULZ

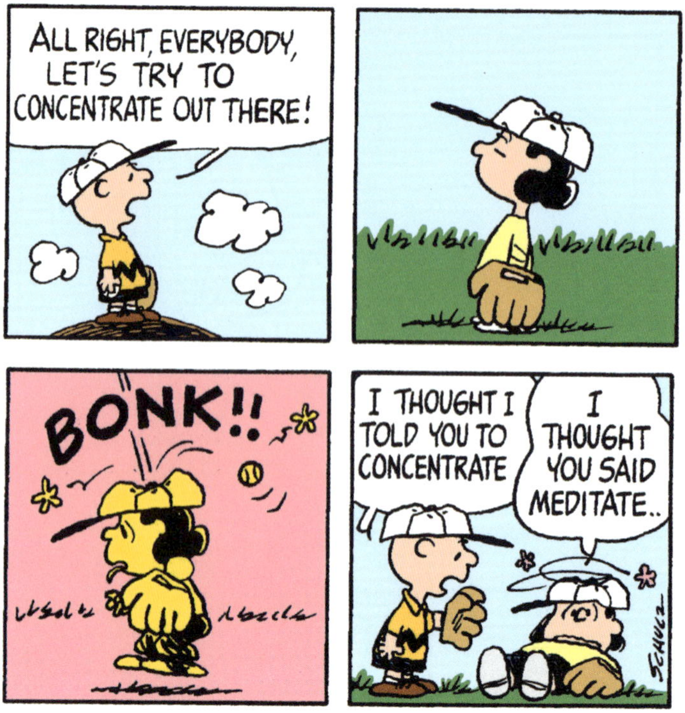
ALL RIGHT, EVERYBODY, LET'S TRY TO CONCENTRATE OUT THERE!
BONK!!
I THOUGHT I TOLD YOU TO CONCENTRATE
I THOUGHT YOU SAID MEDITATE..
SCHULZ

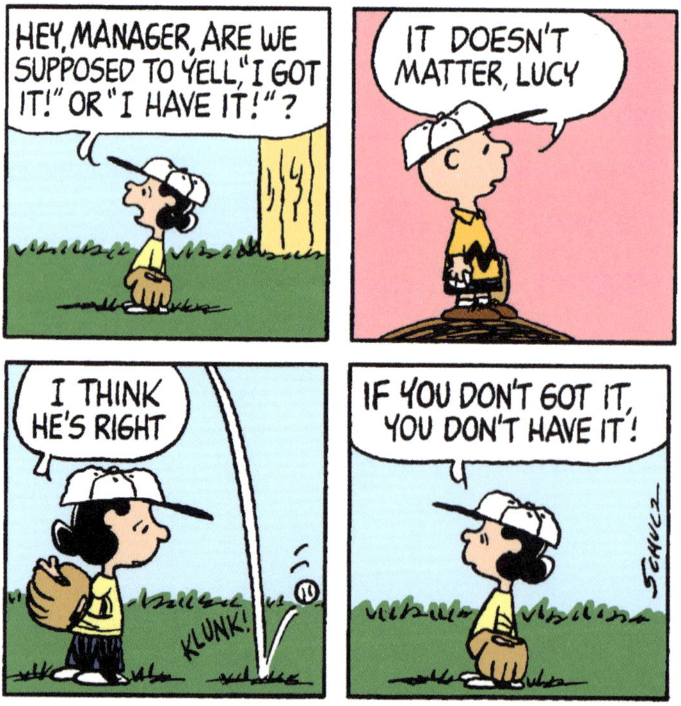
HEY, MANAGER, ARE WE SUPPOSED TO YELL, "I GOT IT!" OR "I HAVE IT!"?
IT DOESN'T MATTER, LUCY
I THINK HE'S RIGHT
KLUNK!
IF YOU DON'T GOT IT, YOU DON'T HAVE IT!
SCHULZ

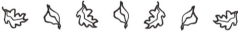

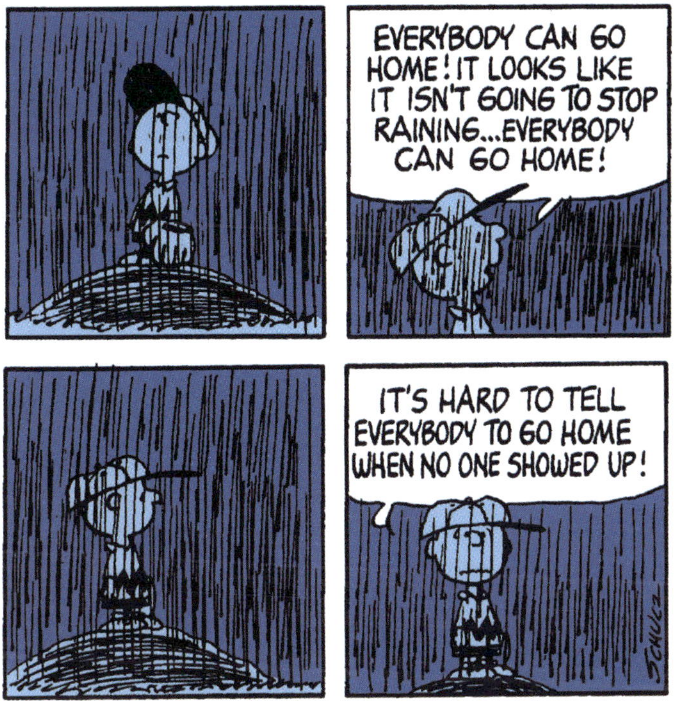
EVERYBODY CAN GO HOME! IT LOOKS LIKE IT ISN'T GOING TO STOP RAINING...EVERYBODY CAN GO HOME!
IT'S HARD TO TELL EVERYBODY TO GO HOME WHEN NO ONE SHOWED UP!
SCHULZ

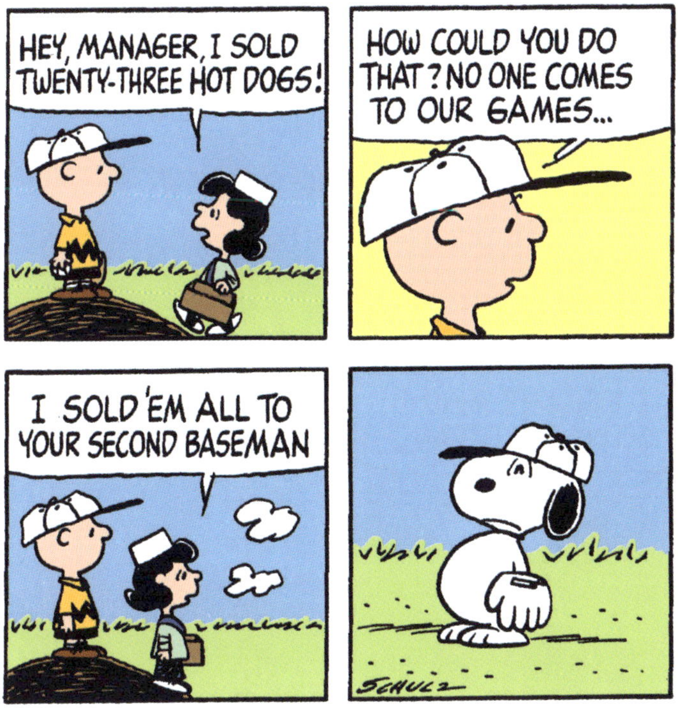
HEY, MANAGER, I SOLD TWENTY-THREE HOT DOGS!
HOW COULD YOU DO THAT? NO ONE COMES TO OUR GAMES...
I SOLD 'EM ALL TO YOUR SECOND BASEMAN
SCHULZ

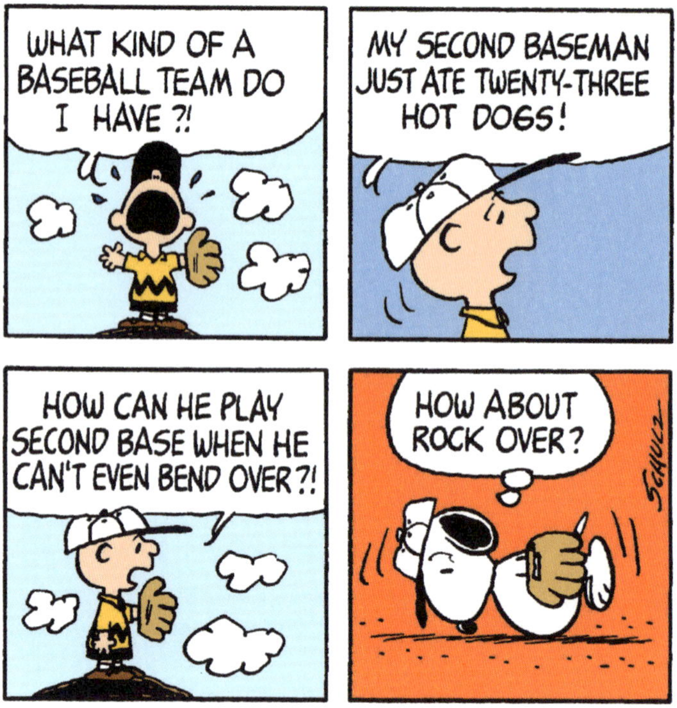
WHAT KIND OF A BASEBALL TEAM DO I HAVE ?!
MY SECOND BASEMAN JUST ATE TWENTY-THREE HOT DOGS!
HOW CAN HE PLAY SECOND BASE WHEN HE CAN'T EVEN BEND OVER ?!
HOW ABOUT ROCK OVER?
SCHULZ

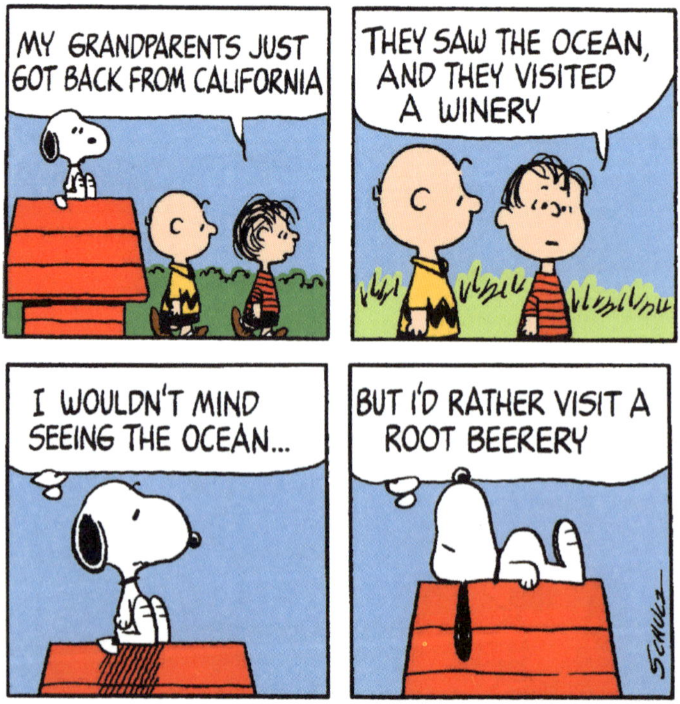
MY GRANDPARENTS JUST GOT BACK FROM CALIFORNIA
THEY SAW THE OCEAN, AND THEY VISITED A WINERY
I WOULDN'T MIND SEEING THE OCEAN...
BUT I'D RATHER VISIT A ROOT BEERERY
SCHULZ

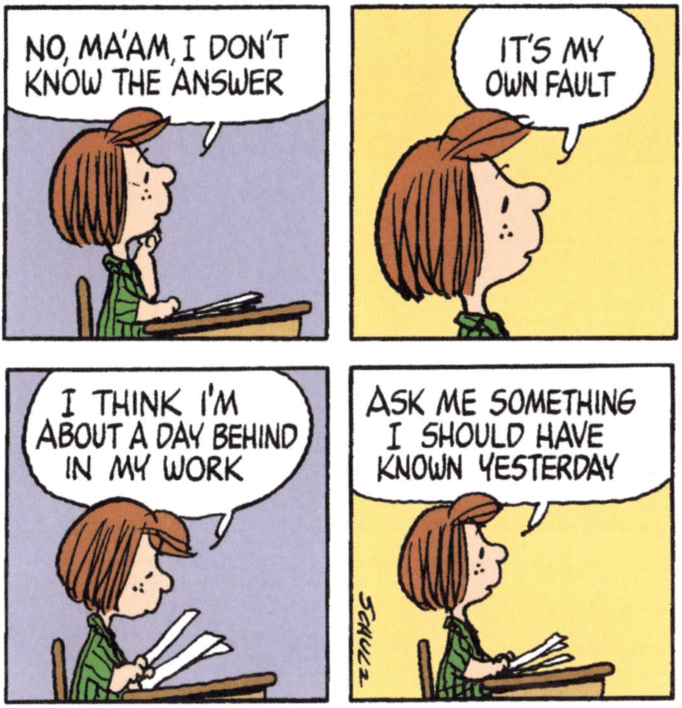
NO, MA'AM, I DON'T KNOW THE ANSWER
IT'S MY OWN FAULT
I THINK I'M ABOUT A DAY BEHIND IN MY WORK
ASK ME SOMETHING I SHOULD HAVE KNOWN YESTERDAY

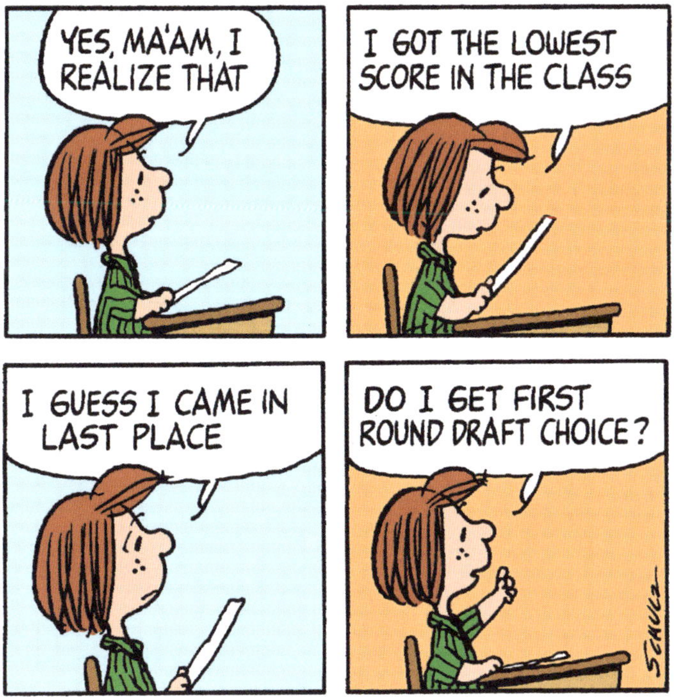
YES, MA'AM, I REALIZE THAT
I GOT THE LOWEST SCORE IN THE CLASS
I GUESS I CAME IN LAST PLACE
DO I GET FIRST ROUND DRAFT CHOICE?

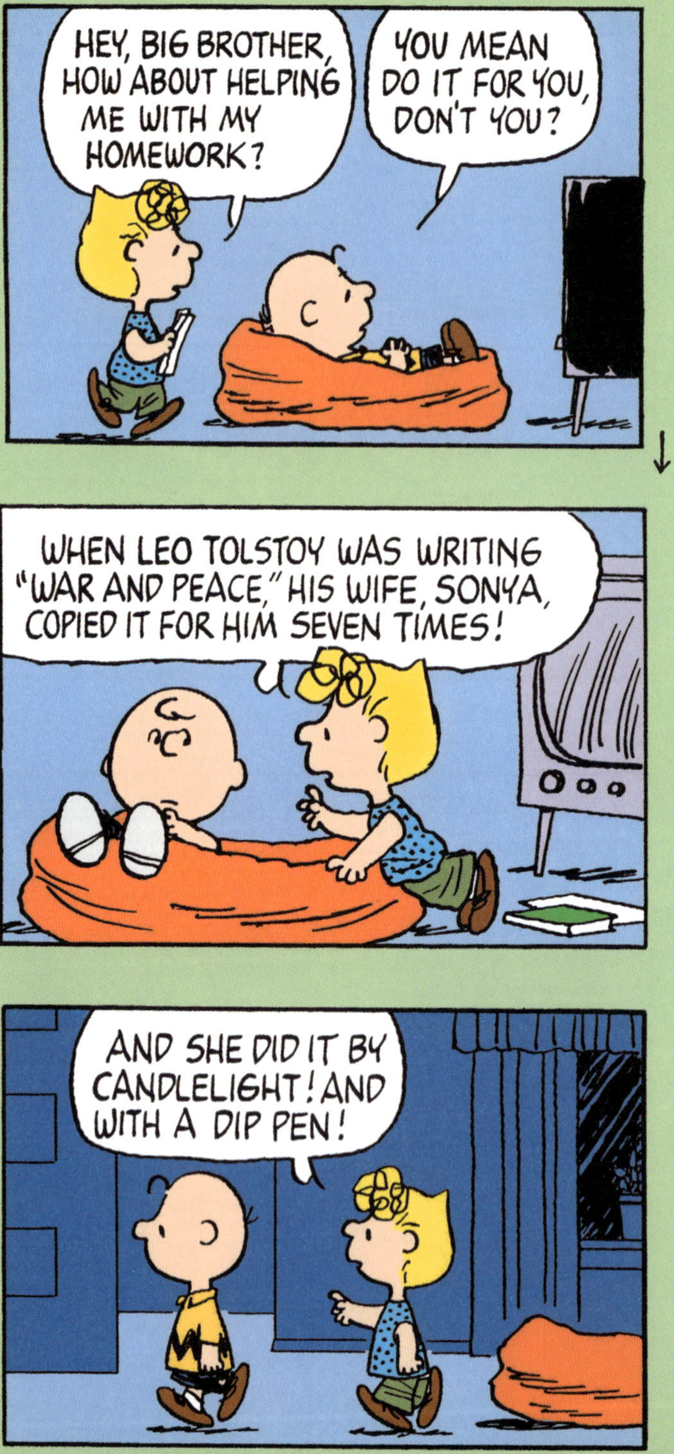
HEY, BIG BROTHER, HOW ABOUT HELPING ME WITH MY HOMEWORK?
YOU MEAN DO IT FOR YOU, DON'T YOU?
WHEN LEO TOLSTOY WAS WRITING "WAR AND PEACE," HIS WIFE, SONYA, COPIED IT FOR HIM SEVEN TIMES!
AND SHE DID IT BY CANDLELIGHT! AND WITH A DIP PEN!

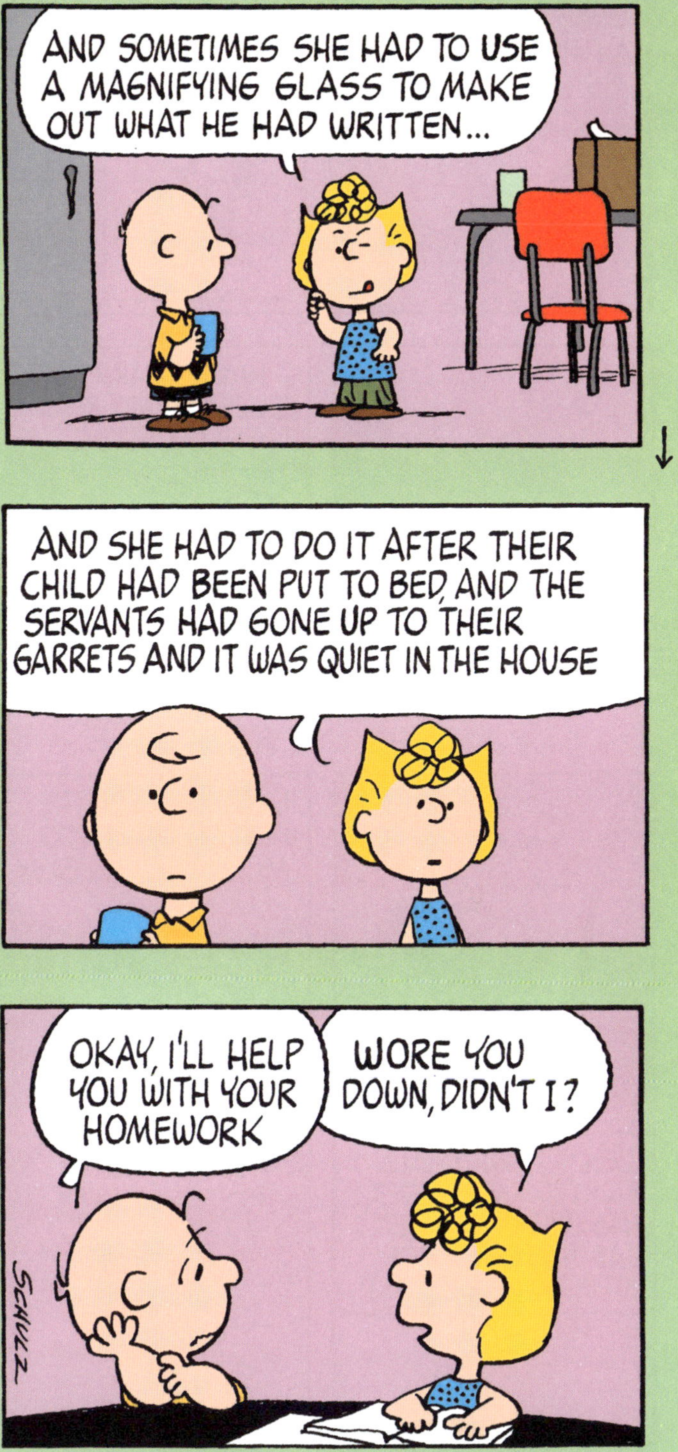
AND SOMETIMES SHE HAD TO USE A MAGNIFYING GLASS TO MAKE OUT WHAT HE HAD WRITTEN...
AND SHE HAD TO DO IT AFTER THEIR CHILD HAD BEEN PUT TO BED, AND THE SERVANTS HAD GONE UP TO THEIR GARRETS AND IT WAS QUIET IN THE HOUSE
OKAY, I'LL HELP YOU WITH YOUR HOMEWORK
WORE YOU DOWN, DIDN'T I?
SCHULZ

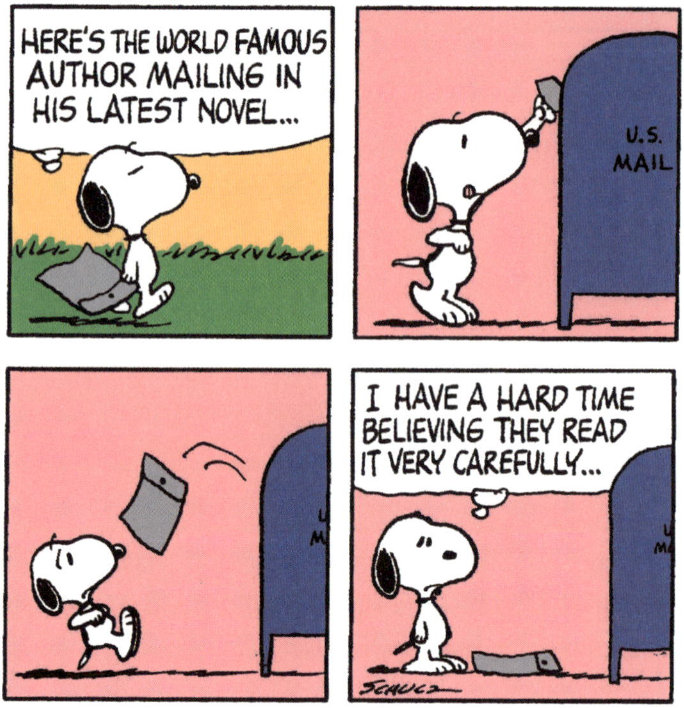
HERE'S THE WORLD FAMOUS AUTHOR MAILING IN HIS LATEST NOVEL...
U.S. MAIL
I HAVE A HARD TIME BELIEVING THEY READ IT VERY CAREFULLY...

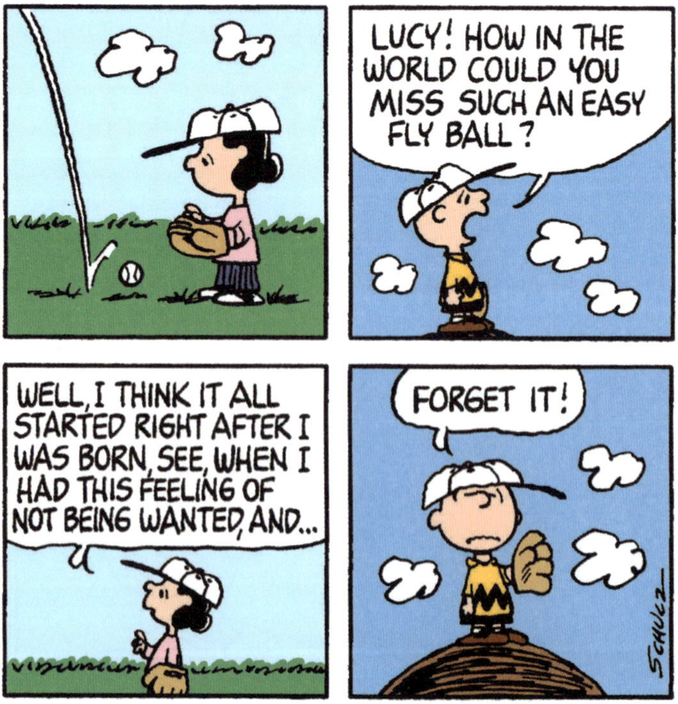
LUCY! HOW IN THE WORLD COULD YOU MISS SUCH AN EASY FLY BALL?
WELL, I THINK IT ALL STARTED RIGHT AFTER I WAS BORN, SEE, WHEN I HAD THIS FEELING OF NOT BEING WANTED, AND...
FORGET IT!

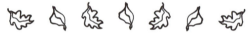

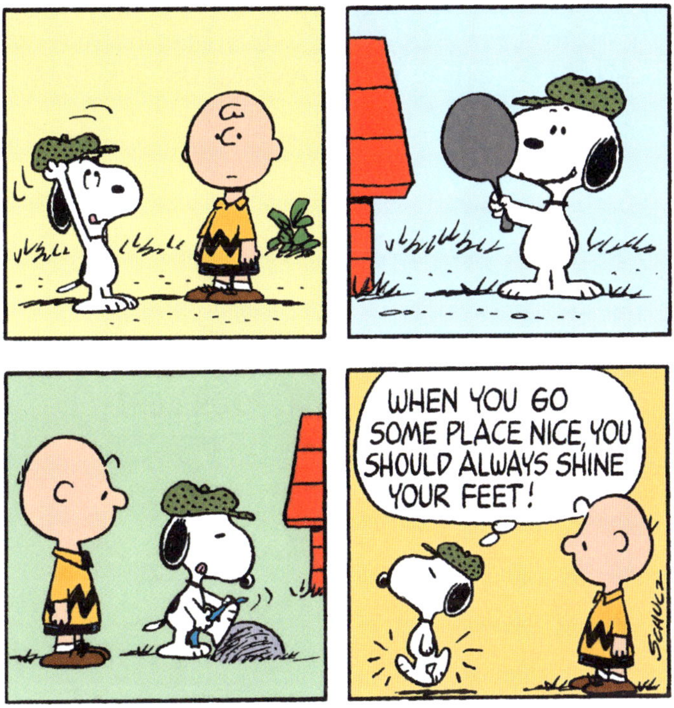
WHEN YOU GO SOME PLACE NICE, YOU SHOULD ALWAYS SHINE YOUR FEET!
SCHULZ

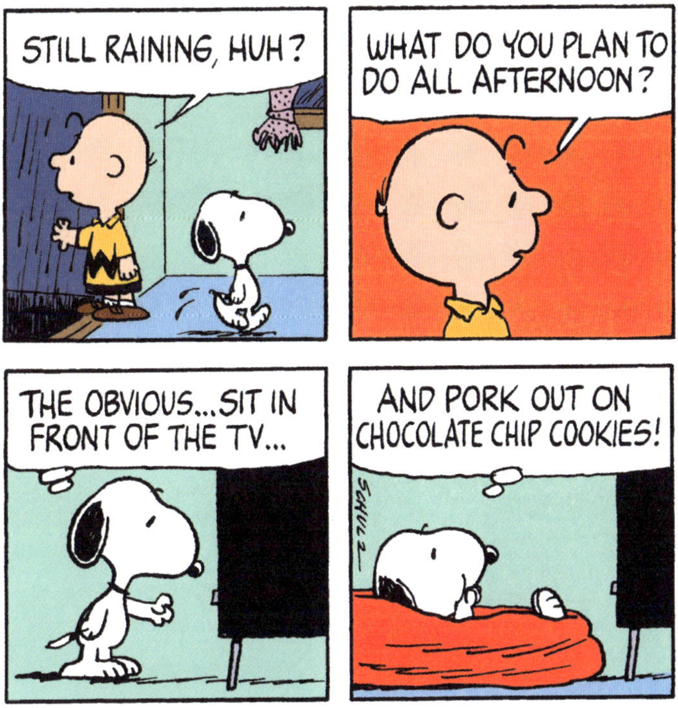
STILL RAINING, HUH?
WHAT DO YOU PLAN TO DO ALL AFTERNOON?
THE OBVIOUS...SIT IN FRONT OF THE TV...
AND PORK OUT ON CHOCOLATE CHIP COOKIES!
SCHULZ

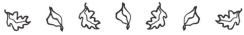

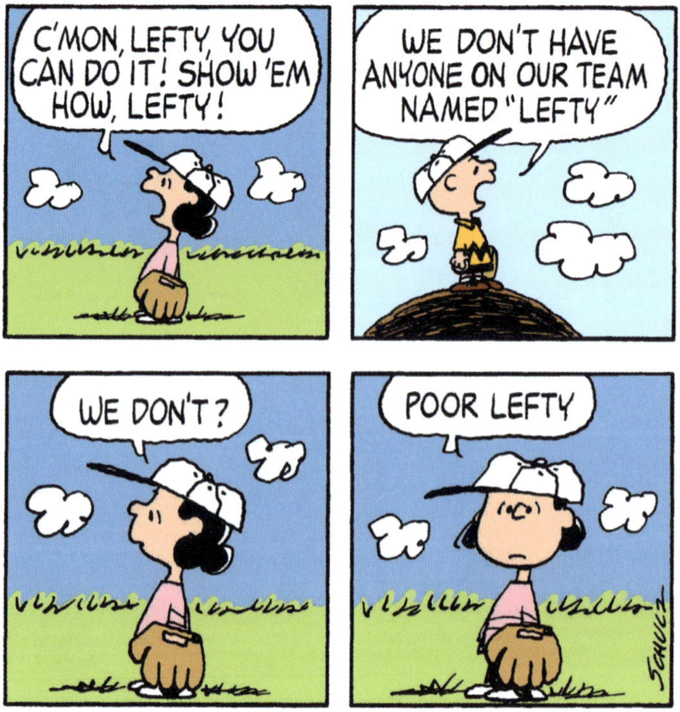
C'MON, LEFTY, YOU CAN DO IT! SHOW 'EM HOW, LEFTY!
WE DON'T HAVE ANYONE ON OUR TEAM NAMED "LEFTY"
WE DON'T?
POOR LEFTY
SCHULZ

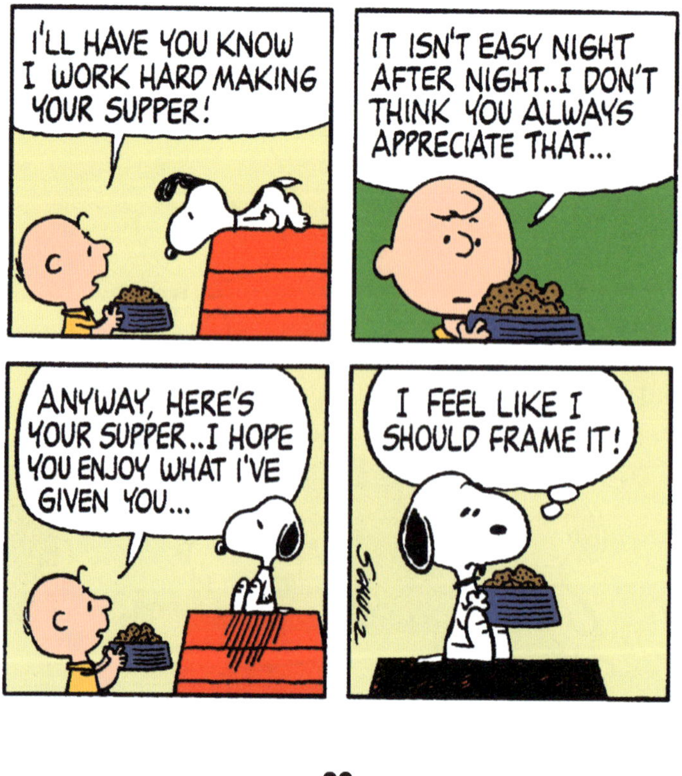
I'LL HAVE YOU KNOW I WORK HARD MAKING YOUR SUPPER!
IT ISN'T EASY NIGHT AFTER NIGHT..I DON'T THINK YOU ALWAYS APPRECIATE THAT...
ANYWAY, HERE'S YOUR SUPPER..I HOPE YOU ENJOY WHAT I'VE GIVEN YOU...
I FEEL LIKE I SHOULD FRAME IT!
SCHULZ

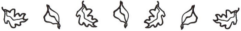

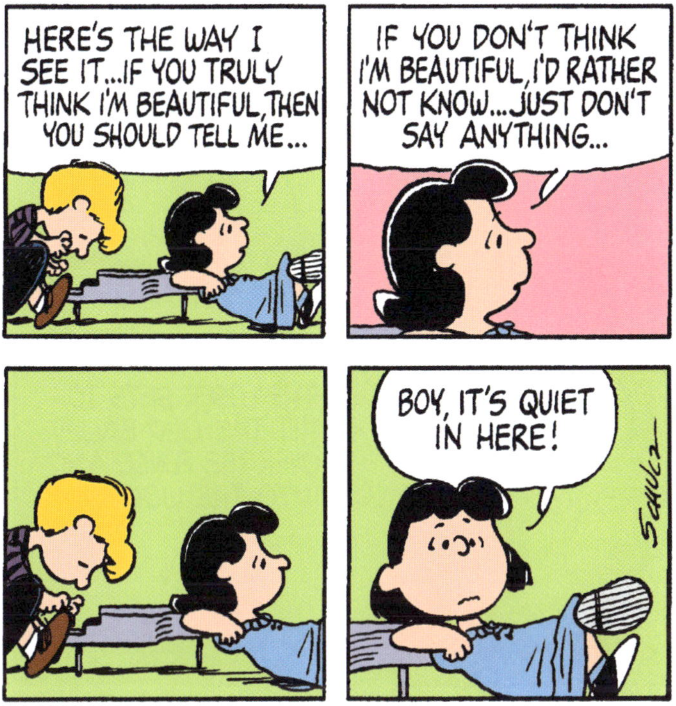
HERE'S THE WAY I SEE IT...IF YOU TRULY THINK I'M BEAUTIFUL, THEN YOU SHOULD TELL ME...
IF YOU DON'T THINK I'M BEAUTIFUL, I'D RATHER NOT KNOW...JUST DON'T SAY ANYTHING...
BOY, IT'S QUIET IN HERE!

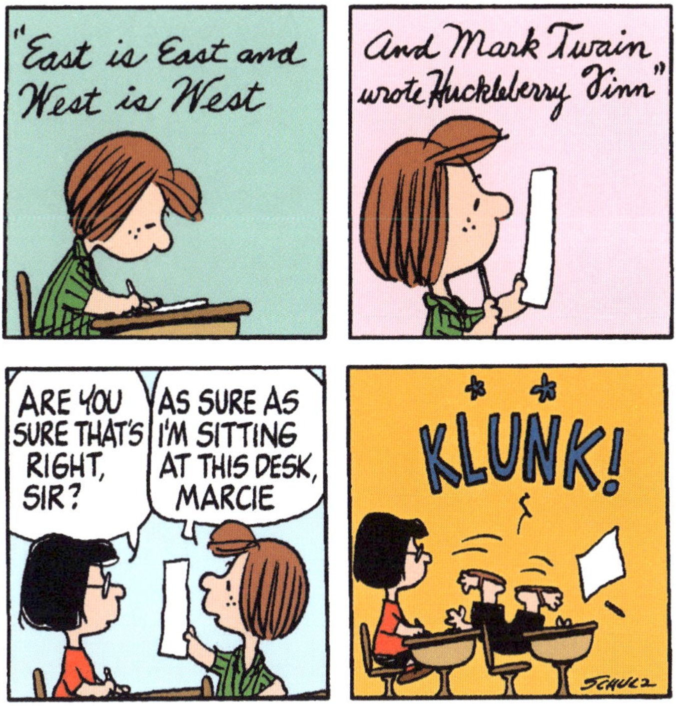
"East is East and West is West
And Mark Twain wrote Huckleberry Finn"
ARE YOU SURE THAT'S RIGHT, SIR?
AS SURE AS I'M SITTING AT THIS DESK, MARCIE
KLUNK!

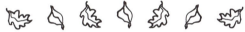

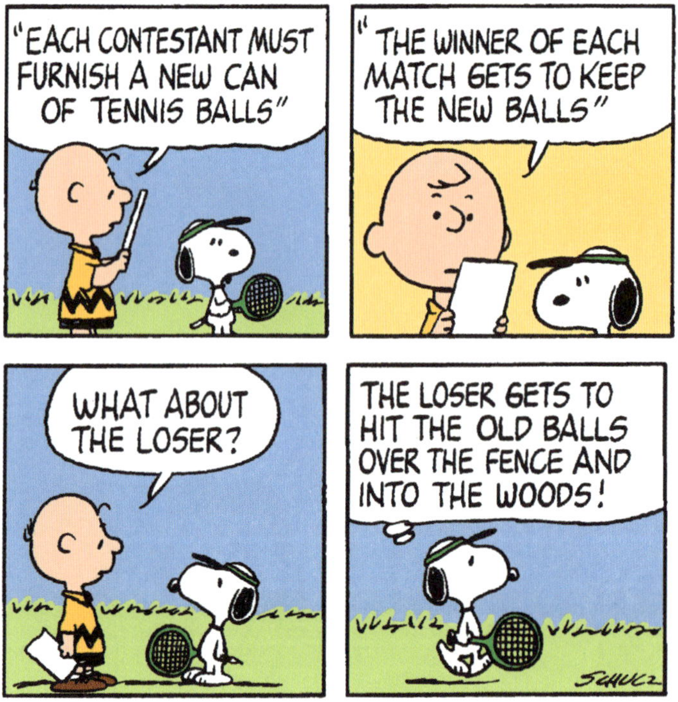
"EACH CONTESTANT MUST FURNISH A NEW CAN OF TENNIS BALLS"
"THE WINNER OF EACH MATCH GETS TO KEEP THE NEW BALLS"
WHAT ABOUT THE LOSER?
THE LOSER GETS TO HIT THE OLD BALLS OVER THE FENCE AND INTO THE WOODS!

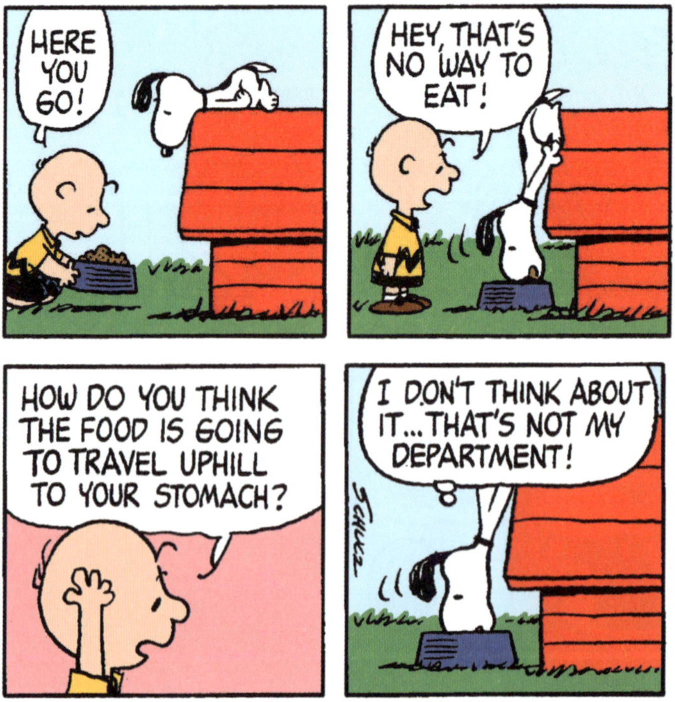
HERE YOU GO!
HEY, THAT'S NO WAY TO EAT!
HOW DO YOU THINK THE FOOD IS GOING TO TRAVEL UPHILL TO YOUR STOMACH?
I DON'T THINK ABOUT IT... THAT'S NOT MY DEPARTMENT!

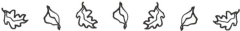

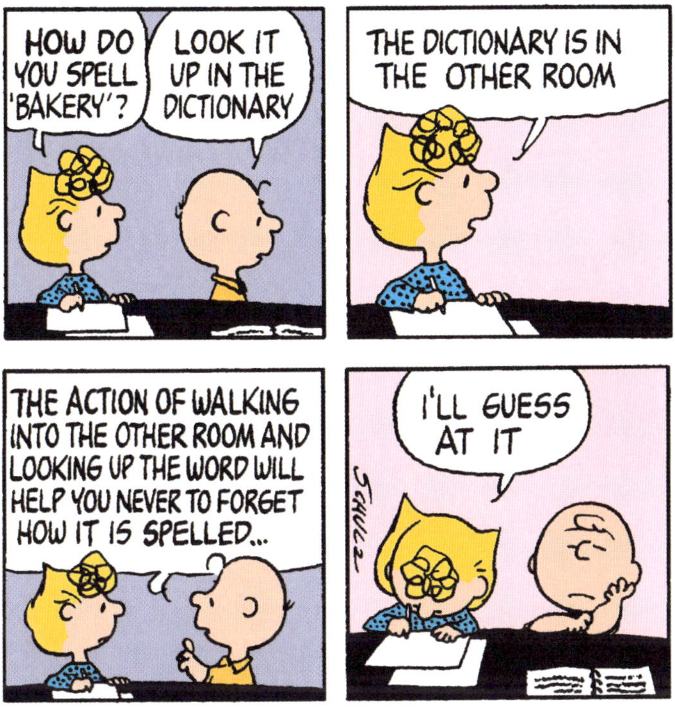
HOW DO YOU SPELL 'BAKERY'?
LOOK IT UP IN THE DICTIONARY
THE DICTIONARY IS IN THE OTHER ROOM
THE ACTION OF WALKING INTO THE OTHER ROOM AND LOOKING UP THE WORD WILL HELP YOU NEVER TO FORGET HOW IT IS SPELLED...
I'LL GUESS AT IT
SCHULZ

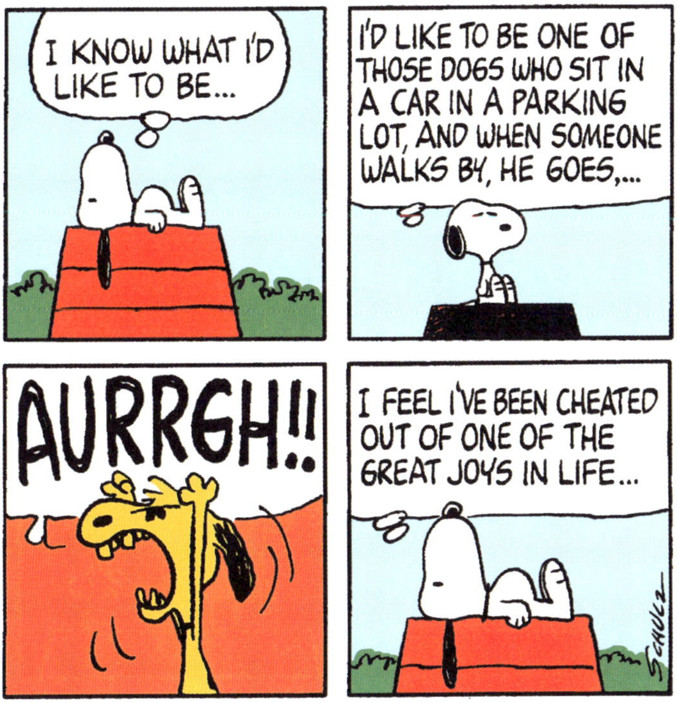
I KNOW WHAT I'D LIKE TO BE...
I'D LIKE TO BE ONE OF THOSE DOGS WHO SIT IN A CAR IN A PARKING LOT, AND WHEN SOMEONE WALKS BY, HE GOES,...
AURRGH!!
I FEEL I'VE BEEN CHEATED OUT OF ONE OF THE GREAT JOYS IN LIFE...
SCHULZ

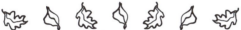

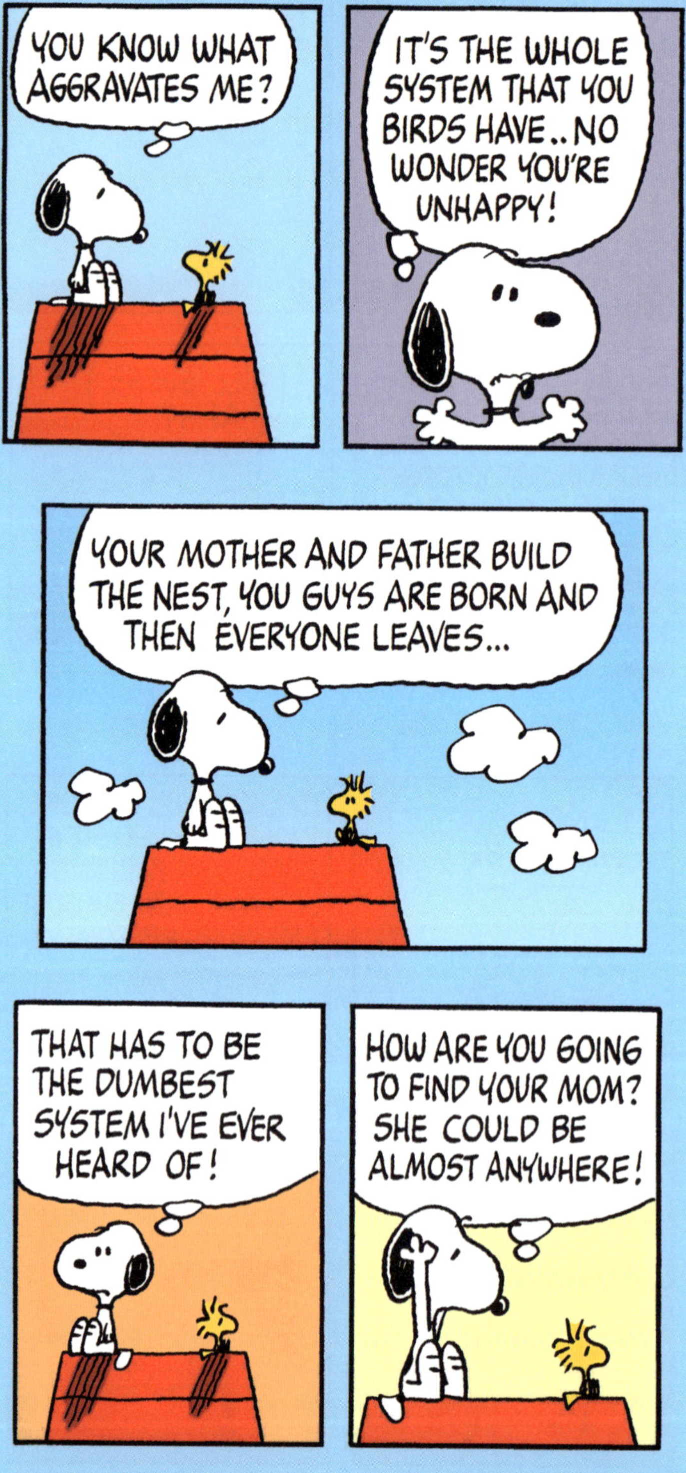
YOU KNOW WHAT AGGRAVATES ME?
IT'S THE WHOLE SYSTEM THAT YOU BIRDS HAVE.. NO WONDER YOU'RE UNHAPPY!
YOUR MOTHER AND FATHER BUILD THE NEST, YOU GUYS ARE BORN AND THEN EVERYONE LEAVES...
THAT HAS TO BE THE DUMBEST SYSTEM I'VE EVER HEARD OF!
HOW ARE YOU GOING TO FIND YOUR MOM? SHE COULD BE ALMOST ANYWHERE!

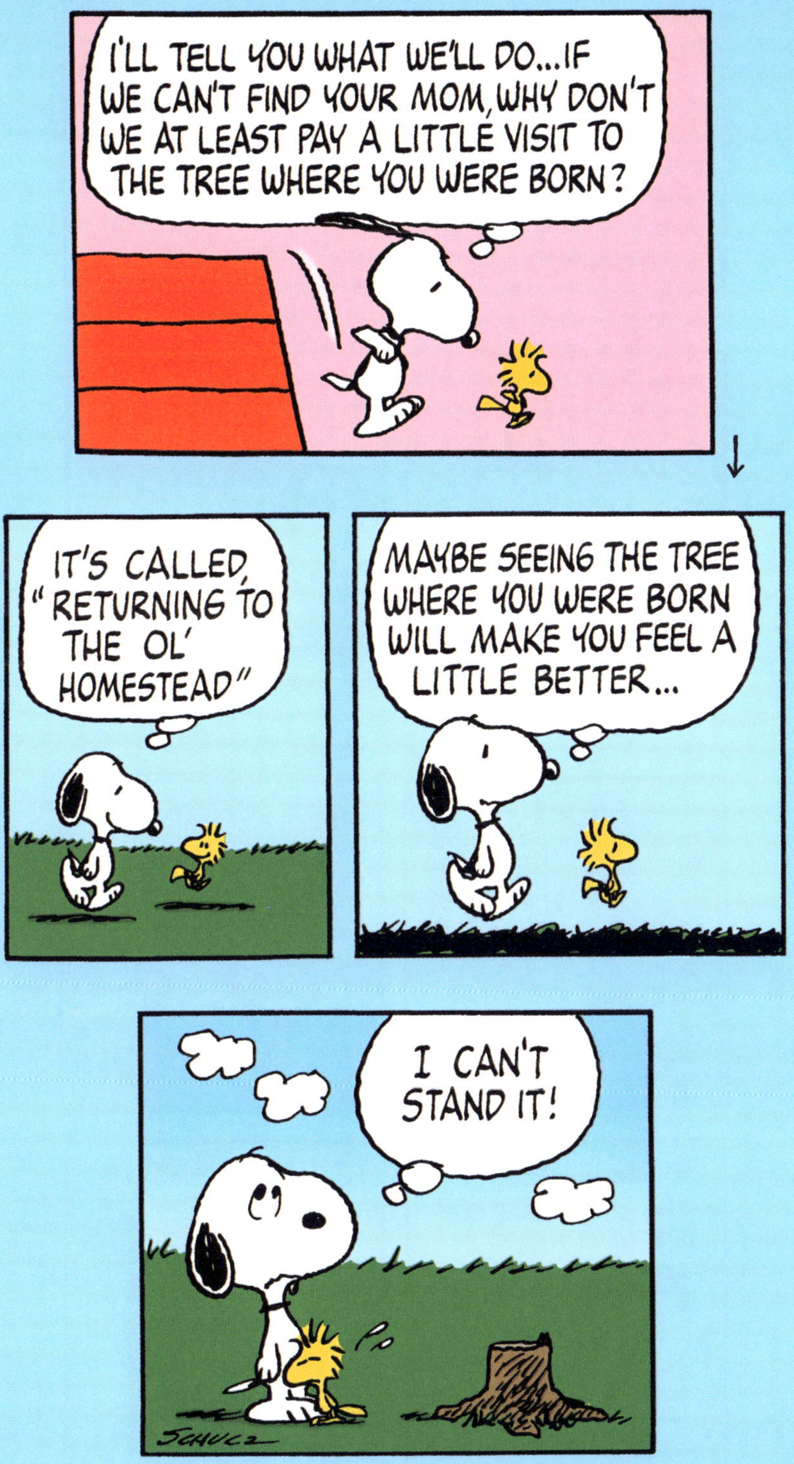
I'LL TELL YOU WHAT WE'LL DO...IF WE CAN'T FIND YOUR MOM, WHY DON'T WE AT LEAST PAY A LITTLE VISIT TO THE TREE WHERE YOU WERE BORN?
IT'S CALLED "RETURNING TO THE OL' HOMESTEAD"
MAYBE SEEING THE TREE WHERE YOU WERE BORN WILL MAKE YOU FEEL A LITTLE BETTER...
I CAN'T STAND IT!
SCHULZ

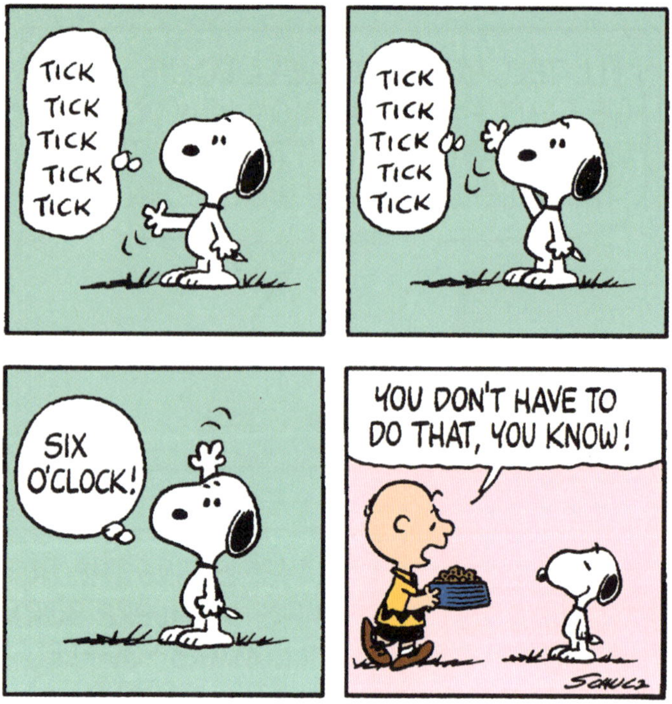
TICK TICK TICK TICK TICK
TICK TICK TICK TICK TICK
SIX O'CLOCK!
YOU DON'T HAVE TO DO THAT, YOU KNOW!
SCHULZ

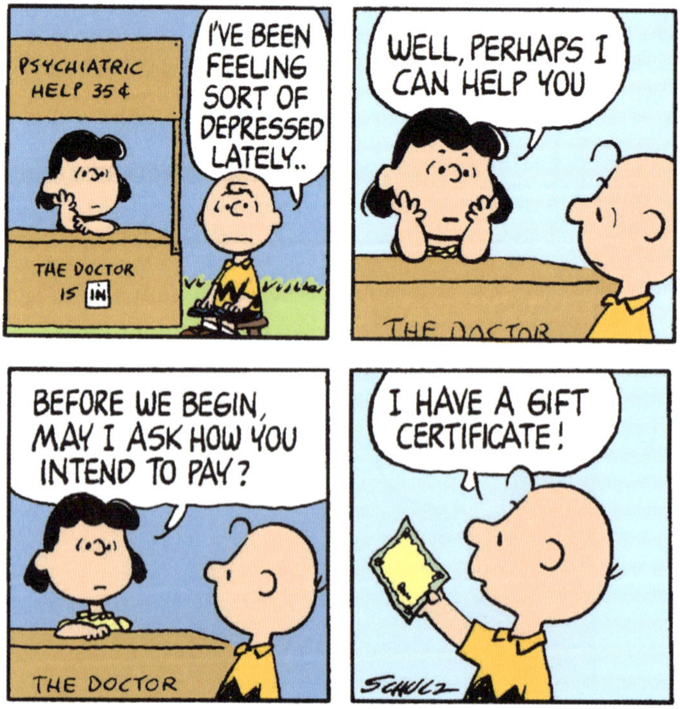
PSYCHIATRIC HELP 35¢
THE DOCTOR IS IN
I'VE BEEN FEELING SORT OF DEPRESSED LATELY..
WELL, PERHAPS I CAN HELP YOU
BEFORE WE BEGIN, MAY I ASK HOW YOU INTEND TO PAY?
THE DOCTOR
I HAVE A GIFT CERTIFICATE!
SCHULZ

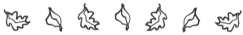

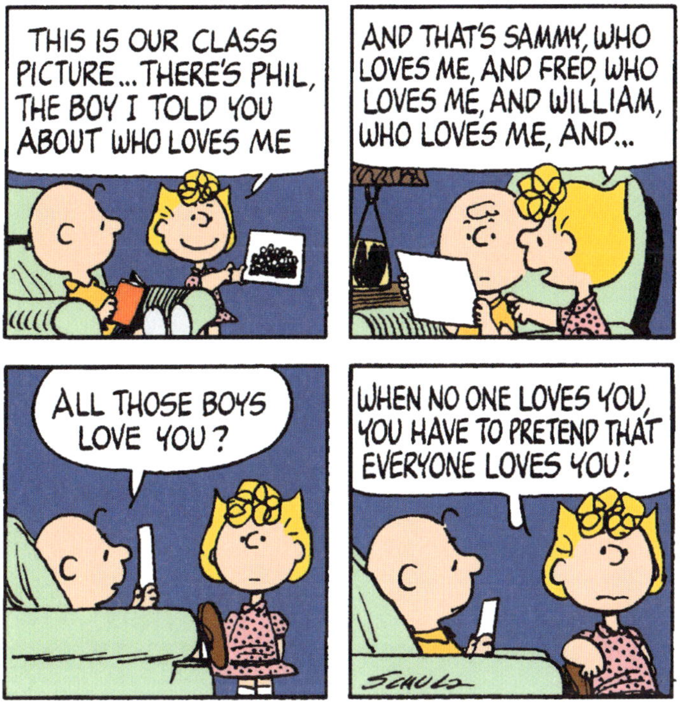
THIS IS OUR CLASS PICTURE...THERE'S PHIL, THE BOY I TOLD YOU ABOUT WHO LOVES ME
AND THAT'S SAMMY, WHO LOVES ME, AND FRED, WHO LOVES ME, AND WILLIAM, WHO LOVES ME, AND...
ALL THOSE BOYS LOVE YOU?
WHEN NO ONE LOVES YOU, YOU HAVE TO PRETEND THAT EVERYONE LOVES YOU!
SCHULZ

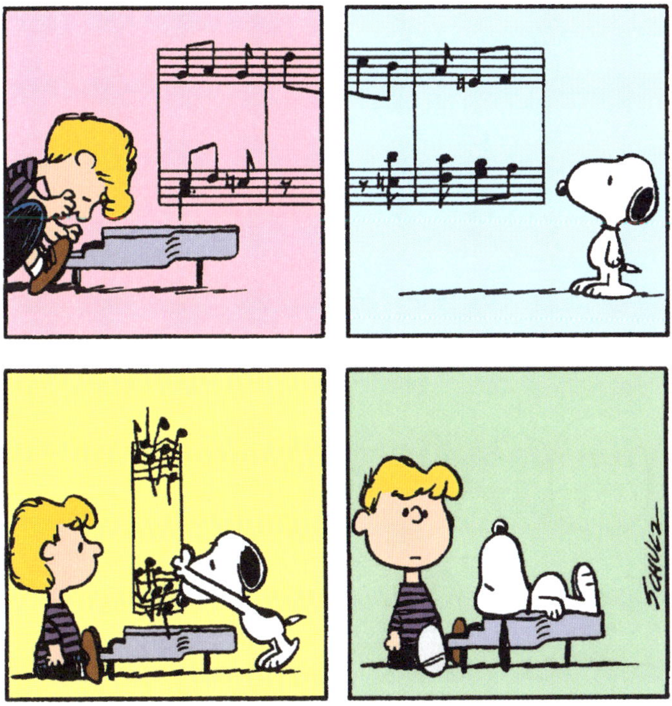
SCHULZ

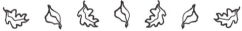

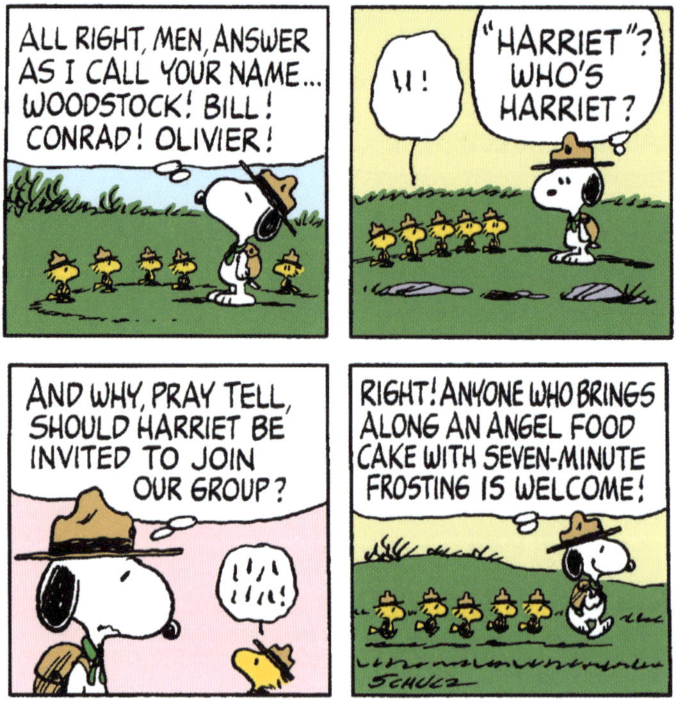
ALL RIGHT, MEN, ANSWER AS I CALL YOUR NAME... WOODSTOCK! BILL! CONRAD! OLIVIER!
"HARRIET"? WHO'S HARRIET?
AND WHY, PRAY TELL, SHOULD HARRIET BE INVITED TO JOIN OUR GROUP?
RIGHT! ANYONE WHO BRINGS ALONG AN ANGEL FOOD CAKE WITH SEVEN-MINUTE FROSTING IS WELCOME!

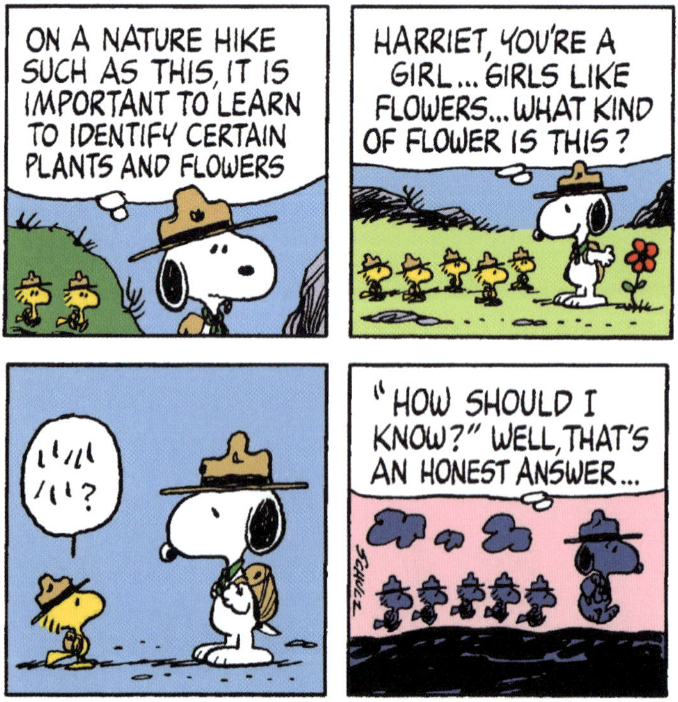
ON A NATURE HIKE SUCH AS THIS, IT IS IMPORTANT TO LEARN TO IDENTIFY CERTAIN PLANTS AND FLOWERS
HARRIET, YOU'RE A GIRL... GIRLS LIKE FLOWERS... WHAT KIND OF FLOWER IS THIS?
"HOW SHOULD I KNOW?" WELL, THAT'S AN HONEST ANSWER...

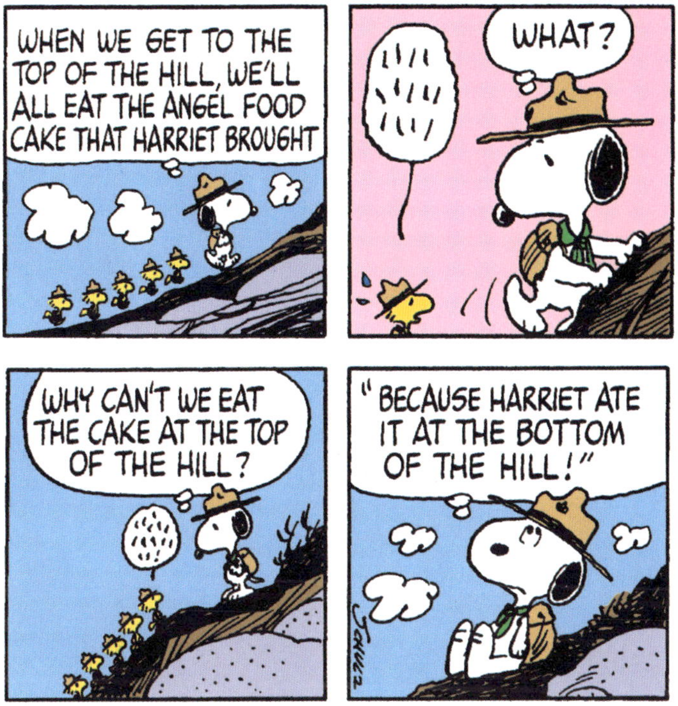
WHEN WE GET TO THE TOP OF THE HILL, WE'LL ALL EAT THE ANGEL FOOD CAKE THAT HARRIET BROUGHT
WHAT?
WHY CAN'T WE EAT THE CAKE AT THE TOP OF THE HILL?
"BECAUSE HARRIET ATE IT AT THE BOTTOM OF THE HILL!"

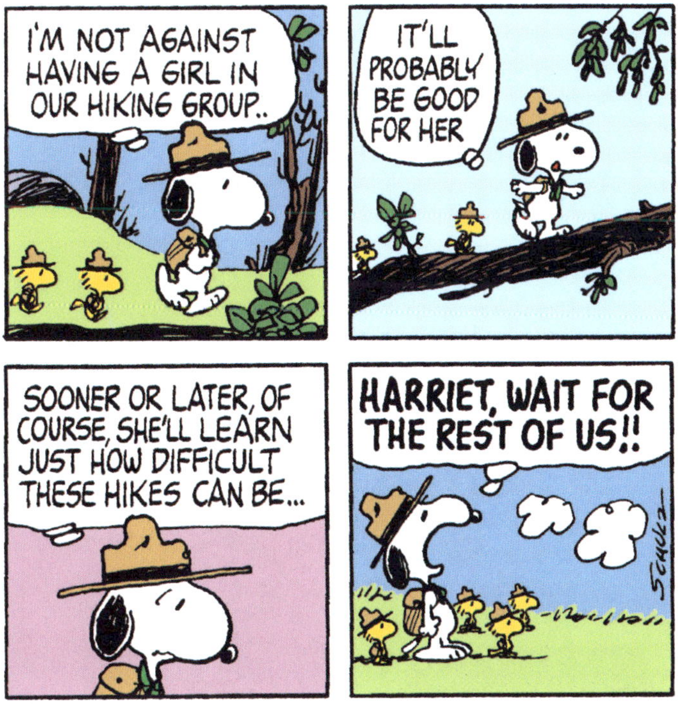
I'M NOT AGAINST HAVING A GIRL IN OUR HIKING GROUP..
IT'LL PROBABLY BE GOOD FOR HER
SOONER OR LATER, OF COURSE, SHE'LL LEARN JUST HOW DIFFICULT THESE HIKES CAN BE...
HARRIET, WAIT FOR THE REST OF US!!

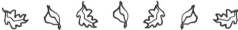

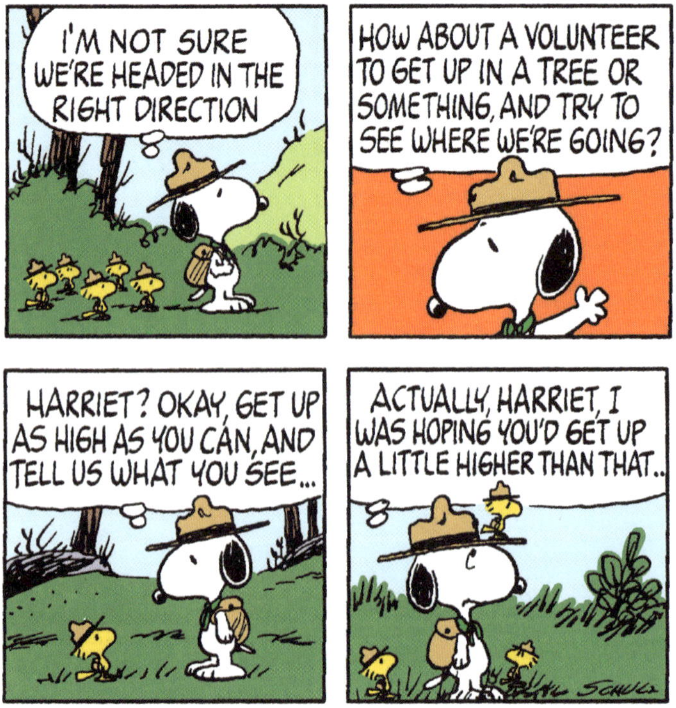
I'M NOT SURE WE'RE HEADED IN THE RIGHT DIRECTION
HOW ABOUT A VOLUNTEER TO GET UP IN A TREE OR SOMETHING, AND TRY TO SEE WHERE WE'RE GOING?
HARRIET? OKAY, GET UP AS HIGH AS YOU CAN, AND TELL US WHAT YOU SEE...
ACTUALLY, HARRIET, I WAS HOPING YOU'D GET UP A LITTLE HIGHER THAN THAT..

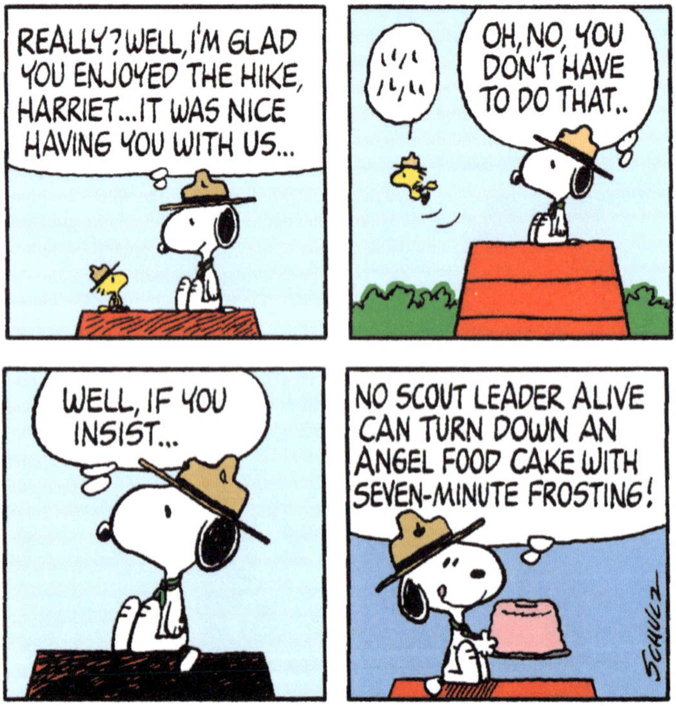
REALLY? WELL, I'M GLAD YOU ENJOYED THE HIKE, HARRIET...IT WAS NICE HAVING YOU WITH US...
OH, NO, YOU DON'T HAVE TO DO THAT..
WELL, IF YOU INSIST...
NO SCOUT LEADER ALIVE CAN TURN DOWN AN ANGEL FOOD CAKE WITH SEVEN-MINUTE FROSTING!

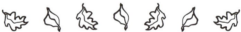

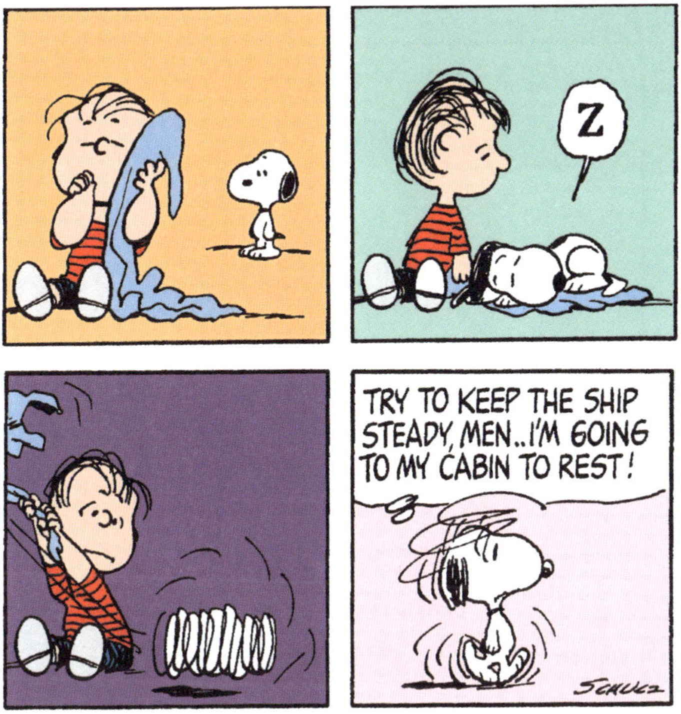
Z
TRY TO KEEP THE SHIP STEADY, MEN..I'M GOING TO MY CABIN TO REST!

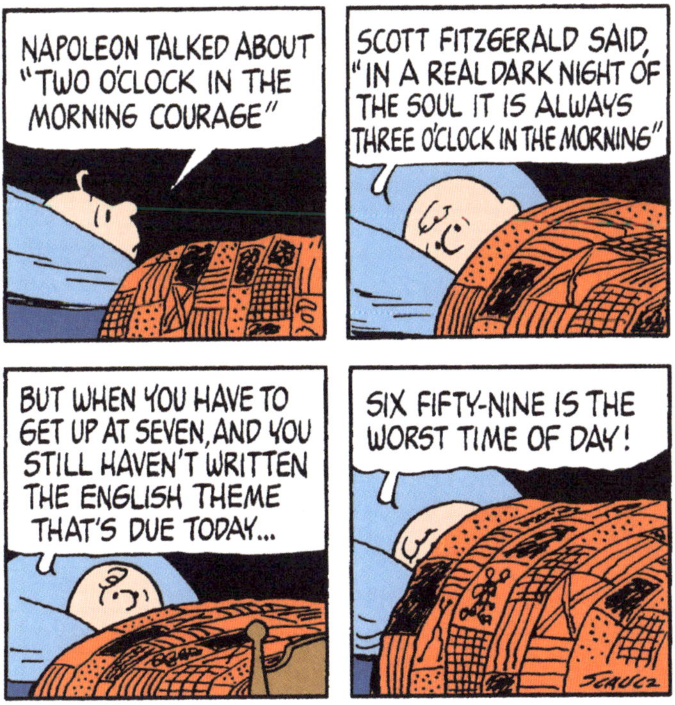
NAPOLEON TALKED ABOUT "TWO O'CLOCK IN THE MORNING COURAGE"
SCOTT FITZGERALD SAID, "IN A REAL DARK NIGHT OF THE SOUL IT IS ALWAYS THREE O'CLOCK IN THE MORNING"
BUT WHEN YOU HAVE TO GET UP AT SEVEN, AND YOU STILL HAVEN'T WRITTEN THE ENGLISH THEME THAT'S DUE TODAY...
SIX FIFTY-NINE IS THE WORST TIME OF DAY!

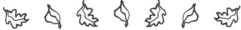

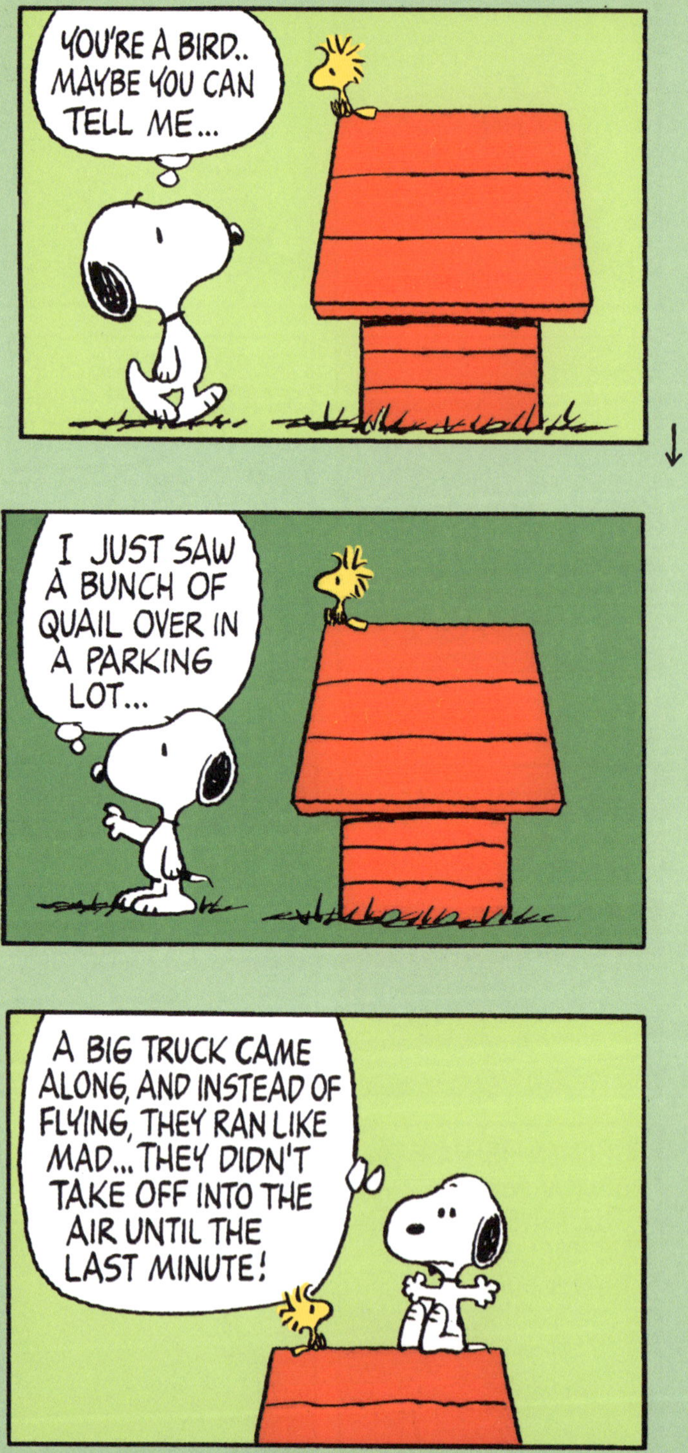
YOU'RE A BIRD.. MAYBE YOU CAN TELL ME...
I JUST SAW A BUNCH OF QUAIL OVER IN A PARKING LOT...
A BIG TRUCK CAME ALONG, AND INSTEAD OF FLYING, THEY RAN LIKE MAD... THEY DIDN'T TAKE OFF INTO THE AIR UNTIL THE LAST MINUTE!

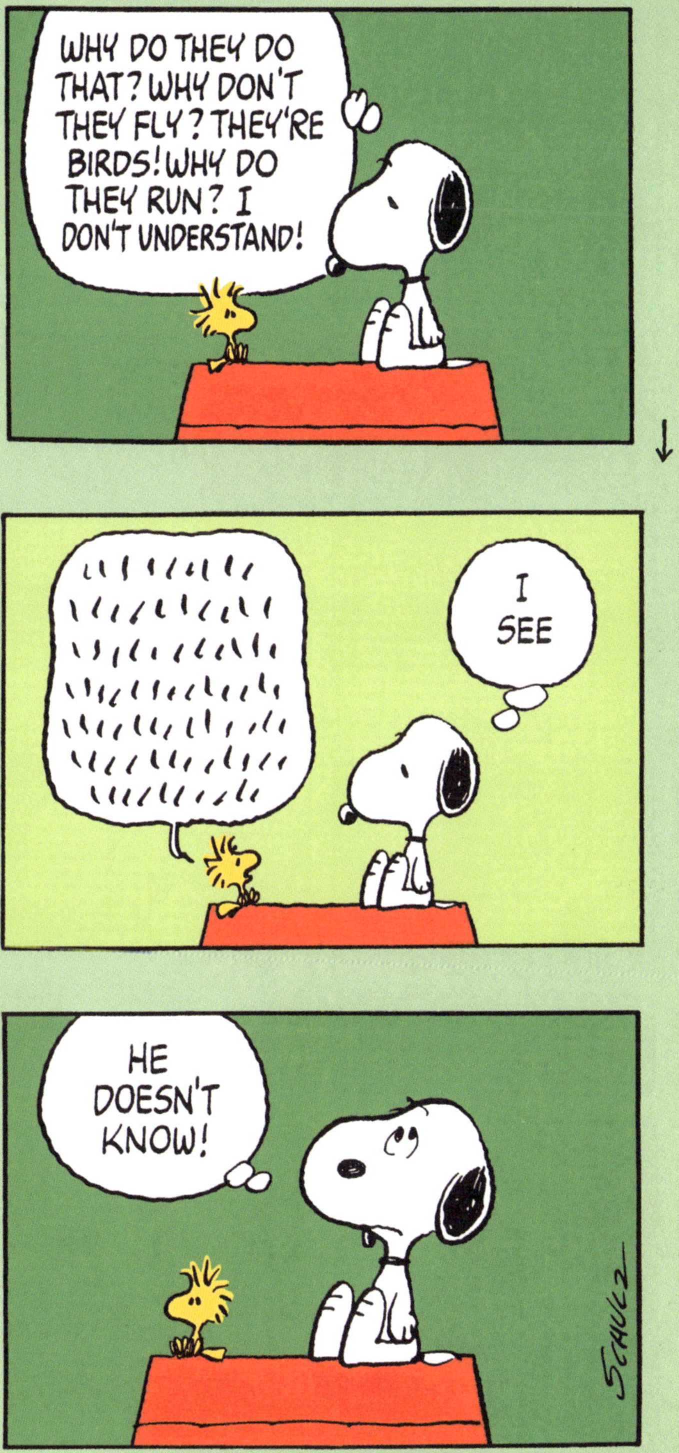
WHY DO THEY DO THAT? WHY DON'T THEY FLY? THEY'RE BIRDS! WHY DO THEY RUN? I DON'T UNDERSTAND!
I SEE
HE DOESN'T KNOW!
SCHULZ

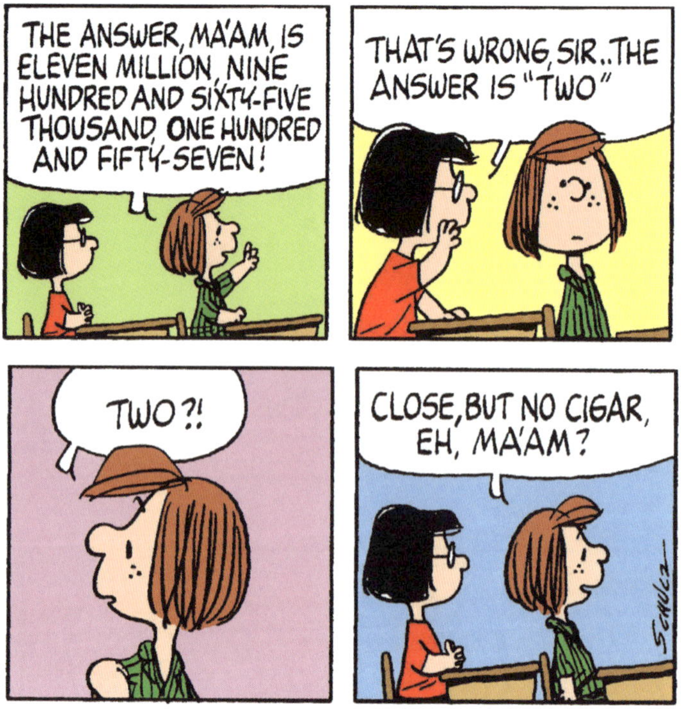
THE ANSWER, MA'AM, IS ELEVEN MILLION, NINE HUNDRED AND SIXTY-FIVE THOUSAND, ONE HUNDRED AND FIFTY-SEVEN!
THAT'S WRONG, SIR..THE ANSWER IS "TWO"
TWO?!
CLOSE, BUT NO CIGAR, EH, MA'AM?
SCHULZ

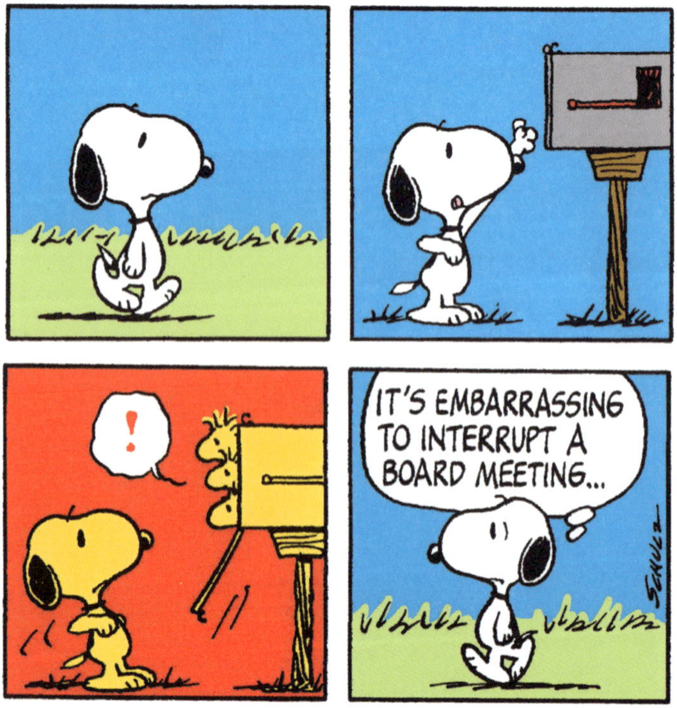
!
IT'S EMBARRASSING TO INTERRUPT A BOARD MEETING...
SCHULZ

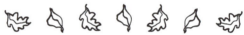

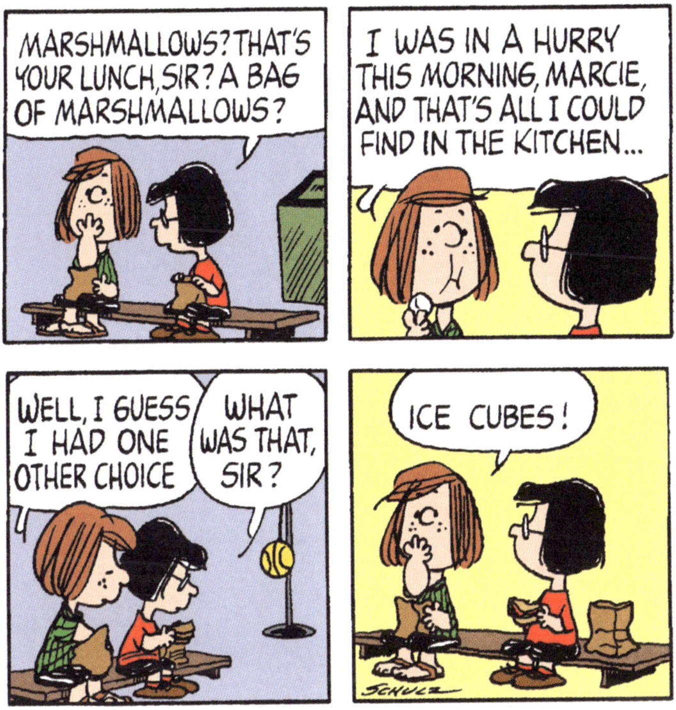
MARSHMALLOWS? THAT'S YOUR LUNCH, SIR? A BAG OF MARSHMALLOWS?
I WAS IN A HURRY THIS MORNING, MARCIE, AND THAT'S ALL I COULD FIND IN THE KITCHEN...
WELL, I GUESS I HAD ONE OTHER CHOICE
WHAT WAS THAT, SIR?
ICE CUBES!

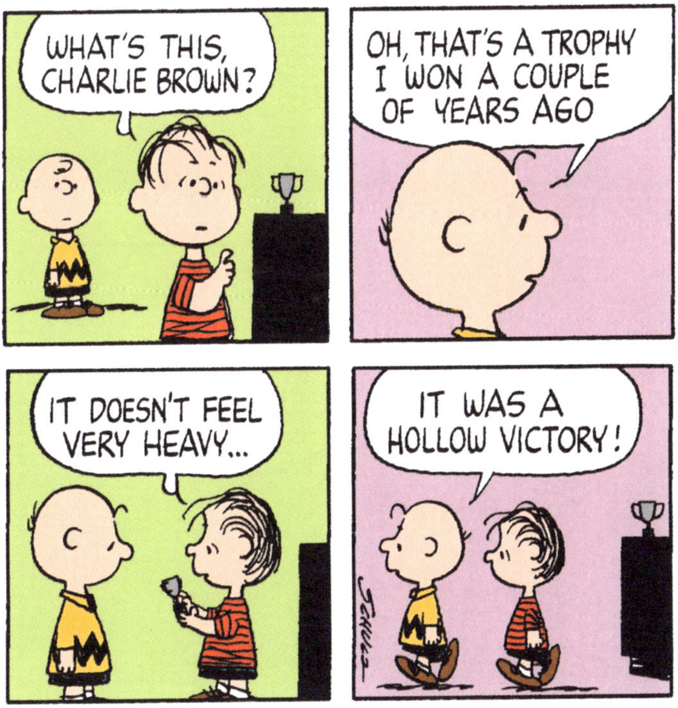
WHAT'S THIS, CHARLIE BROWN?
OH, THAT'S A TROPHY I WON A COUPLE OF YEARS AGO
IT DOESN'T FEEL VERY HEAVY...
IT WAS A HOLLOW VICTORY!

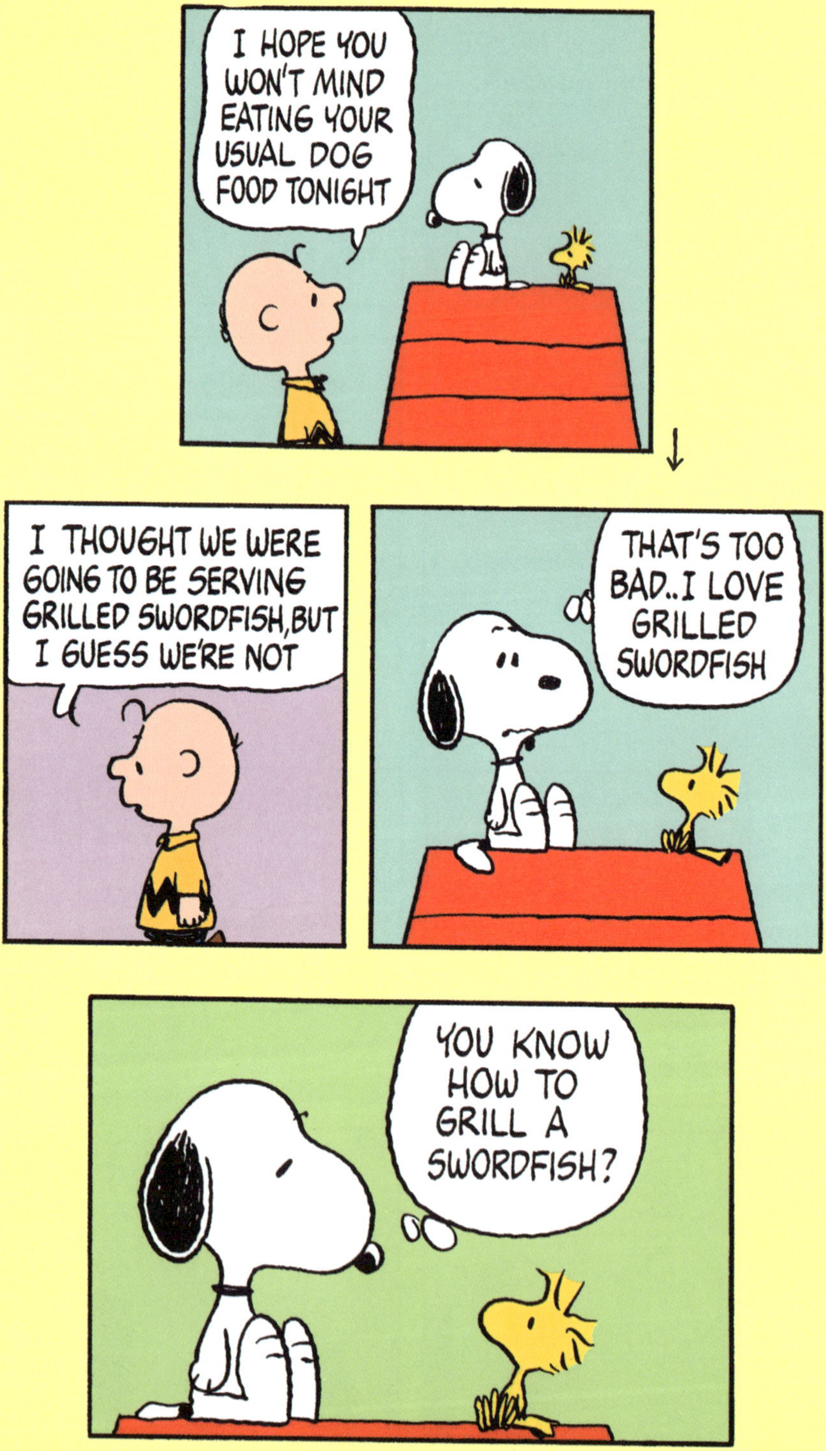
I HOPE YOU WON'T MIND EATING YOUR USUAL DOG FOOD TONIGHT
I THOUGHT WE WERE GOING TO BE SERVING GRILLED SWORDFISH, BUT I GUESS WE'RE NOT
THAT'S TOO BAD..I LOVE GRILLED SWORDFISH
YOU KNOW HOW TO GRILL A SWORDFISH?

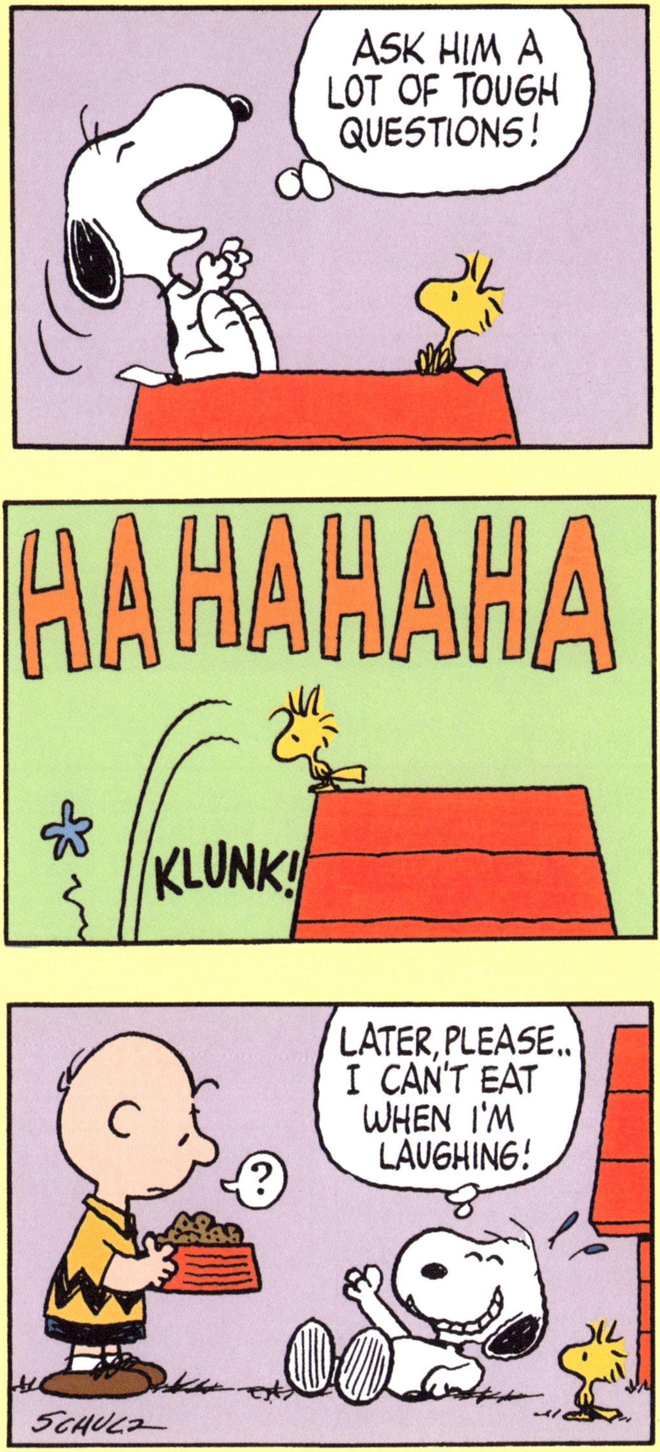
ASK HIM A LOT OF TOUGH QUESTIONS!
HAHAHAHA
KLUNK!
LATER, PLEASE.. I CAN'T EAT WHEN I'M LAUGHING!
?
SCHULZ

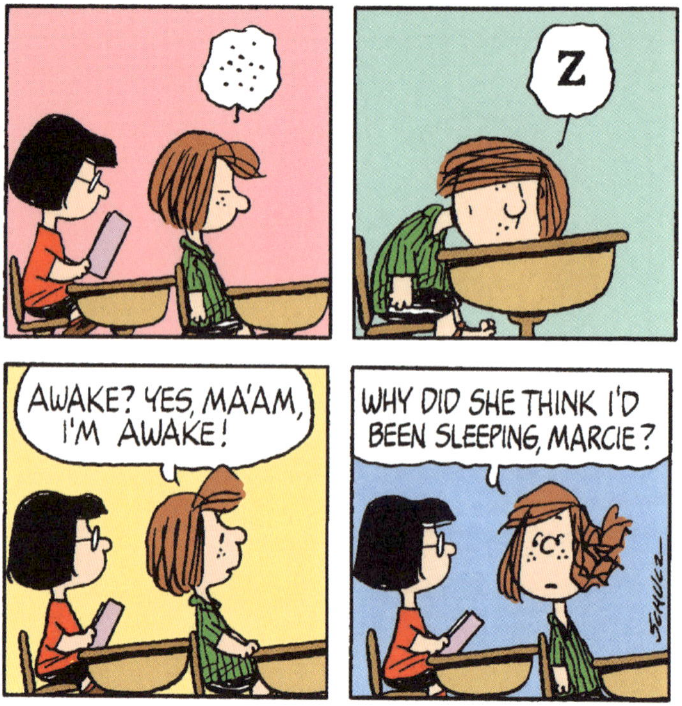
Z
AWAKE? YES, MA'AM, I'M AWAKE!
WHY DID SHE THINK I'D BEEN SLEEPING, MARCIE?
SCHULZ

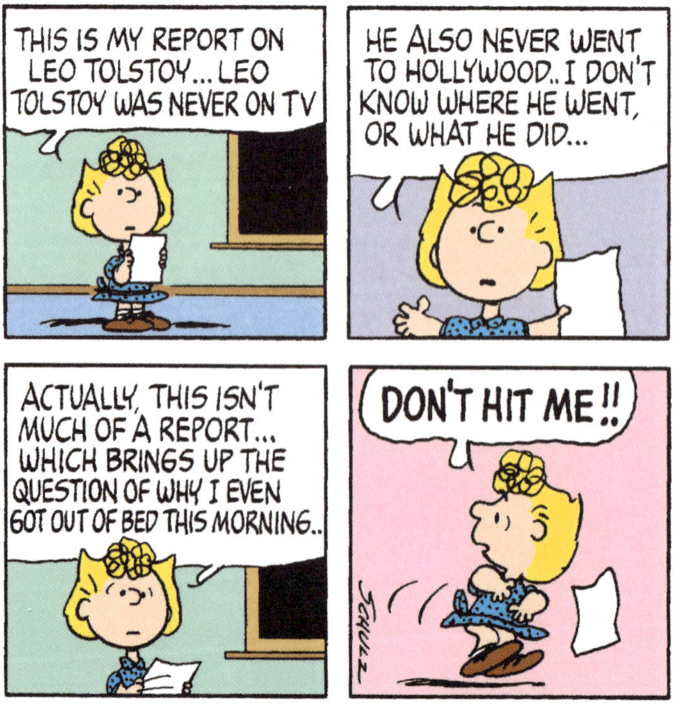
THIS IS MY REPORT ON LEO TOLSTOY... LEO TOLSTOY WAS NEVER ON TV
HE ALSO NEVER WENT TO HOLLYWOOD.. I DON'T KNOW WHERE HE WENT, OR WHAT HE DID...
ACTUALLY, THIS ISN'T MUCH OF A REPORT... WHICH BRINGS UP THE QUESTION OF WHY I EVEN GOT OUT OF BED THIS MORNING..
DON'T HIT ME!!
SCHULZ

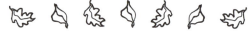

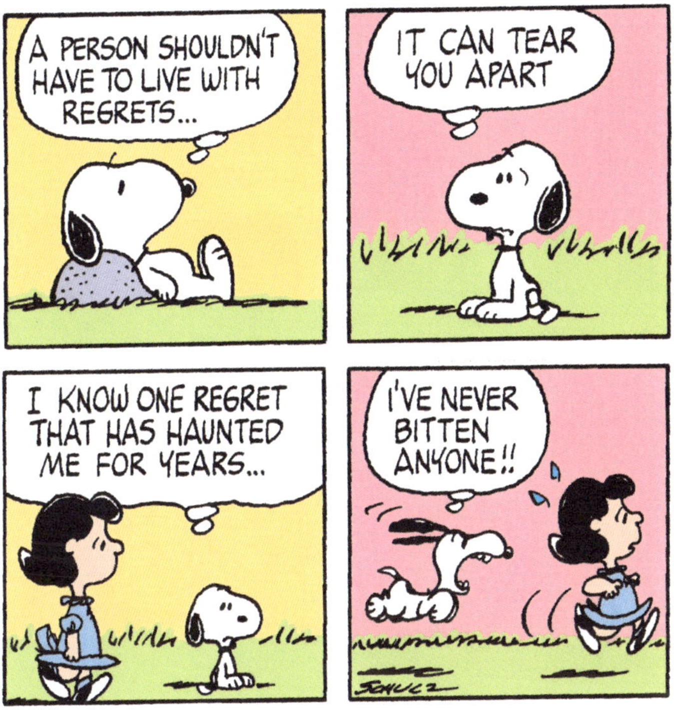
A PERSON SHOULDN'T HAVE TO LIVE WITH REGRETS...
IT CAN TEAR YOU APART
I KNOW ONE REGRET THAT HAS HAUNTED ME FOR YEARS...
I'VE NEVER BITTEN ANYONE!!

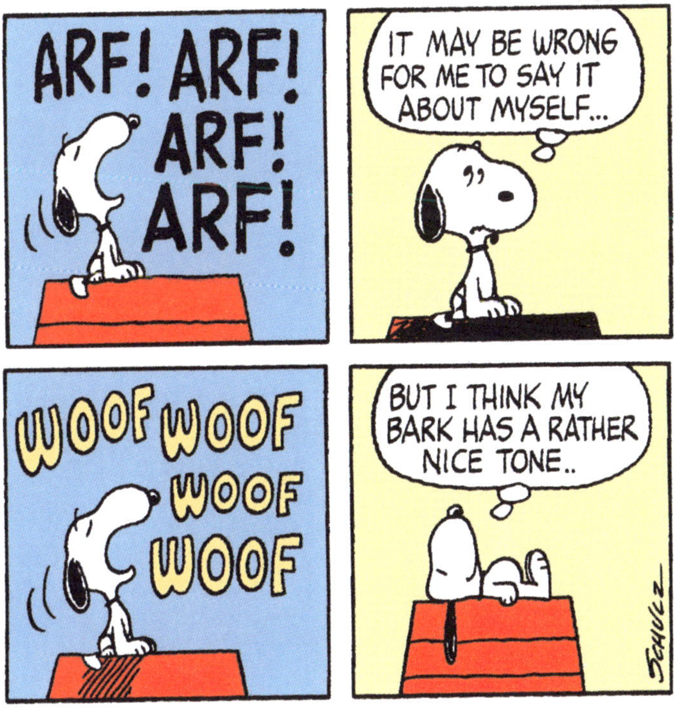
ARF! ARF! ARF! ARF!
IT MAY BE WRONG FOR ME TO SAY IT ABOUT MYSELF...
WOOF WOOF WOOF WOOF
BUT I THINK MY BARK HAS A RATHER NICE TONE..

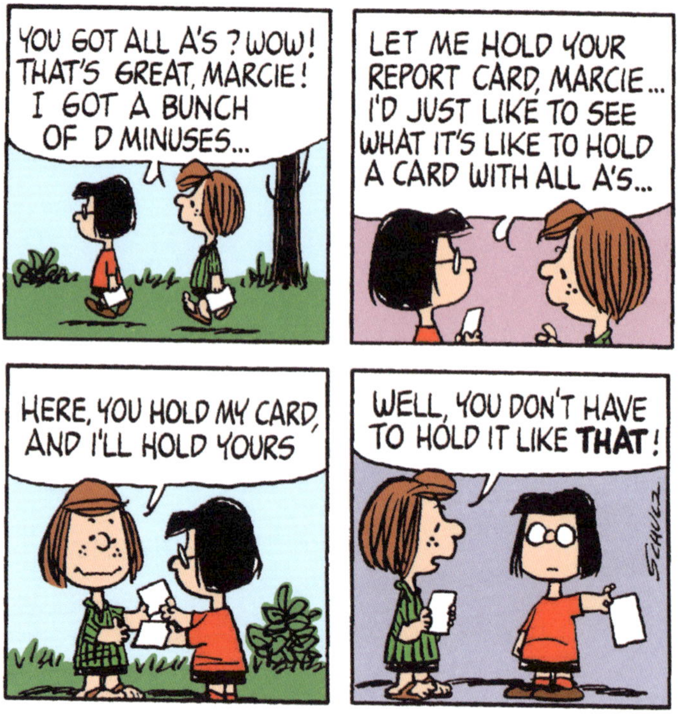
YOU GOT ALL A'S ? WOW! THAT'S GREAT, MARCIE! I GOT A BUNCH OF D MINUSES...
LET ME HOLD YOUR REPORT CARD, MARCIE... I'D JUST LIKE TO SEE WHAT IT'S LIKE TO HOLD A CARD WITH ALL A'S...
HERE, YOU HOLD MY CARD, AND I'LL HOLD YOURS
WELL, YOU DON'T HAVE TO HOLD IT LIKE **THAT**!
SCHULZ

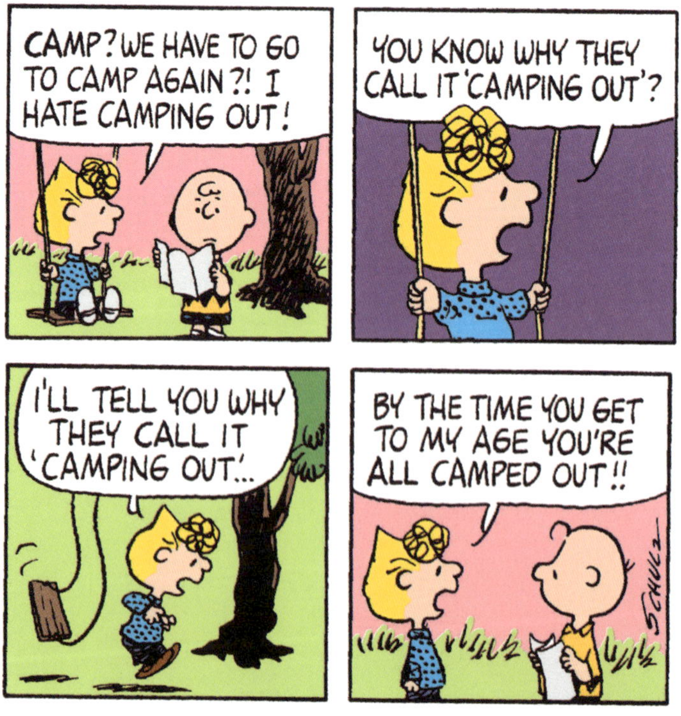
CAMP? WE HAVE TO GO TO CAMP AGAIN?! I HATE CAMPING OUT!
YOU KNOW WHY THEY CALL IT 'CAMPING OUT'?
I'LL TELL YOU WHY THEY CALL IT 'CAMPING OUT'...
BY THE TIME YOU GET TO MY AGE YOU'RE ALL CAMPED OUT!!
SCHULZ

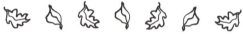

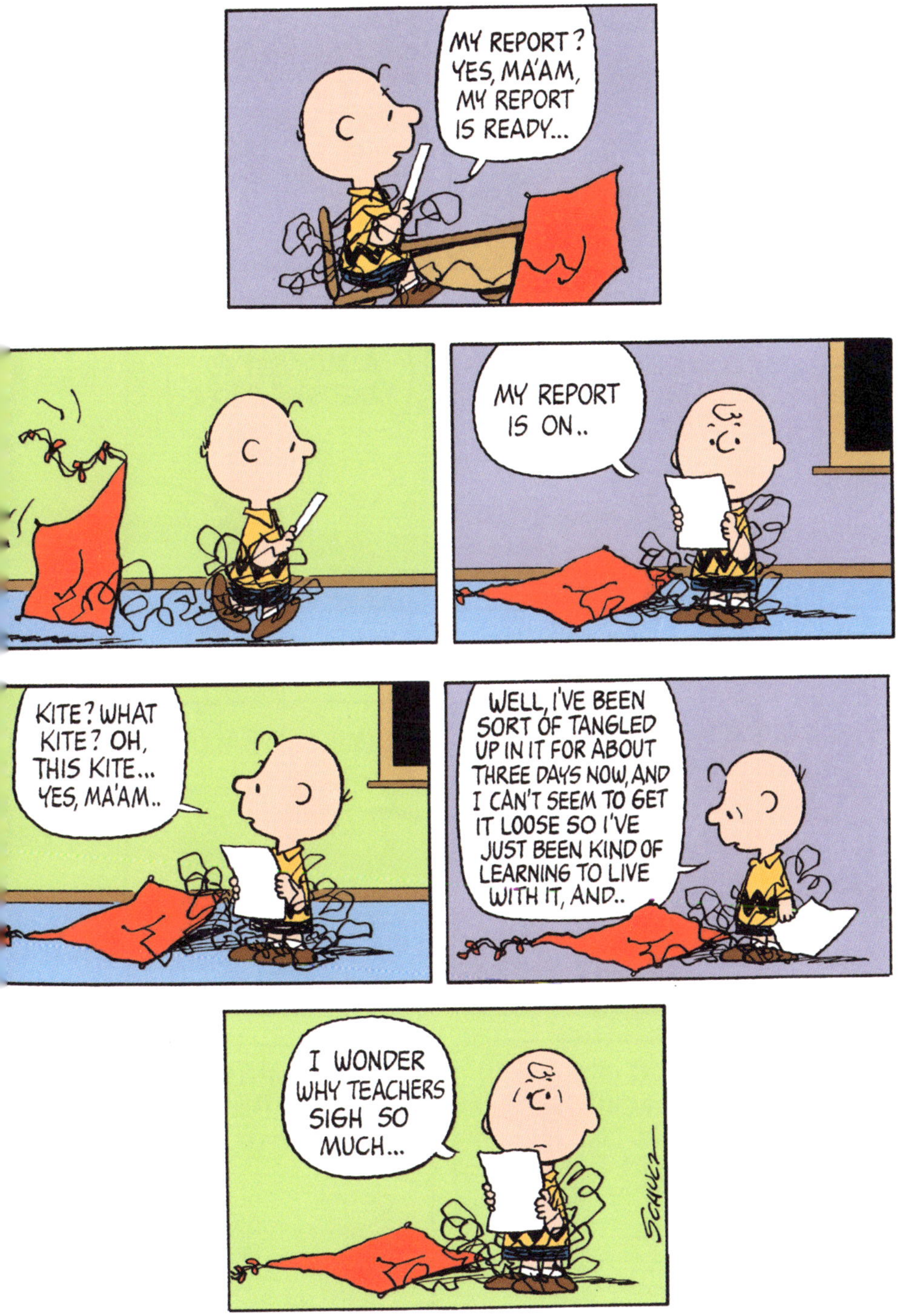
MY REPORT? YES, MA'AM, MY REPORT IS READY...
MY REPORT IS ON..
KITE? WHAT KITE? OH, THIS KITE... YES, MA'AM..
WELL, I'VE BEEN SORT OF TANGLED UP IN IT FOR ABOUT THREE DAYS NOW, AND I CAN'T SEEM TO GET IT LOOSE SO I'VE JUST BEEN KIND OF LEARNING TO LIVE WITH IT, AND..
I WONDER WHY TEACHERS SIGH SO MUCH...
SCHULZ

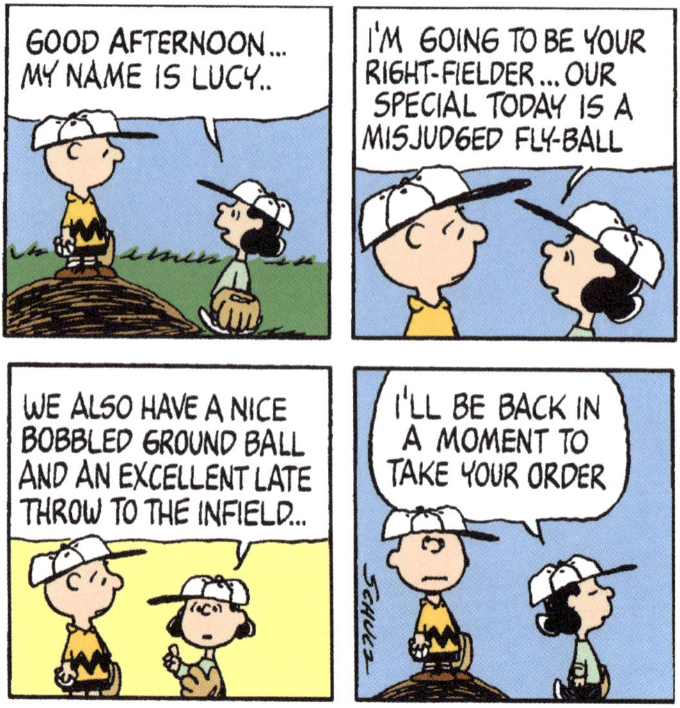
GOOD AFTERNOON... MY NAME IS LUCY..
I'M GOING TO BE YOUR RIGHT-FIELDER... OUR SPECIAL TODAY IS A MISJUDGED FLY-BALL
WE ALSO HAVE A NICE BOBBLED GROUND BALL AND AN EXCELLENT LATE THROW TO THE INFIELD...
I'LL BE BACK IN A MOMENT TO TAKE YOUR ORDER

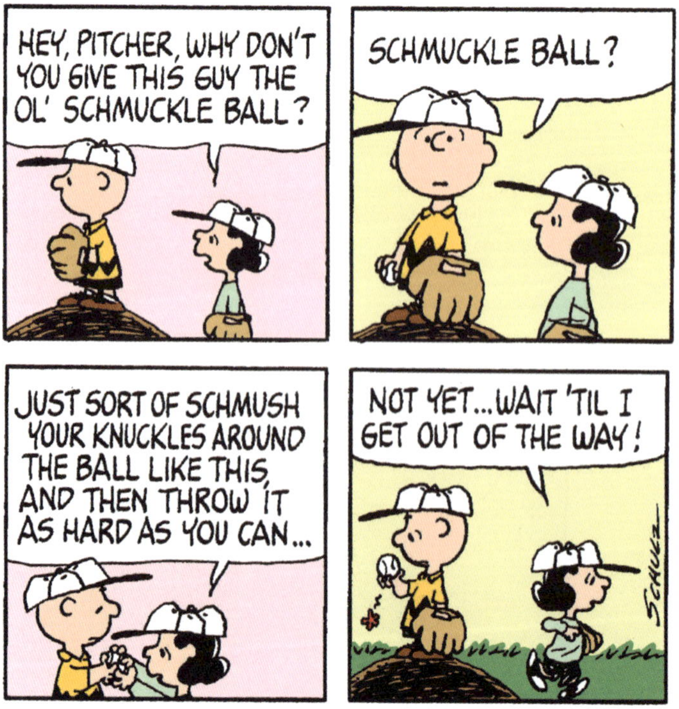
HEY, PITCHER, WHY DON'T YOU GIVE THIS GUY THE OL' SCHMUCKLE BALL?
SCHMUCKLE BALL?
JUST SORT OF SCHMUSH YOUR KNUCKLES AROUND THE BALL LIKE THIS, AND THEN THROW IT AS HARD AS YOU CAN...
NOT YET...WAIT 'TIL I GET OUT OF THE WAY!

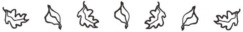

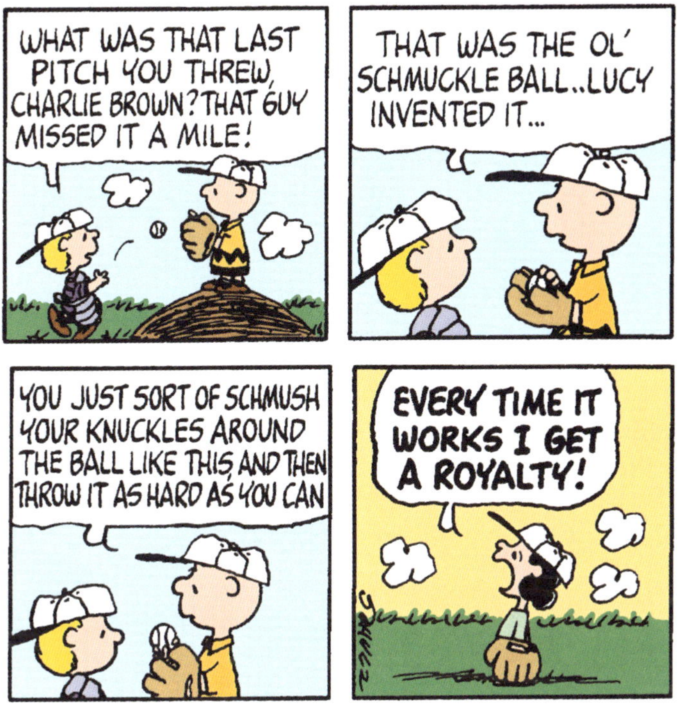
WHAT WAS THAT LAST PITCH YOU THREW, CHARLIE BROWN? THAT GUY MISSED IT A MILE!
THAT WAS THE OL' SCHMUCKLE BALL..LUCY INVENTED IT...
YOU JUST SORT OF SCHMUSH YOUR KNUCKLES AROUND THE BALL LIKE THIS AND THEN THROW IT AS HARD AS YOU CAN
EVERY TIME IT WORKS I GET A ROYALTY!
SCHULZ

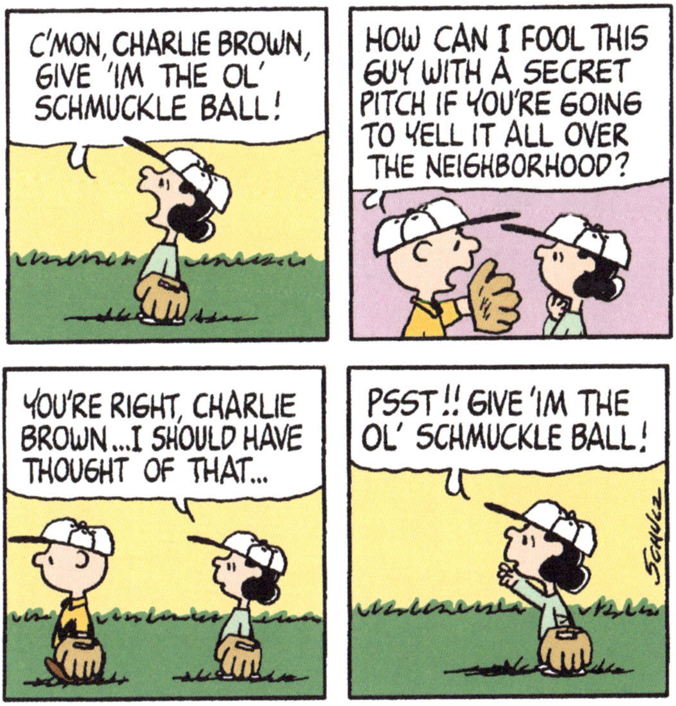
C'MON, CHARLIE BROWN, GIVE 'IM THE OL' SCHMUCKLE BALL!
HOW CAN I FOOL THIS GUY WITH A SECRET PITCH IF YOU'RE GOING TO YELL IT ALL OVER THE NEIGHBORHOOD?
YOU'RE RIGHT, CHARLIE BROWN...I SHOULD HAVE THOUGHT OF THAT...
PSST!! GIVE 'IM THE OL' SCHMUCKLE BALL!
SCHULZ

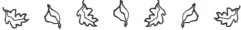

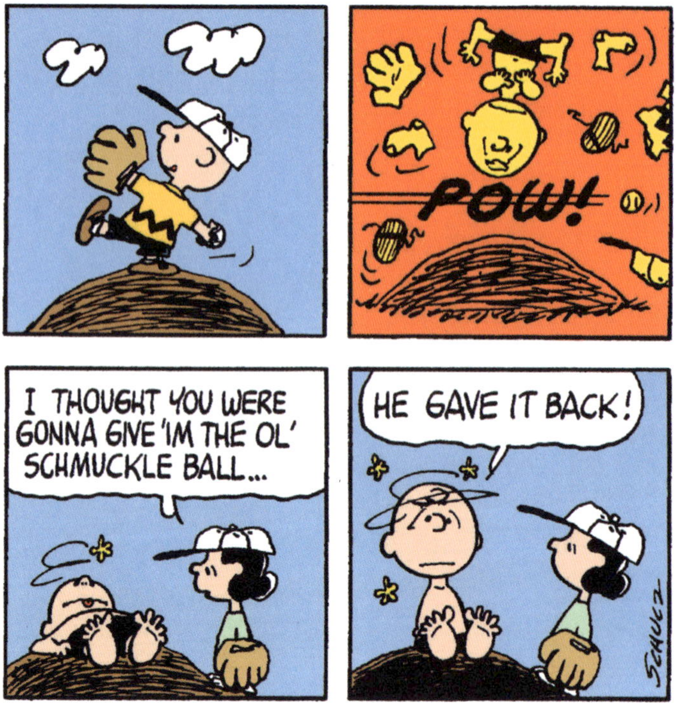
POW!
I THOUGHT YOU WERE GONNA GIVE 'IM THE OL' SCHMUCKLE BALL...
HE GAVE IT BACK!
SCHULZ

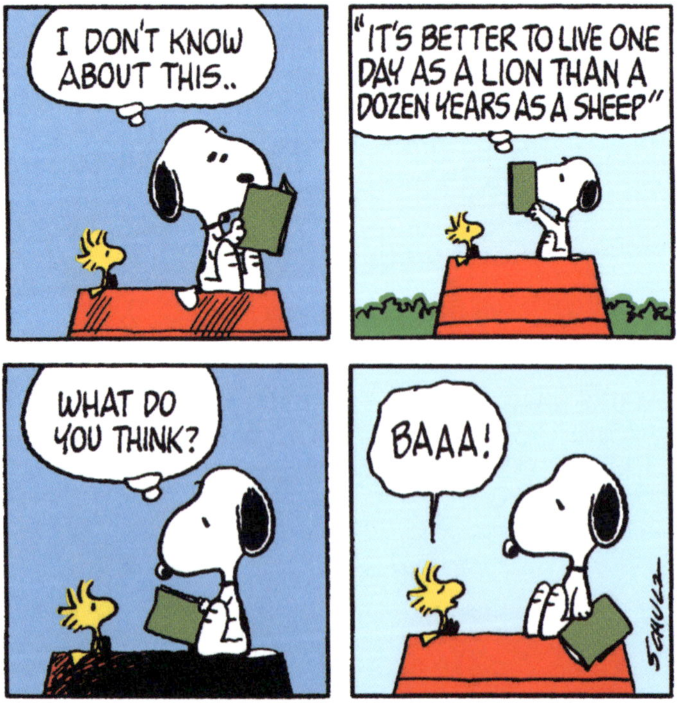
I DON'T KNOW ABOUT THIS..
"IT'S BETTER TO LIVE ONE DAY AS A LION THAN A DOZEN YEARS AS A SHEEP"
WHAT DO YOU THINK?
BAAA!
SCHULZ

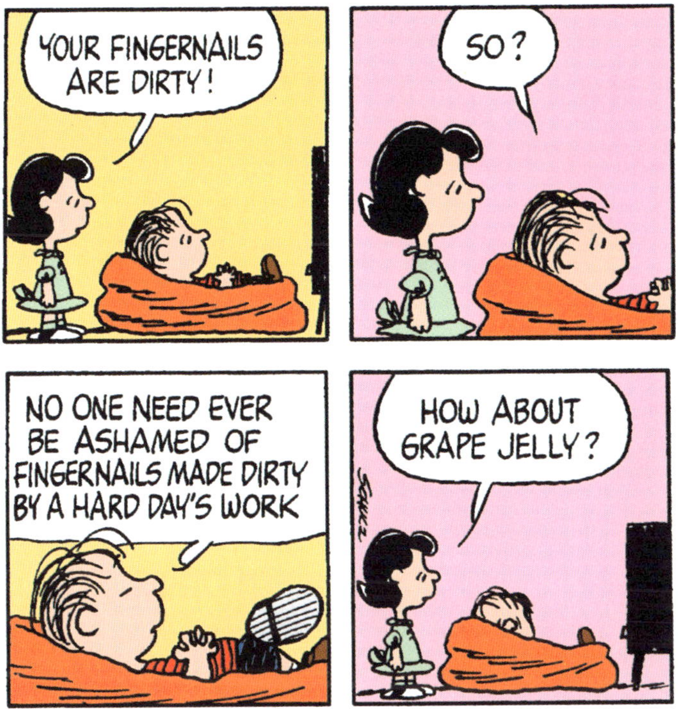
YOUR FINGERNAILS ARE DIRTY!
SO?
NO ONE NEED EVER BE ASHAMED OF FINGERNAILS MADE DIRTY BY A HARD DAY'S WORK
HOW ABOUT GRAPE JELLY?

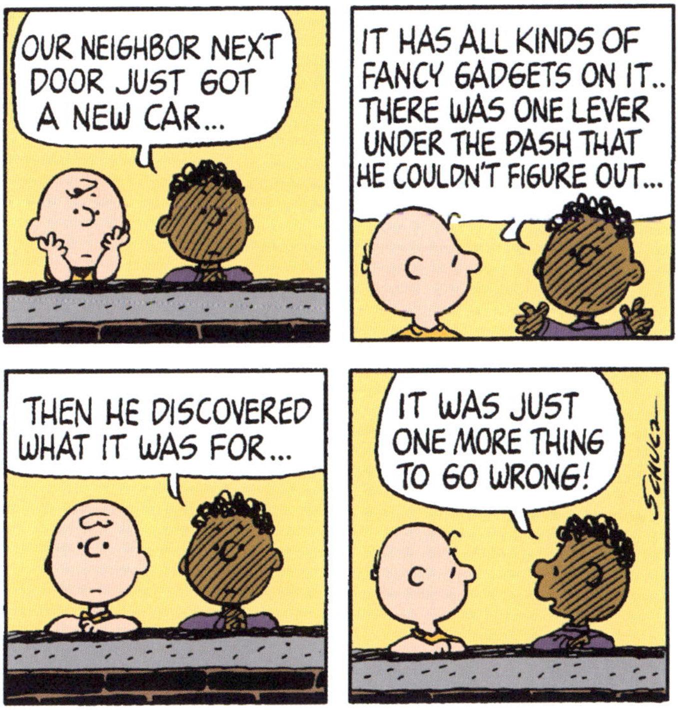
OUR NEIGHBOR NEXT DOOR JUST GOT A NEW CAR...
IT HAS ALL KINDS OF FANCY GADGETS ON IT.. THERE WAS ONE LEVER UNDER THE DASH THAT HE COULDN'T FIGURE OUT...
THEN HE DISCOVERED WHAT IT WAS FOR...
IT WAS JUST ONE MORE THING TO GO WRONG!

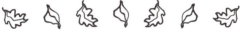

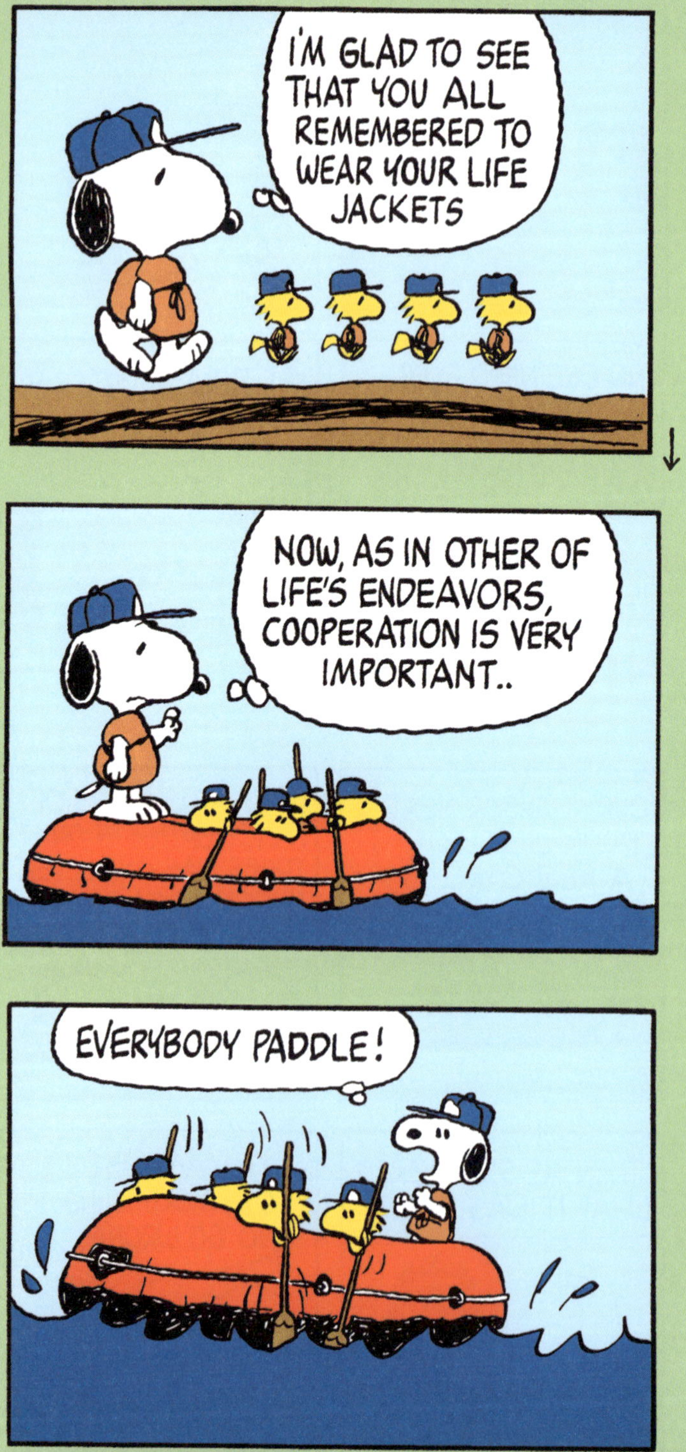
I'M GLAD TO SEE THAT YOU ALL REMEMBERED TO WEAR YOUR LIFE JACKETS
NOW, AS IN OTHER OF LIFE'S ENDEAVORS, COOPERATION IS VERY IMPORTANT..
EVERYBODY PADDLE!

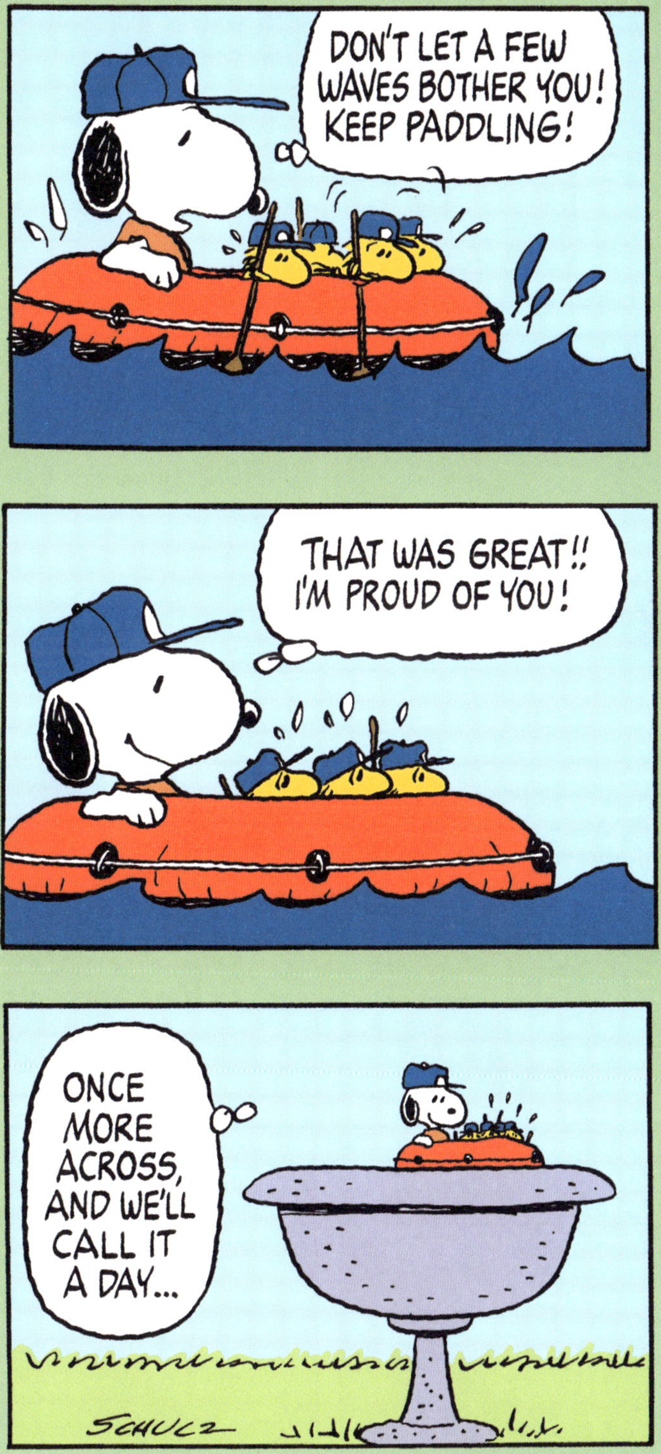
DON'T LET A FEW WAVES BOTHER YOU! KEEP PADDLING!
THAT WAS GREAT!! I'M PROUD OF YOU!
ONCE MORE ACROSS, AND WE'LL CALL IT A DAY...
SCHULZ

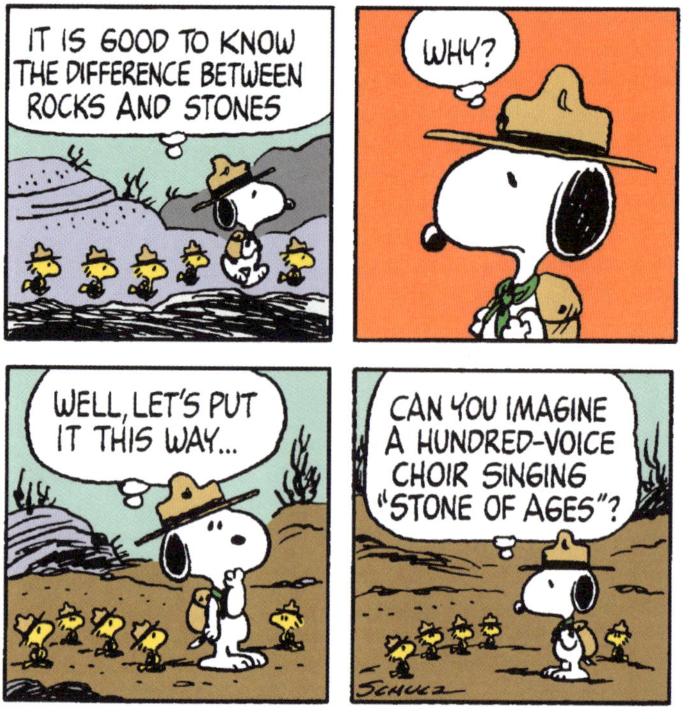
IT IS GOOD TO KNOW THE DIFFERENCE BETWEEN ROCKS AND STONES
WHY?
WELL, LET'S PUT IT THIS WAY...
CAN YOU IMAGINE A HUNDRED-VOICE CHOIR SINGING "STONE OF AGES"?

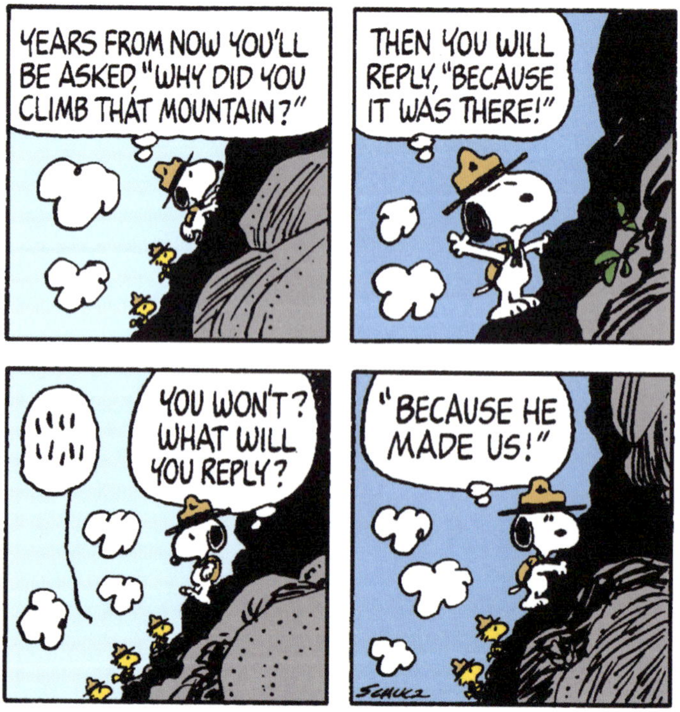
YEARS FROM NOW YOU'LL BE ASKED, "WHY DID YOU CLIMB THAT MOUNTAIN?"
THEN YOU WILL REPLY, "BECAUSE IT WAS THERE!"
YOU WON'T? WHAT WILL YOU REPLY?
"BECAUSE HE MADE US!"

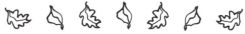

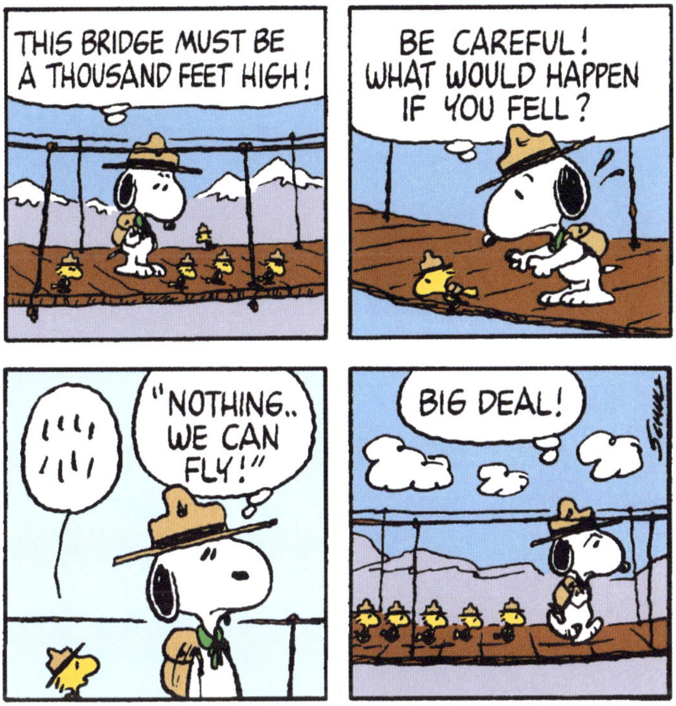
THIS BRIDGE MUST BE A THOUSAND FEET HIGH!
BE CAREFUL! WHAT WOULD HAPPEN IF YOU FELL?
"NOTHING.. WE CAN FLY!"
BIG DEAL!

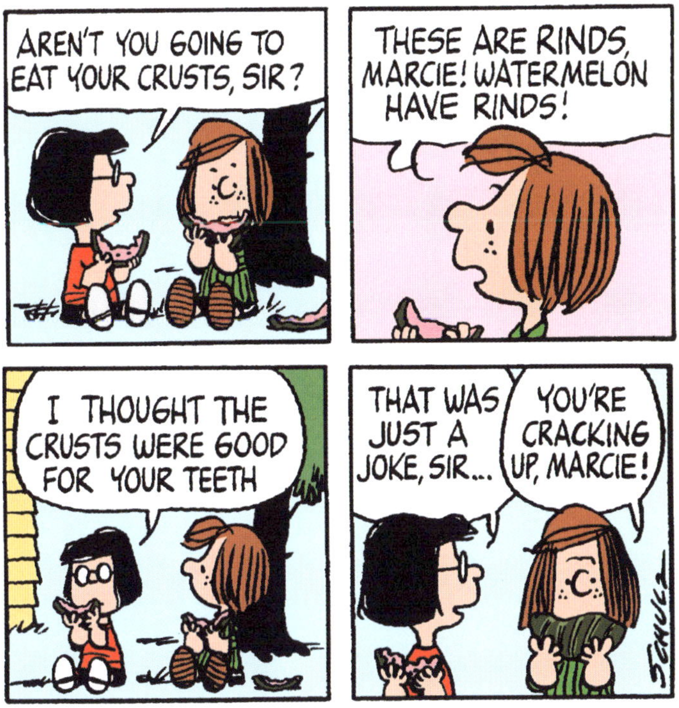
AREN'T YOU GOING TO EAT YOUR CRUSTS, SIR?
THESE ARE RINDS, MARCIE! WATERMELON HAVE RINDS!
I THOUGHT THE CRUSTS WERE GOOD FOR YOUR TEETH
THAT WAS JUST A JOKE, SIR...
YOU'RE CRACKING UP, MARCIE!

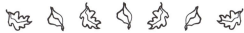

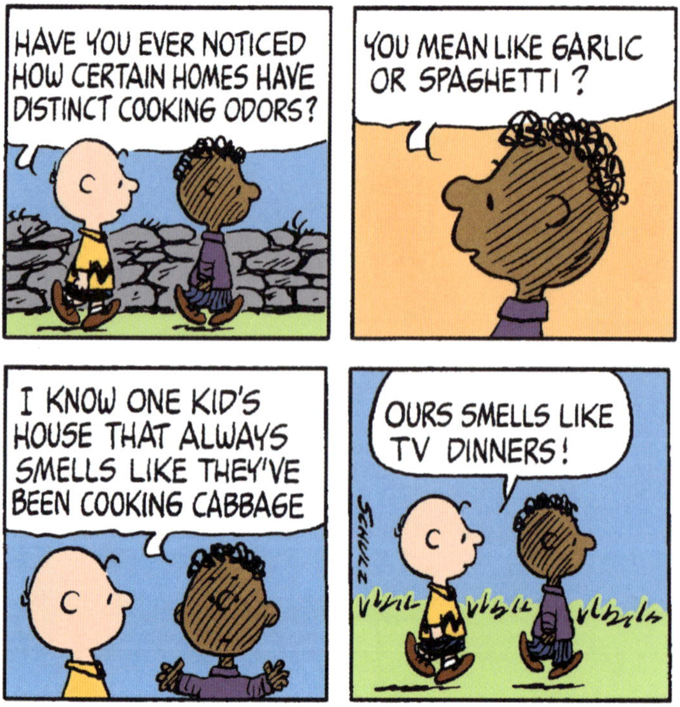
HAVE YOU EVER NOTICED HOW CERTAIN HOMES HAVE DISTINCT COOKING ODORS?
YOU MEAN LIKE GARLIC OR SPAGHETTI ?
I KNOW ONE KID'S HOUSE THAT ALWAYS SMELLS LIKE THEY'VE BEEN COOKING CABBAGE
OURS SMELLS LIKE TV DINNERS!

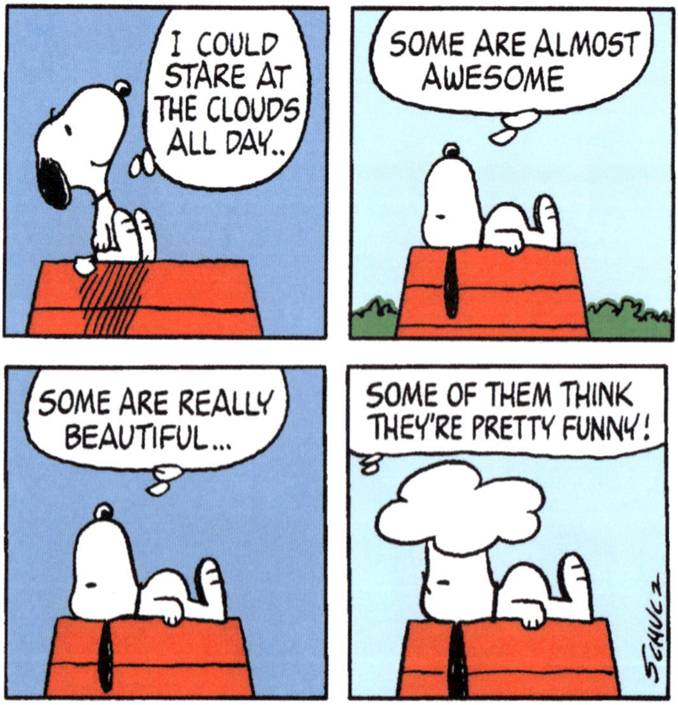
I COULD STARE AT THE CLOUDS ALL DAY..
SOME ARE ALMOST AWESOME
SOME ARE REALLY BEAUTIFUL...
SOME OF THEM THINK THEY'RE PRETTY FUNNY!

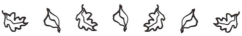

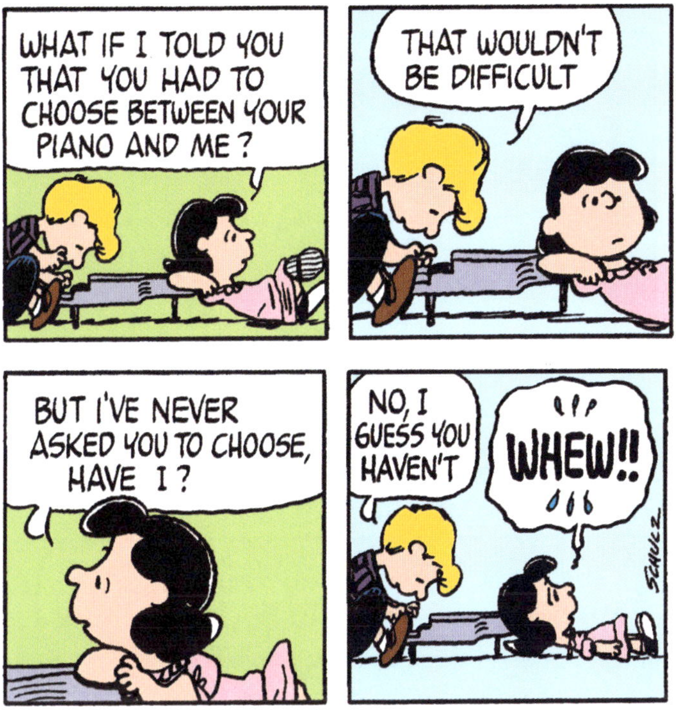
WHAT IF I TOLD YOU THAT YOU HAD TO CHOOSE BETWEEN YOUR PIANO AND ME?
THAT WOULDN'T BE DIFFICULT
BUT I'VE NEVER ASKED YOU TO CHOOSE, HAVE I?
NO, I GUESS YOU HAVEN'T
WHEW!!
SCHULZ

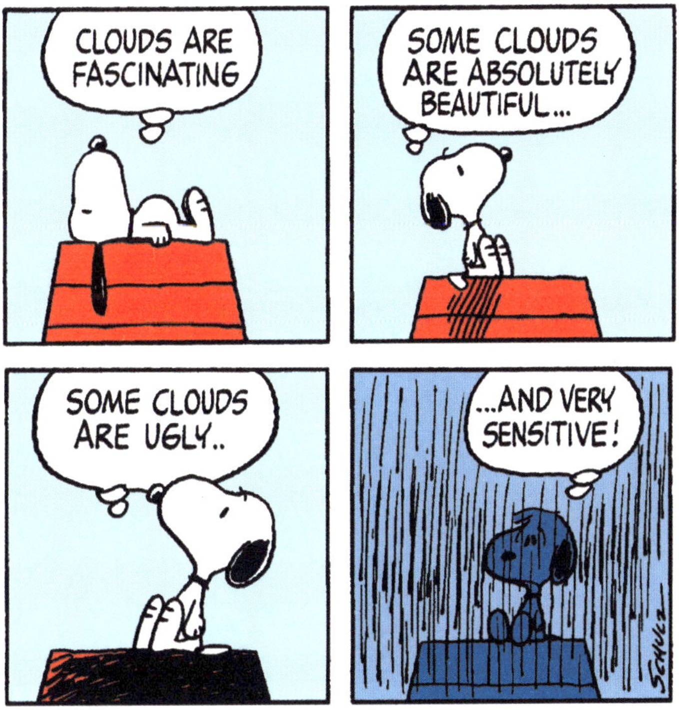
CLOUDS ARE FASCINATING
SOME CLOUDS ARE ABSOLUTELY BEAUTIFUL...
SOME CLOUDS ARE UGLY..
...AND VERY SENSITIVE!
SCHULZ

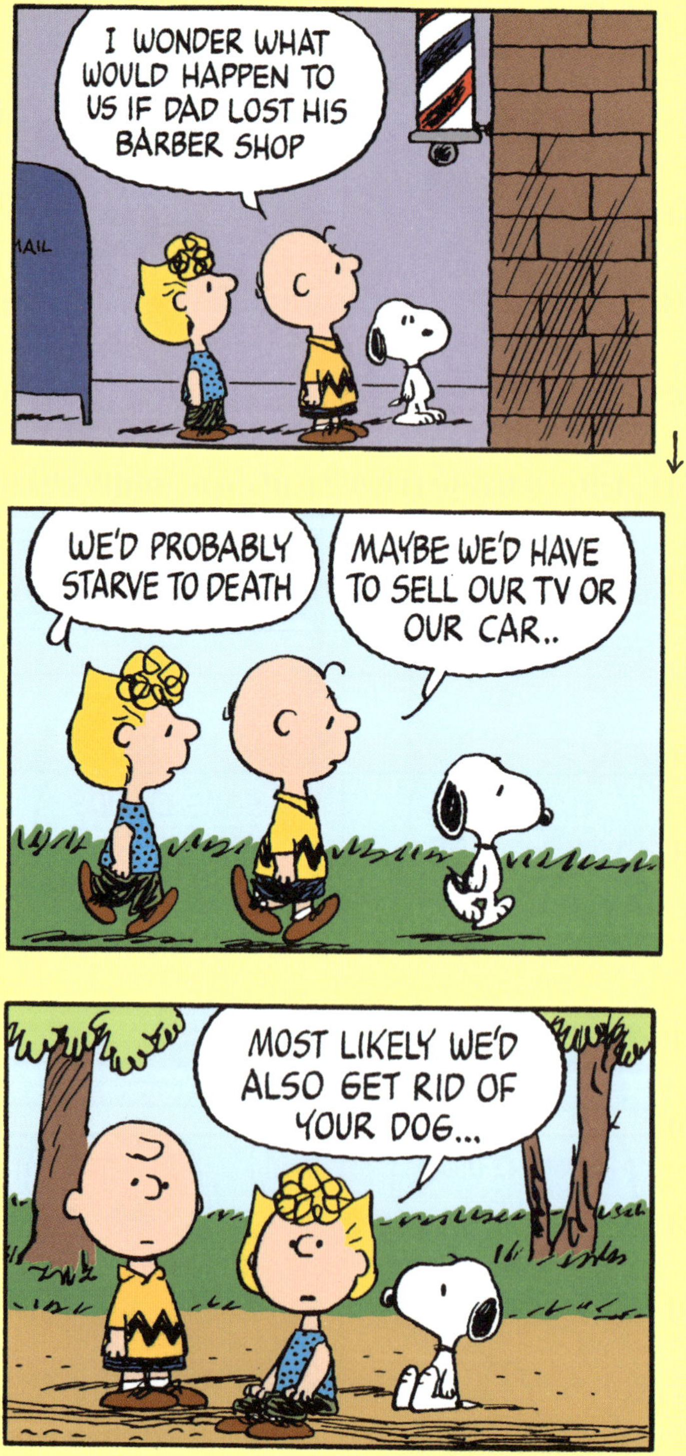
MAIL
I WONDER WHAT WOULD HAPPEN TO US IF DAD LOST HIS BARBER SHOP
WE'D PROBABLY STARVE TO DEATH
MAYBE WE'D HAVE TO SELL OUR TV OR OUR CAR..
MOST LIKELY WE'D ALSO GET RID OF YOUR DOG...

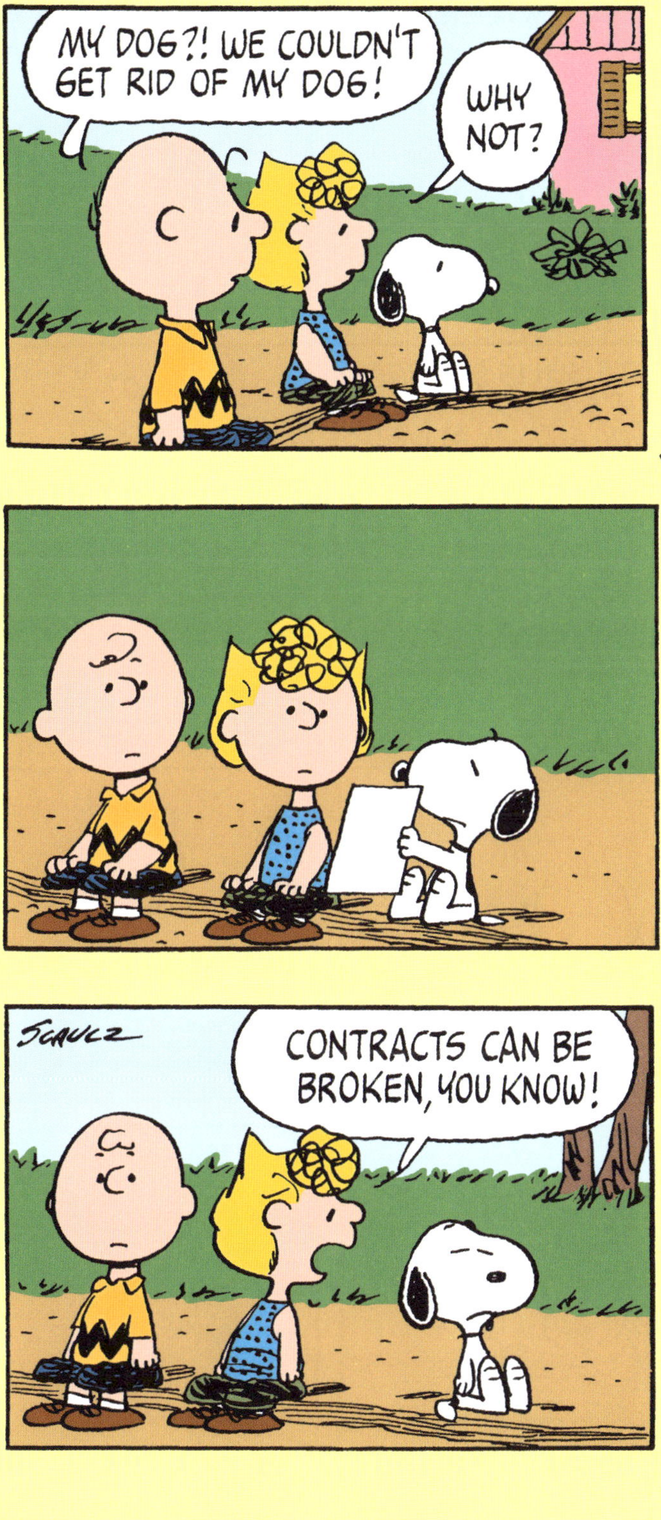
MY DOG?! WE COULDN'T GET RID OF MY DOG!
WHY NOT?
SCHULZ
CONTRACTS CAN BE BROKEN, YOU KNOW!

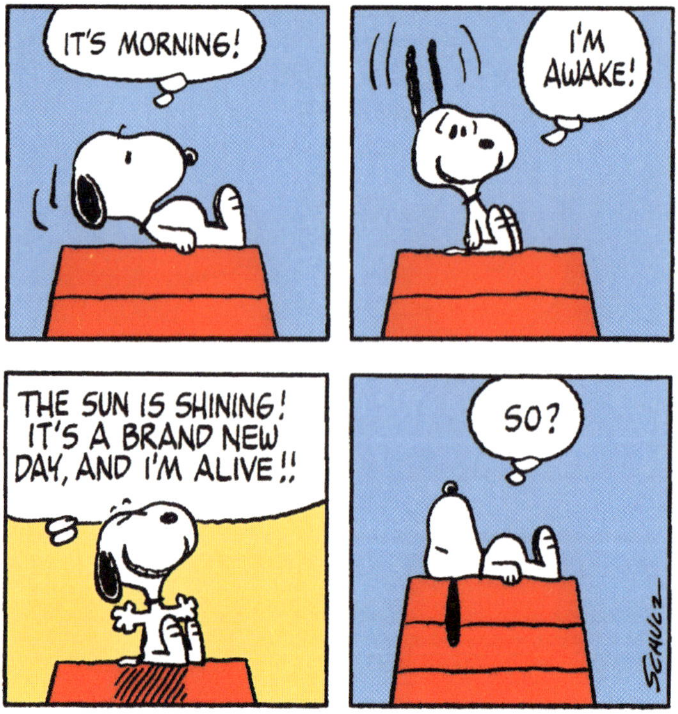
IT'S MORNING!
I'M AWAKE!
THE SUN IS SHINING! IT'S A BRAND NEW DAY, AND I'M ALIVE!!
SO?
SCHULZ

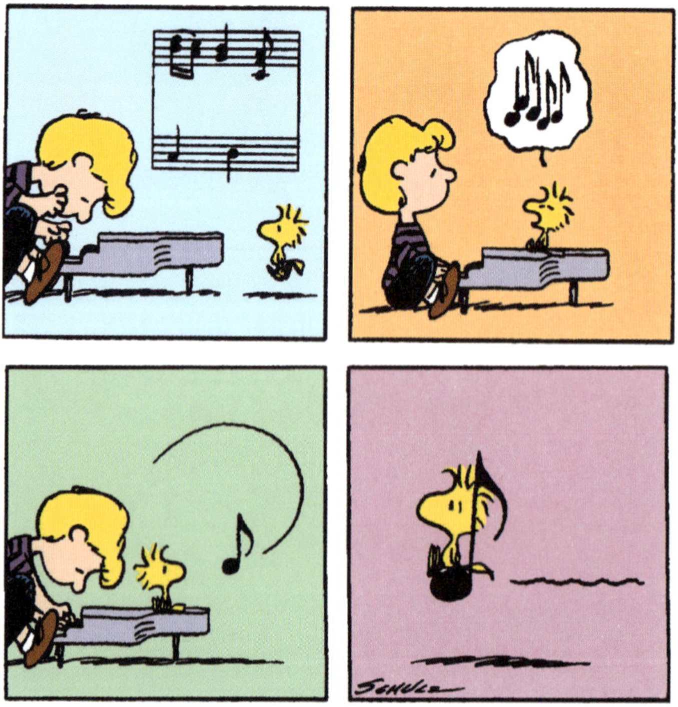
SCHULZ

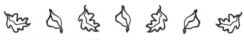

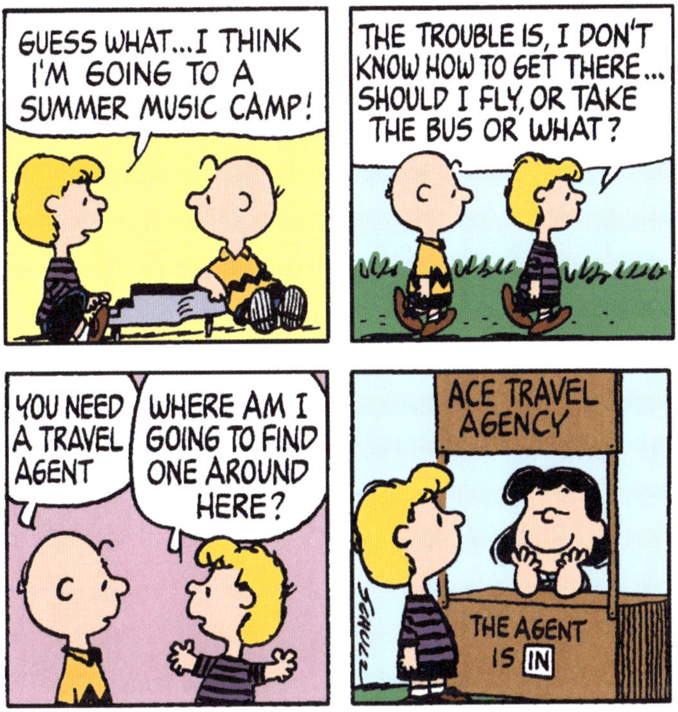
GUESS WHAT...I THINK I'M GOING TO A SUMMER MUSIC CAMP!
THE TROUBLE IS, I DON'T KNOW HOW TO GET THERE... SHOULD I FLY, OR TAKE THE BUS OR WHAT?
YOU NEED A TRAVEL AGENT
WHERE AM I GOING TO FIND ONE AROUND HERE?
ACE TRAVEL AGENCY
THE AGENT IS IN

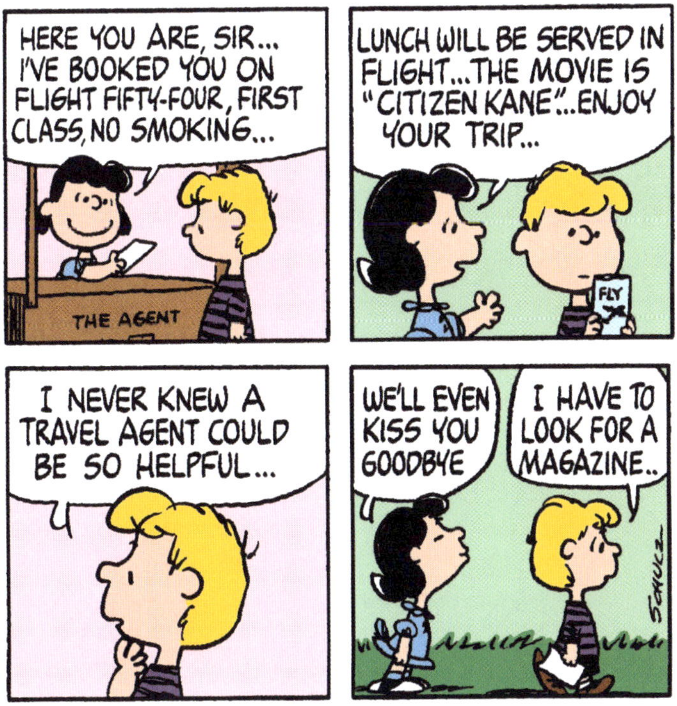
HERE YOU ARE, SIR... I'VE BOOKED YOU ON FLIGHT FIFTY-FOUR, FIRST CLASS, NO SMOKING...
THE AGENT
LUNCH WILL BE SERVED IN FLIGHT...THE MOVIE IS "CITIZEN KANE"...ENJOY YOUR TRIP...
FLY
I NEVER KNEW A TRAVEL AGENT COULD BE SO HELPFUL...
WE'LL EVEN KISS YOU GOODBYE
I HAVE TO LOOK FOR A MAGAZINE..

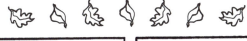

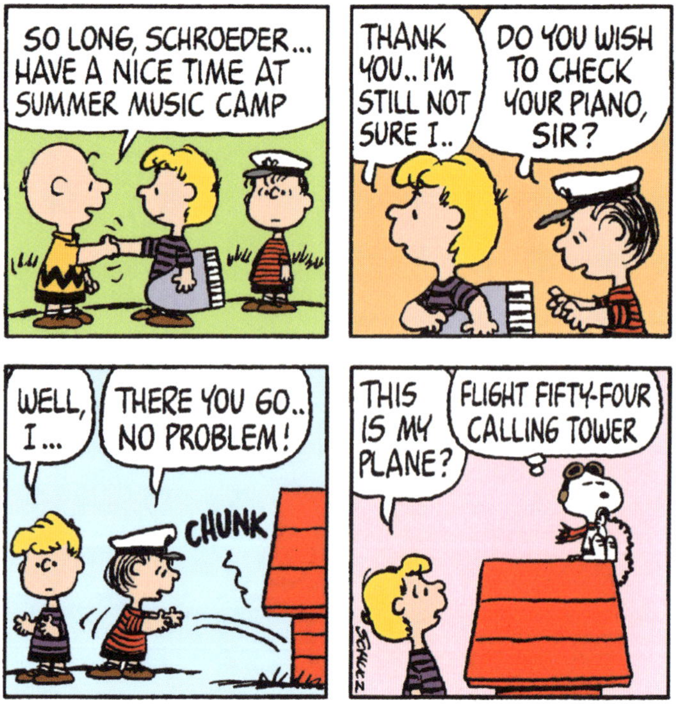
SO LONG, SCHROEDER... HAVE A NICE TIME AT SUMMER MUSIC CAMP
THANK YOU.. I'M STILL NOT SURE I..
DO YOU WISH TO CHECK YOUR PIANO, SIR?
WELL, I...
THERE YOU GO.. NO PROBLEM!
CHUNK
THIS IS MY PLANE?
FLIGHT FIFTY-FOUR CALLING TOWER
SCHULZ

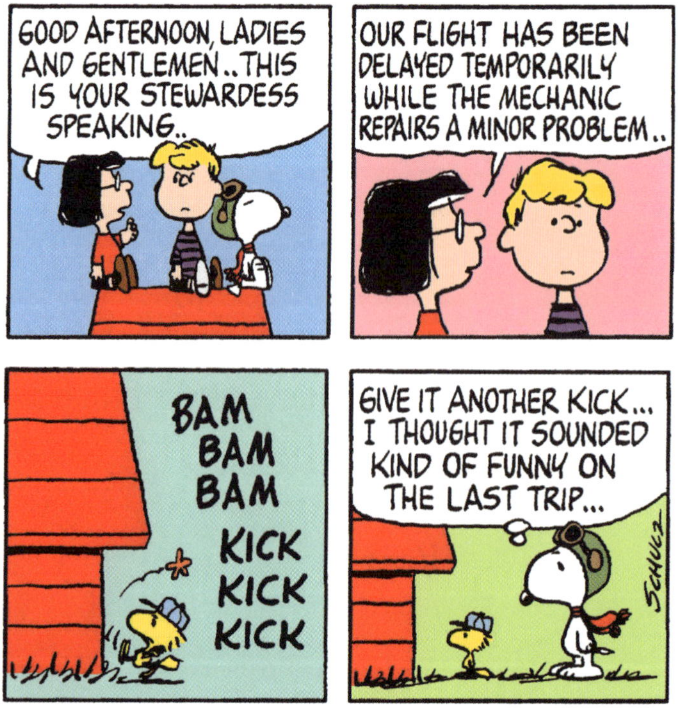
GOOD AFTERNOON, LADIES AND GENTLEMEN.. THIS IS YOUR STEWARDESS SPEAKING..
OUR FLIGHT HAS BEEN DELAYED TEMPORARILY WHILE THE MECHANIC REPAIRS A MINOR PROBLEM..
BAM BAM BAM
KICK KICK KICK
GIVE IT ANOTHER KICK... I THOUGHT IT SOUNDED KIND OF FUNNY ON THE LAST TRIP...
SCHULZ

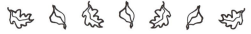

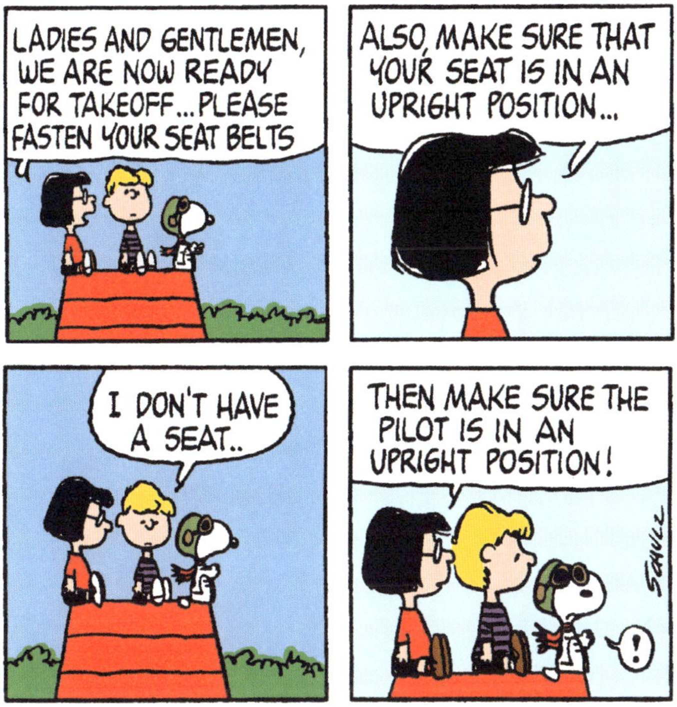
LADIES AND GENTLEMEN, WE ARE NOW READY FOR TAKEOFF...PLEASE FASTEN YOUR SEAT BELTS
ALSO, MAKE SURE THAT YOUR SEAT IS IN AN UPRIGHT POSITION...
I DON'T HAVE A SEAT..
THEN MAKE SURE THE PILOT IS IN AN UPRIGHT POSITION!
!
SCHULZ

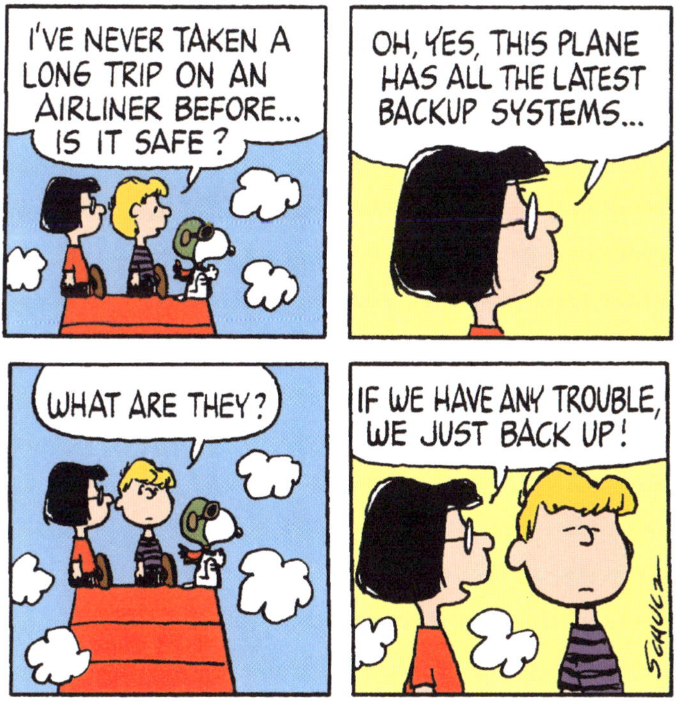
I'VE NEVER TAKEN A LONG TRIP ON AN AIRLINER BEFORE... IS IT SAFE?
OH, YES, THIS PLANE HAS ALL THE LATEST BACKUP SYSTEMS...
WHAT ARE THEY?
IF WE HAVE ANY TROUBLE, WE JUST BACK UP!
SCHULZ

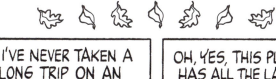

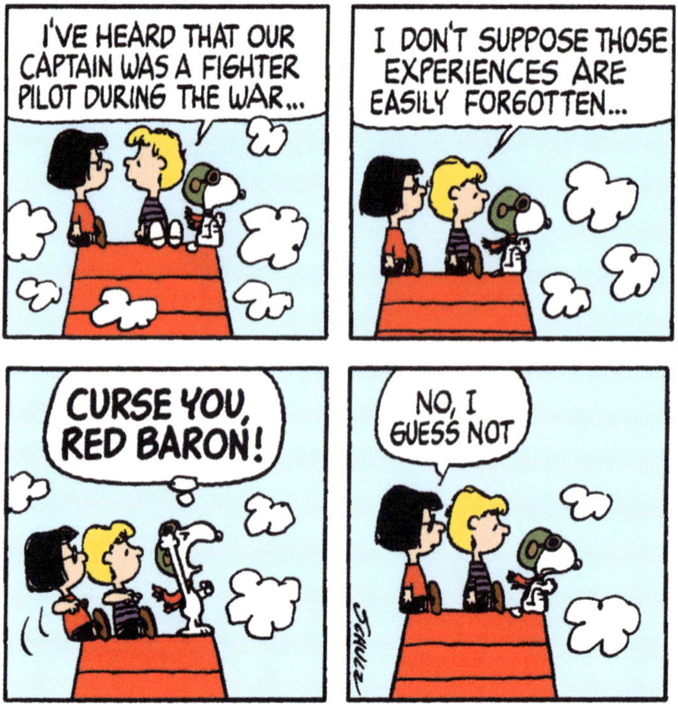
I'VE HEARD THAT OUR CAPTAIN WAS A FIGHTER PILOT DURING THE WAR...
I DON'T SUPPOSE THOSE EXPERIENCES ARE EASILY FORGOTTEN...
CURSE YOU, RED BARON!
NO, I GUESS NOT
SCHULZ

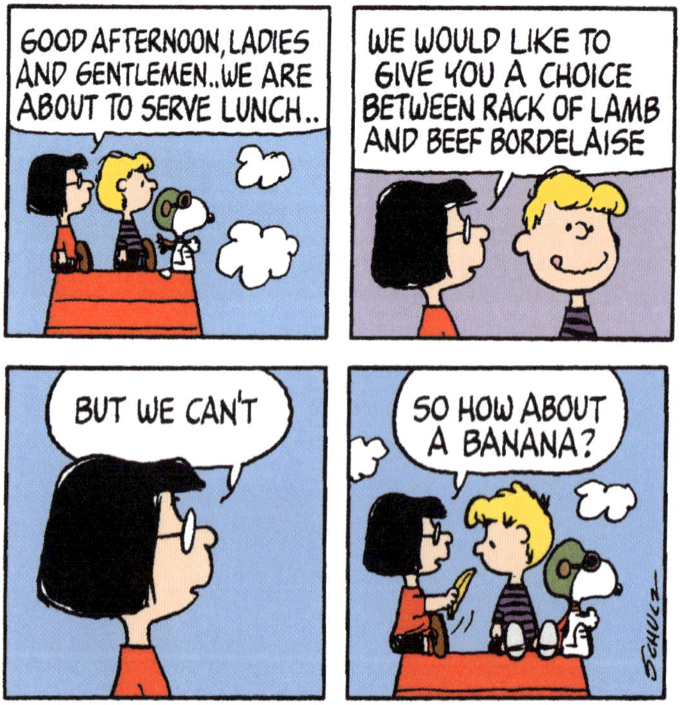
GOOD AFTERNOON, LADIES AND GENTLEMEN..WE ARE ABOUT TO SERVE LUNCH..
WE WOULD LIKE TO GIVE YOU A CHOICE BETWEEN RACK OF LAMB AND BEEF BORDELAISE
BUT WE CAN'T
SO HOW ABOUT A BANANA?
SCHULZ

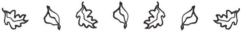

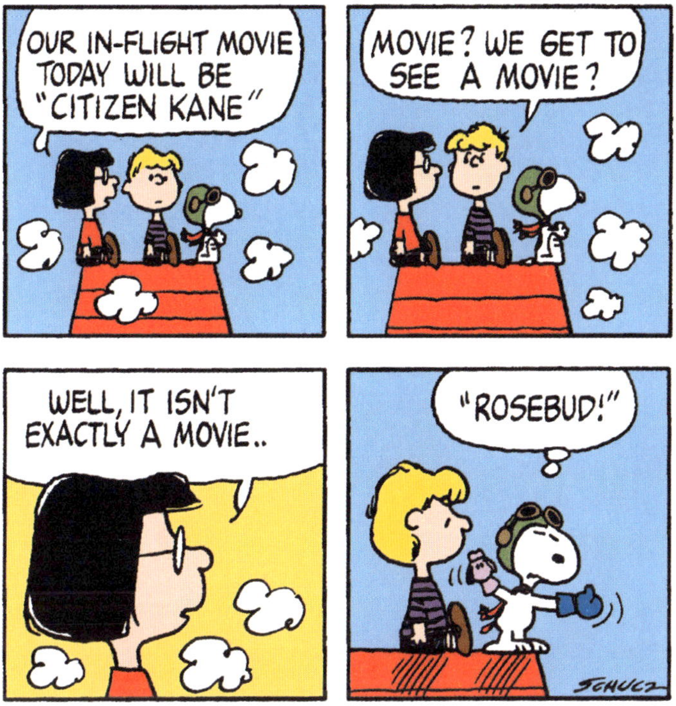
OUR IN-FLIGHT MOVIE TODAY WILL BE "CITIZEN KANE"
MOVIE? WE GET TO SEE A MOVIE?
WELL, IT ISN'T EXACTLY A MOVIE..
"ROSEBUD!"

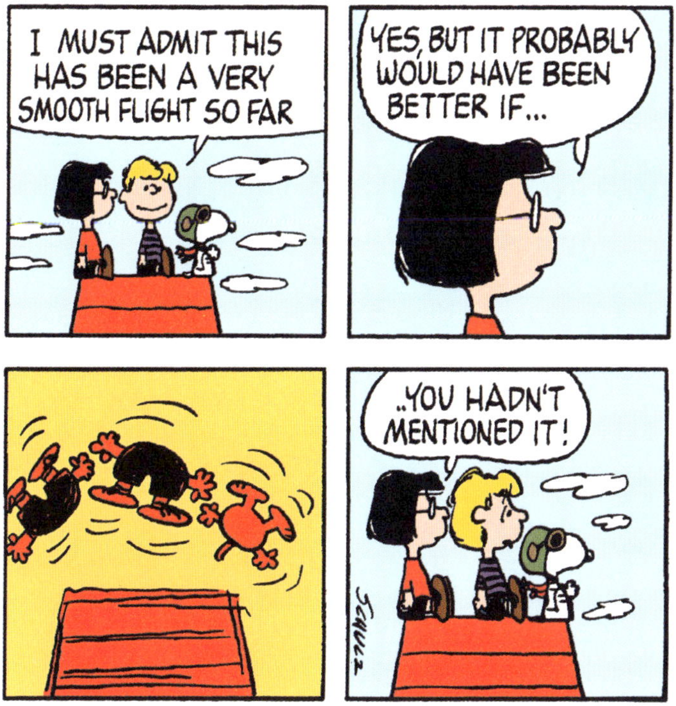
I MUST ADMIT THIS HAS BEEN A VERY SMOOTH FLIGHT SO FAR
YES, BUT IT PROBABLY WOULD HAVE BEEN BETTER IF...
..YOU HADN'T MENTIONED IT!

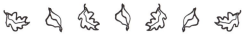

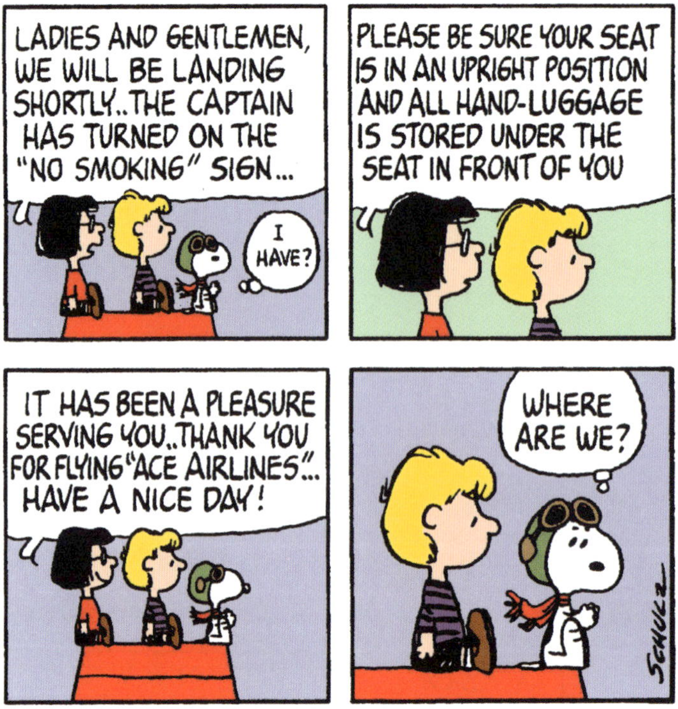
LADIES AND GENTLEMEN, WE WILL BE LANDING SHORTLY..THE CAPTAIN HAS TURNED ON THE "NO SMOKING" SIGN...
I HAVE?
PLEASE BE SURE YOUR SEAT IS IN AN UPRIGHT POSITION AND ALL HAND-LUGGAGE IS STORED UNDER THE SEAT IN FRONT OF YOU
IT HAS BEEN A PLEASURE SERVING YOU..THANK YOU FOR FLYING "ACE AIRLINES"... HAVE A NICE DAY!
WHERE ARE WE?
SCHULZ

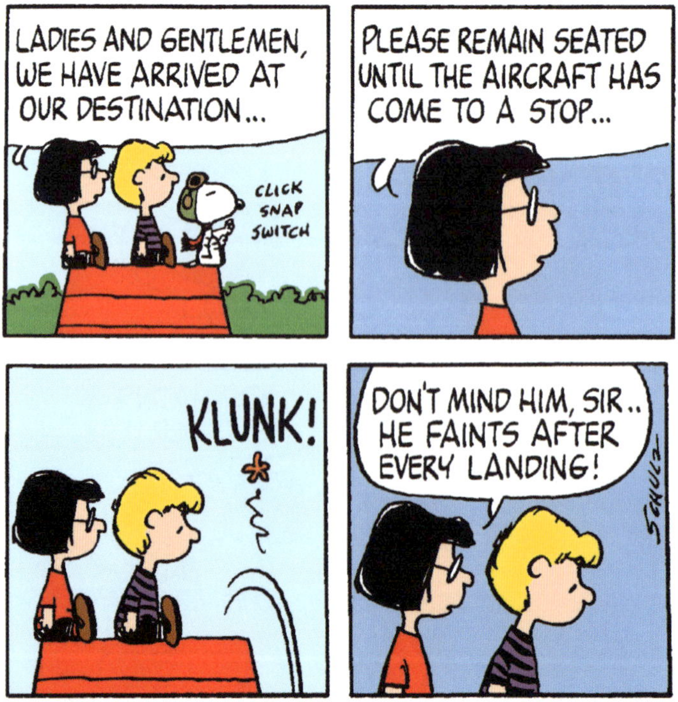
LADIES AND GENTLEMEN, WE HAVE ARRIVED AT OUR DESTINATION...
CLICK
SNAP
SWITCH
PLEASE REMAIN SEATED UNTIL THE AIRCRAFT HAS COME TO A STOP...
KLUNK!
DON'T MIND HIM, SIR.. HE FAINTS AFTER EVERY LANDING!
SCHULZ

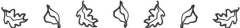

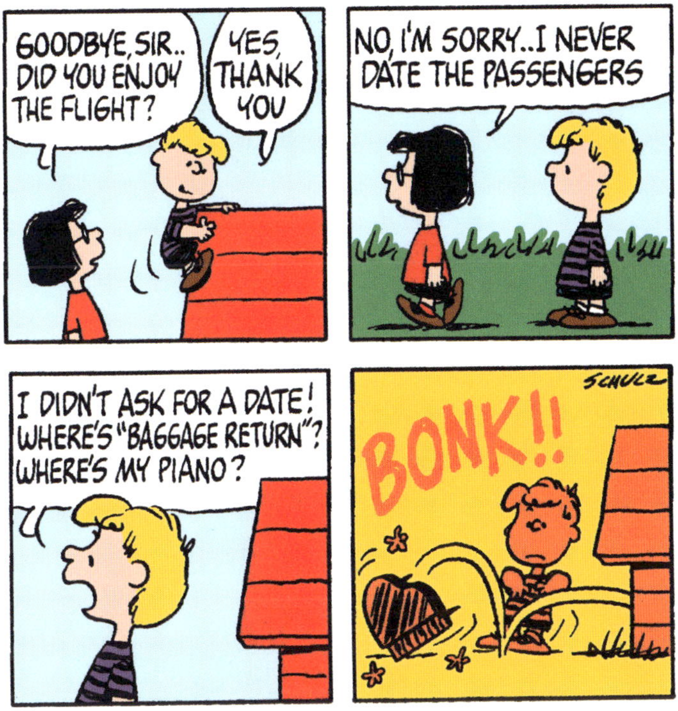
GOODBYE, SIR.. DID YOU ENJOY THE FLIGHT?
YES, THANK YOU
NO, I'M SORRY..I NEVER DATE THE PASSENGERS
I DIDN'T ASK FOR A DATE! WHERE'S "BAGGAGE RETURN"? WHERE'S MY PIANO?
BONK!!
SCHULZ

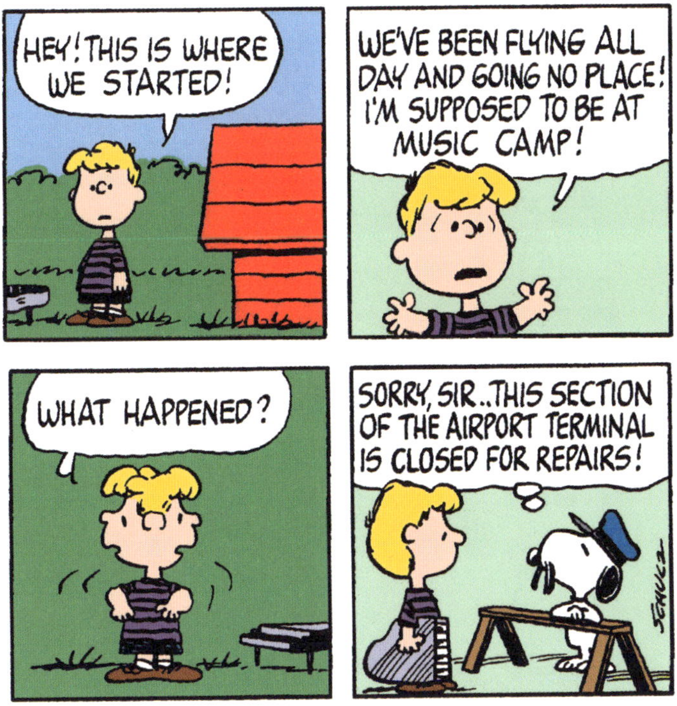
HEY! THIS IS WHERE WE STARTED!
WE'VE BEEN FLYING ALL DAY AND GOING NO PLACE! I'M SUPPOSED TO BE AT MUSIC CAMP!
WHAT HAPPENED?
SORRY, SIR..THIS SECTION OF THE AIRPORT TERMINAL IS CLOSED FOR REPAIRS!
SCHULZ

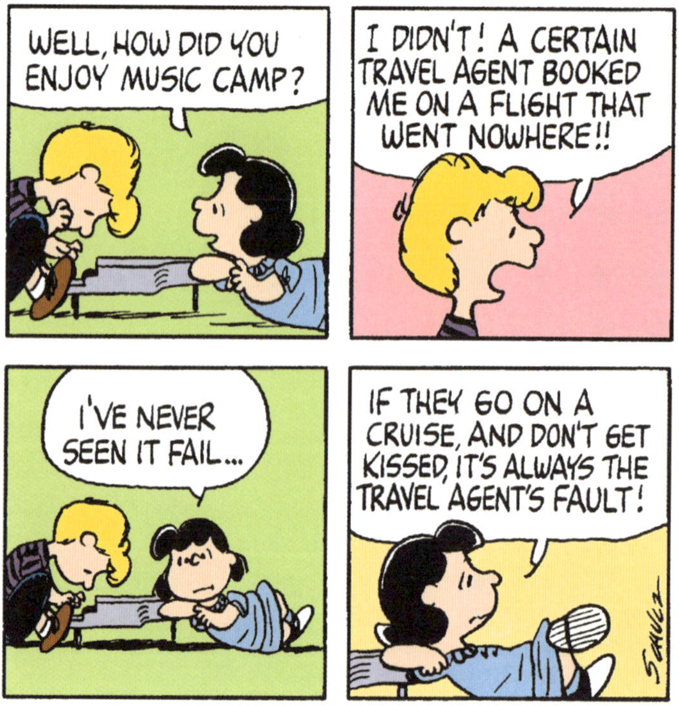
WELL, HOW DID YOU ENJOY MUSIC CAMP?
I DIDN'T! A CERTAIN TRAVEL AGENT BOOKED ME ON A FLIGHT THAT WENT NOWHERE!!
I'VE NEVER SEEN IT FAIL...
IF THEY GO ON A CRUISE, AND DON'T GET KISSED, IT'S ALWAYS THE TRAVEL AGENT'S FAULT!

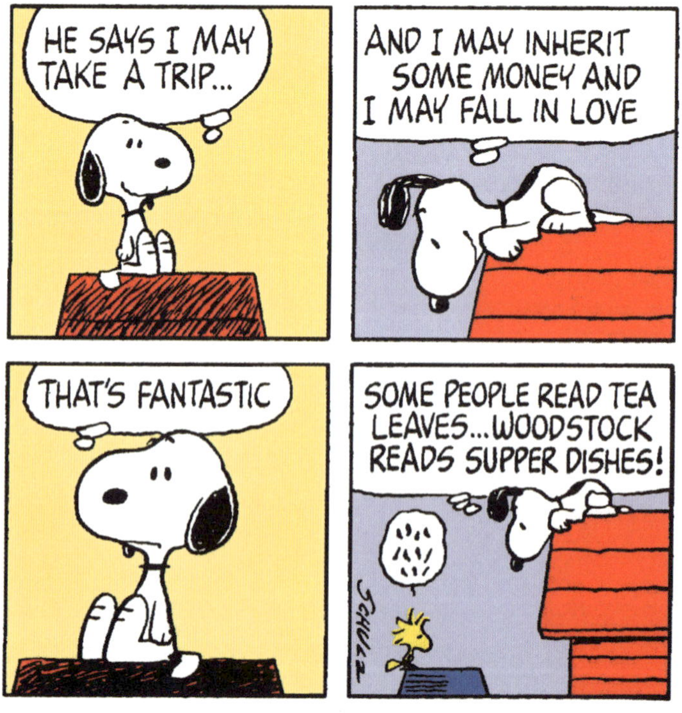
HE SAYS I MAY TAKE A TRIP...
AND I MAY INHERIT SOME MONEY AND I MAY FALL IN LOVE
THAT'S FANTASTIC
SOME PEOPLE READ TEA LEAVES...WOODSTOCK READS SUPPER DISHES!

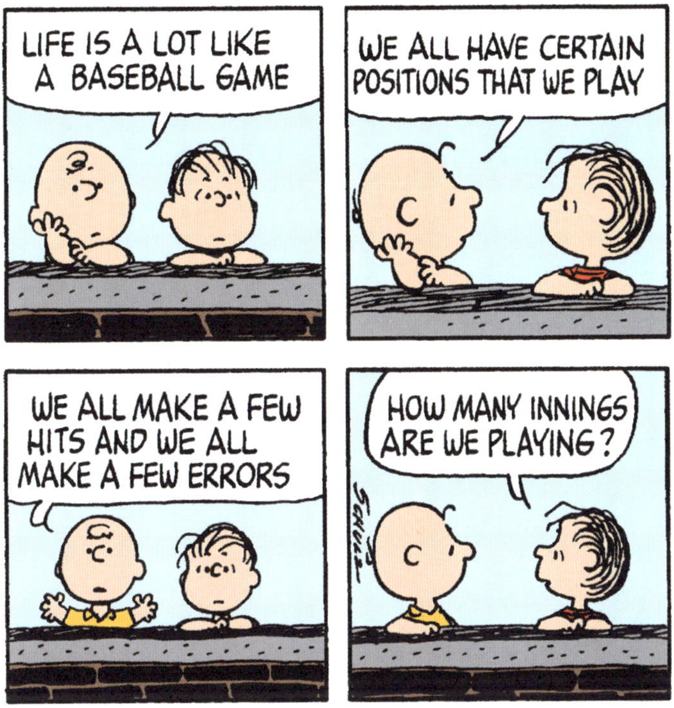
LIFE IS A LOT LIKE A BASEBALL GAME
WE ALL HAVE CERTAIN POSITIONS THAT WE PLAY
WE ALL MAKE A FEW HITS AND WE ALL MAKE A FEW ERRORS
HOW MANY INNINGS ARE WE PLAYING?
SCHULZ

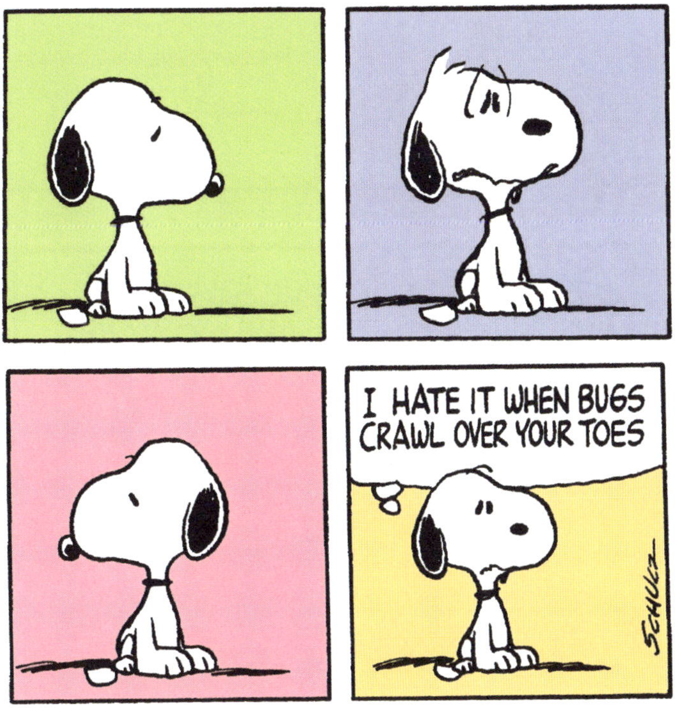
I HATE IT WHEN BUGS CRAWL OVER YOUR TOES
SCHULZ

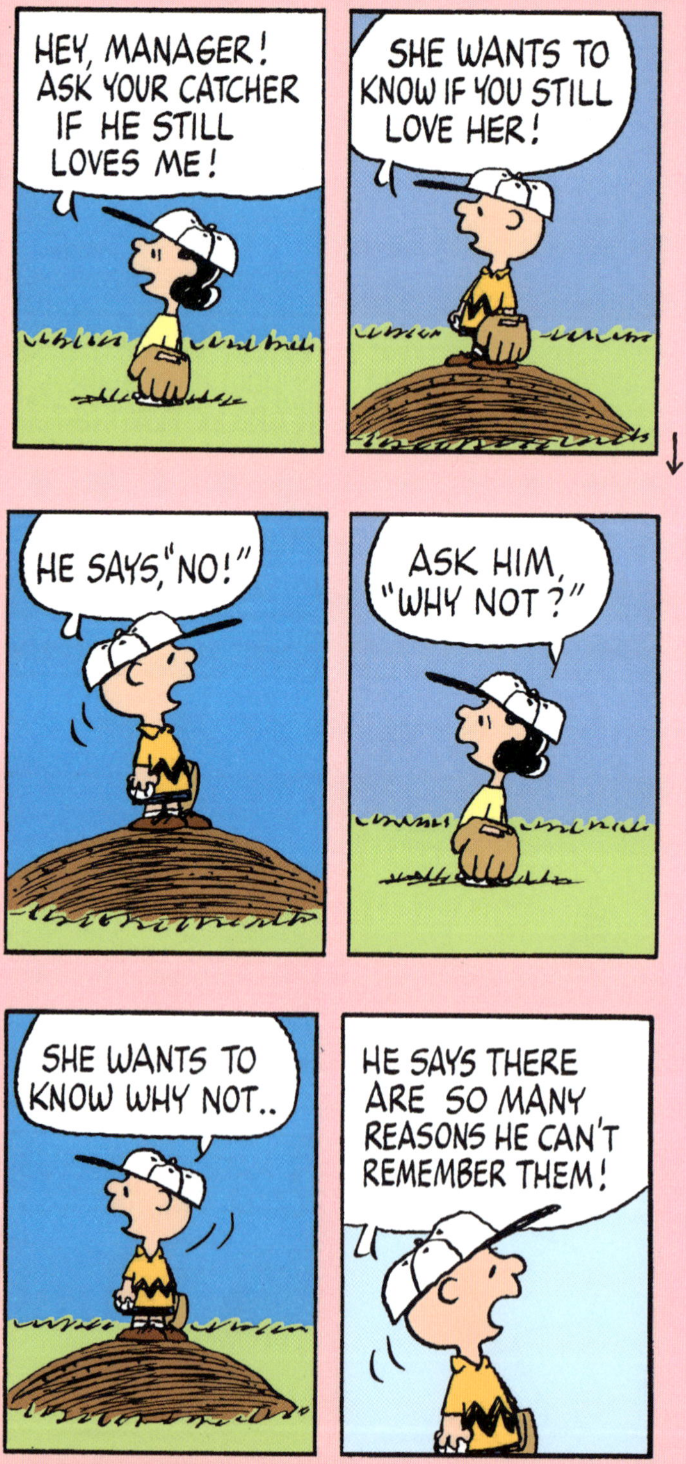
HEY, MANAGER! ASK YOUR CATCHER IF HE STILL LOVES ME!
SHE WANTS TO KNOW IF YOU STILL LOVE HER!
HE SAYS, "NO!"
ASK HIM, "WHY NOT?"
SHE WANTS TO KNOW WHY NOT..
HE SAYS THERE ARE SO MANY REASONS HE CAN'T REMEMBER THEM!

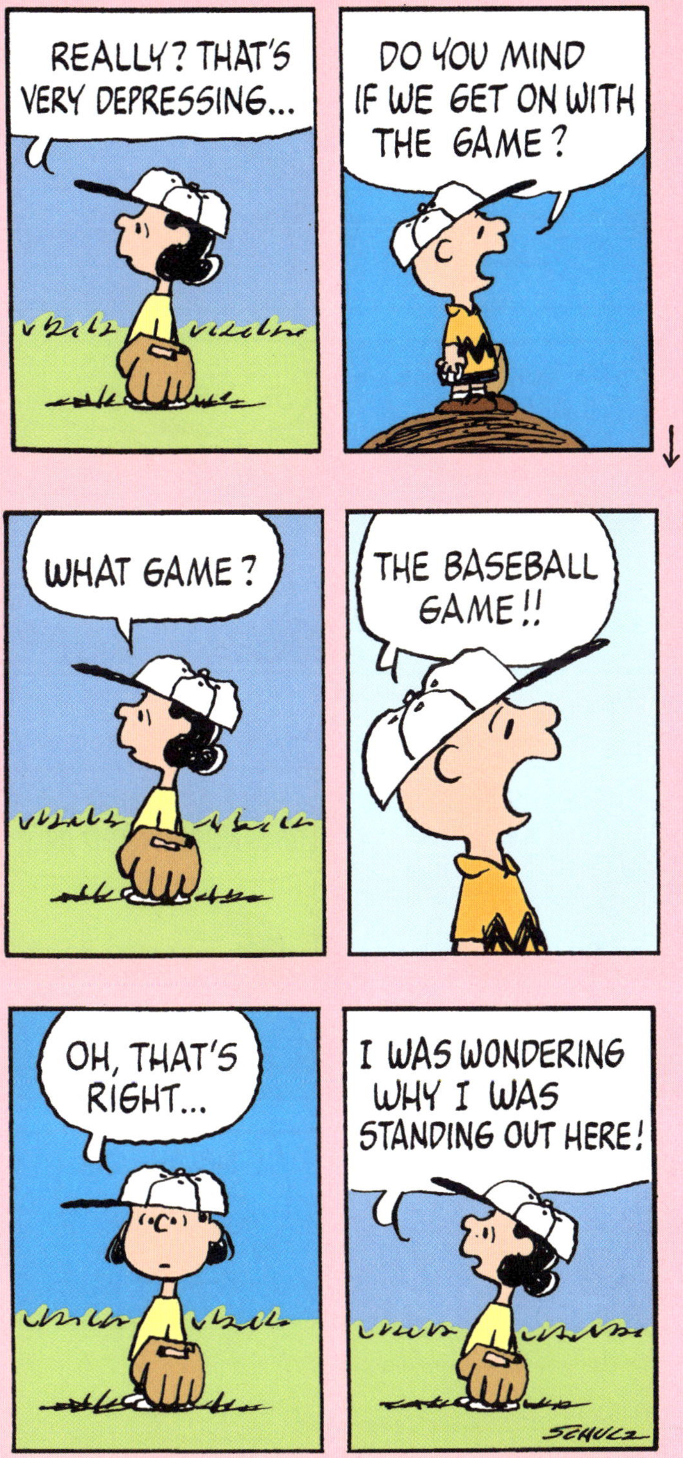
REALLY? THAT'S VERY DEPRESSING...
DO YOU MIND IF WE GET ON WITH THE GAME?
WHAT GAME?
THE BASEBALL GAME!!
OH, THAT'S RIGHT...
I WAS WONDERING WHY I WAS STANDING OUT HERE!
SCHULZ

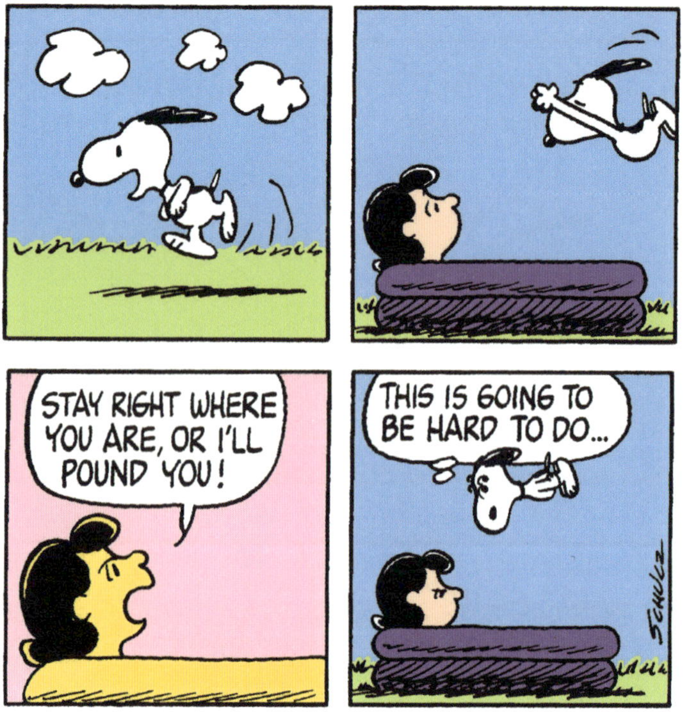
STAY RIGHT WHERE YOU ARE, OR I'LL POUND YOU!
THIS IS GOING TO BE HARD TO DO...
SCHULZ

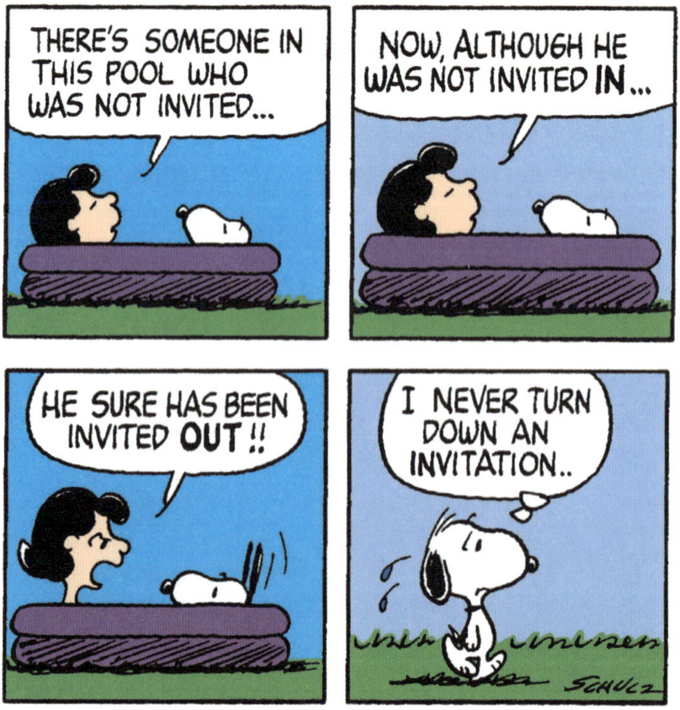
THERE'S SOMEONE IN THIS POOL WHO WAS NOT INVITED...
NOW, ALTHOUGH HE WAS NOT INVITED **IN**...
HE SURE HAS BEEN INVITED **OUT**!!
I NEVER TURN DOWN AN INVITATION..
SCHULZ

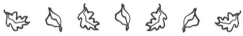

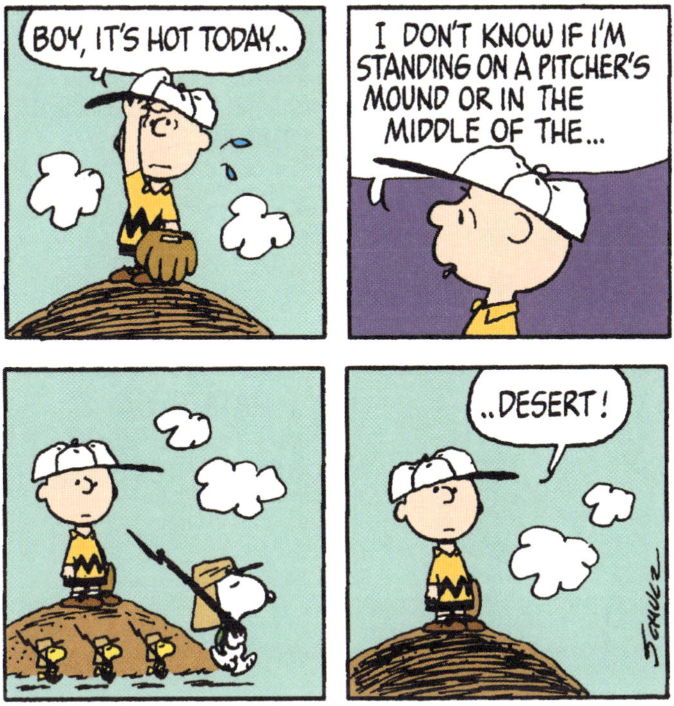
BOY, IT'S HOT TODAY..
I DON'T KNOW IF I'M STANDING ON A PITCHER'S MOUND OR IN THE MIDDLE OF THE...
..DESERT!
SCHULZ

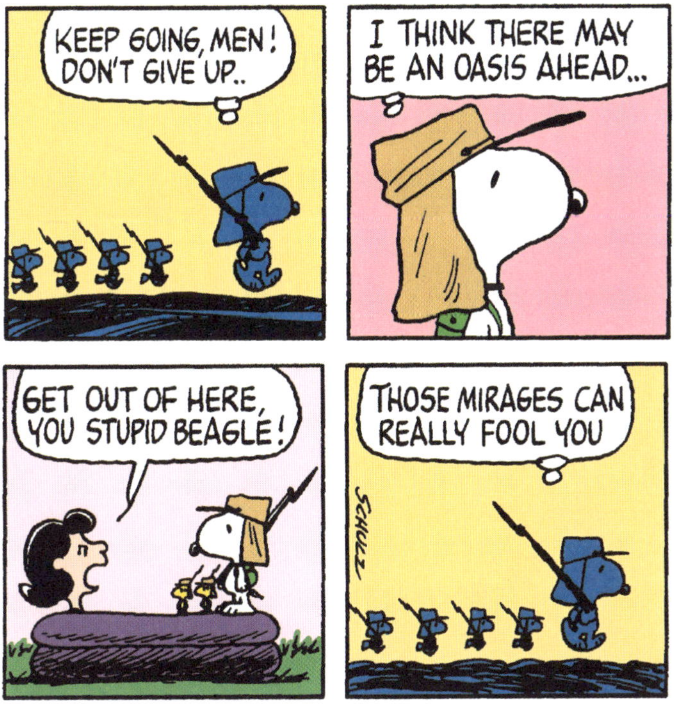
KEEP GOING, MEN! DON'T GIVE UP..
I THINK THERE MAY BE AN OASIS AHEAD...
GET OUT OF HERE, YOU STUPID BEAGLE!
THOSE MIRAGES CAN REALLY FOOL YOU
SCHULZ

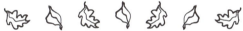

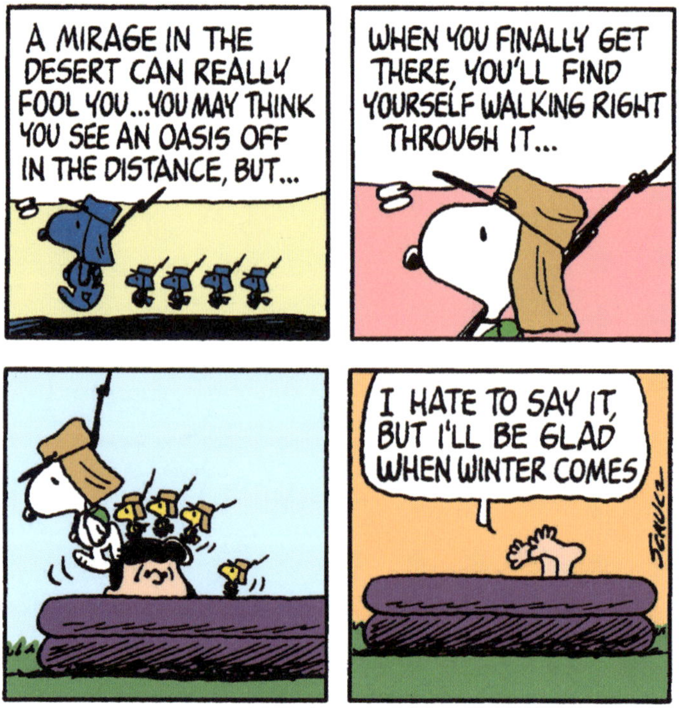
A MIRAGE IN THE DESERT CAN REALLY FOOL YOU...YOU MAY THINK YOU SEE AN OASIS OFF IN THE DISTANCE, BUT...
WHEN YOU FINALLY GET THERE, YOU'LL FIND YOURSELF WALKING RIGHT THROUGH IT...
I HATE TO SAY IT, BUT I'LL BE GLAD WHEN WINTER COMES

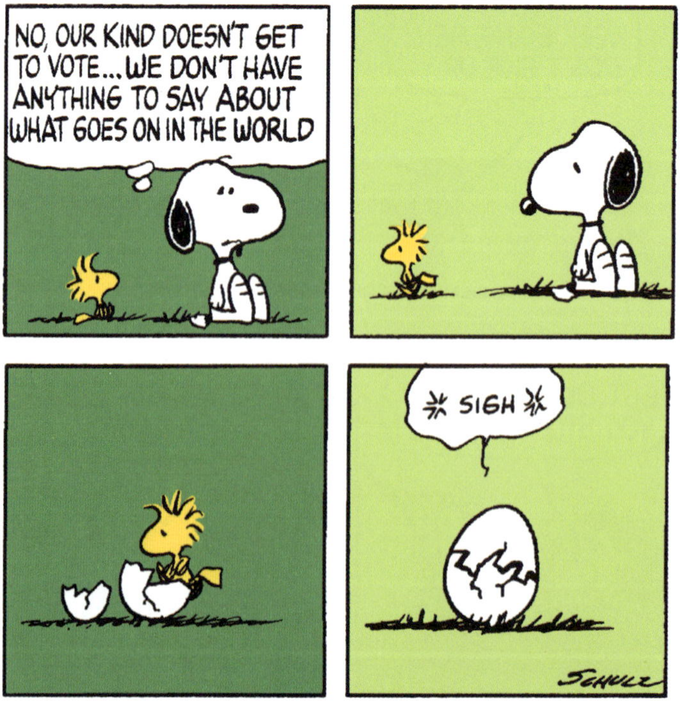
NO, OUR KIND DOESN'T GET TO VOTE...WE DON'T HAVE ANYTHING TO SAY ABOUT WHAT GOES ON IN THE WORLD
SIGH

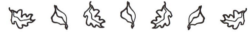

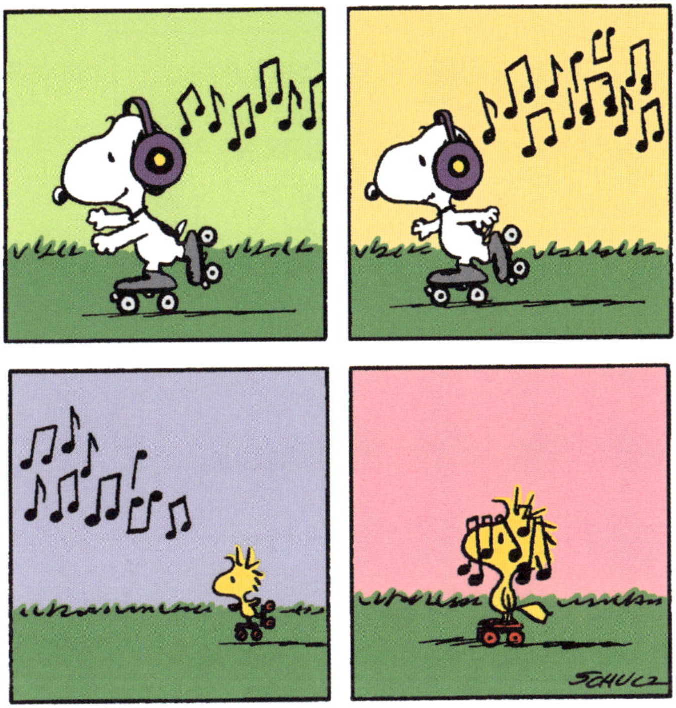

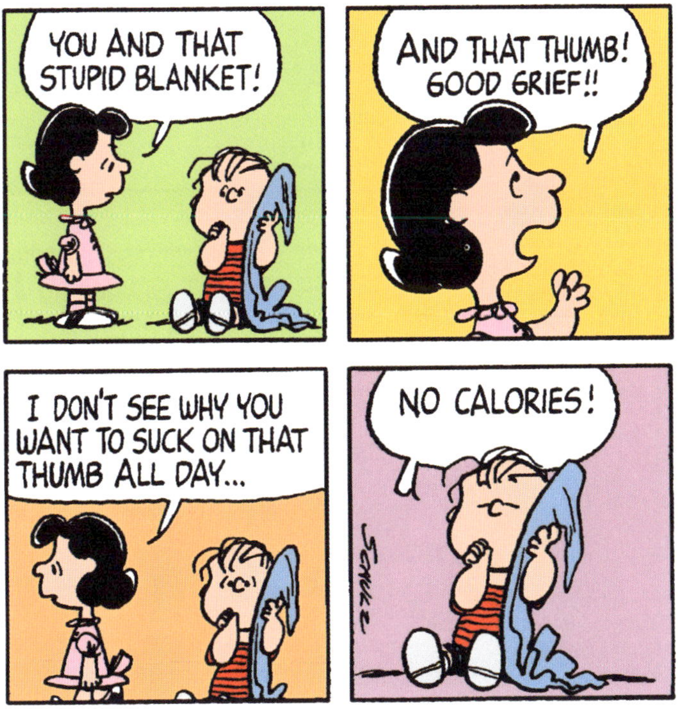
YOU AND THAT STUPID BLANKET!
AND THAT THUMB! GOOD GRIEF!!
I DON'T SEE WHY YOU WANT TO SUCK ON THAT THUMB ALL DAY...
NO CALORIES!

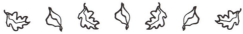

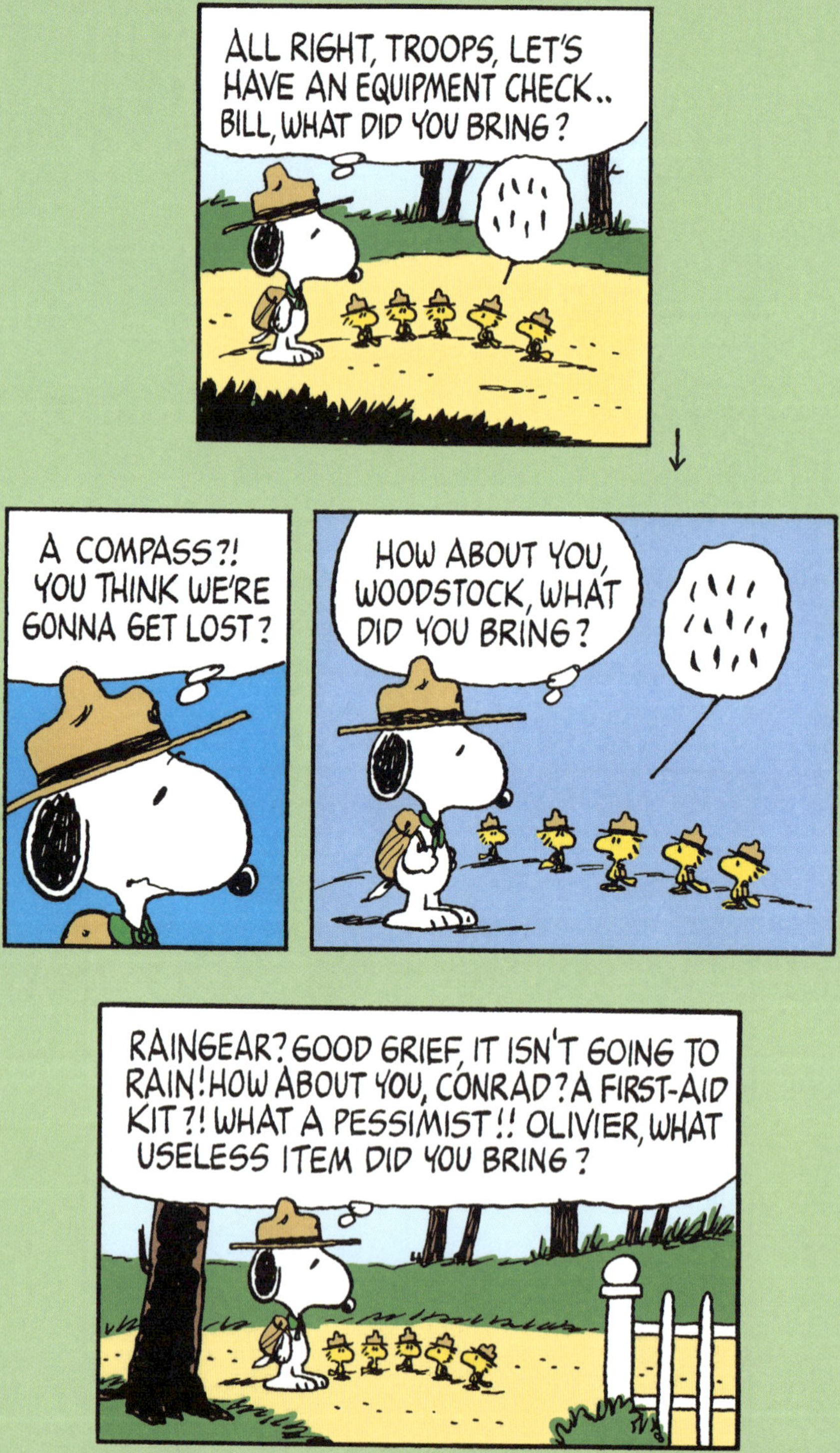
ALL RIGHT, TROOPS, LET'S HAVE AN EQUIPMENT CHECK.. BILL, WHAT DID YOU BRING?
A COMPASS?! YOU THINK WE'RE GONNA GET LOST?
HOW ABOUT YOU, WOODSTOCK, WHAT DID YOU BRING?
RAINGEAR? GOOD GRIEF, IT ISN'T GOING TO RAIN! HOW ABOUT YOU, CONRAD? A FIRST-AID KIT?! WHAT A PESSIMIST!! OLIVIER, WHAT USELESS ITEM DID YOU BRING?

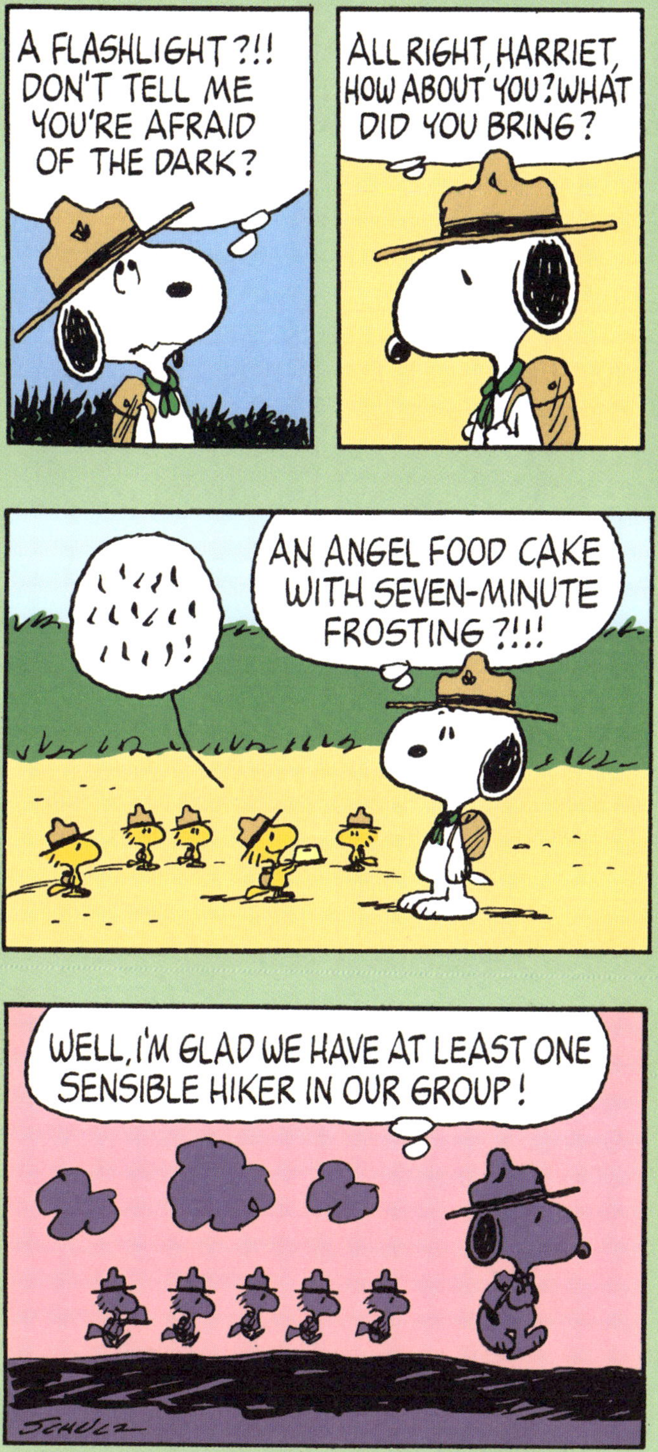
A FLASHLIGHT?!! DON'T TELL ME YOU'RE AFRAID OF THE DARK?
ALL RIGHT, HARRIET, HOW ABOUT YOU? WHAT DID YOU BRING?
AN ANGEL FOOD CAKE WITH SEVEN-MINUTE FROSTING?!!!
WELL, I'M GLAD WE HAVE AT LEAST ONE SENSIBLE HIKER IN OUR GROUP!
SCHULZ

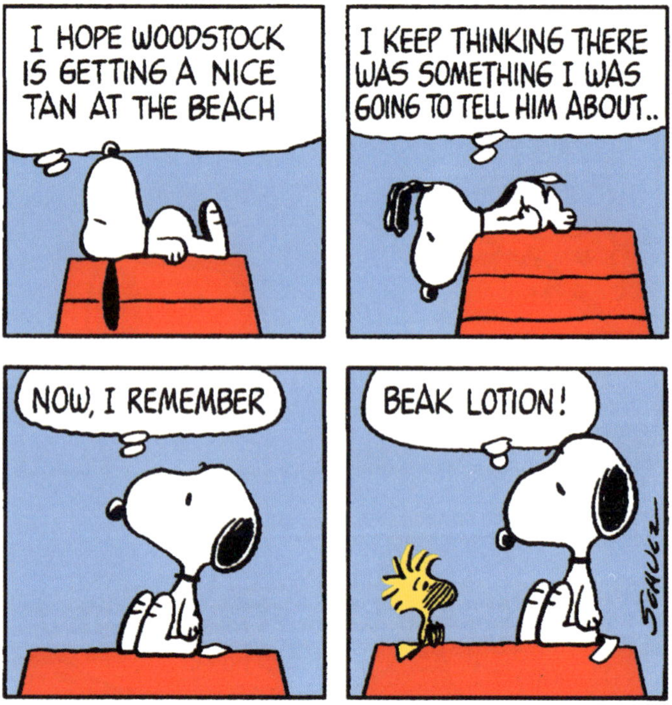
I HOPE WOODSTOCK IS GETTING A NICE TAN AT THE BEACH
I KEEP THINKING THERE WAS SOMETHING I WAS GOING TO TELL HIM ABOUT..
NOW, I REMEMBER
BEAK LOTION!
SCHULZ

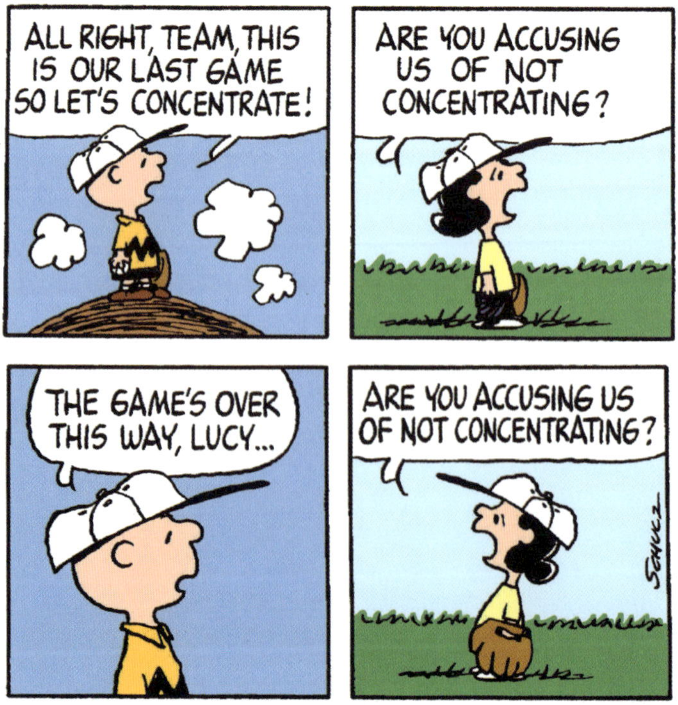
ALL RIGHT, TEAM, THIS IS OUR LAST GAME SO LET'S CONCENTRATE!
ARE YOU ACCUSING US OF NOT CONCENTRATING?
THE GAME'S OVER THIS WAY, LUCY...
ARE YOU ACCUSING US OF NOT CONCENTRATING?
SCHULZ

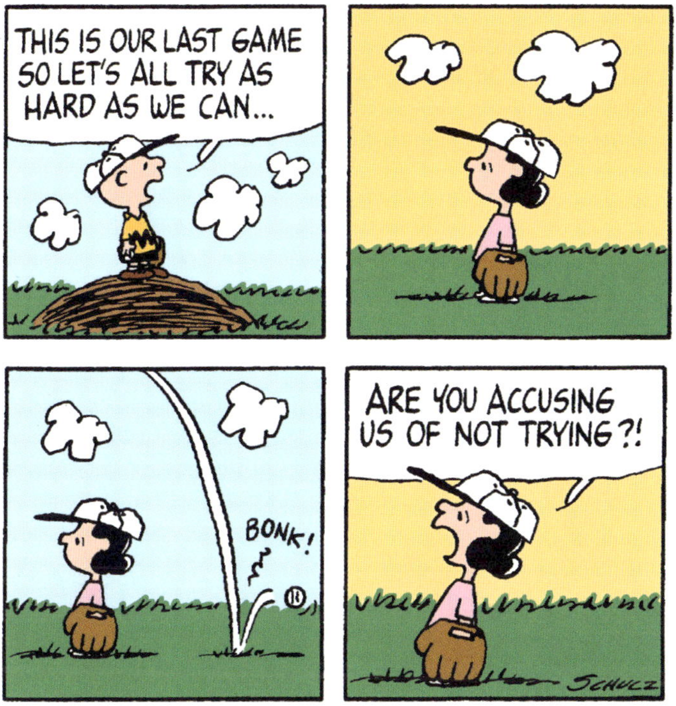
THIS IS OUR LAST GAME SO LET'S ALL TRY AS HARD AS WE CAN...
BONK!
ARE YOU ACCUSING US OF NOT TRYING?!
SCHULZ

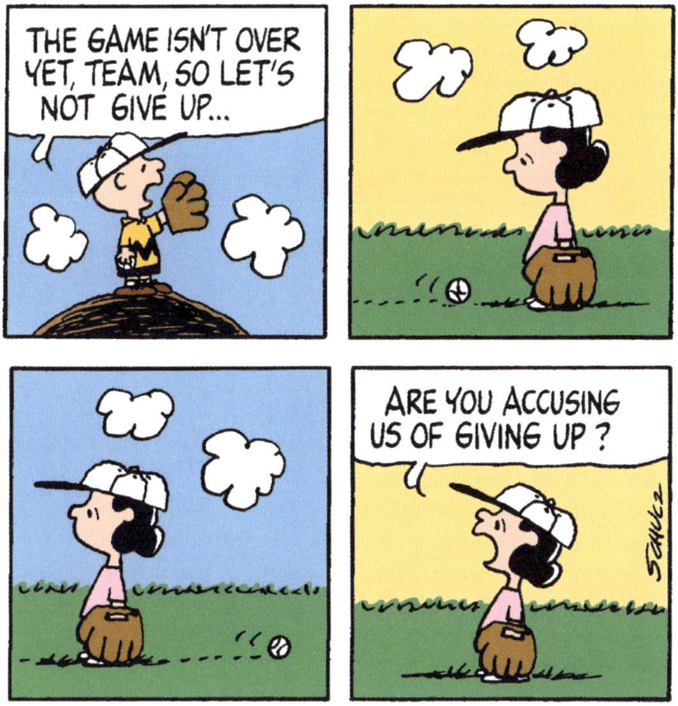
THE GAME ISN'T OVER YET, TEAM, SO LET'S NOT GIVE UP...
ARE YOU ACCUSING US OF GIVING UP?
SCHULZ

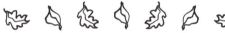

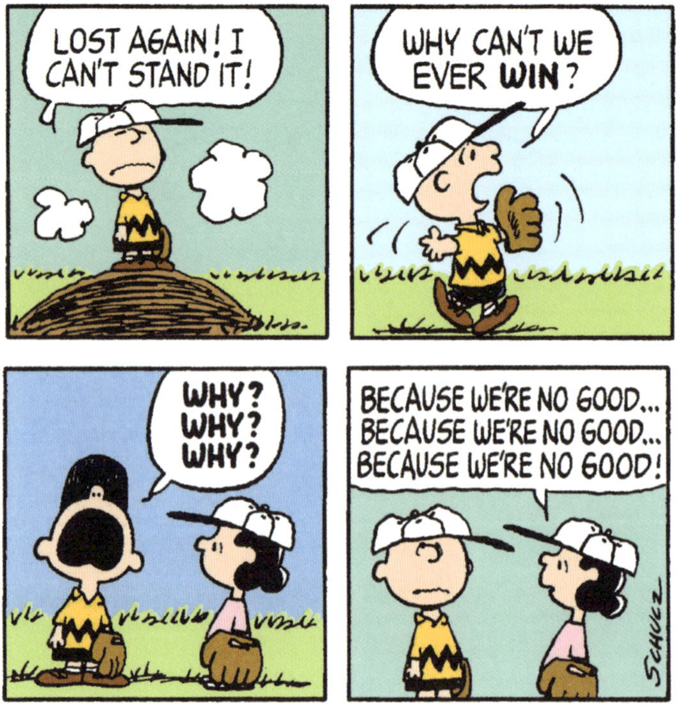
LOST AGAIN! I CAN'T STAND IT!
WHY CAN'T WE EVER **WIN**?
WHY? WHY? WHY?
BECAUSE WE'RE NO GOOD... BECAUSE WE'RE NO GOOD... BECAUSE WE'RE NO GOOD!
SCHULZ

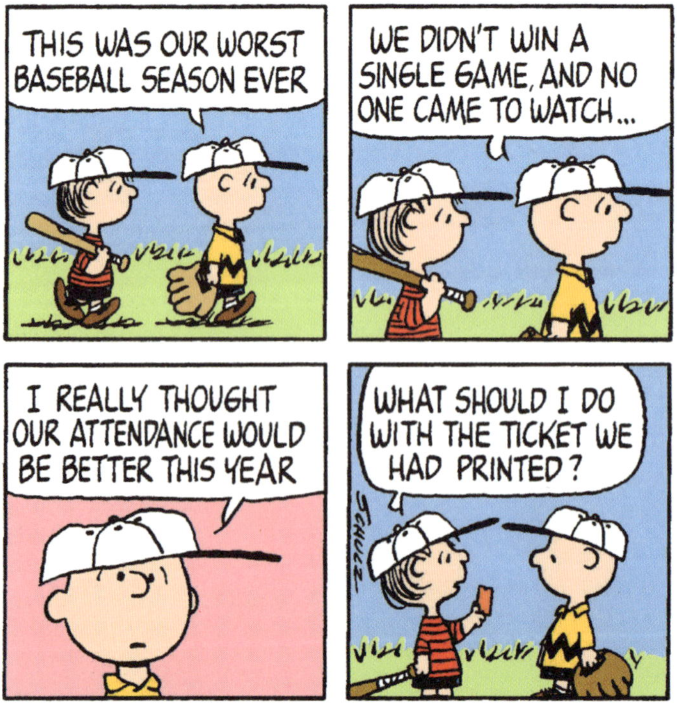
THIS WAS OUR WORST BASEBALL SEASON EVER
WE DIDN'T WIN A SINGLE GAME, AND NO ONE CAME TO WATCH...
I REALLY THOUGHT OUR ATTENDANCE WOULD BE BETTER THIS YEAR
WHAT SHOULD I DO WITH THE TICKET WE HAD PRINTED?
SCHULZ

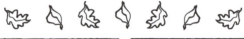

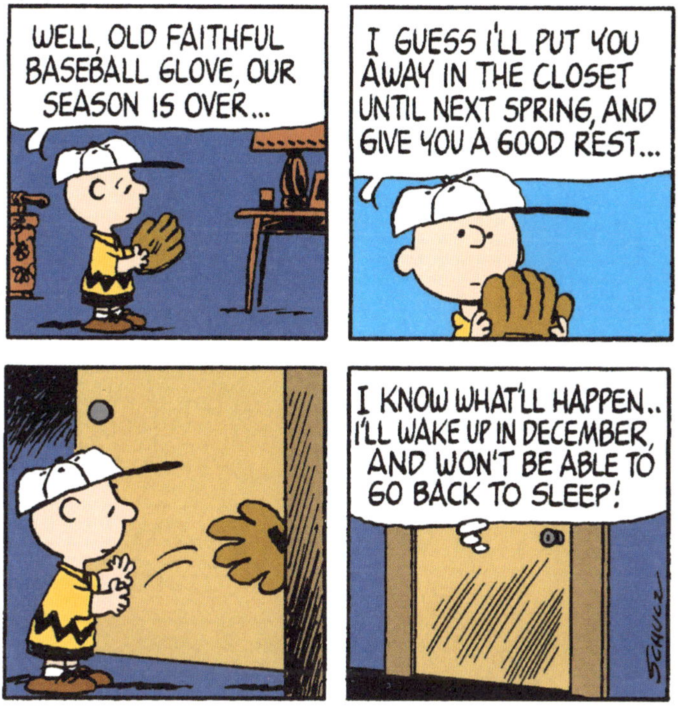
WELL, OLD FAITHFUL BASEBALL GLOVE, OUR SEASON IS OVER...
I GUESS I'LL PUT YOU AWAY IN THE CLOSET UNTIL NEXT SPRING, AND GIVE YOU A GOOD REST...
I KNOW WHAT'LL HAPPEN.. I'LL WAKE UP IN DECEMBER, AND WON'T BE ABLE TO GO BACK TO SLEEP!
SCHULZ

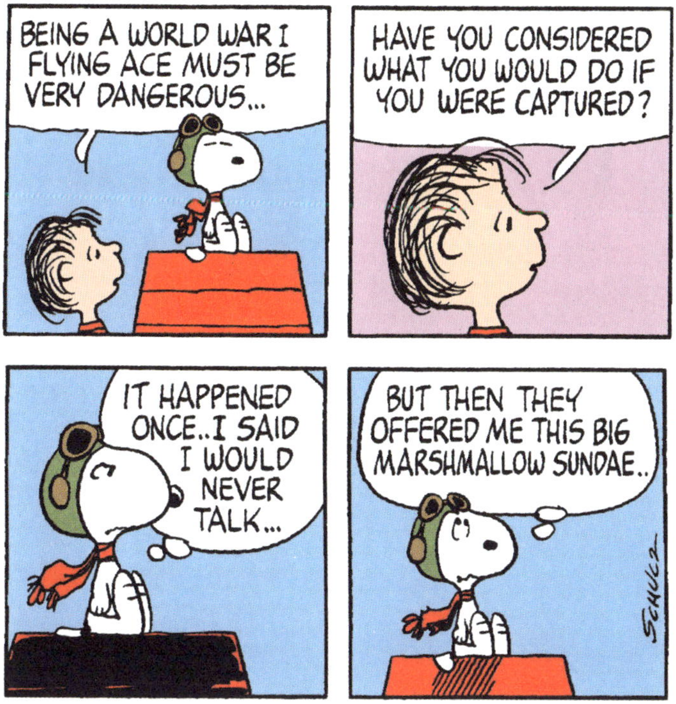
BEING A WORLD WAR I FLYING ACE MUST BE VERY DANGEROUS...
HAVE YOU CONSIDERED WHAT YOU WOULD DO IF YOU WERE CAPTURED?
IT HAPPENED ONCE..I SAID I WOULD NEVER TALK...
BUT THEN THEY OFFERED ME THIS BIG MARSHMALLOW SUNDAE..
SCHULZ

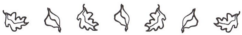

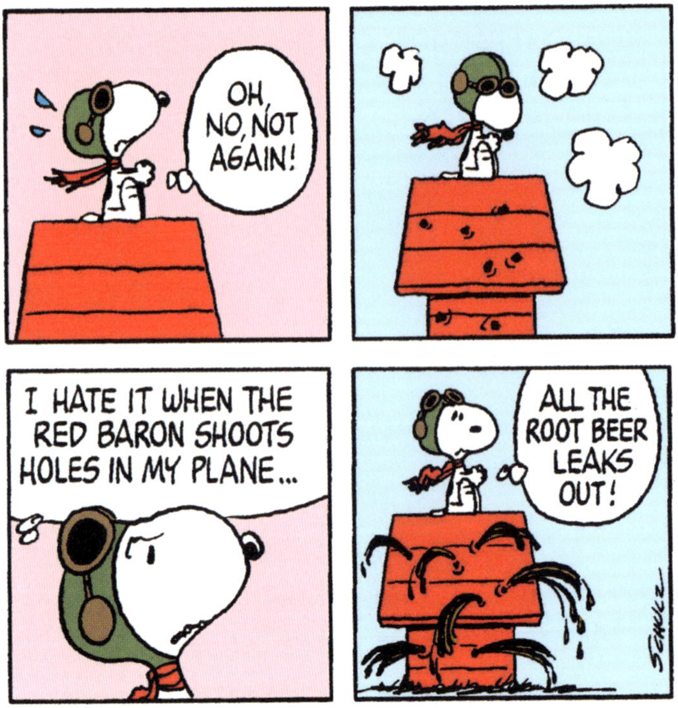
OH, NO, NOT AGAIN!
I HATE IT WHEN THE RED BARON SHOOTS HOLES IN MY PLANE...
ALL THE ROOT BEER LEAKS OUT!
SCHULZ

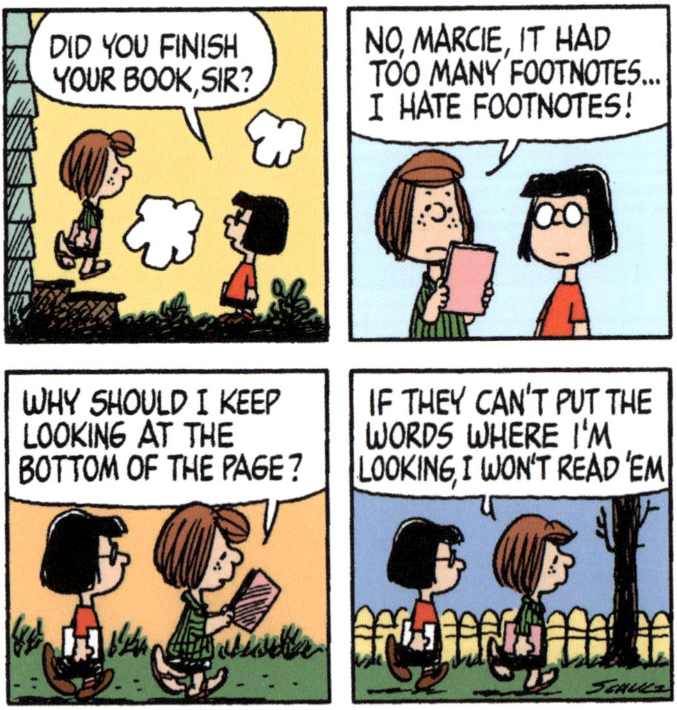
DID YOU FINISH YOUR BOOK, SIR?
NO, MARCIE, IT HAD TOO MANY FOOTNOTES... I HATE FOOTNOTES!
WHY SHOULD I KEEP LOOKING AT THE BOTTOM OF THE PAGE?
IF THEY CAN'T PUT THE WORDS WHERE I'M LOOKING, I WON'T READ 'EM
SCHULZ

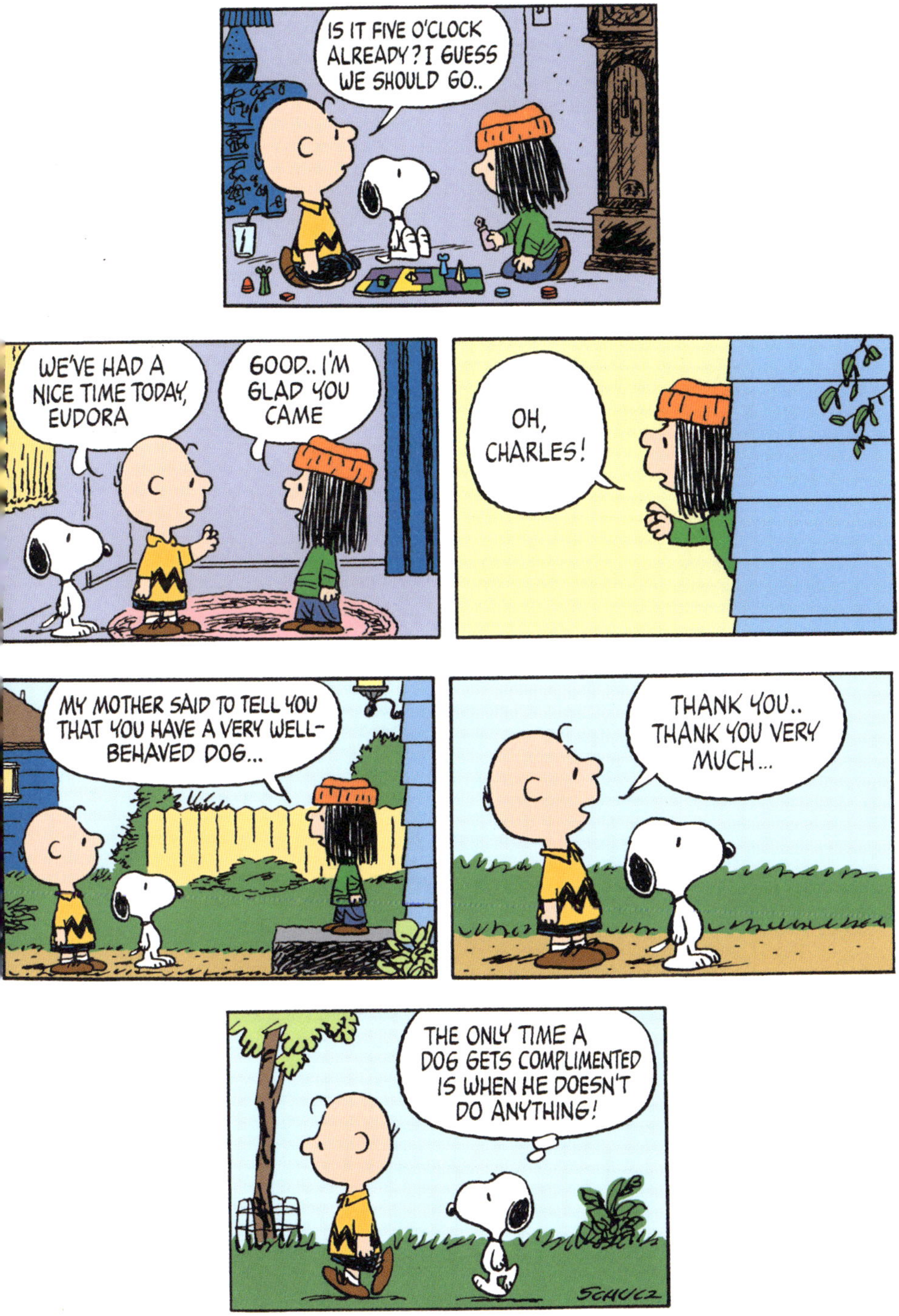
IS IT FIVE O'CLOCK ALREADY? I GUESS WE SHOULD GO..
WE'VE HAD A NICE TIME TODAY, EUDORA
GOOD.. I'M GLAD YOU CAME
OH, CHARLES!
MY MOTHER SAID TO TELL YOU THAT YOU HAVE A VERY WELL-BEHAVED DOG...
THANK YOU.. THANK YOU VERY MUCH...
THE ONLY TIME A DOG GETS COMPLIMENTED IS WHEN HE DOESN'T DO ANYTHING!
SCHULZ

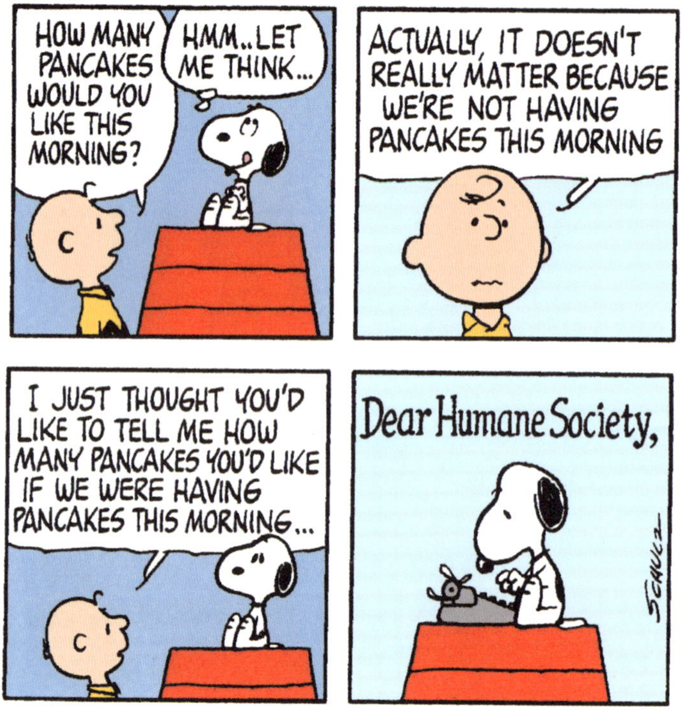
HOW MANY PANCAKES WOULD YOU LIKE THIS MORNING?
HMM..LET ME THINK...
ACTUALLY, IT DOESN'T REALLY MATTER BECAUSE WE'RE NOT HAVING PANCAKES THIS MORNING
I JUST THOUGHT YOU'D LIKE TO TELL ME HOW MANY PANCAKES YOU'D LIKE IF WE WERE HAVING PANCAKES THIS MORNING...
Dear Humane Society,
SCHULZ

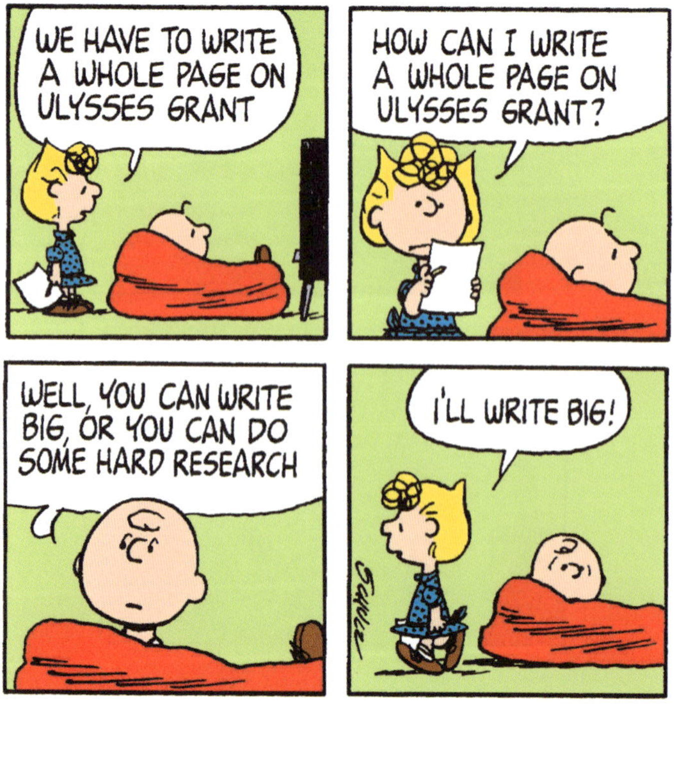
WE HAVE TO WRITE A WHOLE PAGE ON ULYSSES GRANT
HOW CAN I WRITE A WHOLE PAGE ON ULYSSES GRANT?
WELL, YOU CAN WRITE BIG, OR YOU CAN DO SOME HARD RESEARCH
I'LL WRITE BIG!
SCHULZ

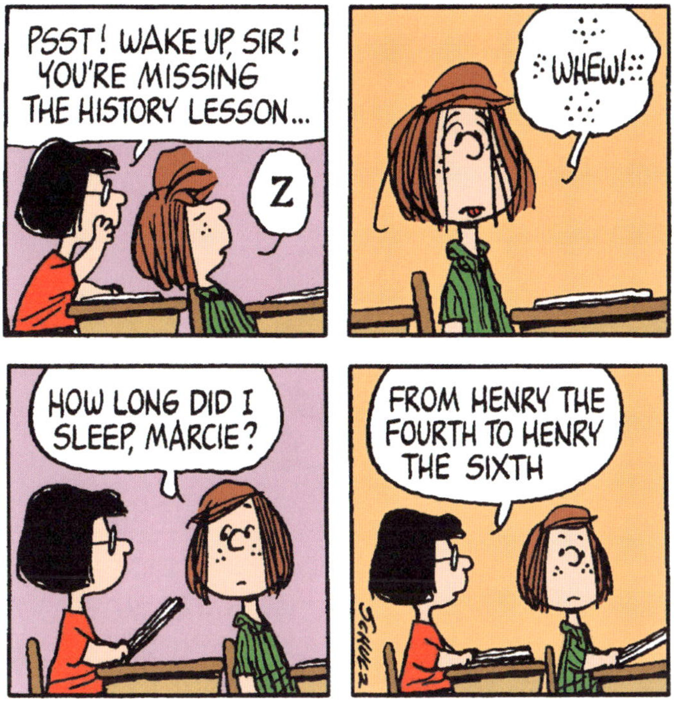
PSST! WAKE UP, SIR! YOU'RE MISSING THE HISTORY LESSON...
Z
WHEW!
HOW LONG DID I SLEEP, MARCIE?
FROM HENRY THE FOURTH TO HENRY THE SIXTH
SCHULZ

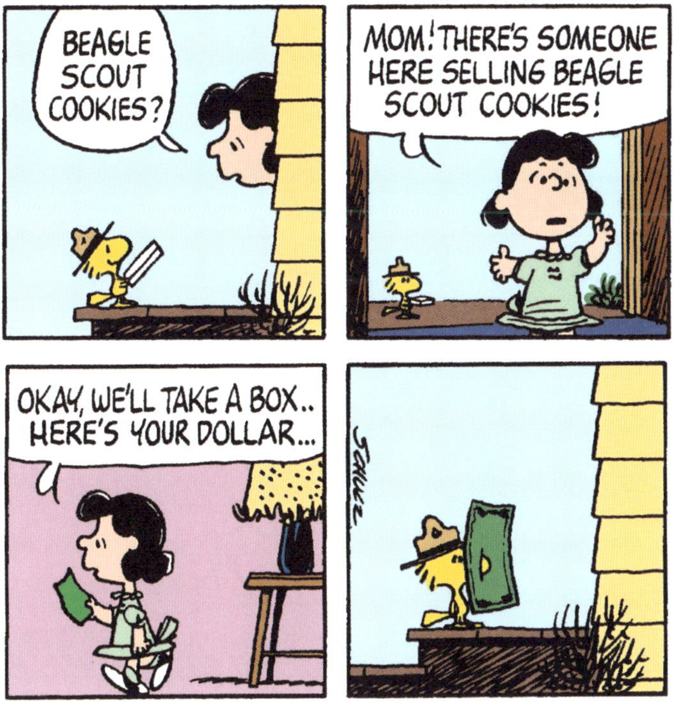
BEAGLE SCOUT COOKIES?
MOM! THERE'S SOMEONE HERE SELLING BEAGLE SCOUT COOKIES!
OKAY, WE'LL TAKE A BOX.. ..HERE'S YOUR DOLLAR...
SCHULZ

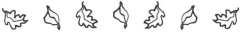

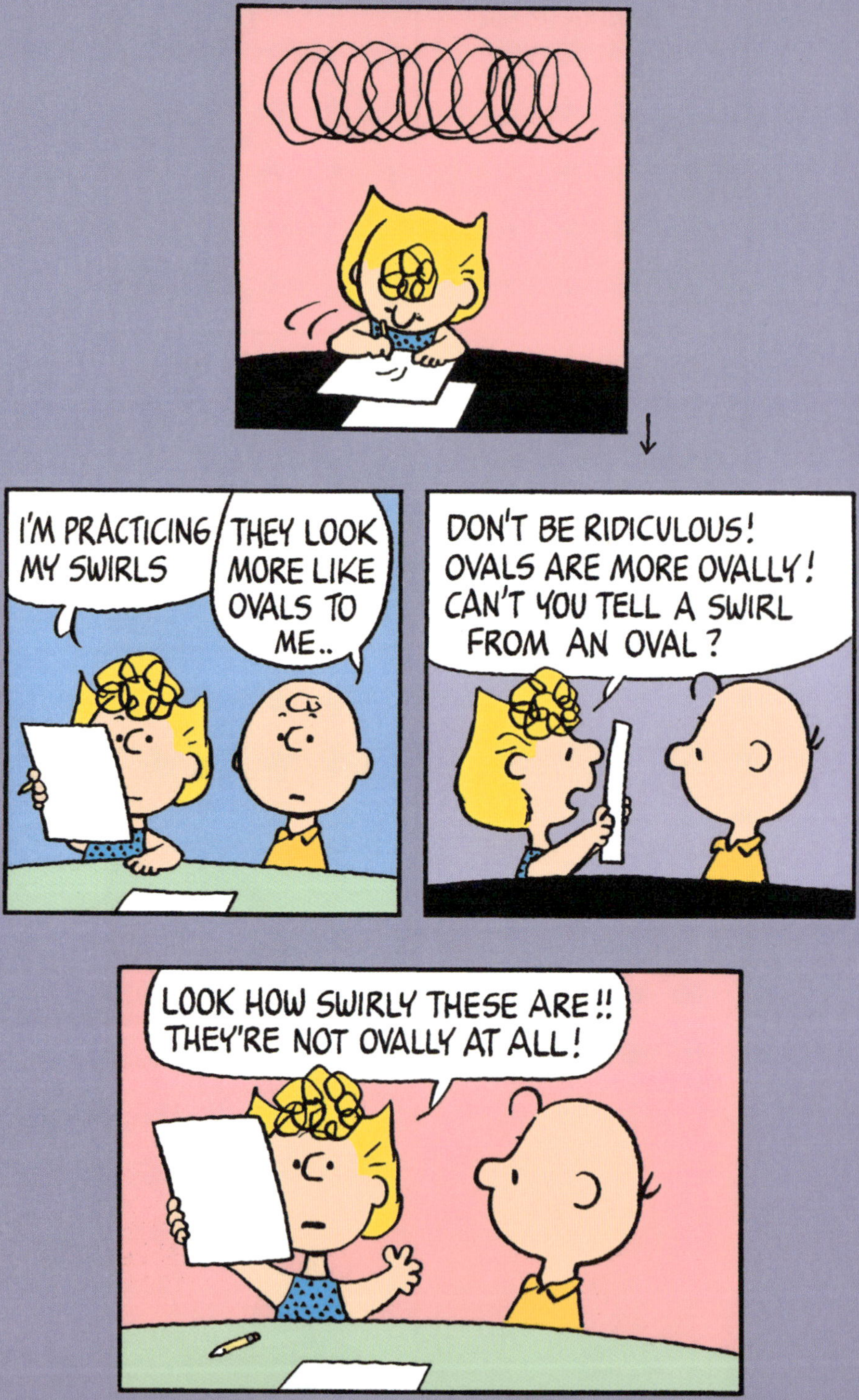
I'M PRACTICING MY SWIRLS
THEY LOOK MORE LIKE OVALS TO ME..
DON'T BE RIDICULOUS! OVALS ARE MORE OVALLY! CAN'T YOU TELL A SWIRL FROM AN OVAL?
LOOK HOW SWIRLY THESE ARE!! THEY'RE NOT OVALLY AT ALL!

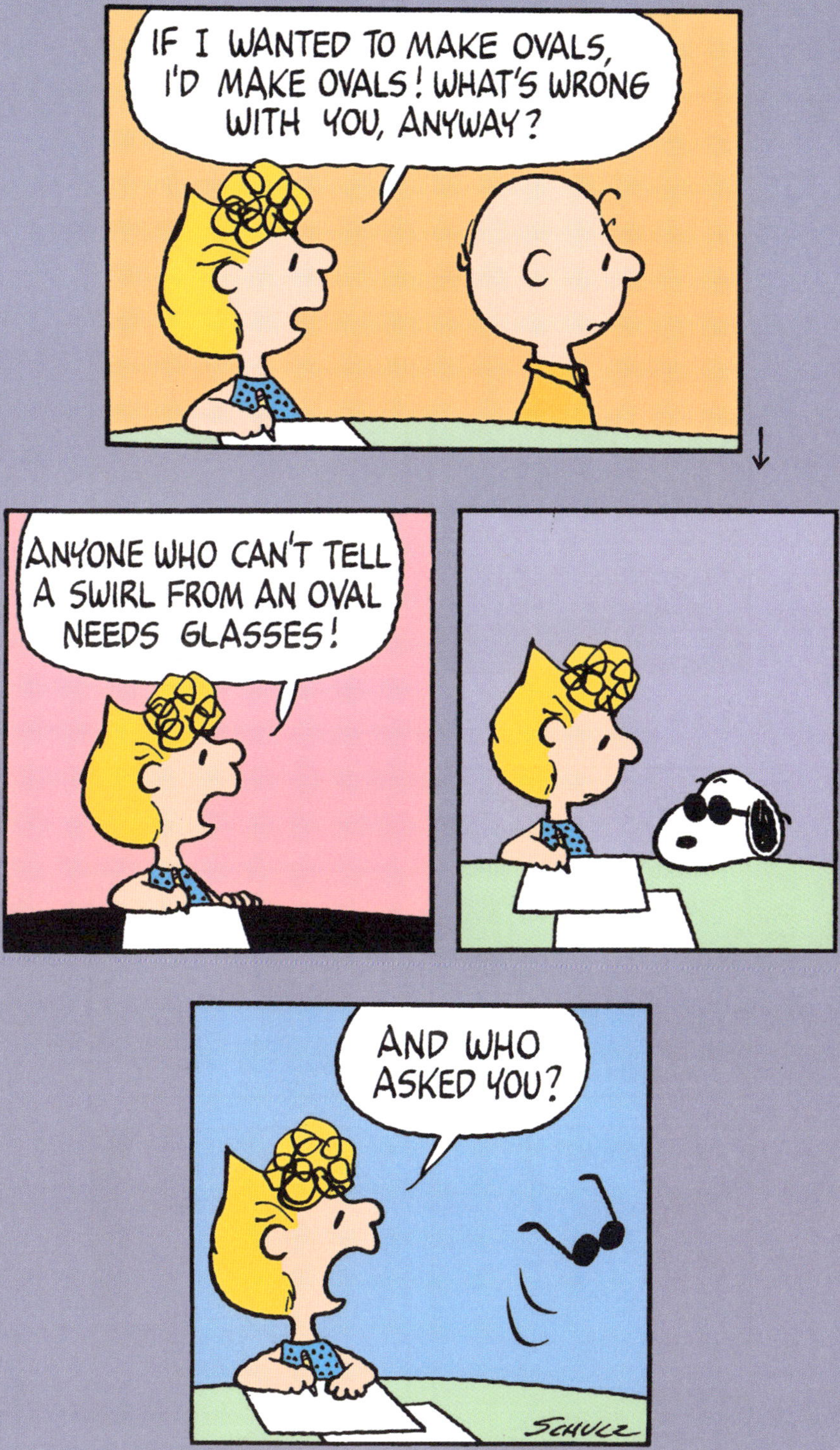
IF I WANTED TO MAKE OVALS, I'D MAKE OVALS! WHAT'S WRONG WITH YOU, ANYWAY?
ANYONE WHO CAN'T TELL A SWIRL FROM AN OVAL NEEDS GLASSES!
AND WHO ASKED YOU?
SCHULZ

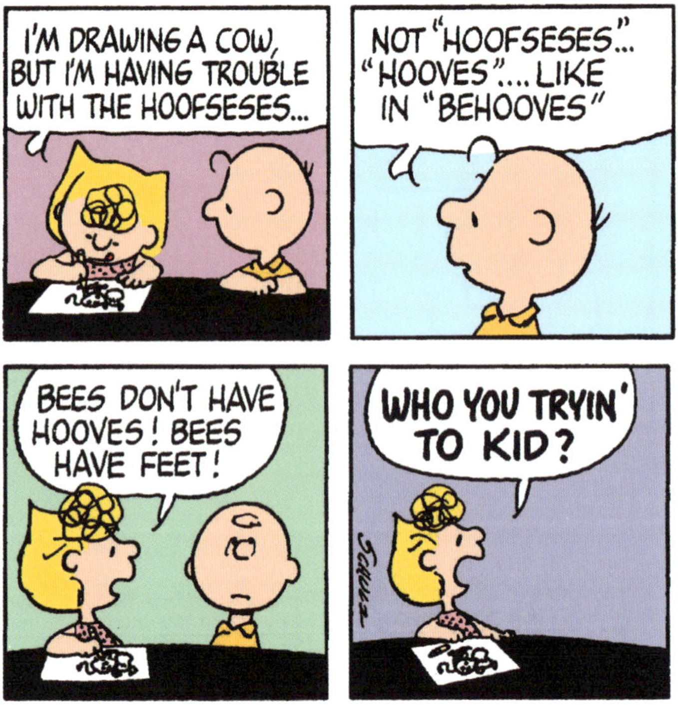
I'M DRAWING A COW, BUT I'M HAVING TROUBLE WITH THE HOOFSESES...
NOT "HOOFSESES"... "HOOVES".... LIKE IN "BEHOOVES"
BEES DON'T HAVE HOOVES! BEES HAVE FEET!
WHO YOU TRYIN' TO KID?
SCHULZ

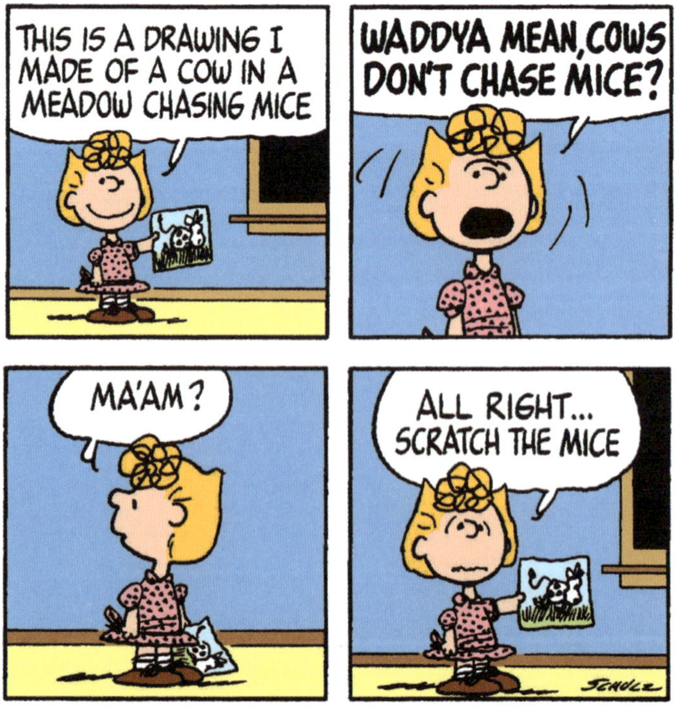
THIS IS A DRAWING I MADE OF A COW IN A MEADOW CHASING MICE
WADDYA MEAN, COWS DON'T CHASE MICE?
MA'AM?
ALL RIGHT... SCRATCH THE MICE
SCHULZ

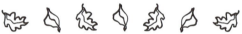

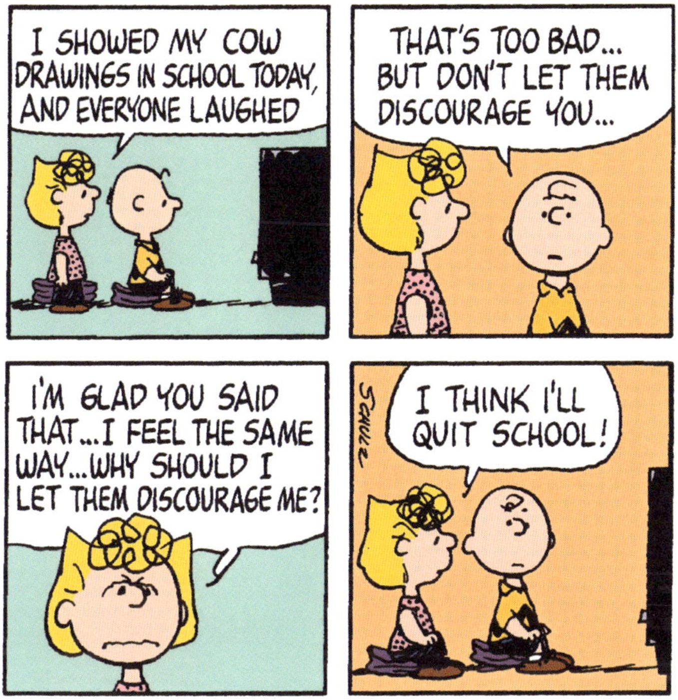
I SHOWED MY COW DRAWINGS IN SCHOOL TODAY, AND EVERYONE LAUGHED
THAT'S TOO BAD... BUT DON'T LET THEM DISCOURAGE YOU...
I'M GLAD YOU SAID THAT...I FEEL THE SAME WAY...WHY SHOULD I LET THEM DISCOURAGE ME?
I THINK I'LL QUIT SCHOOL!

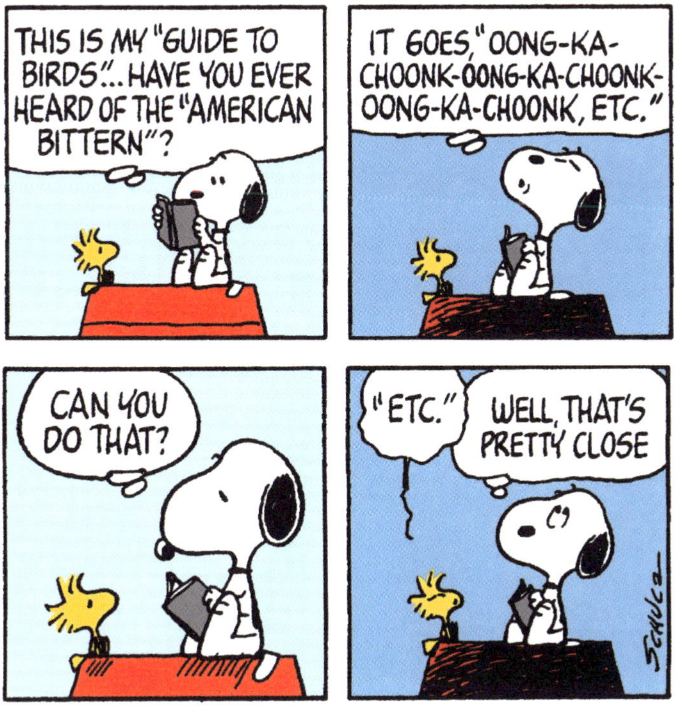
THIS IS MY "GUIDE TO BIRDS"...HAVE YOU EVER HEARD OF THE "AMERICAN BITTERN"?
IT GOES, "OONG-KA-CHOONK-OONG-KA-CHOONK-OONG-KA-CHOONK, ETC."
CAN YOU DO THAT?
"ETC."
WELL, THAT'S PRETTY CLOSE

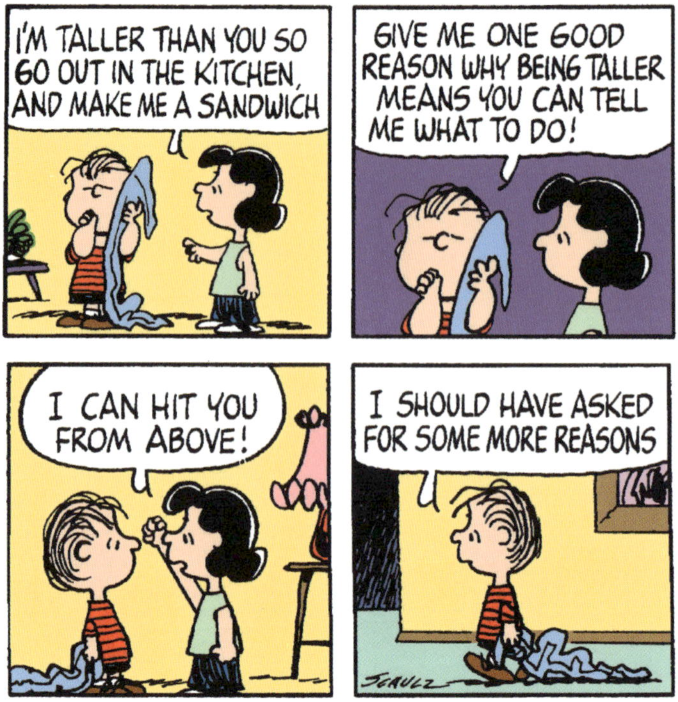
I'M TALLER THAN YOU SO GO OUT IN THE KITCHEN, AND MAKE ME A SANDWICH
GIVE ME ONE GOOD REASON WHY BEING TALLER MEANS YOU CAN TELL ME WHAT TO DO!
I CAN HIT YOU FROM ABOVE!
I SHOULD HAVE ASKED FOR SOME MORE REASONS

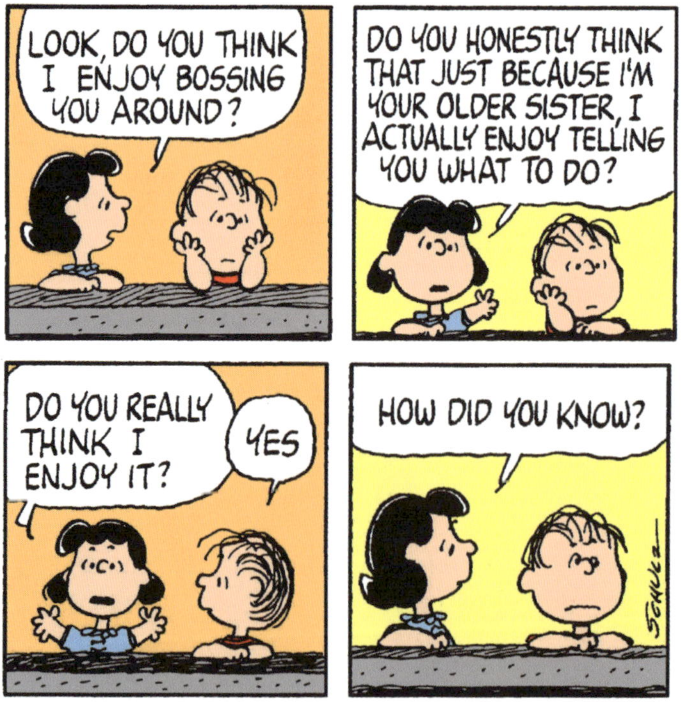
LOOK, DO YOU THINK I ENJOY BOSSING YOU AROUND?
DO YOU HONESTLY THINK THAT JUST BECAUSE I'M YOUR OLDER SISTER, I ACTUALLY ENJOY TELLING YOU WHAT TO DO?
DO YOU REALLY THINK I ENJOY IT?
YES
HOW DID YOU KNOW?

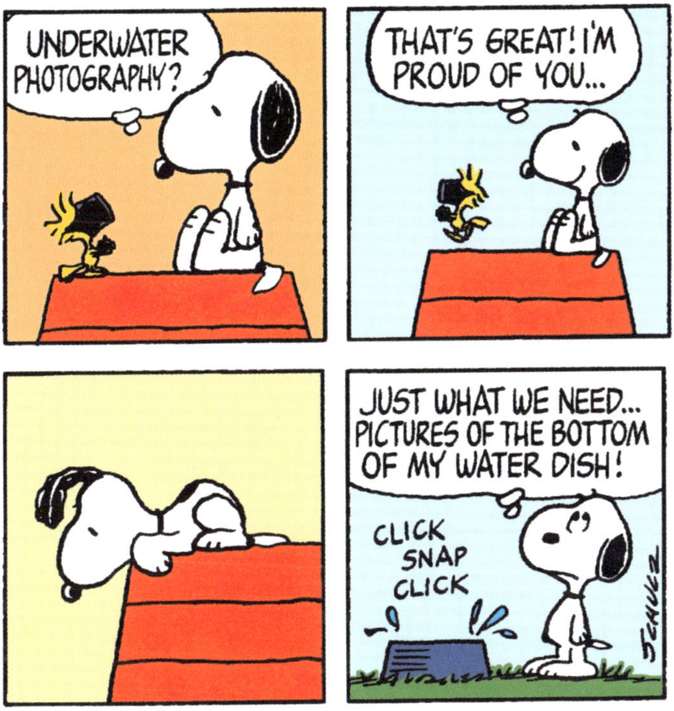
UNDERWATER PHOTOGRAPHY?
THAT'S GREAT! I'M PROUD OF YOU...
JUST WHAT WE NEED... PICTURES OF THE BOTTOM OF MY WATER DISH!
CLICK
SNAP
CLICK
SCHULZ

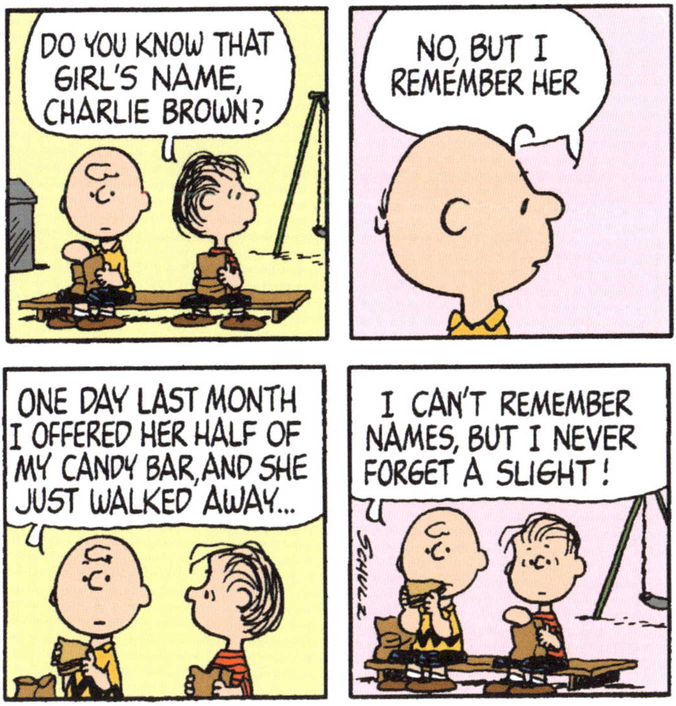
DO YOU KNOW THAT GIRL'S NAME, CHARLIE BROWN?
NO, BUT I REMEMBER HER
ONE DAY LAST MONTH I OFFERED HER HALF OF MY CANDY BAR, AND SHE JUST WALKED AWAY...
I CAN'T REMEMBER NAMES, BUT I NEVER FORGET A SLIGHT!
SCHULZ

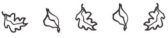

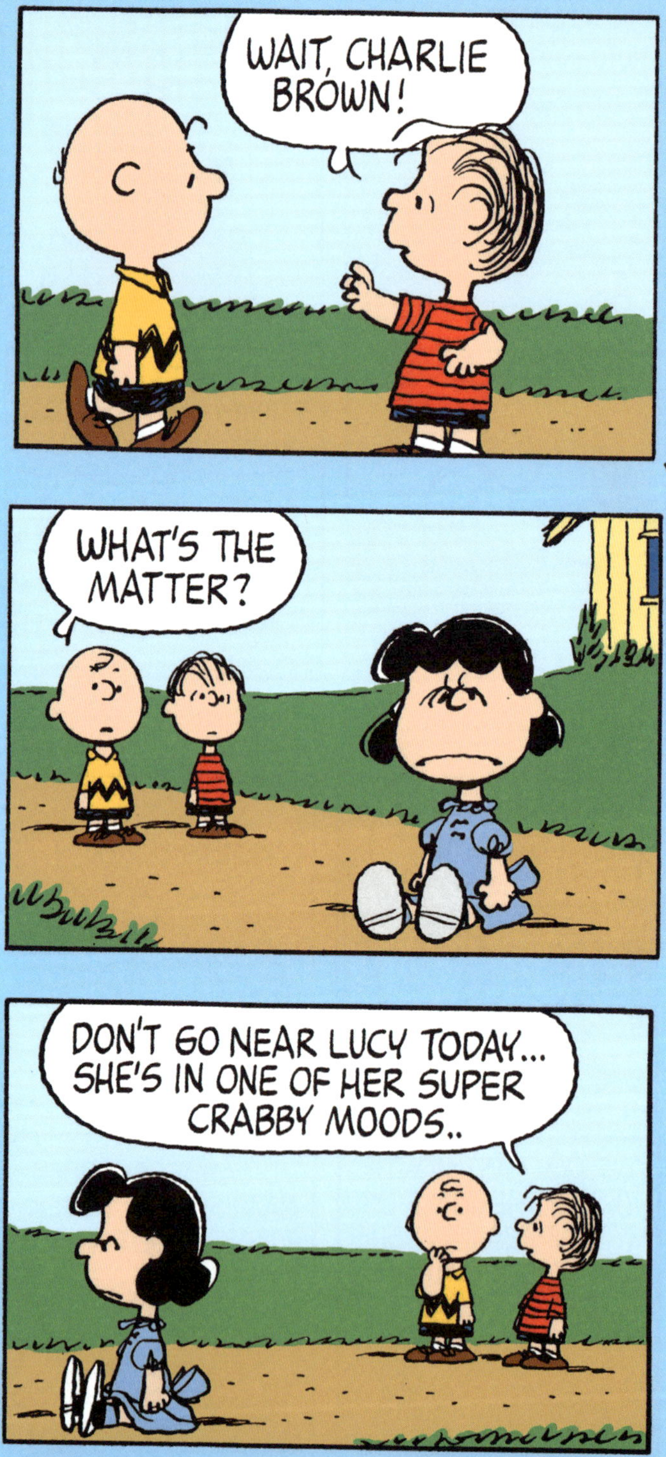
WAIT, CHARLIE BROWN!
WHAT'S THE MATTER?
DON'T GO NEAR LUCY TODAY... SHE'S IN ONE OF HER SUPER CRABBY MOODS..

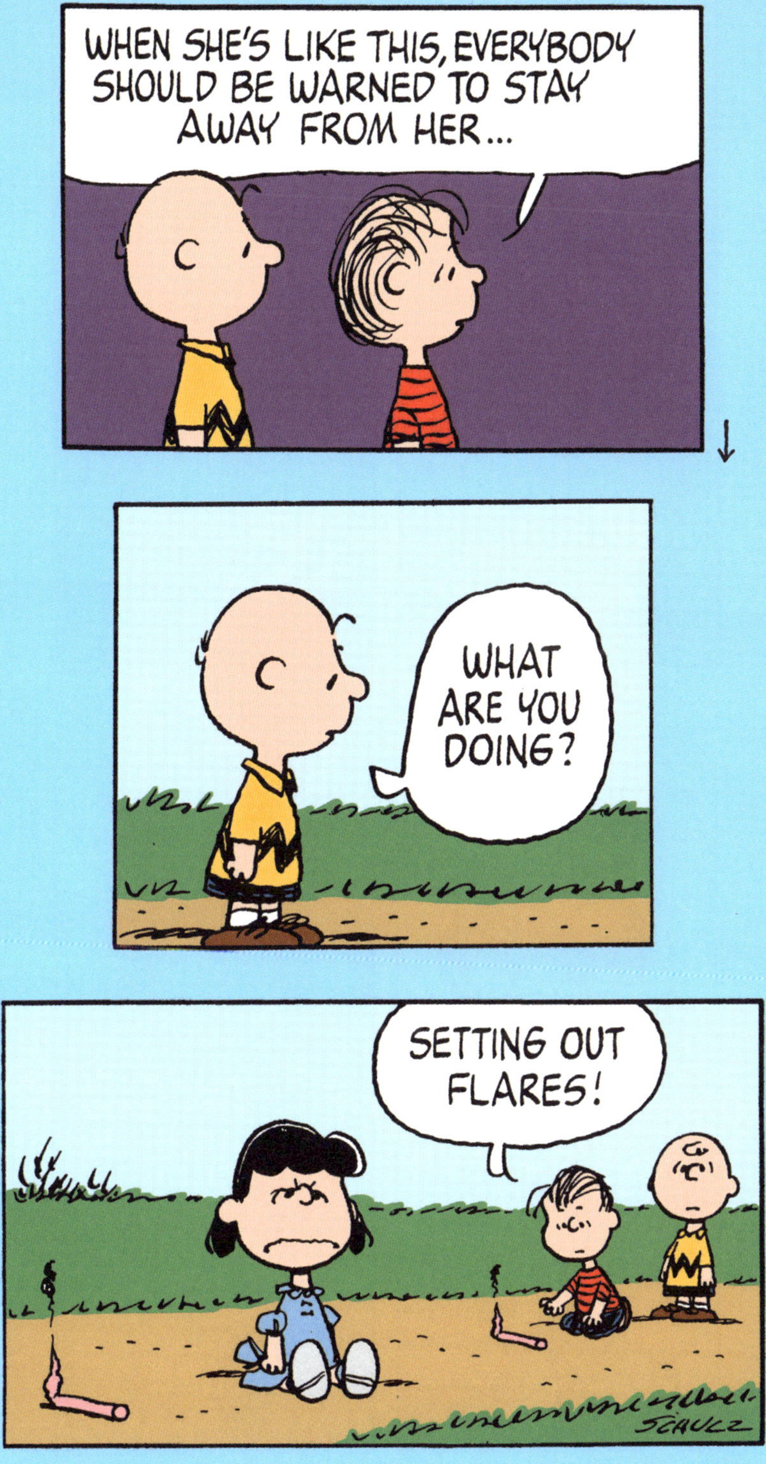
WHEN SHE'S LIKE THIS, EVERYBODY SHOULD BE WARNED TO STAY AWAY FROM HER...
WHAT ARE YOU DOING?
SETTING OUT FLARES!
SCHULZ

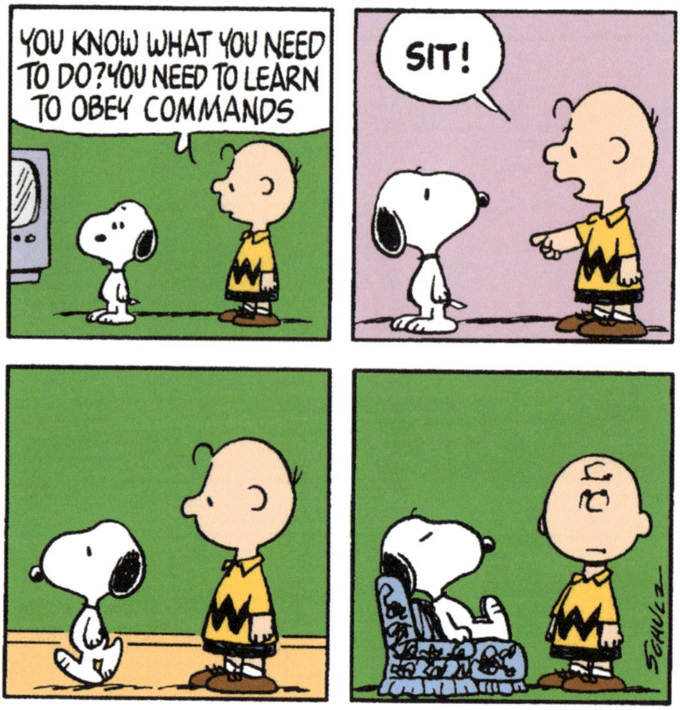
YOU KNOW WHAT YOU NEED TO DO? YOU NEED TO LEARN TO OBEY COMMANDS
SIT!
SCHULZ

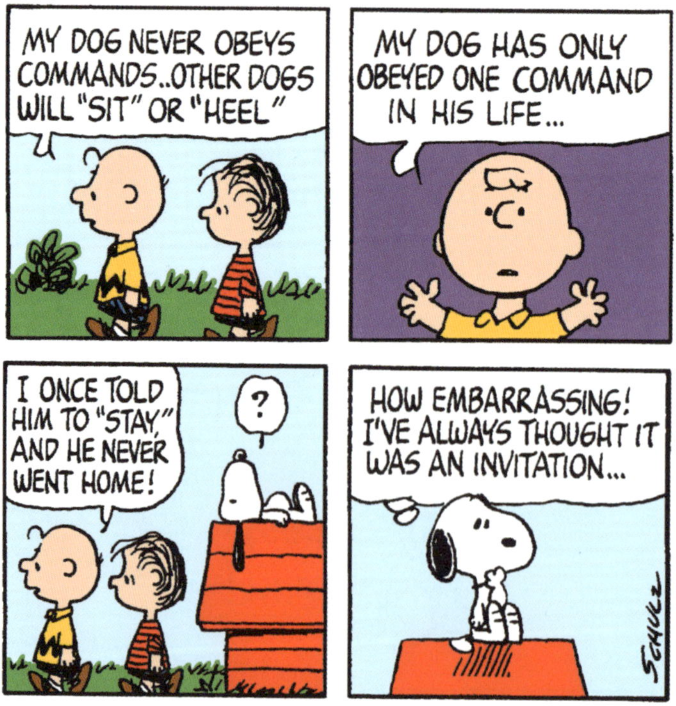
MY DOG NEVER OBEYS COMMANDS..OTHER DOGS WILL "SIT" OR "HEEL"
MY DOG HAS ONLY OBEYED ONE COMMAND IN HIS LIFE...
I ONCE TOLD HIM TO "STAY," AND HE NEVER WENT HOME!
?
HOW EMBARRASSING! I'VE ALWAYS THOUGHT IT WAS AN INVITATION...
SCHULZ

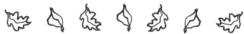

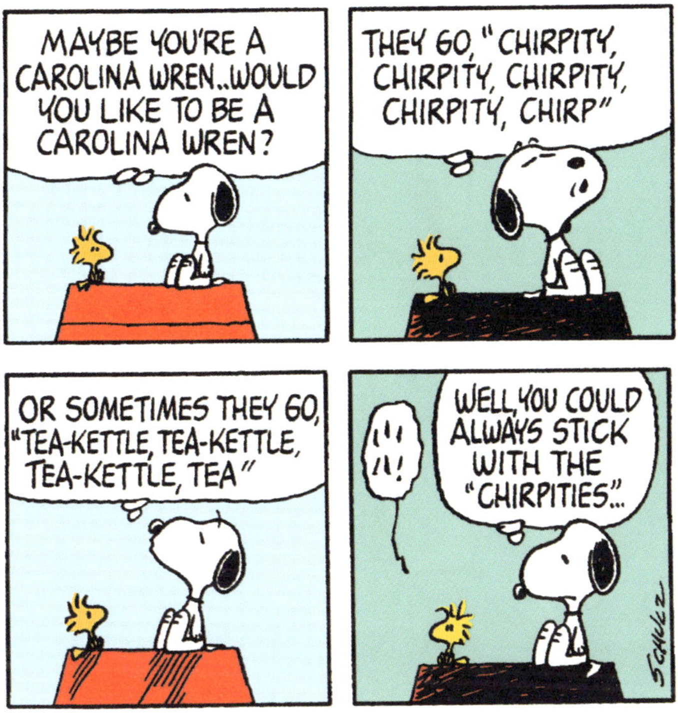
MAYBE YOU'RE A CAROLINA WREN..WOULD YOU LIKE TO BE A CAROLINA WREN?
THEY GO, "CHIRPITY, CHIRPITY, CHIRPITY, CHIRPITY, CHIRP"
OR SOMETIMES THEY GO, "TEA-KETTLE, TEA-KETTLE, TEA-KETTLE, TEA"
WELL, YOU COULD ALWAYS STICK WITH THE "CHIRPITIES"...
SCHULZ

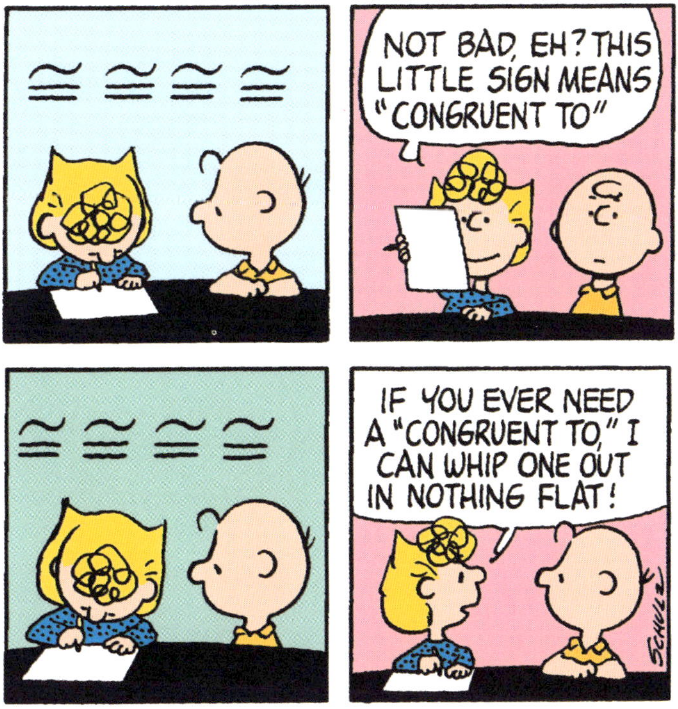
NOT BAD, EH? THIS LITTLE SIGN MEANS "CONGRUENT TO"
IF YOU EVER NEED A "CONGRUENT TO," I CAN WHIP ONE OUT IN NOTHING FLAT!
SCHULZ

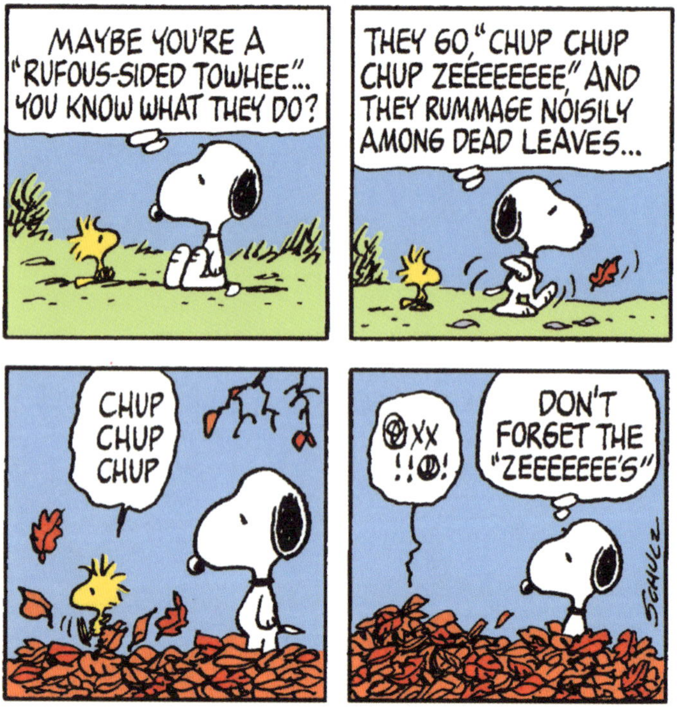
MAYBE YOU'RE A "RUFOUS-SIDED TOWHEE"... YOU KNOW WHAT THEY DO?
THEY GO, "CHUP CHUP CHUP ZEEEEEEEE," AND THEY RUMMAGE NOISILY AMONG DEAD LEAVES...
CHUP CHUP CHUP
DON'T FORGET THE "ZEEEEEEE'S"
SCHULZ

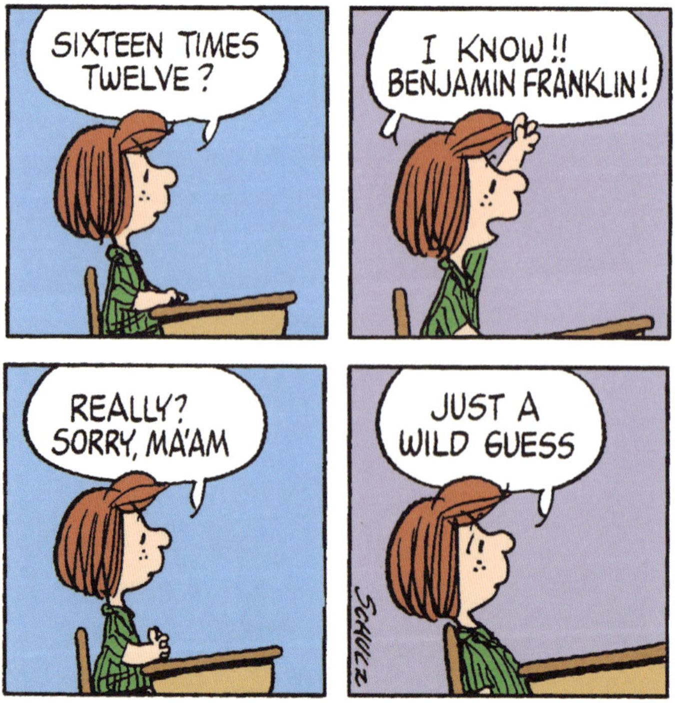
SIXTEEN TIMES TWELVE?
I KNOW!! BENJAMIN FRANKLIN!
REALLY? SORRY, MA'AM
JUST A WILD GUESS
SCHULZ

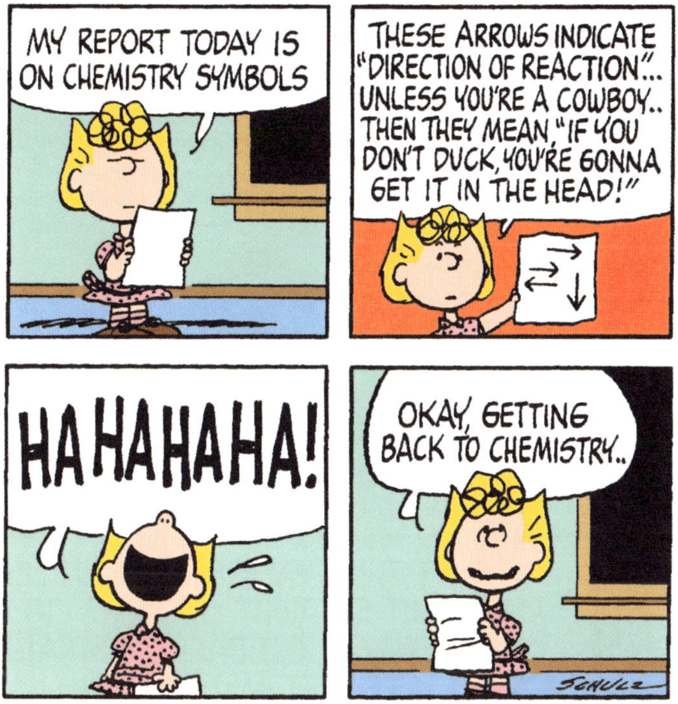
MY REPORT TODAY IS ON CHEMISTRY SYMBOLS
THESE ARROWS INDICATE "DIRECTION OF REACTION"... UNLESS YOU'RE A COWBOY.. THEN THEY MEAN, "IF YOU DON'T DUCK, YOU'RE GONNA GET IT IN THE HEAD!"
HAHAHAHA!
OKAY, GETTING BACK TO CHEMISTRY..
SCHULZ

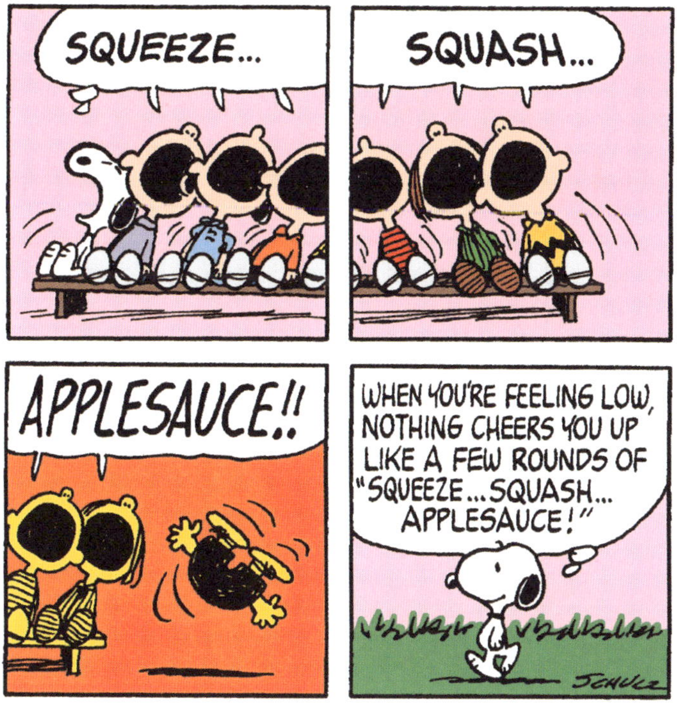
SQUEEZE...
SQUASH...
APPLESAUCE!!
WHEN YOU'RE FEELING LOW, NOTHING CHEERS YOU UP LIKE A FEW ROUNDS OF "SQUEEZE...SQUASH... APPLESAUCE!"
SCHULZ

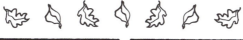

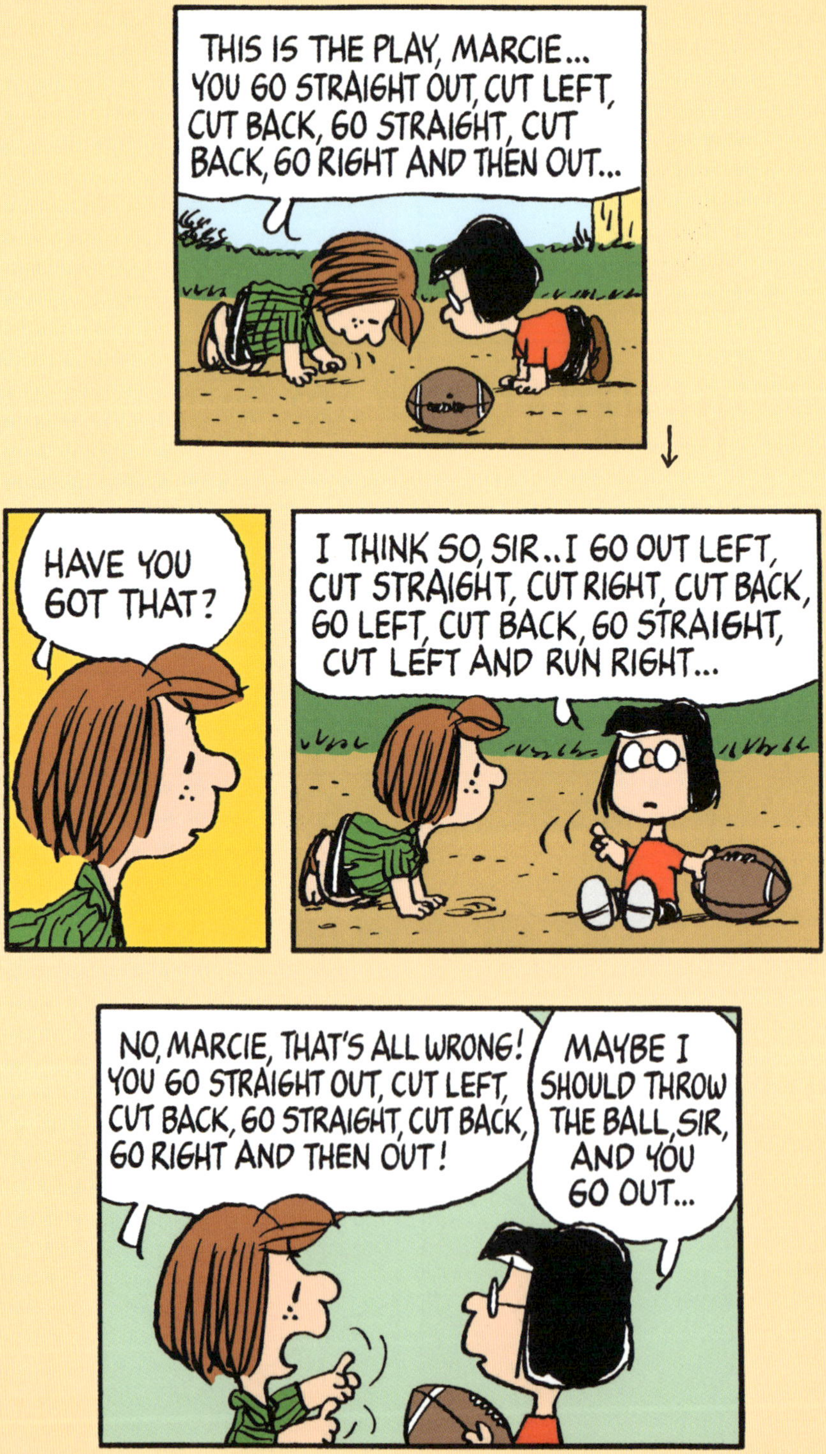
THIS IS THE PLAY, MARCIE... YOU GO STRAIGHT OUT, CUT LEFT, CUT BACK, GO STRAIGHT, CUT BACK, GO RIGHT AND THEN OUT...
HAVE YOU GOT THAT?
I THINK SO, SIR..I GO OUT LEFT, CUT STRAIGHT, CUT RIGHT, CUT BACK, GO LEFT, CUT BACK, GO STRAIGHT, CUT LEFT AND RUN RIGHT...
NO, MARCIE, THAT'S ALL WRONG! YOU GO STRAIGHT OUT, CUT LEFT, CUT BACK, GO STRAIGHT, CUT BACK, GO RIGHT AND THEN OUT!
MAYBE I SHOULD THROW THE BALL, SIR, AND YOU GO OUT...

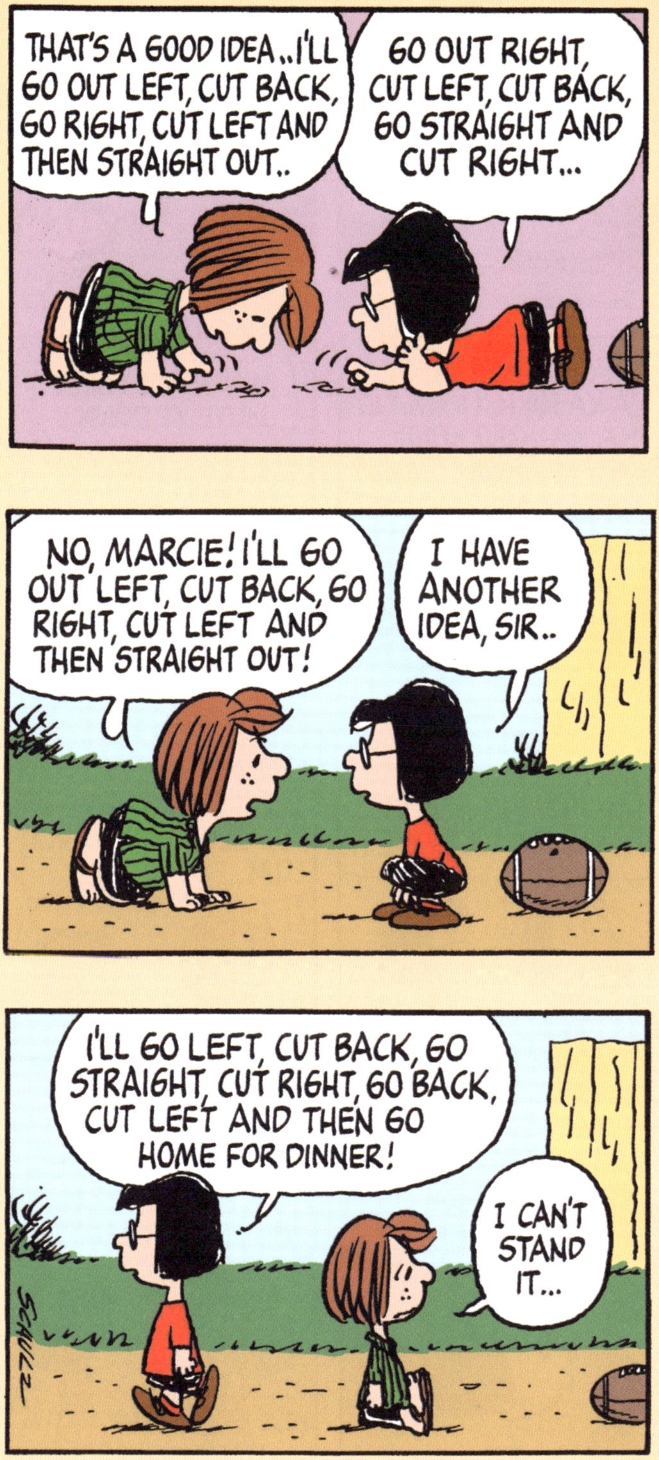
THAT'S A GOOD IDEA..I'LL GO OUT LEFT, CUT BACK, GO RIGHT, CUT LEFT AND THEN STRAIGHT OUT..
GO OUT RIGHT, CUT LEFT, CUT BACK, GO STRAIGHT AND CUT RIGHT...
NO, MARCIE! I'LL GO OUT LEFT, CUT BACK, GO RIGHT, CUT LEFT AND THEN STRAIGHT OUT!
I HAVE ANOTHER IDEA, SIR..
I'LL GO LEFT, CUT BACK, GO STRAIGHT, CUT RIGHT, GO BACK, CUT LEFT AND THEN GO HOME FOR DINNER!
I CAN'T STAND IT...
SCHULZ

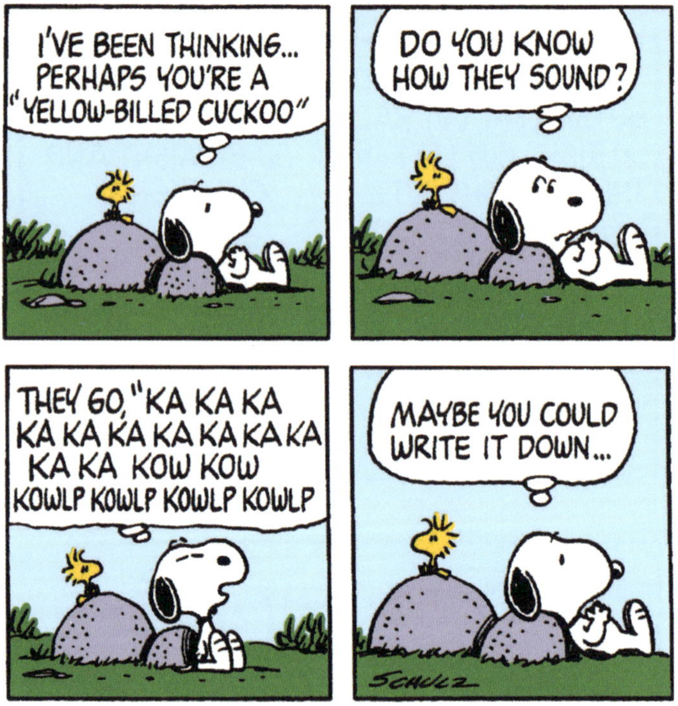
I'VE BEEN THINKING... PERHAPS YOU'RE A "YELLOW-BILLED CUCKOO"
DO YOU KNOW HOW THEY SOUND?
THEY GO, "KA KA KA KA KA KA KA KA KA KA KA KA KOW KOW KOWLP KOWLP KOWLP KOWLP
MAYBE YOU COULD WRITE IT DOWN...
SCHULZ

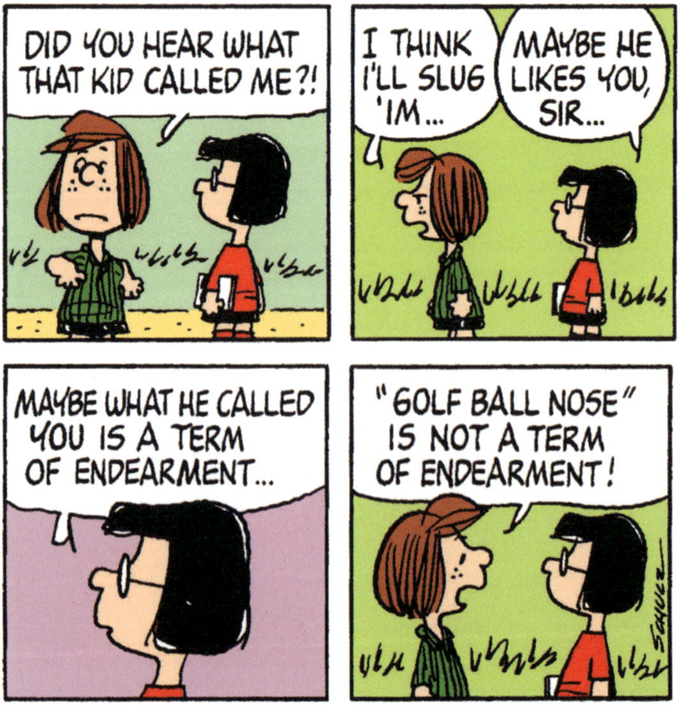
DID YOU HEAR WHAT THAT KID CALLED ME?!
I THINK I'LL SLUG 'IM...
MAYBE HE LIKES YOU, SIR...
MAYBE WHAT HE CALLED YOU IS A TERM OF ENDEARMENT...
"GOLF BALL NOSE" IS NOT A TERM OF ENDEARMENT!
SCHULZ

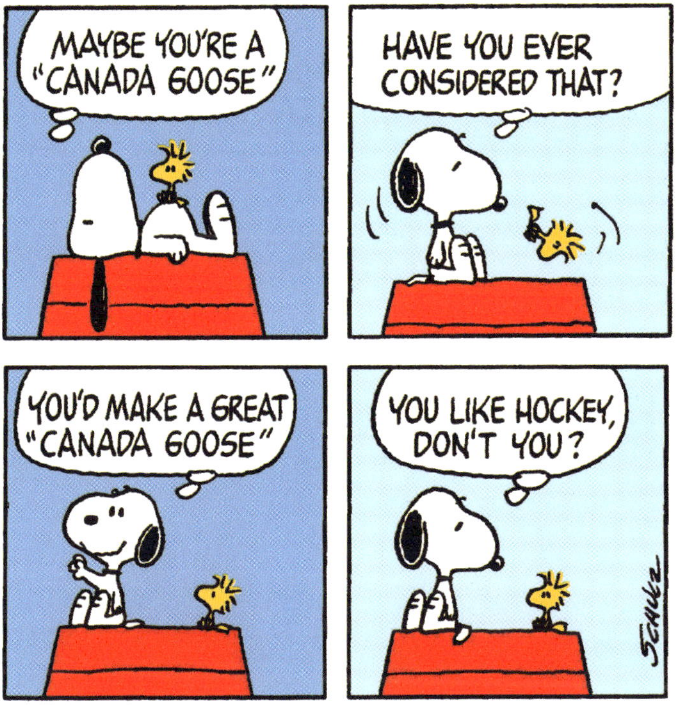
MAYBE YOU'RE A "CANADA GOOSE"
HAVE YOU EVER CONSIDERED THAT?
YOU'D MAKE A GREAT "CANADA GOOSE"
YOU LIKE HOCKEY, DON'T YOU?
SCHULZ

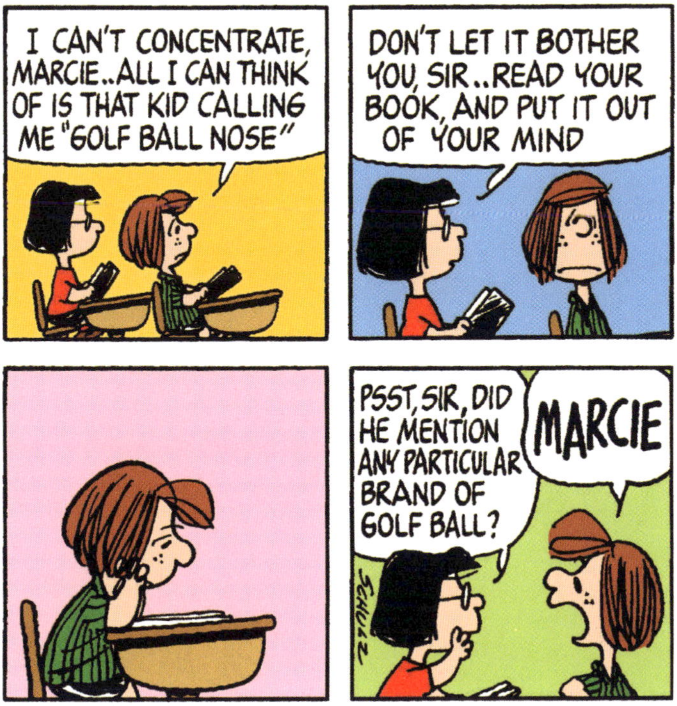
I CAN'T CONCENTRATE, MARCIE..ALL I CAN THINK OF IS THAT KID CALLING ME "GOLF BALL NOSE"
DON'T LET IT BOTHER YOU, SIR..READ YOUR BOOK, AND PUT IT OUT OF YOUR MIND
PSST, SIR, DID HE MENTION ANY PARTICULAR BRAND OF GOLF BALL?
MARCIE
SCHULZ

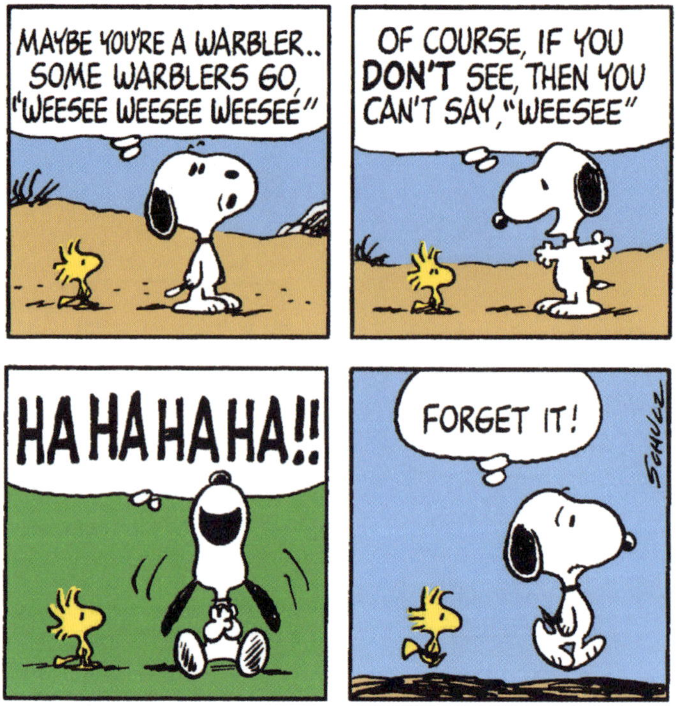
MAYBE YOU'RE A WARBLER.. SOME WARBLERS GO, "WEESEE WEESEE WEESEE"
OF COURSE, IF YOU **DON'T** SEE, THEN YOU CAN'T SAY, "WEESEE"
HA HA HA HA!!
FORGET IT!
SCHULZ

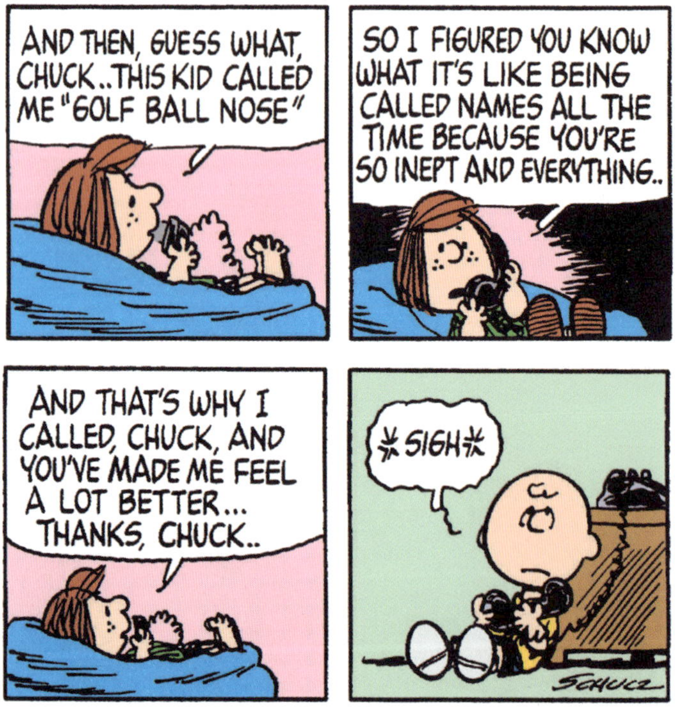
AND THEN, GUESS WHAT, CHUCK..THIS KID CALLED ME "GOLF BALL NOSE"
SO I FIGURED YOU KNOW WHAT IT'S LIKE BEING CALLED NAMES ALL THE TIME BECAUSE YOU'RE SO INEPT AND EVERYTHING..
AND THAT'S WHY I CALLED, CHUCK, AND YOU'VE MADE ME FEEL A LOT BETTER... THANKS, CHUCK..
SIGH
SCHULZ

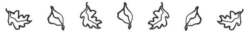

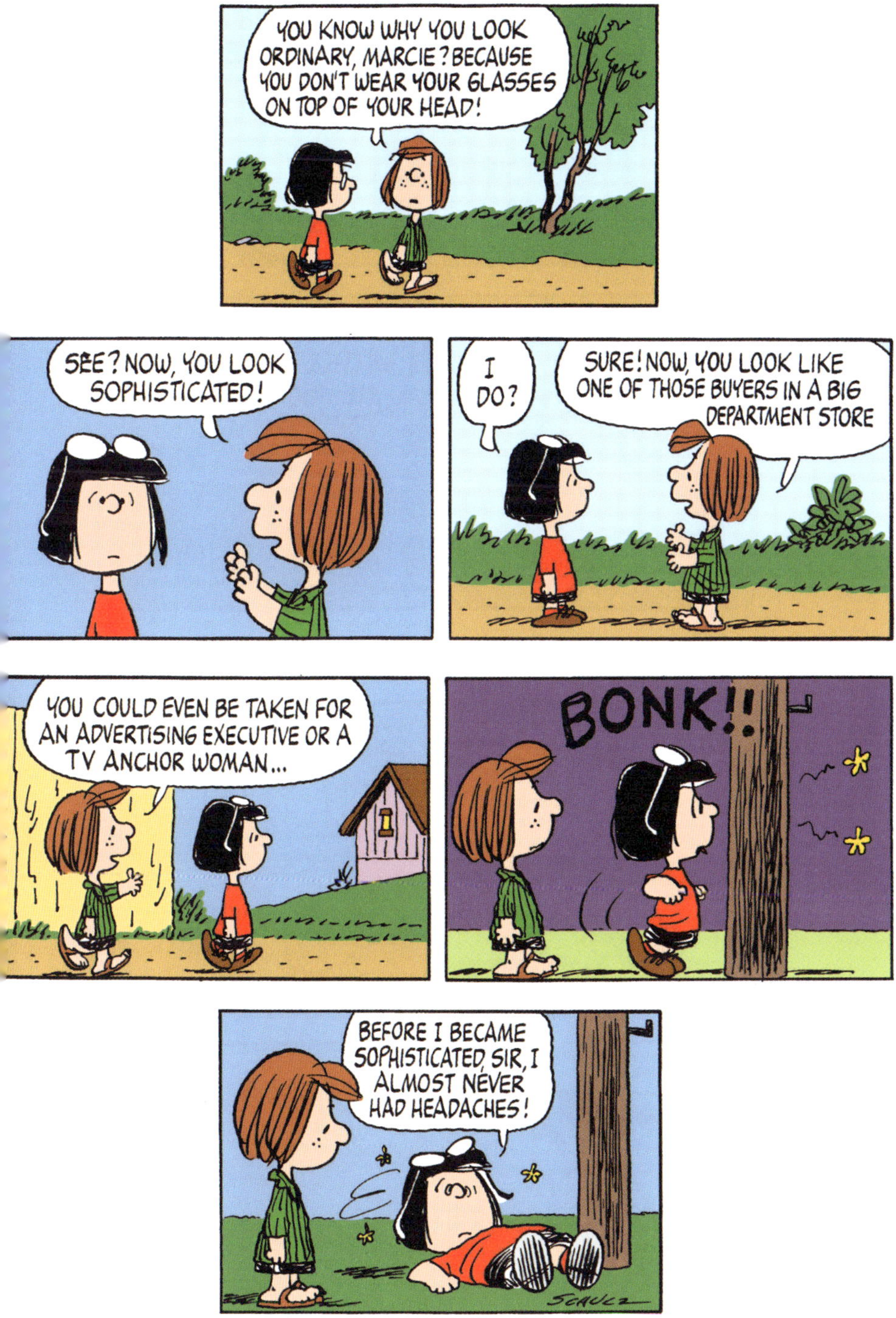
YOU KNOW WHY YOU LOOK ORDINARY, MARCIE? BECAUSE YOU DON'T WEAR YOUR GLASSES ON TOP OF YOUR HEAD!
SEE? NOW, YOU LOOK SOPHISTICATED!
I DO?
SURE! NOW, YOU LOOK LIKE ONE OF THOSE BUYERS IN A BIG DEPARTMENT STORE
YOU COULD EVEN BE TAKEN FOR AN ADVERTISING EXECUTIVE OR A TV ANCHOR WOMAN...
BONK!!
BEFORE I BECAME SOPHISTICATED, SIR, I ALMOST NEVER HAD HEADACHES!
SCHULZ

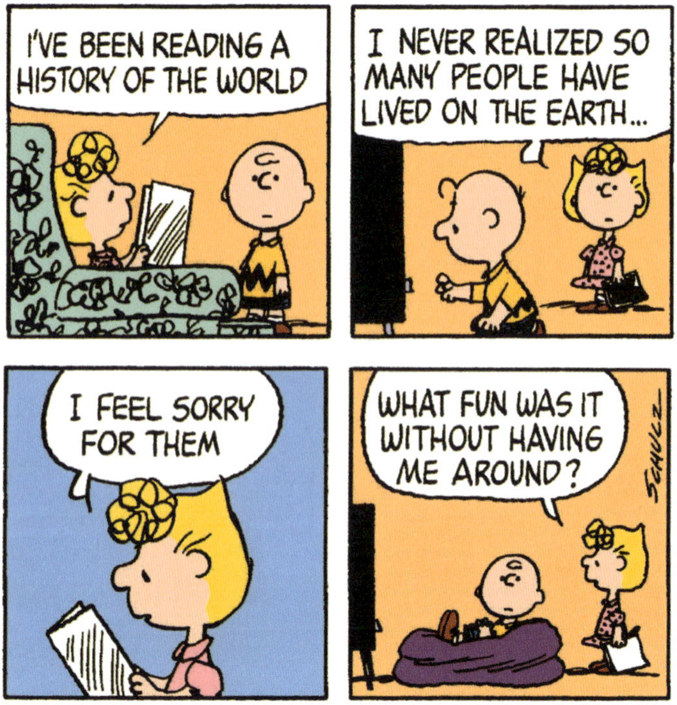
I'VE BEEN READING A HISTORY OF THE WORLD
I NEVER REALIZED SO MANY PEOPLE HAVE LIVED ON THE EARTH...
I FEEL SORRY FOR THEM
WHAT FUN WAS IT WITHOUT HAVING ME AROUND?
SCHULZ

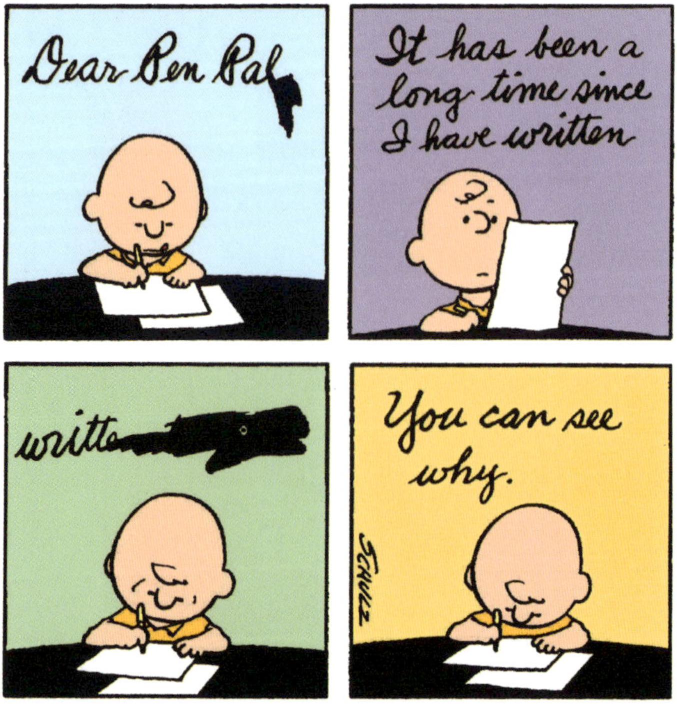
Dear Pen Pal
It has been a long time since I have written
writte
You can see why.
SCHULZ

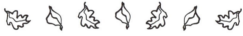

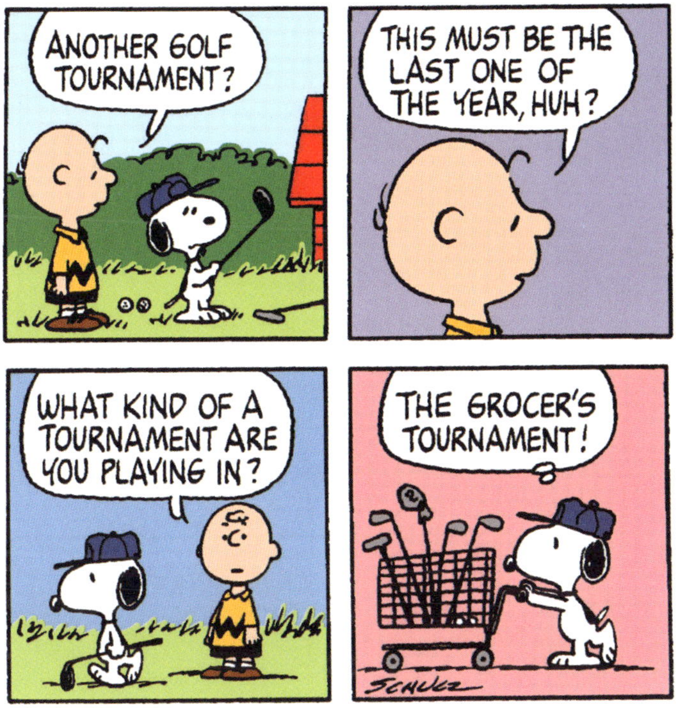
ANOTHER GOLF TOURNAMENT?
THIS MUST BE THE LAST ONE OF THE YEAR, HUH?
WHAT KIND OF A TOURNAMENT ARE YOU PLAYING IN?
THE GROCER'S TOURNAMENT!

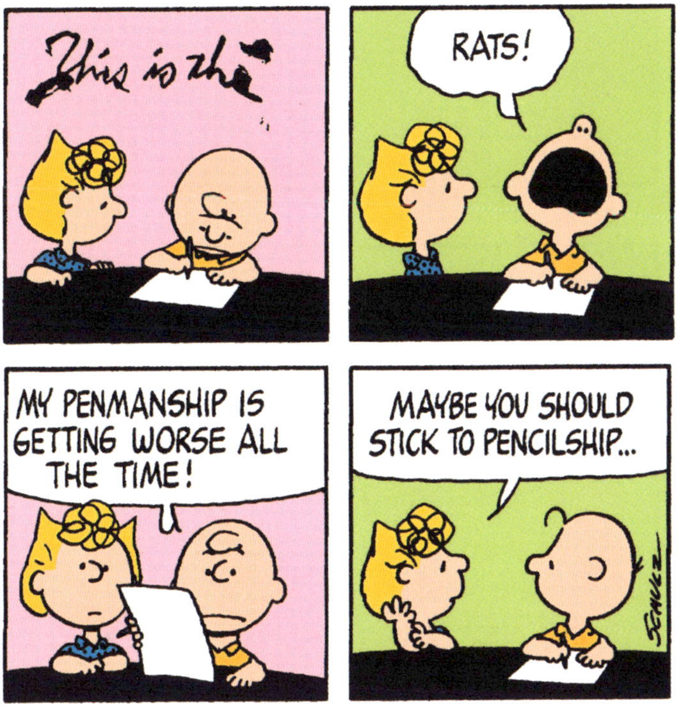
This is the
RATS!
MY PENMANSHIP IS GETTING WORSE ALL THE TIME!
MAYBE YOU SHOULD STICK TO PENCILSHIP...

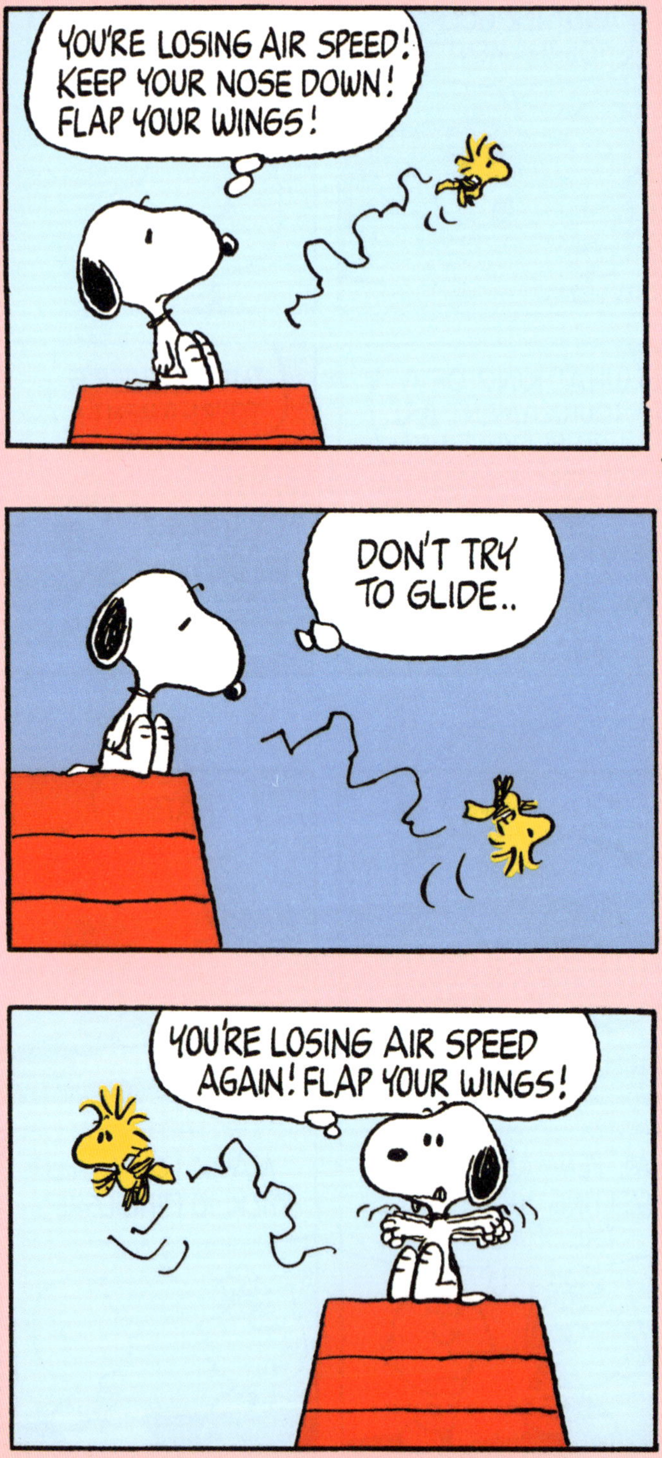
YOU'RE LOSING AIR SPEED! KEEP YOUR NOSE DOWN! FLAP YOUR WINGS!
DON'T TRY TO GLIDE..
YOU'RE LOSING AIR SPEED AGAIN! FLAP YOUR WINGS!

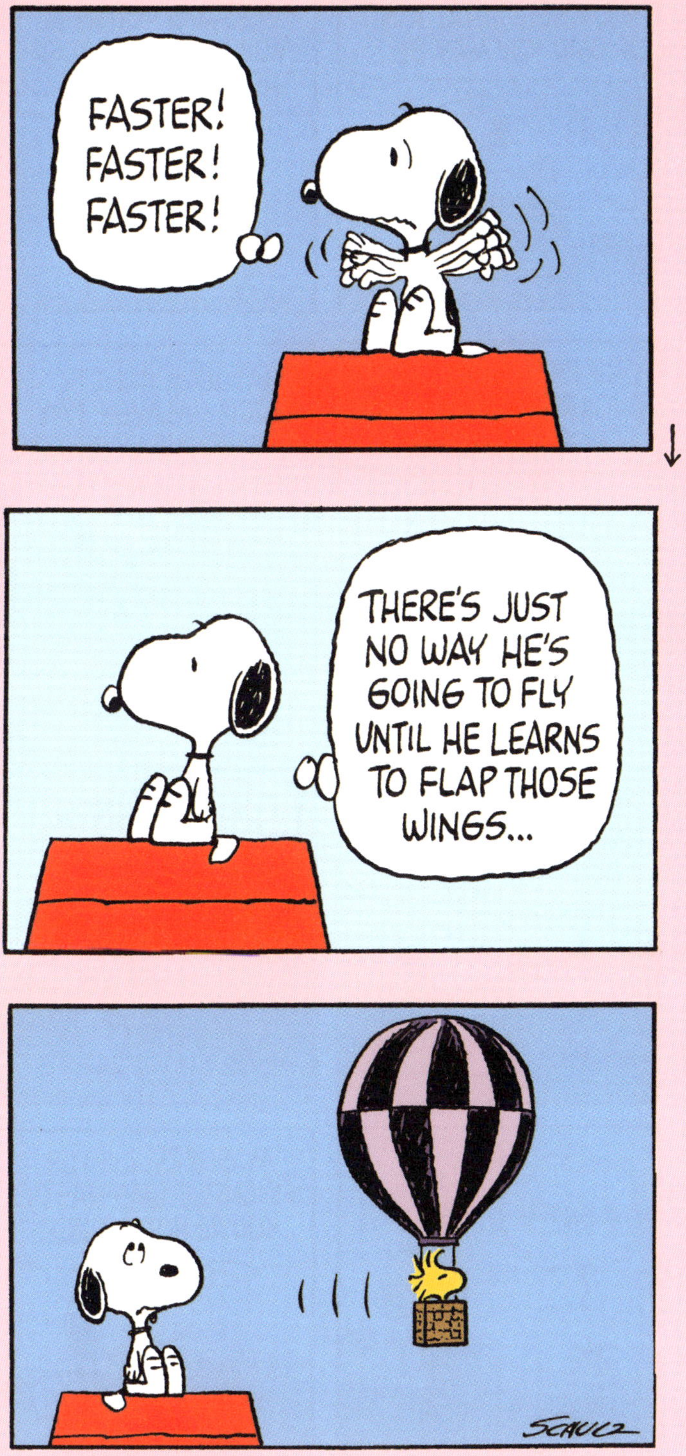
FASTER! FASTER! FASTER!
THERE'S JUST NO WAY HE'S GOING TO FLY UNTIL HE LEARNS TO FLAP THOSE WINGS...
SCHULZ

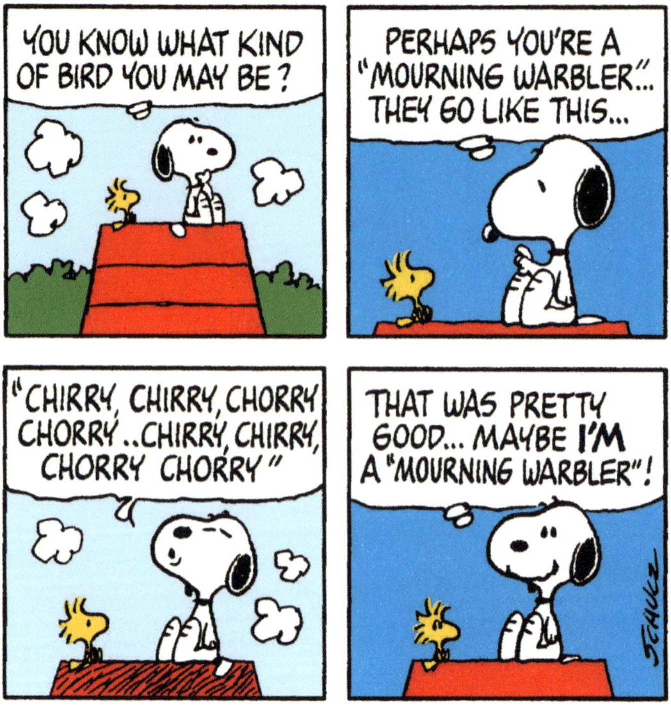
YOU KNOW WHAT KIND OF BIRD YOU MAY BE?
PERHAPS YOU'RE A "MOURNING WARBLER"... THEY GO LIKE THIS...
"CHIRRY, CHIRRY, CHORRY CHORRY ..CHIRRY, CHIRRY, CHORRY CHORRY"
THAT WAS PRETTY GOOD... MAYBE **I'M** A "MOURNING WARBLER"!

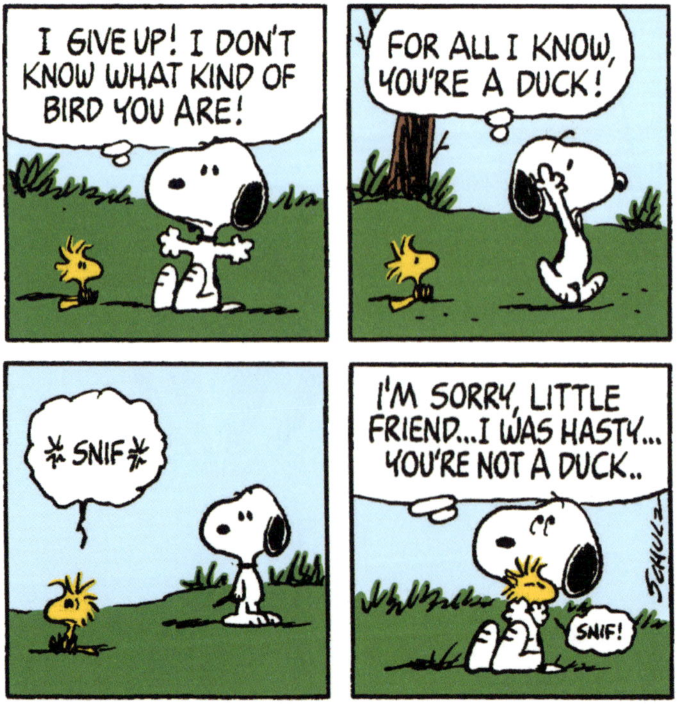
I GIVE UP! I DON'T KNOW WHAT KIND OF BIRD YOU ARE!
FOR ALL I KNOW, YOU'RE A DUCK!
SNIF
I'M SORRY, LITTLE FRIEND...I WAS HASTY... YOU'RE NOT A DUCK..
SNIF!

Make Your Own Miniature Kite!

MATERIALS NEEDED: 8.5 x 11 craft paper of different colors, safety scissors, extra-strength glue stick, pencil, ruler, paper straws (two for each kite), string or baker's twine, craft glue, ribbon or decorative string, glitter glue

INSTRUCTIONS:

1. Using two pieces of paper that can be different colors or patterns, fold the sheets in half on the longest edge so that the new size is 5.5 x 8.5. Use scissors to cut each piece of paper along the fold line.

2. With an extra-strength glue stick, glue one piece of paper to the back of the first one and smooth the page down.

3. Use a pencil to mark four dots on each side of the paper that will form the shape of your kite. The points at the top and bottom should be at the halfway mark across the page. The dots on the long edges should be about 3 inches down the page, measured from the top. Once you mark the dots, you can use a ruler to trace lines connecting them.

4. Cut out the shape of your kite with safety scissors.

5. Measure out about 24 inches of twine, and tie one end of the twine a third of the way down the paper straw. Add a drop of glue to secure the knot in place. The knot should be at the middle of the cross on the kite.

6. Cut the other paper straw into three pieces. Tie the opposite end of the twine to the middle of one of the paper straw pieces to make a kite handle. Add a drop of glue to keep the string from sliding off the handle.

7. Cut about 18 inches of lightweight ribbon or decorative string to make the kite tail. Tie one end of the string to the bottom of the longest straw, at the opposite end from the first knot. Add a drop of glue to secure the knot in place.

8. Decide which side you want to be the front (or top) of the kite, and lay it down so that the bottom of the kite is facing up.

9. Using a ruler and pencil, connect the corners of the kite to form a cross. Squeeze out a line of craft glue along the cross, and place the straws onto the glue to make the kite frame. Make sure the first knot of twine is at the center of the cross and the second knot is placed at the bottom of the kite. Let the glue dry for 5 minutes.

10. Decorate your kite with glitter glue or draw fun faces and designs with markers. Tie some short ribbons along the kite tail for decoration.

Now your kite is ready to fly. Just watch out for that evil kite-eating tree!

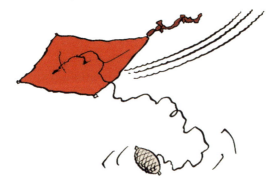

*As a variation of this project, use pasta noodles instead of paper straws. Or, make the kite size smaller and use tissue paper to make kites that you can hang in the window for decoration. Have fun!

Make an Edible Woodstock's Nest

With an adult's help, make this sweet treat for you and your friends to enjoy.

INGREDIENTS: 1 5-oz. can of chow mein noodles; 1 12-oz. package of chocolate chips; 1 bag of small jelly beans; peanut butter (or alternative cashew or almond butter); wax paper; paper plates. (Makes about 15 nests.)

INSTRUCTIONS:

1. Put a piece of wax paper on each plate.
2. Put chow mein noodles in a large bowl.
3. Melt chocolate chips in the microwave or over low heat on the stove.
4. Pour chocolate over noodles and mix.
5. Place a heaping tablespoonful of the mixture on the wax paper on each plate. Have an adult test to see when it's cool enough to form the mixture into nests.
6. Stick the jelly beans down with peanut butter inside the nest.

Charles M. Schulz and *Peanuts* Fun Facts

- Charles Schulz drew 17,897 comic strips throughout his career.
- Schulz was first published in Ripley's newspaper feature *Believe It or Not* in 1937. He was fifteen years old and the drawing was of the family dog.
- From birth, comics played a large role in Schulz's life. At just two days old, an uncle nicknamed Schulz "Sparky" after the horse Spark Plug from the *Barney Google* comic strip. And that's what he was called for the rest of his life.
- In a bit of foreshadowing, Schulz's kindergarten teacher told him, "Someday, Charles, you're going to be an artist."
- Growing up, Schulz had a black-and-white dog that later became the inspiration for Snoopy—the same dog that Schulz drew for Ripley's *Believe It or Not*. The dog's name was Spike.

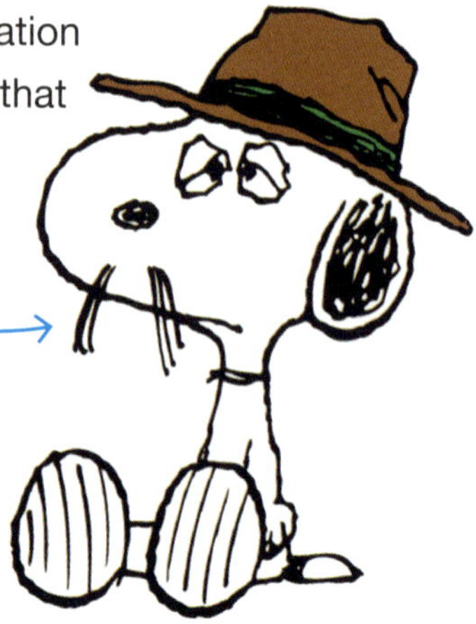

- Charles Schulz earned a star on the Hollywood Walk of Fame in 1996.

Peanuts is distributed internationally by Andrews McMeel Syndication.

Charlie Brown: All Tied Up copyright © 2019 by Peanuts Worldwide, LLC. All rights reserved. Printed in China. No part of this book may be used or reproduced in any manner whatsoever without written permission except in the case of reprints in the context of reviews.

Andrews McMeel Publishing
a division of Andrews McMeel Universal
1130 Walnut Street, Kansas City, Missouri 64106

www.andrewsmcmeel.com

www.peanuts.com

19 20 21 22 23 SDB 10 9 8 7 6 5 4 3 2 1

ISBN: 978-1-5248-5226-9

Library of Congress Control Number: 2019932570

Made by:
Shenzhen Donnelley Printing Company Ltd.
Address and location of manufacturer:
No. 47, Wuhe Nan Road, Bantian Ind. Zone,
Shenzhen China, 518129
1st Printing—7/22/19

ATTENTION: SCHOOLS AND BUSINESSES
Andrews McMeel books are available at quantity discounts with bulk purchase for educational, business, or sales promotional use. For information, please e-mail the Andrews McMeel Publishing Special Sales Department: specialsales@amuniversal.com.

Check out more *Peanuts* kids' collections from Andrews McMeel Publishing.

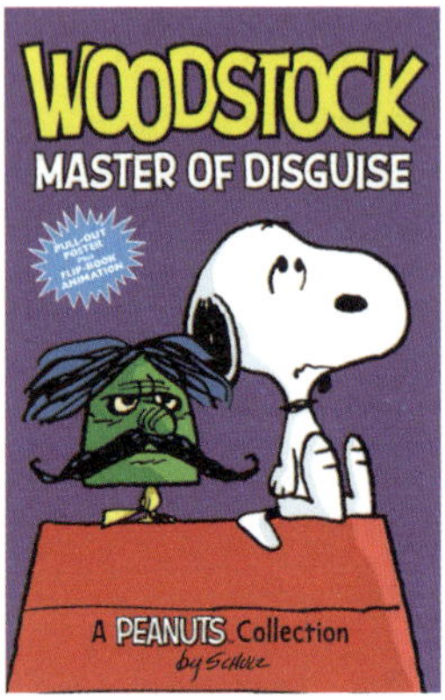
WOODSTOCK
MASTER OF DISGUISE
A PEANUTS Collection

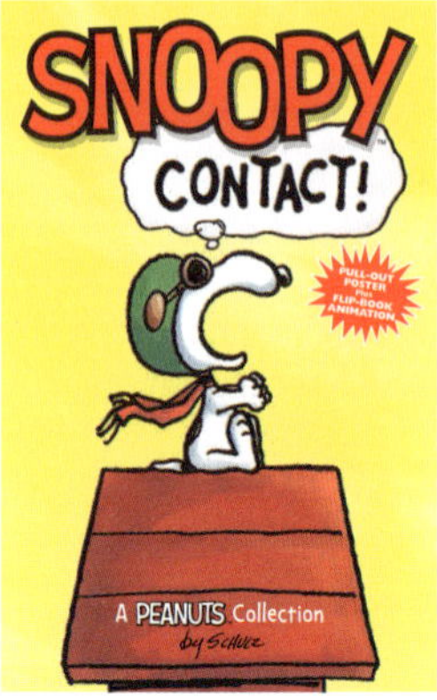
SNOOPY
CONTACT!
A PEANUTS Collection

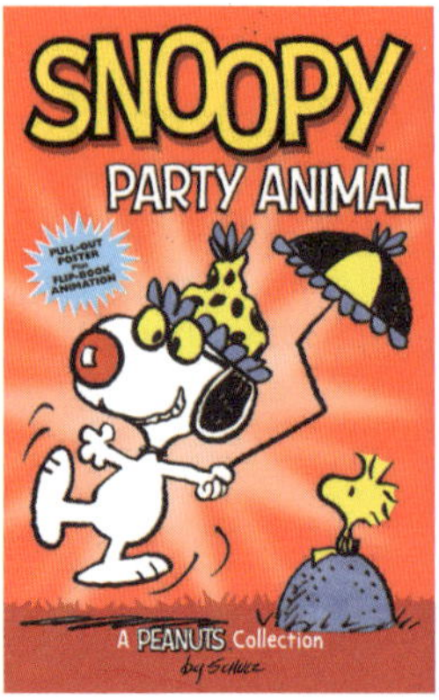
SNOOPY
PARTY ANIMAL
A PEANUTS Collection

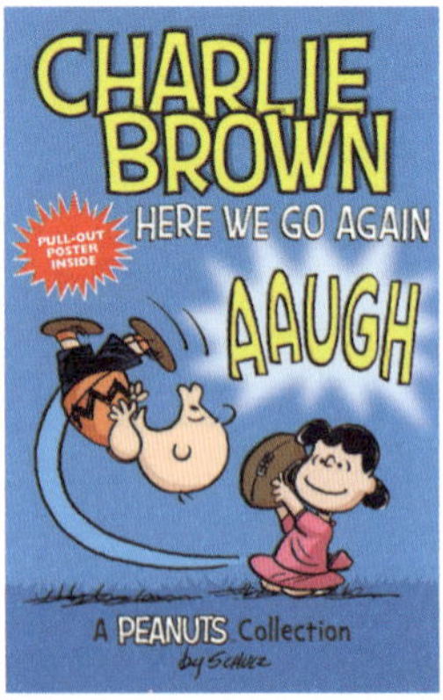
CHARLIE BROWN
HERE WE GO AGAIN
AAUGH
A PEANUTS Collection

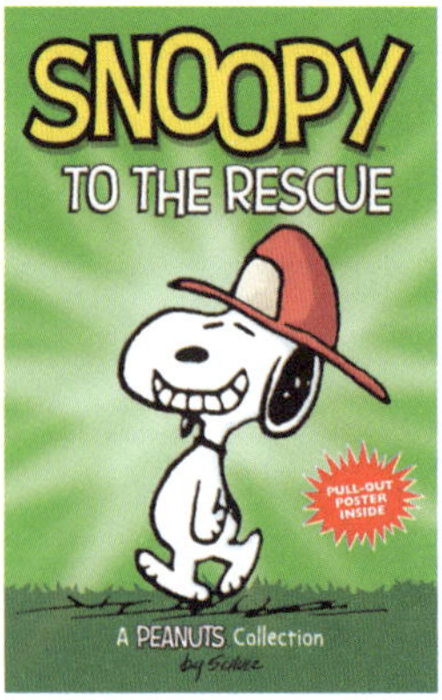
SNOOPY
TO THE RESCUE
A PEANUTS Collection

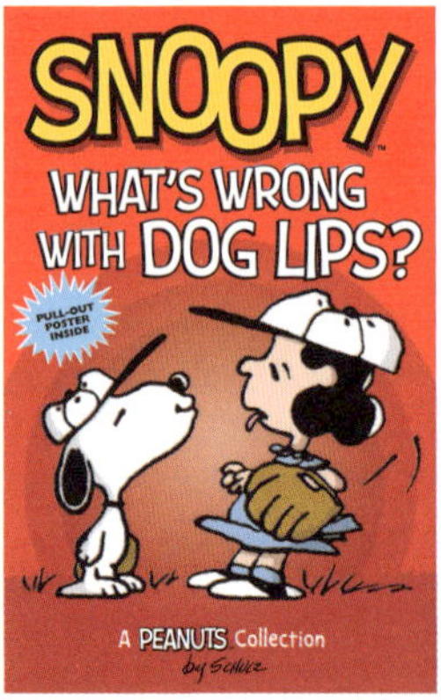
SNOOPY
WHAT'S WRONG WITH DOG LIPS?
A PEANUTS Collection

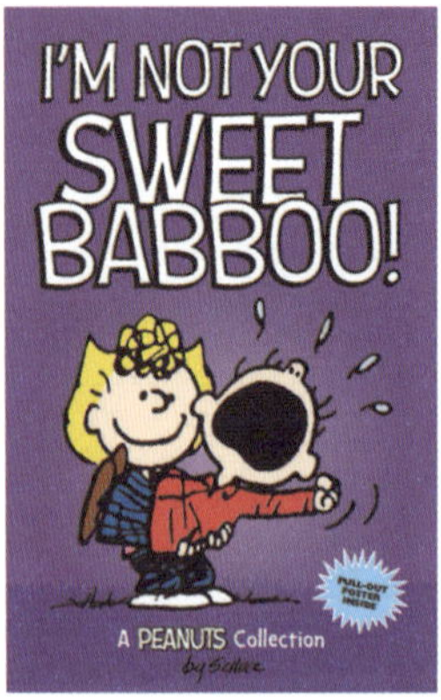
I'M NOT YOUR SWEET BABBOO!
A PEANUTS Collection

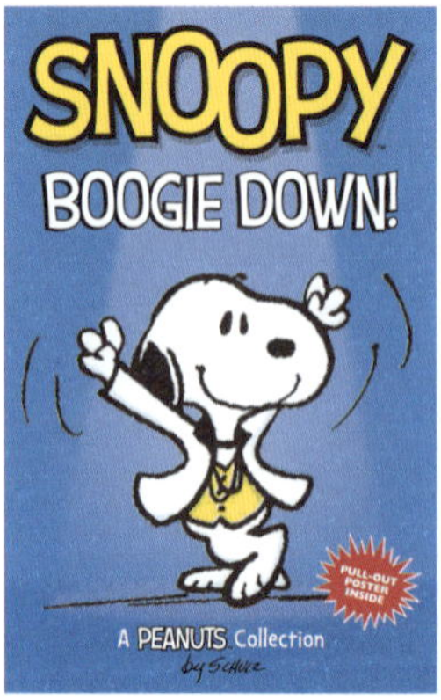
SNOOPY
BOOGIE DOWN!
A PEANUTS Collection

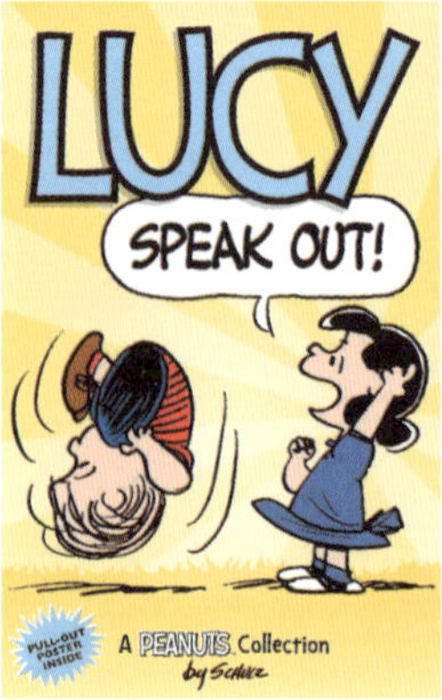
LUCY
SPEAK OUT!
A PEANUTS Collection